CONTEMPORARY
AMERICAN PHILOSOPHY
VOL. I

PROFESSOR G. H. PALMER

CONTEMPORARY AMERICAN PHILOSOPHY

PERSONAL STATEMENTS

VOL. I

BY

G. H. PALMER
G. P. ADAMS
H. B. ALEXANDER
A. C. ARMSTRONG
J. E. BOODIN
H. C. BROWN
M. W. CALKINS
M. R. COHEN

G. W. CUNNINGHAM
D. DRAKE
G. J. DUCASSE
W. G. EVERETT
W. FITE
W. E. HOCKING
T. DE LAGUNA
J. A. LEIGHTON

EDITED BY

GEORGE P. ADAMS

AND

WM. PEPPERELL MONTAGUE

LONDON: GEORGE ALLEN & UNWIN LTD
NEW YORK: THE MACMILLAN COMPANY

FIRST PUBLISHED IN 1930

THESE ESSAYS ARE

AFFECTIONATELY DEDICATED TO

GEORGE HERBERT PALMER

THE FRIEND AND TEACHER

OF SO MANY AMERICAN PHILOSOPHERS

PREFACE

PLANS for bringing out one or two volumes of *Contemporary American Philosophy* were suggested and definitely set in motion shortly after the publication, in 1924, of the first volume of *Contemporary British Philosophy*. The project was entrusted to a committee of the American Philosophical Association, made up of three Divisional Committees, of the Eastern, Western, and Pacific Divisions of the Association, whose chairmen were to act as the American Editors of the volumes.

The contributors to the volumes were selected on the basis of a referendum vote of the membership of the three Divisions of the American Philosophical Association. The Editors regret that either through the more or less accidental omissions in this hastily taken referendum or through sudden illness, as in the case of Professor Addison Moore, a number of colleagues whose essays would have been greatly valued are not here represented. Each contributor was requested to state his principal philosophic beliefs, the reasons supporting them, and the manner in which he had reached them. It is hoped that the publication of these philosophic autobiographies will serve the purpose of clarifying the minds of the writers, and of helping their students to a better understanding of their various specific doctrines. An explicit confession of the temperamental sympathies and prejudices of a philosopher, and of such of his life's circumstances as seem to him to have been relevant in shaping his conclusions, may possess as much philosophic value both to the writer and to his readers as the conclusions to which they contribute. And the honest attempt to psycho-analyse one's mind may and should result in a wholesomely humiliating realization of the extent to which one's own beliefs (and not merely those of one's neighbours) are determined by subjective causes rather than by objective reasons.

These considerations are offered by the Editors in defence of a book which might appear at first sight as an inappropriately egotistic collection of studies. The degree to which the defence is an adequate one, and the extent to which American teachers of Philosophy are severally justified in confessing their faiths, must of course be left for the readers of the volumes to decide.

After the Committee had become organized and had its plans well under way, it suffered a severe loss in the death of Professor Alfred H. Lloyd, of the University of Michigan, Chairman of the Committee of the Western Division. His colleagues take this occasion to record their appreciation of the great interest in the plans for these volumes which Professor Lloyd manifested, and their profound regret that he did not live to see their fruition.

It is doubtful whether these volumes would have appeared had it not been for the constant encouragement and help which the American Editors have received from the Editor of the British volumes and of the Library of Philosophy, Professor John H. Muirhead, and they cannot refrain from expressing, on behalf of all the contributors, their appreciation of Professor Muirhead's generous aid and unflagging interest.

GEORGE P. ADAMS
WM. PEPPERELL MONTAGUE

CONTENTS

12 CONTEMPORARY AMERICAN PHILOSOPHY

THE American Philosophy Association dedicates its new volume of discussions to me and asks me to write the introductory paper. I am somewhat puzzled by the honour. It cannot be due to any signal contribution on my part to philosophical doctrine, such as has been made by several of my colleagues, by James, Royce, Münsterberg, Santayana, Perry, McDougall. My name is connected with none of the many fighting faiths which have enriched American thought during the eighty-seven years of my life. There is no distinctively Palmerian philosophy. But I have viewed the whole marvellous expansion of thought which has gone on from the restricted outlook of Hopkins, Porter, Bowen, and McCosh to the wide horizons of Dewey, Montague, Hocking, and Whitehead.

What, then, is the mental condition of one who has seen it all, seen it too instructed by a pretty wide acquaintance with the general history of philosophy? This may well be the question I am asked to answer. Of argumentation over single problems enough will be offered by other contributors to these volumes. They are still in the field of conflict. Something more personal I can supply. By making my paper largely biographic I can treat myself as a kind of representative of the philosophic young men of my time. I can tell of the haphazards, discouragements, helps, and changes of public opinion through which they have forced their way from the stagnation of early thought into the tumultuous activity of the present time, and beyond this into individual careers and positive personal beliefs. Of course each of us is unique. No man is completely typical. Yet there are sufficient resemblances among the buffetings which we all have had to encounter to make a single candid story of them interesting and instructive. The plot of the story may fit us all, even if the incidents vary. So I shall try to set down here an old man's memories of the struggles through which he has passed in reaching the criticized convictions about ultimate things on which he now relies.

GEORGE HERBERT PALMER

INTRODUCTION

By PROFESSOR GEORGE HERBERT PALMER

Born Boston, Mass., 1842; Emeritus Professor of Philosophy, Harvard University.

INTRODUCTION

PART I

I

FAIRLY to follow the growth of a mind, one must begin by inspecting the soil wherefrom its roots drew nourishment. From what heritage did I set out? I am of English stock. My father's ancestor came over in 1636 and settled at Little Compton, Rhode Island. A few years later, John Peabody, the ancestor of my mother, settled at Boxford, Massachusetts, and on his farm I am of the seventh generation. Half of each year of my youth I lived in the country, the other half in Boston, where on March 19, 1842, I was born. In the same house with me were born my seven brothers and sisters. My father, a business man, was of modest means, so that we early learned the careful use of money. No waste was allowed, and we understood that there would be little property to be divided after the death of our parents. But expenditures for education, books, music, travel, charity, and the dignified furnishing of the home were lavish. After attendance at the Boston public schools, all four boys went to Phillips Academy, Andover, two subsequently to Harvard College. Two by their own choice entered business. Self-reliance was secured by my father's principle that every healthy child who had been well brought up should be turned out of the home at twelve. That was my age when I entered Andover. Studious opportunities for girls were scanty then. But from the best there were each of my sisters took what suited her disposition.

Two strong philosophic influences dominated my childhood, one personal, one institutional. To-day it is fashionable to decry authority in education and allow the child to form its own beliefs. But where shall he get material to form them of? In reality we do not enter the world so poor. Each of us starts with what I may call an intellectual bank-stock, consisting of the conclusions those preceding us have reached in regard to the best modes of living. Knives and forks, three meals a day, electricity, the state, the family, are notions we were not left to invent, but to adopt and criticize.

An uncle of mine, a professor of Latin in Amherst College, had loved the old English poet, George Herbert, and suggested to my mother to give me his name, "so that I might always have a friend." A rich endowment indeed! For though Herbert's range is limited, he is an exquisite lyric artist who spent the few years of his ardent and hesitating life in perplexity over the counter attractions of the one and the many, God and the world. In him religious aspiration is peculiarly fresh and genuine. No less so are the allurements of sex, station, sweet sounds, rich clothes, fine phrases, high society. He always remains a double-minded man, at his death entrusting the manuscript of his poems to his friend as "a picture of the conflicts of my soul with God." What a stimulus to reflection would a thoughtful boy find in such a volume!

But the philosophic influence which was supreme over my youth, and has left its honoured mark on my age, was Puritanism. My father was a deacon in an Orthodox Church. Four uncles were Orthodox ministers. Religion of that positive type entered into every hour of my happy home. In a former paper I have set forth the facts and features of the Puritan home, and shown how far from true are the current caricatures of it. While profoundly serious—more romantically serious than many natures could well bear—there was nothing morose or sour about it. If its people had such traits independently, these no doubt appeared peculiarly unlovely in a religious setting. But for stout and cheerful souls it was an ennobling faith, providing abundant room for the play of all that is worthy in human character.

According to it man and God are not separable. A complete man, such as once appeared, would be a revelation of God himself. There are, however, lower and higher sides in our nature, the former expressing our adaptation to the physical and temporary world we inhabit. These, therefore, require continual subordination to the rational order. Indeed, the exercise of this subordination—not suppression—is a precious opportunity for that self-discipline which is the very purpose of our existence. We are born only half made, and must not take any casual impulse as if it rightly belonged to us. Pick and choose. Life is designed as a training school where each orderly advance makes another more possible. So life here prepares for life hereafter, and in that new life there will be nothing arbitrary. Its woe or happiness is the unobstructed expression of what we have come to value. I have sometimes thought that the deepest thing in Puritanism was its insistence on orderly connection. Or was that deepest thing the immediacy of the divine presence? The Puritan stood face to face with God, and owned responsibility to no one else. No Church or State could bind him. In his conscience and his Bible—and between the two he felt no divergence—he heard the authentic voice of God.

There are plenty of loose joints in such a creed, especially in its extreme individualism and lack of a community sense. But all will acknowledge that it provides an incomparable body of material for a youthful philosopher to wrestle with. In Germany, under the name of Pietism, it started the career of Kant. And nobody can understand the early history of America without perceiving that the Puritanism of New England furnishes its backbone.

Such was the rich intellectual "bank-stock" I set out with. But the physical stock was discouragingly poor. I was born a weakling, not expected to live from year to year. Spinal and heart trouble were in the family on my mother's side; on my father's constipation, rupture, and the attendant disturbances. My whole nervous system was over-sensitive and easily upset. Hardly one of my early years went by without a long illness. There may have been disorder in the brain, for up to about my fortieth year headaches were almost continuous, and I have never slept a night through in my life. I have undergone six surgical operations, the last when I was eighty-three. It is hardly necessary to add that I was a shy boy, avoiding people and finding writing and speaking extremely difficult. I do not complain of these conditions. Most of us break down at some time. He is fortunate to whom ill-health comes early and who thus learns betimes how to take care of himself. Since the nervous collapse that sent me home from Germany in 1869, I have been building up a body capable of meeting strains undisturbed. And that is the test of health.

Going to Andover at twelve to prepare for college, I was stopped two years later by granulation of the eyelids. Hard little particles nearly as large as peas formed on the under surface and nearly closed the lids. I was obliged to give up study and be put in charge of a surgical oculist. After six months' treatment he advised an entire change of climate, if possible a sea voyage. On a barque of five hundred tons I, at fifteen, with a brother two years older as companion, sailed for Egypt. There we spent a month in a country as yet hardly affected by Western civilization. It was a memorable experience for a youngster, but produced no improvement in the eyes. All thought of education had to be abandoned, and I took a place in a wholesale dry goods store.

After rather more than a year a friend took me to a physician in general practice, who thought my trouble might not be merely local but due to a generally bad condition of the system. With no instruments or lotions, but using simple homeopathic medicine, he brought the lids in the course of a few months to entire smoothness. To let the eyes grow strong they should have had an entire year's rest. But the prospect of entering Harvard was too inviting. I found that by exercising in the open air for most of the day I could study for an hour or two. As my doctor did not absolutely forbid the plan, I took a tutor and crawled into Harvard in 1860 with six conditions, but with feeble eyesight for the rest of my life. From service in the Civil War I was rejected on account of my eyes.

II

Harvard education reached its lowest point during my college course. When I entered it it was a small local institution with 996 students in all its departments and thirty teachers in the college Faculty. C. C. Felton was its President. Nearly all its studies were prescribed, and these were chiefly Greek, Latin, and Mathematics. There was one course in Modern History, one in Philosophy, a half course in Economics. There was no English Literature, but in the Sophomore year three hours a week were required in Anglo-Saxon. A feeble course or two in Modern Languages was allowed to those who wished it. There were two or three courses in Natural Science, taught without laboratory work. All courses were taught from text-books and by recitations. Though lectures were announced in several subjects, among them English Literature, not more than half a dozen of these were given in a year. Professor Cooke, it is true, lectured to the Sophomores an hour each week on Chemistry. But though we were all required to attend, there was no examination. All teaching was of a low order. The personality of only two teachers impressed me—Torrey in History, Gurney in Latin, perhaps I should add Sophocles in Greek, through his picturesque remoteness.

Such a curriculum—and it was no worse than in other colleges—would seem to have been arranged by a lunatic and to be valuable only as preparing the way for an Eliot. But that would be a mistaken judgment. While students found little to attract them in the official programme, they had four free years to devote to sports, society, discussion, friendships, and the pursuit of individual tastes. There was enormous waste, of course. But any of us who cared for intellectual things enjoyed an elective system of our own. I, up to the limit of my eyesight, read Poetry, Philosophy, and History, committing great quantities of Poetry to memory at times when I could not read. Tennyson was my master. All his changes from edition to edition I copied into a pocket volume, and was fairly introduced by him to Poetry as a Fine Art. Art for me became henceforth a close ally of Philosophy and Religion.

What I most wanted from Harvard was systematic training in Philosophy. But Professor Bowen offered only a single course, and that more elementary than any of the more than thirty now on the Harvard list. A slender acquaintance with the Scotch School—Reid, Stewart, Hamilton—was something. Something came from a source peculiarly barren—Lewes's *Biographical History of Philosophy*. It is an ignorant book, written to prove that there is no such thing as Philosophy. But the style is pleasing, and the exhibit of an age-long struggle by man to comprehend himself, his world, and his maker was what I needed at that particular moment. It was my first encounter with historic thought.

In striking contrast with this pretender a genuine man appeared and made an epoch in my intellectual life, John Stuart Mill. His book on *Liberty* was published the year before I entered college, his *Utilitarianism* in my Junior year. Through these I experienced for the first time the luxury of loyalty, of feeling myself a follower and propagandist. In the *Utilitarianism* I had gained a moral creed, and I made my Commencement part a defence of it. Everything that Mill wrote I read eagerly. And though before long I came to see that the best parts of Mill were his inconsistencies, these in no way lessened my admiration. They rather increased it as signs of his candour and freedom from partisanship. Here was a beautiful soul, somewhat too modest and inclined to lean—on his father, on Bentham, on Mrs. Taylor, on Miss Taylor—and showing in his face the tragedy produced by the conflict between the new idealism of Coleridge and Wordsworth and the traditional empiricism in which he grew up. While Mill's philosophy provided me no resting-place, I have never ceased to think gratefully of the man. On my first visit to England I went to the House of Commons and found my hero not the calm listener I had imagined, but restless in his seat and continually ejaculating the strange "Hear, Hear!" with which members approve what is said. In the early nineties Mrs. Palmer and I made a pilgrimage to Avignon to see the house where Mill spent his last years in sight of his wife's grave.

Herbert Spencer never affected me in any such way. His technical knowledge of Philosophy was slight and his personality inferior. Nor was I much moved by the bitter Darwinian controversy. Darwin himself was admirably restrained, but his defenders and assailants were alike blunderers when they assumed that religion was at stake over the question whether creation was accomplished at once or by successive stages. On the whole, I thought those wisest who did not count evolution an affair of chance. These three men—Mill, Spencer, and Darwin—were the chief agents in breaking up American stupor and starting fruitful philosophic discussion.

III

On leaving college I felt I had absorbed more than I had digested, and I resolved to take a year of comparative leisure for reviewing and rethinking what I had read. Accordingly I accepted a position as sub-master in the Salem High School. I was to teach half a dozen elementary subjects with which I was entirely familiar. But I never worked harder in my life. To be acquainted with a subject sufficiently for one's own purposes is not the same thing as the mastery needed for impartation. The entire year was devoted to the study of teaching. Already I had made a beginning in this finest of the Fine Arts. During the winter vacation of my Freshman year I took the place of an absent teacher in the State Reform School. I waked my boys in the morning, presided over their three meals, had them as pupils during the forenoon, for two hours in the evening sat with them in their games, talks, and readings, and put them to bed at 9.30. I found them attachable and interesting. Few had known anything like a home or had learned to love anybody. Being somewhat cleverer than the average and more adventurous, they had committed some petty crime and were arrested. Most of them afterwards served in the war. During the later years of my college course I gave two evenings a week to Boston Mission Schools, where all ages, all nationalities, all colours, and both sexes gathered to be taught reading, writing, and other beginnings of wisdom.

The boys and girls of Salem were of different stuff. They came of a cultivated inheritance and a preliminary training, and were less afraid of their bashful instructor than he of them. I can feel again the sinking of heart as the closing door shut me into my recitation room with half a dozen pupils from whom I could not escape for an hour. Precious sufferings these. By them a self-centred youth becomes gradually transformed into a public-minded man. Another profitable hardship the school gave: it initiated me into tact. The two Principals, man and woman, were powerful characters but markedly divergent in temperament. I admired both and learned as much from one as from the other. But they soon declared war and throughout the year were hardly on speaking terms with one another. We all three lived in the same house, sat at the same table, and each required to be treated with considerate care.

These two abilities—the ability to face an intelligent class unabashed and the ability to meet differently constituted people with kindly tact—were begun in me at Salem School. Each was evidently essential for a teacher of philosophy; yet to make a beginning on them obliged me temporarily to suspend all philosophic work. To devote myself now exclusively to this central interest became my urgent aim.

IV

In most colleges the little philosophy attempted was usually taught by the President, a minister. If an independent teacher was also employed, he was a minister. Under Puritanism theology and philosophy were pretty closely identified. Before the days of Johns Hopkins, too, the best opportunity for continuous study of philosophy was in a Divinity School. I accordingly entered Andover Seminary in September 1865. Among the hundred students I met there I gained some lifelong friends, chief among them W. J. Tucker, afterwards President of Dartmouth, and J. H. Lee, an Amherst graduate who had just returned from the war with tastes similar to mine.

With Lee I formed a studious alliance. We read philosophy three hours a day, at first in its history, then in the English and Scotch writers, later in Kant. By the end of our second year both he and I felt the need of a broader outlook, especially clearer insight into German Idealism. A glimpse of this we had already gained through the writings of Coleridge and F. D. Maurice. Of course a first reading of Kant had bewildered more than enlightened us. We longed for a German university. One morning Lee returned from a week-end at home with the announcement that his father had told him to spend next year abroad. When this was reported in my home my brother-in-law offered to send me also. I hesitated, knowing that he was far from rich. But as we all saw that it would be a turning-point in my life and would make me of public value, I finally accepted the great gift—a gift the more generous since none of my family shared my philosophic interests. I hoped, too, that the brain trouble that had been growing more oppressive might be helped by a change of climate.

As neither Lee nor I knew any language but our own, we planned to sail in May 1867, and spend the intervening months before the universities opened in getting up our German in a family in Stuttgart to whom we had introductions. We would then divide our year between Leipzig and Berlin. The voyage and journey were exhilarating. European travel was less common then than now. To us Europe had always been a fairy tale, and here it was proved real. We ran rapidly over Ireland, England, Holland, and the Rhineland, mostly on foot and in daily wonderment, until we settled in comfortable quarters in picturesque Stuttgart and began our attack on German. As no other language was spoken in the house our progress was rapid. In July we heard of Tübingen as one of the quaint spots of Germany, hardly changed since the Middle Age, and we walked across the hills to see it. Both of us were completely fascinated. We decided to move there at once and to spend our first semester there.

There for two years I was enrolled as a student, with great profit and enjoyment from the lectures of Professor Sigwart and Professor Herzog and from the intimate personal acquaintance which these gentlemen allowed me. But on the whole my foreign stay was a period of catastrophe and disappointment.

During the summer my brother and sister, who had sent me abroad, crossed the ocean on business and urged me to join them in their Paris apartment. Some happy weeks were spent with them, with the Louvre pictures and with the bookstalls along the Quai. But one Saturday a telegram from Sheffield, England, called me instantly to the death-bed of a friend. It was a stormy night and the Channel boats were crowded. The crossing usually required two or three hours; that night it took nine. I have never known so wild a sea. The waves swept the decks, the hatches broke loose, and everybody was drenched. We landed in the morning with clothes wet through, and before they could be dried all passengers were called to the waiting train and the long railroad ride. My head was in a bewildered state. I managed to return from England the next day, but as soon as I entered the Paris apartment I fell on the floor unconscious, and for six weeks thereafter had my wits only at intervals. The illness was pronounced typhus fever in the brain. Possibly enough, something of the sort might have occurred if I had not been so badly exposed. The brain had long been weak, the German food was abominable, hygiene and drainage had there no existence.

But the upsetting was not without its compensations. For physician it gave me Mme. Hahnemann, the second wife of the discoverer of homeopathy, a stately lady past seventy, in full vigour of body and mind, to whom I became warmly attached. Then as I grew able to move about a little I visited the magnificent Exposition of 1867, where Japan for the first time startled Europe with its unique art. In the Louvre and several of the other galleries I studied often, for art was now taking its permanent place in my mind as the supplement and concrete embodiment of philosophy. Evenings an eccentric man of genius, Edward Silsbee, read aloud to me. He was a devotee of Shelley. The Shelley manuscripts at Harvard and Oxford are his gift. I, a sworn Wordsworthian, could give him only a fragment of the admiration he desired. These were, therefore, gainful weeks. They brought everything except abstract Philosophy. To get this I was anxious to return to Tübingen at the earliest moment. My brother and sister were already in America. Though my doctor advised against haste, I set off as the bleak autumn was changing to winter. It was a bad blunder. I overestimated my strength. A relapse occurred, and I was forced back to Paris for another month.

By the time I was settled again in Tübingen half of my precious year was gone. Lee was to return to America in the spring, and my brain was so unsteady that I was warned not to strain it by severe study. I therefore visited still more frequently the homes of my

Professors, especially that of Sigwart, absorbing philosophy instead of studying it. Finally Herzog suggested my beginning a thesis for the Doctorate on the concept of Sin in the Agamemnon of Æschylus. At Harvard I had tasted the delights of Greek literature, and little as was my knowledge of Greek grammar, I had from time to time read several dramas with a friend. Now in broken health I turned to these enchantments as a refuge. Sometimes alone, sometimes with a like-minded companion, I read Homer through, much of Herodotus, all the surviving plays of Æschylus and Sophocles, half of those of Aristophanes, two or three of Euripides, for whom I never greatly cared. Half a dozen of the lighter dialogues of Plato kept philosophy alive, but into the magic world of the *Republic* I did not enter till much later, and I never got much from the *Laws* and the *Theætetus*.

It will be seen that my Greek studies were not serious. A lawless personal taste directed them no less than when I read Goethe, Heine, Keats, or Chaucer, to whom a friend had early introduced me. No doubt such eager amateurism yields something missed by the academic scholar. The two should go together. And in my work for the Ph.D. I more nearly united them.

But I have anticipated, and brought over into my first year much belonging to the opening of the second. For there was to be a second. When my father learned of my misfortunes he wrote and offered me another chance. So I spent the summer in a quiet German village where I could have good care and small expense. By the time the new semester opened I was much improved in health, able, indeed, to get real profit from philosophic lectures and from work on my thesis. I need not then recount the experiences of these months, but may skip to the Christmas holidays.

My brother and sister had again come abroad, this time themselves in search of health. They were spending the winter in Italy and invited me to join them in Rome for the holidays. An interesting time it was to be there. Pius Ninth's Œcumenical Council was in session, and Catholic leaders from all over the world filled the streets. Each Sunday I heard Cardinal Manning render Catholicism plausible to the many English Protestants then in Rome. He was an imposing figure and an admirable pleader, as good as Browning's Bishop Blougram. That old Rome ruled by the Pope was worth seeing. The masking for the Carnival was brilliant, the horse-race down the Corso unique, the services at St. Peter's vulgarly superb, and the Pope's blessing of the crowded Piazza majestic.

But Popes knew nothing of hygiene. The rotten streets of Rome bred a special type of malaria with Roman fever as its product. I was soon attacked. I fled to Florence in time to escape the full force of the fever, but the virus went off in a series of huge boils as prostrating as the fever itself. More than a month passed before I was able to move about and study the frescoes and the lovely Tuscan sculpture. My excellent Italian doctor assured me that I could not expect to be myself again under a year. It was plain that I must abandon Germany, Sigwart, my thesis, and go home. At my little hotel in Florence I had found a dear friend and Harvard classmate, Frank Washburn, whose experiences abroad had been almost as disappointing as mine. He, too, was minded for America. Travelling together slowly, a pair of cripples, we reached Boston in early spring. Europe had given me little of what I came for, but it had been a great maturing time. A scholar is hardly grown up until he makes another language and another national outlook his own.

I hoped the quiet of a Boxford summer would put vigour enough into me to allow me a final year at Andover. I entered there in September 1869. But complete nervous collapse brought me back two months later to Boxford for the winter. And here let me say that I never became a minister nor applied for licence to preach. I saw that my business in life must be the critical analysis of thought, of moral and religious thought, and that any appeals I might wish to make to the emotions and wills of men must be subservient to this and depend for success on the literary power hard work would enable me to attain. In my early youth it would have been accounted presumptuous for a young man to aim at a professorship of philosophy. He must be "called" to this. He did not nominate himself. My hope had been to master my subject, preach a few years, and then to be so called. But a change in the educational estimate of philosophy had been coming about, especially since the appearance of President Eliot. It was not reckoned so audacious as formerly to aim directly at a college position.

Toward spring an eccentric country doctor began to build me up, without medicine, but with minute instructions on diet and mental conduct. He was a mental healer before medical fashions gave him the right to be. He taught me how to live. The building of a body is a slow business, but I knew myself on the way to it, and saw that with study, persistence, and daily self-denial it could be accomplished as certainly as the building of a barn. Now in old age I am in health that may be called perfect—no cold for five years, no headache for nearly twice that time.

V

In May I sent out applications to several western colleges for a place in philosophy. None of them replied. One day I met Professor

Kelsey, the temporary President of Michigan, Angell's predecessor. As we parted, I asked if there were no opening in philosophy at Michigan. He thought there might be, would look it up and write. While waiting for the letter I asked Professor Gurney of Harvard if I might use his name as a reference. He readily gave it, but said he thought I made a mistake in treating my subject as final and then looking for a college where it might be taught; better turn the matter round. Choose a first-class college and teach whatever they would accept. If I had power, it would be discovered and I should ultimately be in the place that fitted me. Daring advice! which I resisted. But three days later I received from President Eliot an appointment in Greek. I replied that I could not decide at once but must await an expected letter from the West. "And how long?" "A fortnight. If nothing then comes I shall be obliged to accept Harvard." Nothing came. Twenty-five years later President Angell showed me on the Faculty Record my appointment to an Assistant Professorship at Michigan, and underneath it in a different hand "Declined." All were dead who knew the circumstances. The only explanation I can imagine is a letter lost in the mail. The opening of the term was near, a teacher must be secured at once, nothing was heard from me, and my name was crossed off. My entire career was thus changed by a single mishap. So interlocked are luck and purpose in the game of life.

When I told Professor Goodwin that an objection to my entering his department was that I knew no Greek and could not write a Greek sentence if my life depended on it, he was most kind, saying that teachers drilled in Greek grammar were common, but trained in Greek literature rare. One of these would not harm his department. It harmed me though. Most of my time the first year had to be spent on moods and tenses. In an attempt to make my students perceive what these were for I offered, as we finished a Book of the Odyssey, to translate the whole at a sitting for all who cared to come. A large number came. Copies of the text were provided and the closest possible rendering was used. Hence arose the voluntary Greek Readings, a plan soon adopted in other departments. In successive years I read the whole Odyssey through twice, and in 1884 published a revolutionary version of it.

At the beginning of 1872 Professor Peterson resigned his position of Assistant Professor of Philosophy. I resigned my Tutorship in Greek and was appointed instructor in philosophy for a single year on a salary of $1,000. This was soon increased by $500, the salary of the Curatorship of the Gray Collection of Engravings, and by the large fees from three private pupils, the last I ever consented to take. Henceforth all my time was to be given to my own subject, in which I was appointed Assistant Professor in 1873, Full Professor in 1880.

VI

But here I must insert a section more frankly autobiographic, and sketch in a few words an influence which was the chief formative agency of the first half of my life. Naturally, so diffident and self-centred a person had few youthful love affairs. Their place was taken by one abiding loyalty. For ten years I followed Ellen Margaret Wellman, of Brookline. She lived but a few doors from my sister and was an intimate in my sister's household. No doubt I am prejudiced, but I believe everyone living in Brookline at that time acknowledged her as pre-eminent in fascination and accomplishments. A little creature, weighing less than a hundred pounds, all grace, vivacity, and charm, abounding in health and spirits, totally unacquainted with fear, either of man or nature, all she did or said was unique, though never queer.

Those were the days when girls did not go to college or take part in public affairs. But the education the best of them gave themselves, induced a refinement all their own. Miss Wellman was exquisite in all things, as a musician, actor, dancer, talker. She had read widely and with discerning taste. French was nearly as familiar to her as English. With all her brilliancy, too, and perpetual humour, she was deeply religious, a follower of Swedenborg and the mainstay of her little Church. Several years older than I, she allowed me during my Harvard and Andover days all the friendship I could ask—with occasional intimations of a limit beyond which not—until a catastrophe occurred, parting us for a time, but ultimately uniting.

A favourite brother of hers was in the class below me at Harvard. He looked forward to a scholarly life, but was struck down the year after graduation with quick consumption. He was bitterly rebellious. With her usual unselfish ardour, she abandoned all other interests to identify herself with him. She must be his only nurse. She did not leave his room by day and slept on the floor beside him at night. When he died he was at peace with himself and God. Up to that time she had never known a day's illness; from that time she knew no day of health, and she never regretted the sacrifice.

The following year she spent in the Azores, with little improvement in health, but great enjoyment. Her ability to enjoy no weakness could check. I was abroad all this time. We exchanged a few letters, only a few. But when I came home, broken too, the love of years could no longer be hidden. It had ripened in us both. Through much opposition from both families, on grounds of age, religion, and health, we came to our joyful wedding on June 15, 1871.

The specifically intellectual profits of an ideally happy marriage cannot be summarized. They are too subtle and permeating. But I will venture to name a few of the more conspicuous. Inclusive of all else was the wholehearted companionship which gave a deeper significance to all I did. She taught me to talk; for we talked all day, seldom of trivialities or gossip, but of things worth talking about. Able to go about but little, she entered the more completely into my work. The publication of my Odyssey was due to her urging, and to her it is dedicated. Innumerable students were drawn by her to our home, and her swift sympathies contributed something to the modern friendly Harvard spirit. Then, too, I felt it an enlargement that the sources from which we instinctively drew our spiritual sustenance were so different. She read her Swedenborg every day, and in the early years hoped to see me a convert. But at the last I think she liked me better as I was.

I should add also that the knowledge that we could be together only a short time sanctified those precious years and deepened their influence. For two years after her hæmorrhage came she could only speak in whispers. But this in no wise checked her gaiety or charm. We talked of her approaching death as freely as of any other incident. She advised me, after it should occur, to take rooms in the college buildings, herself selected the rooms, and planned how our furniture should be disposed. On February 10, 1879, she died. For eight and a half years thereafter, till Alice Freeman appeared, I lived among my boys in Stoughton Hall. My life with Alice Freeman has been detailed at such length elsewhere that it requires no recapitulation here.

VII

At the beginning of my teaching in philosophy I was merely the assistant of Professor Bowen. He directed all my work, even what books my classes should use. The Heads of Departments in those days took their positions seriously. Logic was required of all Juniors, and I was set to teach it in Jevons's *Elementary Lessons*. The class was divided into six sections, each of which I was to meet twice a week. Anything less nutritive can hardly be imagined. Jevons has carefully eliminated all philosophy from his clever and shallow little book, so that my twelve hours a week of work would seem to have been completely unprofitable to me and to my class. But they were not so, and I mention these repellent circumstances because I suspect they are by no means peculiar to me.

Beginnings are apt to be barren. Whatever gains can be extracted from them must generally be collateral, affecting the whole personality. These years proved excellent for the interminable study of teaching. In this I had made a fair start at Salem. But I had not yet gone beyond the bounds contemplated in the common saying, "I am ready to teach pupils who are ready to learn." A higher order of teaching should be demanded of a college professor. He should be able to interest his students in his subject and make them wish to learn. In all my dealings with elementary and required work this was ever my problem, and I thought myself fortunate to have had it impressed on me so early in my career.

For many years Professor Bowen taught a course in Cartesianism with Bouillier's *History* as a manual. In 1874 he asked me to offer this as an advanced course, and for elementary work to take the whole Junior class together instead of in sections. Of course I welcomed this, my first serious encounter with philosophy. Only I resolved to deal with it in the original, in Descartes' *Methode* and *Principes* and Malebranche's *Entretiens*. To refresh my knowledge of French, Mrs. Palmer and I spent the summer of 1873 at Saint-Germain. This course I taught for several years with great delight and profit. Descartes has ever since been one of my closest philosophic friends. For the required course a series of wretched books were used—Porter, Bain, Hamilton, etc.—the best of them being Ferrier's unfinished *History of Greek Philosophy*. This enabled me to bring some genuine problems before my boys. When, too, Professor Everett, of the Divinity School, was absent for a year, I had the luxury of teaching Kant's *Critique* in his place.

It will be seen that at this time all the philosophic teaching at Harvard was historical, the presentation and criticism of notable men of the past. This was the general practice of American colleges, whether cause or effect of the low condition of philosophic thought one cannot say. Probably, as is usually the case in social phenomena, it was both. Such habits start in modesty and the conscious need of knowledge; but if persisted in to the exclusion of creative work, they are enfeebling. Learning and originality are not easily reconciled, essential though both are. At present too little history is studied. Our young philosophers lack balance. Fifty years ago they lacked courage. The coming of constructive courses made an epoch in American philosophy. I like to think I was the first to offer one at Harvard in 1889. It was announced as "Phil. IV, A Theory of Ethics Considered Constructively—Lectures, Theses, and Private Reading." Into this course I put the utmost of my powers for twenty-five years. Because it acquired a certain historic importance through attracting many men who have since won distinction, I will describe its method in some detail.

No one could take it who had not already spent a year on philosophy. In its first term every student was obliged to write two elaborate papers, one of them dealing with some eminent writer who approached ethics from an empiric standpoint, followed by one from an idealist. But in each paper there was to be a sharp division. In a first section the writer was to make the best defence he could of his author's position, regardless of his own views, and not in the author's words; in a second, those views were to be stated. The theses of the second Half Year were on abstract problems— Freedom, Value, Vice, Punishment, etc.—where only the writer's own observations and reasonings were allowed. Meanwhile, I was expounding systematically my own beliefs, interposing at frequent intervals an hour of debate. My system was divided, not altogether wisely, into two parts. The first, under the title "Goodness," discussed the moral individual; the second, on "Duty," the claims of society. Throughout I endeavoured to impress on my men that until we had rid our minds of all notions of "radical" and "conservative" and confined our attention to evidence alone, there was no possibility of useful thinking.

Desiring to avoid large numbers and restrict the class to serious men who were ready to make some sacrifice to enter it, I chose for my hour 3.30 in the afternoon. The course being known, too, as far from soft, loafers and dullards avoided it, and its members were a stimulus to one another and to me. One compliment it received I have always cherished. A committee from one of the tables in Memorial Hall waited on me with complaint of my students who dined there. They made themselves a nuisance. They were forever discussing ethics, and so insistently that nobody had a chance for a word on anything else. That was impolite, 1 owned. But inwardly I glowed.

And since I have said so much about Phil. IV, I will venture to touch on two points more. While I never wrote a lecture, and kept only a continually altered note-book, I found that after going over the same ground for several years I became liable to routine, to reliance on memory rather than fresh thinking, I accordingly learned to drop the course every fourth or fifth year, and when I returned it was re-created. I noticed, however, that it was best the third year after my return, not the first. Royce taught another of these standard contructive courses, Phil. II, Metaphysics. Similar ones were springing up all over the country and were, in my judgment, factors in breaking up the early philosophic stupor. Notable examples of these were Garman's at Amherst, Howison's in California, Hyde's at Bowdoin. The regular quantum of my teaching after I became Chairman of the Department was a Seminary, once a week for two hours; an advanced course, three hours; and a half course, elementary, three hours, usually the History of Greek or Modern Philosophy. Believing that elementary work requires the greatest skill in its teacher, we kept it entirely in charge of Full Professors and assigned our young men, who were generally specialists, to advanced work.

VIII

With the Department of Philosophy I was connected earlier than any of its other members. I have watched its entire development and have had my share in shaping its policies. Up to the time of my resignation in 1913 it included the following Full Professors—I name them in the order of seniority—Palmer, James, Royce, Münsterberg, Santayana; and four closely affiliated allies, C. C. Everett in the Philosophy of Religion, F. G. Peabody in Social Ethics, E. C. Moore in Christian Morals, and P. H. Hanus in Education, B. Rand always being our Librarian. It was a remarkable group. President Tucker, of Dartmouth, once remarked to me that he thought it not merely the strongest department of Philosophy the country had ever seen, but the strongest department of any kind. Its powers, too, were increased by duration, seven of those I have named being associated together for more than twenty years. I was in it forty-one. All, too, had published largely and made a name in general literature as well as in their technical subjects. The professors appointed since my time have fully maintained the standard there set. As Full Professors there are R. B. Perry. M. deWulf, W. E. Hocking, R. C. Cabot, W. MacDougall, A. N. Whitehead. My colleagues were men of genius who, independently, would have had a deep influence anywhere. But I believe that influence was doubled by certain ethical features in the organization of our department. Since these features have attracted little notice, though in my judgment they are well worth reproducing elsewhere, I name them here.

1. The former controlling Head of the Department was abandoned. A Chairman took his place. This officer called our meetings, presided at them, and was our medium of communication with the President. Every few years he was changed. In the course of time most of our professors served in this way and so became acquainted with administrative as well as teaching duties. Occasionally even an Assistant Professor was Chairman. But neither he nor any other professor had authority over the rest. All were equal and independent. When we met for discussion, or to draw up our programme of studies for the following year, we did so as a company of gentlemen all alike anxious to strengthen the department. If two mentioned the same topic as the subject they proposed for their course on the new programme, we talked it over and considered whether we had better double up, as is sometimes well, or fill a vacancy elsewhere.

One of the two professors always gladly withdrew, postponing his topic to a later year. The Chairman led the discussion and made suggestions, but exercised no control. The fact that no professor of ours was a subordinate gave dignity to the position and enabled us to call men of superior grade. I never knew anyone invited to join our staff who refused. This organization through a chairman is now, I believe, employed in many departments at Harvard, but extends itself slowly through other colleges.

2. We avoided "breeding-in" and directly aimed at diversity in our staff. When a new member was proposed, we at once asked whether he had not the same mental attitude as someone we had already. If so, we did not want him. There is therefore no Harvard "School" of philosophy. As soon as our students leave college they are sure to encounter all sorts of beliefs. We wished them to have a chance to study these beliefs under the guidance of an expert believer and then to have the difficulties in them presented by an expert opponent. This, we held, accomplishes best the great aim of a college: it leads a student to think for himself, to acquire the mastery of his mind. It so protects his after-years and saves him from subjection to the casual opinions of his little circle. We endeavoured to train leaders, not followers.

3. These differences of opinion in our staff were always openly acknowledged. In our lectures we were accustomed to attack each other by name, James forever exposing the follies of the idealists, particularly of Royce and me, Royce in turn showing how baseless all empiricism is, lacking a metaphysical ground. One year James and Royce combined in a course on metaphysics, Royce occupying the first half-year, James the second. One November Royce asked me to take charge of his advanced course for six weeks while he was lecturing at Aberdeen. I told him I hardly could, for I dissented from everything thus far in his lectures. He said he was aware of this, and for that reason had asked me. He thought my coming would enrich the course. I took it and devoted myself to pulling up all the young plants which Royce had carefully set out. When he came home he ordered a thesis on the entire work of the half-year, and he told me it was the best thesis he had ever received. Our students were not misled by these our attacks on each other. They knew that we were all warm friends, few departments more so. But truth was sacred, and criticism, the surest way of approaching it, was a friendly not a hostile process. We wished our students to cultivate the critical habit, learn to be dispassionate, and not allow personal feelings to encroach on intellectual judgments. James has admirably defined philosophy as the obstinate attempt to think clearly, and nowhere is such obstinacy more needed than for purging one's judgment from

personal bias. We were glad to be examples of this, of the honour
paid to diversity, and the assurance that infinite reality might be
approached from many points of view. And what happiness to
work under conditions of entire freedom, where suspicions were
unknown and friendships profound!

IX

In several of the interpolated years when I suspended my teaching
in Phil. IV, I traced the course of English Ethics from Hobbes to
Mill. Hobbes was always a favourite of mine. His eager thought,
his frankness, and forthright utterance made me like to return to
him often. I incline to think him our earliest writer of pure prose.
His predecessors and contemporaries who wrote something that
looks like prose did not think of it as a colourless medium through
which thought might shine. They coloured it with beauty and meant
to have at least half the reader's attention given to the diction, as
in poetry. With Hobbes the thought is all. He cannot pause for
anything else. The *Leviathan* is an impassioned cry to his readers
to save the nation from impending ruin. The State of Nature is a
state of war, where each seeks his own, regardless of his neighbour's
welfare. The only escape is a social compact, where each agrees to
give up something of what he desires on condition that others do
the same. This is not done out of altruism. There is no such thing.
It is merely an enlarged selfishness that, by abandoning immediate
pleasure, reaps through peace a richer harvest.

Here Hobbes set the ethical problem for the next two hundred
years. Many solutions were tried. I shall not refer them to their
authors. Roughly and briefly as I state them here, it would be unfair
to do so. I am not writing history, but merely noting steps in my own
progress. Hobbes was told he had libelled nature. It contained two
instincts, not one. Sometimes one is uppermost, sometimes the other.
Moreover, from our earliest years, those about us insisted on our
paying attention to their comfort and would not otherwise give us
what we wanted. Thus through association the two impulses become
blended and we give the more honourable name to the mixture.
Or there is a kind of pleasure in helping the neighbour; another kind
in helping oneself. But the former is so much "higher" than the
latter that a little of it outweighs much of the other. Sympathy,
the swift experience of what others are experiencing, is too obvious
a fact in daily life not to have influenced ethics. Or again, Hobbes
is right. Our instincts prompt us to pursue only our own pleasure.
But in the Bible God bids us seek that of our neighbour also, and

threatens us with eternal misery if we do not. It is possible even to ignore questions of *meum* and *tuum* and make morality a simple problem of bulk. "Aim at producing the greatest happiness of the greatest number" will then be our maxim.

No one of these theories, not even that of Hobbes, fails to honour the claims of society. These are paramount. Apart from society all agree there is no morality. The problem is to find a connection between the claims of society and those of myself. Why should an individual self, a person, go outside himself for an ultimate ground of obligation? Must not life be its own justification? What shall a man give or take in exchange for his life? The oftener I returned to this historic movement the more urgent its central problem appeared. I early saw that self-realization must be our constant moral aim, but only by degrees I detected ambiguity in the phrase.

A child thinks of himself as a single independent being and has never happened to notice that no such being exists. In reality, a single person is a contradiction in terms. The smallest conceivable unit of personality is threefold—father, mother, child. It is true that as we grow the relations of father and mother largely fall away, but this is only because they are superseded by relations more comprehensive. That is, a person is an individual being plus his relations, and these relations are what constitute him to be what he is. What is there in me, I may well ask, that I have not received? What would I be if I were not an American, if I were not a Harvard man, if I had not had the friends I have had, or read the books I have read?

Such relations are not external, like those of space and time. They are constitutive. Therefore, when I call morality the fullness of self-realization, the complex character of the self must be borne in mind. I doubted if the English writers had felt this ambiguity of the self and I devised a couple of phrases to keep the two meanings unmistakable. These I have since used in my classes and books with decided advantage. Occasionally, and for a special purpose, I need to fix attention on myself in contrast to others. This I call the separate or abstract self. The real self, the self plus, I call the conjunct self.

In speaking, however, of the separate self as abstract and artificial, I do not deny that each of us is unique, different from all others, made so by the very relations which produce the conjunction. Still further, the weighty facts of praise and blame, and the very existence of morals, testify to some central agency in the conjunct self which enables me to contrast myself as permanent and causal with what happens to me. Rightly I say, "I have this feeling," not "I am this feeling." Otherwise it would be as absurd to censure me for a trespass as to censure the wind for blowing. In my book on Freedom I hope I have made this plain. In Royce's philosophy there is something similar to this conjunctive notion. In his early papers, when analysing time, he points out how, though we must often speak of a present moment, nothing of the sort really exists, but only a relation to foregoing and oncoming time. And more elaborately in his last book the community is set forth as the fulfilment of the spiritual individual.

I like my term, the conjunct self, better, because it holds before the mind with less explanation the nature of morality, the meaning of virtue and vice. Virtue, the service of the conjunct self, calls upon us whenever we act, however slight the action may be, to see that more than our unitary personality is involved. I was walking down one of the paths in the College Yard the other day and saw a man in front of me reading a letter. When he had read it he tore it up and threw it on the ground. He had done with it; it was of no more use to him. He threw it down, never asking himself whether it was going to be agreeable to other people. That is the very essence of vice. Wherever we trace iniquity it will always be seen to amount to this, the setting up of the abstract or unitary self against the conjunct.

Something like this seems to have been in the mind of the early etymologists when they coined the word obligation. Translated syllable by syllable, this is ob-lig-ation, tied-in-ness, an excellent expression. Duty springs from relations beyond the separate self. There is the same suggestion in con-science, which bids us know, through connections. When a plate of apples is passed to me and I select the best one, there is nothing wrong in my having a good apple. I am selfish only when I do not consider others and am ready to make my gain out of their loss.

There was one of my predecessors at Harvard who was always careful not to ask a question of his class in Ethics until he had made sure that they could answer it. In those distant days we had only one connection with Boston, an omnibus which ran once an hour. The professor took this to illustrate selfishness. "Mr. Jones, if you were going to Boston this cold morning and as you walked to the hourly you saw a crowd moving in the same direction, then remembering that the bus had only a single blanket, you dashed past and secured the blanket—what would you call that?" "Presence of mind," said the student, a sensible answer for the separate self.

Pleasure is dangerous through its attempt to realize the self in an instant without reference to the rest of life. Evil patriotism tries to isolate itself, to the disparagement of other nations; just patriotism cherishes the characteristics of its own people because they form a distinctive contribution which it can make to internationalism. How disgusting to see a religious sect thinking of itself as the whole thing, instead of trying to be a worthy member of the Universal Church! The jeering soldiery at the foot of the cross laughed at the folly of him who hung on it. "He saved others, himself he could not save." But he was saving that inclusive self of which they were ignorant. Well might Socrates say that the Delphic maxim, "know thyself," is the starting-point of morality. And I did not discover this starting-point until several years after I had been teaching Ethics! I think this is characteristic of progress in philosophy. It is seldom an even advance, but on a sudden an obstructing wall goes down and to the prepared eye discloses a broad prospect.

X

It is hard to estimate how great a debt we owe to daily companions, especially to those who differ from us so widely as to set before us a supplementary pattern of humanity. My debt to the men who diversified my department is simply enormous.

Hardly less is it to the mighty master of us all, so simple, so dignified, President Eliot. He knew little of technical philosophy, but he honoured the truth and truth-seekers everywhere. Our growth he watched with steadfast interest and gave us all the assistance we could ask. I was associated with him for thirty-nine of the forty years of his presidency; and living next door to him for half that time I was privileged with an intimacy which transformed reverence to love. Besides his all-comprehending intellect and his patiently persistent will I saw his tenderness and the ardour of his domestic affections, and I have felt that he was well described in a couplet of my god-father's, George Herbert:

> " He life's way knows
> Whom all his passions follow—as he goes."

No personal inclination ever diverted him from an approved end. In consequence of this dispassionate attitude, his estimates of men were almost unerring. He liked to surround himself with strong men, and this the more if such associates were critical of his policies. Edward Hooper, Alexander Agassiz, and Major Higginson were choices of his. From him I learned more about the wise guidance of life—and this is philosophy in the concrete—than from any other single man. Perhaps he was the greatest man I ever studied.

I am not sure. For another massive personality shaped me for ten years and in ways more strictly philosophic, Edward Caird. For a long time he was Professor of Philosophy at Glasgow University and probably more influential over Scotch thought than any teacher of his time. Then he became Jowett's successor at Balliol. In those days German Idealism was challenging the Empiricism of Bain and Spencer. When Caird's first book on Kant appeared Eliot Cabot, the biographer of Emerson, called my attention to it. I saw at once its importance for me and wrote Caird asking to become his pupil for the summer of 1878. He replied that he had taken no pupils for several years, finding his summer necessary for refreshment. I took the next steamer to Glasgow and found him one Saturday morning reading Æschylus in the Greek. He was a man over six feet tall, brawny throughout, shy in manner, and with a strong Scotch accent. After we had talked a couple of hours, he said: "Won't you bring in on Monday afternoon a paper on Hume for discussion?" I did so and he ordered another on Kant's *Æsthetic* for Tuesday. Thereafter I spent two hours a day with him, and when he went to Ireland for the remainder of his vacation he invited me to join him. Some fears I had that all was not going well at home made me decline and return to America. That was the first of six summers, not always continuous, spent with this stimulating friend.

Our procedure was always the same. We took a furnished house and had the owner cook for us, often in the English Lake Country, sometimes in the Highlands where Gaelic was the native language and little English was known. After a simple breakfast we worked in our respective rooms at our respective studies till luncheon-time. When that was over, nothing could induce Caird to return to books. We must walk for three hours, accompanied by Mrs. Caird and a shaggy poodle dog known to Glasgow students as the *Ding an sich*. It always rained. I have gone six weeks without seeing the sun. These walks were our seasons of earnest discussion. Returning in time to bathe, to send our wet clothes to the kitchen and to eat a hearty dinner, we then read aloud till ten o'clock, when Mrs. Caird and I withdrew and left Caird himself for three hours more over books in all languages. A fresh box of them came from Mudie's each week.

He read with extreme rapidity and held at easy command all he had once known. I do not think he had paid much attention to physical science, but in all the varieties of humanism—History, Government, Economics, Ethics, Religion—he was prodigiously learned. He loved the English poets, too, but more still Dante and Goethe. In religion a Presbyterian, in politics an extreme Liberal, a propagandist for women's education and suffrage, he belonged to a club composed half of professors and half of working men which met for discussion on alternate weeks at each other's houses.

What I sought him for chiefly was his Hegelianism. He might fairly be called a sectarian Hegelian, for he could find no fault with his master, and knew all his innumerable pages. I have gained more from Hegel than from any other philosopher, but I never became an Hegelian. Hegel has too slender a sense of personality and practically none of sin or conscious wrong-doing, a fundamental ethical fact. Freedom is his sacred word, but with him it means natural necessity and has nothing to do with the alternative choice of common speech. My Anti-Hegelianism I have developed at length in my book on Freedom. My relations with Caird were like those with James, of friendly and perpetual antagonism.

XI

Two questions were proposed at the beginning of this paper. What agencies have operated in America during the last half-century to transform indifference into the enthusiasm which has recently brought six hundred teachers from all over the globe to do philosophy honour in the Harvard Yard? Over the answer to this first question I have lingered long in an endeavour to trace the helps and hindrances which attended my slow, but probably fairly representative progress. An answer to the second question, about the conclusions reached by an average mind after passing through this transitional period, I have reserved as the topic of the remainder of this paper. Before treating it, however, I had better sum up *in abstracto* the working agencies of advance which hitherto I have presented only historically.

Table of influences aiding philosophic advance:

1. Resort to Germany for graduate study.
2. Professors make a specialty of single subjects.
3. Ph.D. first given at Harvard in 1873 to W. E. Byerly.
4. Possibility of aiming at a professorship even though not a minister.
5. Philosophic staffs employed in place of Presidents or single professors.
6. For courses beyond elementary, textbooks and mere criticism of authors abandoned and orderly constructive work expected of professors.
7. Lectures substituted for recitations, with assistants for quizzes and theses.
8. Books reserved in the Library and large private reading demanded of students.
9. Sabbatical years introduced at Harvard in 1878.
10. Descriptive pamphlets issued in 1889 by Harvard Philosophy Department.

PART II

XII

In religion all philosophy culminates, or rather from it all philosophy flows. To it and to its nearest of kin, Ethics, my life has been given. In the remainder of this paper I shall set forth as simply as possible the beliefs about the two, to which the philosophic wanderings hitherto described have conducted me. And in discussing religion I shall confine myself to Christianity as its universal type. For as we have it to-day it is all-inclusive and readily finds room within itself for the many precious half-truths of the other ethnic faiths.

My ethical beliefs are sufficiently stated in Section VIII, pp. 35–38. As regards religion it will be understood that I am not exploring its rise like the ethnologist, nor analysing its relation to branches of philosophy other than Ethics. I merely wish to show what place I believe it may rightfully claim in the practical affairs of to-day. But at the start a warning is needed against looking in the wrong direction to find its function. It has no use as a linkage. When in tracing the connection of events some necessary step is unknown, it will not do to call in God to bridge the chasm. Eventually Science will discover the absent link and religion will be discredited. I have no doubt that God's agency was needed for this link, but no more than for every other. The old-fashioned miracle, where God intervenes to meet an exigency not anticipated in the plan of the world, is out of date. I at least hold that scientific sequence is never broken.

The place where I find God is at the upper end of the line. Without the presupposition of God, Science is fragmentary and baseless. He is the antecedent condition of all being, the unitary ground of existence. Things of space and time are ever perishing, with them man has never been content. Knowing himself to be in some measure akin to what is beyond these, he has ever been stretching himself up, toward an object superior to himself, an object to which he may give himself in uncalculating loyalty. Science needs this transcendent object to impart an "always" to its truths. A person needs it as an object of loyal devotion. Religion begins, as does love everywhere, with the vision of a person or a cause greater than ourselves, to which, approaching with bowed head, we may give ourselves up, regardless of personal gain.

XIII

Because Science has been concerned with observation, it has with
entire propriety come slowly to the conception of a unitary ground
of existence. Primitive races begin with taking each event detachedly
and asking no questions. More advanced, they group together
similar phenomena and attribute these to the presence of an indwelling god. There is a god of the sky, of the sea, of the winds, of love,
of music. This is polytheism and marks a decided advance in rationality. Men are no longer content to see something happen, but feel
obliged to connect it plausibly with something else. And this can
be best accomplished by thinking of gods of many groups, all
separate. A further advance is hinted at by Homer, when in half a
dozen instances he uses θεός in the sense of a general divine agency,
Now until about a century ago Science had not advanced beyond
this point. It talked of heat, light, gravitation, electricity, etc., as
separate agencies. But the discovery of the correlation of energies
proved that each of these may, under appropriate conditions, be transformed into the others. Whatever happens in one group is affected
by the whole. A unitary ground is now recognized with which all
things, if fully traced, can be seen to be rationally connected. Therefore I think we may say that to-day, just in proportion as people are
rational, no matter what their occupations, they acknowledge something like a god. They do not all call it by that name. Frequently
it is called Nature.

But as soon as we are convinced that the one and the many are
inseparable, so that wherever we behold a manifold we regularly
presuppose a one in the background, two questions at once await
us: Is this uniting one an intelligent being? And if so, what is his
moral character?

XIV

To the first of these questions I know only a single plausible
answer. For if we must conceive a groundwork of all that is, something
in which we live and move and have our being, I do not see how we
can leave out of it the element of intelligence. Evolution has gone on
throughout the ages culminating in intelligence as its final stage.
Can the compendium of all being be destitute of this? Is it not more
sensible to think that intelligence has always been involved in
existence, but has been only gradually disclosed? Such, at least, is
my belief. Darwinism, attempting to exclude intelligence, is to-day
widely discredited.

Furthermore, the view of intelligence as an original factor in the creation of the world seems demonstrated empirically when we find intelligence in Nature responding to intelligence in us. The world is adapted to intelligent habitation. While much in it is still blind, the more intelligent we become, the more at home here we are. We are not mistaken in talking about laws of Nature. Such paths of intelligent order through what at first sight looked chaotic can even be expressed in mathematical terms without error and so enable us to construct a rational science. Would such construction be possible if we did not posulate reason as latent in all things?

XV

Let me here interpose a few collateral remarks which must be borne in mind as we proceed. It is often said there is no use in going off into philosophical and theological discussion, for such doctrines are always changing. The philosophy of one age is not that of another. When, then, we come upon a department of life that cannot hold its own, why not let it alone? To this I should reply that doctrines of philosophy do change continually. They never become permanently fixed. I should only have to add that this is far less true of philosophy and theology than it is of any other human interest. One might say with truth that the only fixed matter in the world is change. Change is a universal law. Nothing escapes it. In every department of human life it goes on, in every department of non-human life. But there are two kinds of change. There is one sort that sees it was mistaken and sets out again, only to have its new point of view pushed aside by the next that appears. This certainly is a depressing sort of change, but it is not the only kind. There are changes which carry their past with them, which see a deeper meaning than was perceived before and are continually evolving it.

Now when we ask: "What are the changes of religion, theology, or philosophy?" it must be said that they are predominantly of this second sort. Let anyone who doubts that the destructive changes in these departments are less than in others, examine any alcove of books on physical science in the Harvard Library. He will find that most of those written fifty years ago are entirely superseded to-day. They are dead things. What is asserted in them is not true. It is gone. Other doctrines have come up and taken their place. Then if one goes into the alcoves on theology and philosophy, he will see that a large part of the speculations and pronouncements of more than two thousand years are vital still.

They are not completely accurate. They stop far too short. There was a depth of meaning in them originally, which was not at the time fully discovered. But they can be read to-day with instruction for all. What we are trying to undertake at present is largely a deepening of what is there. They have not been superseded. I would not overstate the contrast, real though it is. Looking back through the ages a scientist will stand out here and there as germinal, opening fruitful paths for his successors. But the history of physical science is of no such consequence in furthering discovery to-day as is the history of philosophy.

When, then, we consider the nature of an ultimate being, a god or ground of all things, and see that it must include intellect, we must not expect that this will be precisely the same god as was conceived two thousand years ago, or even a hundred years ago. It has been changing all the time because it has been deepening its meaning. I might go farther and say that when any one of us lays hold for himself of that mighty thought, it will appear with a special meaning, different for each of us. No one of us can comprehend in full anything so large. We may look in a certain direction with some assurance that it is a right direction, but our business is chiefly to see how far it can be adopted into our lives, to illuminate and give them strength. That will undoubtedly differ with different persons. We ought not to be shocked at finding that the way in which I approach religion is different from the way in which my neighbour does. Because each of us is but a fragmentary being we must content ourselves with fragmentary insights.

XVI

Preliminary education, I have pointed out, supplies us authoritatively with what is generally agreed upon in our community as regards the important facts of life. The university has a different aim. We come to it for purposes of criticism, to gain control of our own minds, to judge how far our inherited bank-stock of beliefs fits our case. What do these mean and mean for me? Nothing is good that has not been criticized and criticized continually. Some people are afraid of criticism. They say, "Oh, if you send a boy to college, he will go to doubting everything." Certainly! That is what he is here for. He cannot come to personal certitude till he has doubted. But I should not agree with the assumption that doubt means simply casting aside. Doubt has a positive office as well. It should bring out into fuller significance ideas which have been hidden under the incrustations of time. And such clarified beliefs are, in fact, commonly the result. All dictation is taken off during these maturing years. At least we try to take it off at Harvard. Yet it would not be easy to find elsewhere a larger body of serious-minded, yes reverent, young men.

A peculiarly damaging doubt, however, will early occur to any reflecting mind. Suppose intelligence is inwrought in the framework of things. How vast is that framework! Our world occupies but a pinhead of space in the universe, and in that world I am but one person among incalculable billions. Is it not absurdly presumptuous to imagine that a God of all creation will attend individually to me, hear my prayer, and be pleased or offended at my conduct? Here is a doubt which disturbed the Psalmist and most modest-minded persons ever since. The Psalmist writes: "When I consider thy heavens the work of thy fingers, the moon and the stars which thou hast ordained, what is man that thou art mindful of him?"

Now I believe that this inevitable doubt establishes the very opposite of what it at first suggests. To our minds, the one and the many are usually set in contrast. In attending to the large, we are almost bound to overlook the small. But God, the intelligence of Nature, can have no such limitations. How absurd if he had! Gravitation and electricity are needed for some of the larger suns in the Milky Way. But since there is not enough of these agencies to go round, objects less than an inch in size cannot have them! Is it not more sensible to hold that not a sparrow falls to the ground without our Father? The obvious fact that God is infinite in nowise hinders his being minutely regardful.

Hitherto I have been approaching God on his least personal side, as the intelligence presupposed in the order of Nature. Such an approach proceeds on the principle that with like conditions like results always follow. Without this assurance that Nature presents a fixed order, science would be impossible. Yet no proof of the principle can be given. It is not a fact directly observed, as, for example, that sunshine is hot and snow cold. Nor is it demonstrable from anything else. When the sun rose this morning it brought with it no proof that it would rise again to-morrow. That is a working hypothesis which subsequent experience shows to yield valuable results. When in any case seemingly similar conditions yield an issue different from what was had before we do not accept the result, we suspect we have misread either the original conditions or the final issue. But in testing the matter we are obliged to employ the very assumption of unproved order once again. In short, this working hypothesis is unescapable. To deny it is to accept it. And this is scientific faith, not the credulity of the schoolboy: "Faith is believing what you know isn't so." Scientific faith, though blind at the start, yields verifiable results.

When we turn to the moral or personal world, the situation is much the same. In Section IX I have maintained that the only possible ultimate aim of action is self-realization. There is nothing of greater worth than life to justify living. Only the self to be realized must be the conjunct self. If I set up a separate self and try to realize it, I confront no self at all. To find myself, I must go outside myself in loyalty to a personality beyond myself, and then, through subsequent experience, verify that a life more abounding has, in fact, resulted. Nor will this, if rightly done, be but the experience of a single instance. The moral life proceeds under the working hypothesis of loyalty to a perpetually larger personality. This is religious faith. Religion is allegiance to this unitary basis of all personal being.

XVII

How can we gain fuller acquaintance with God thus involved in our very constitution? By resorting to those who, by their superior power, show that they have had the deepest experience of him. This is our method in other departments of human life. Take the recognition of beauty. We have not discovered beauty. It is not anything of my individual creation. It has been in the world a good while and has affected men profoundly. To ascertain its meaning, I might turn to Leonardo, who was not only a great producer of beauty, but speculated also on its nature. Shall he tell me what to admire? Yes and no. I am glad to listen to him, or to any other great master of beauty, and have him point out what it is that he counts beautiful. But I shall not take it on his authority. I shall listen only because I am justified in believing that these men have seen farther into beauty than any others I happen to know, and I want them to open my dull mind and lead me to see what they have seen. I shall then, casting aside authority, decide whether their teaching accords with my experience and tends toward my strength.

Now precisely this seems to me the way in which I grow in my conception of religion. I shall turn to those who, I believe, and who, indeed, the world believes, have had the deepest comprehension and experience of religion and who have united it most closely with life. I should like to come under their tuition and have them explain to me what they have found. Then I shall ask myself whether I can make use of their judgments for strengthening my conjunct life.

To-day, in our Western civilization, we have two chief aids in our comprehension of religion. They are widely unlike. One of them is a series of pictures describing the experience of a race that is universally recognized as pre-eminent in its understanding of religion, that is, we have the Bible. It gives us a series of pictures of a marvellous people, and lets us see it grow in its conception of God. It began in the most elementary way where God appeared merely as a tribal deity, capable of all sorts of iniquity himself, and approving iniquity in others. Then we can trace that people criticizing such conceptions and mounting ever higher through a thousand years until in some of the Psalms there are examples of the most exalted lyric poetry that exists in any language and all of it impassioned with the experience of God. Here we are taught by an ascending series of pictures, that is, through history, the meaning of God.

On the other hand, men have busied themselves with consciously reflecting about these matters and have tried to formulate them into the most graphic and rational doctrines. An institution has been erected on this theoretic basis. We have the Church.

To each of us these two authorities appeal. Each tries to point out what we should think about God. Our business is to get as much illumination from both of them as we possibly can, and then subject it to personal criticism.

XVIII

Here, then, I am obliged to pass over into an individual confession of faith. I do not altogether commend it to others. They may find modes of approach that fit them better than mine. But when I ask myself where shall I find the deepest insight into the being of God, and learn how he can be best connected with my personal life, I have no doubt where it can be had. In Jesus of Nazareth. Confessedly his thoughts about God have shaped all mankind as those of nobody else have. We justly reckon all time with reference to his birth. Even those who maintain that he never lived acknowledge that the legends about him present ideals of incomparable value. Just the same, therefore, as when I sought to learn about beauty, I studied the acts and thoughts of Leonardo da Vinci in precisely the same way I turn to Jesus of Nazareth.

All sorts of stories about him have come down to us. They were carefully gathered, sifted, and reported according to the best understanding of those who knew him. This precious deposit I have, and I scrutinize it reverently, but I cannot accept every word that is there. I have to verify it in my own experience, asking, Would it strengthen me if I, too, thought in that way? I am told that Jesus was hungry as he walked across the plain. He saw a fig-tree in the distance and came to it, expecting something to eat. Not finding anything, he cursed the fig-tree. The story is out of character for him and for me. It is the petulance of a boy over things that work against him, a temper of mind that I try to avoid. But so common is it that something of the sort was sure to drift into the record. Such stories, however, mean nothing to me. I cannot say they are all false, for much that originally I might have called false I now see to be true. Fifty years ago, those of us who tried to accept the New Testament had to carry a pretty heavy load when we read how Jesus, by a word, made sickness cease. These miracles we could not understand. We knew of no such powers in ourselves. It seemed as if such tales had better have been omitted from the narrative. We now see that their absence from the record would have discredited it. To-day it would require credulity to imagine such a being as Jesus moving through the world without such manifestations. We have discovered psychiatric powers in ourselves that were already familiar to him. How much farther their influence may extend, we are still uncertain. A miracle is only a physical change prompted by a person.

But more than by unworthy stories, more than by a too easy acceptance of the power of mind over matter, I am disturbed by occasional phrases which may be construed as identifying the nature of Jesus with that of God himself. This would strike a blow at the work of Jesus in redeeming men. It is true the number of such passages in the Gospels is small, and to get such a meaning from them they must be read with extreme literalness. "I and the Father are one." "He that hath seen me hath seen the Father." "All that the Father hath are mine." These are all from the Fourth Gospel. In the three Synoptic Gospels Jesus is sharply distinguished from God. God is his Father and mightier than he. His power is "given" him. He is commonly said to be "sent" by God. In two passages—and those, too, in John—he speaks of himself and God as "us" and "we." His will and God's are contrasted. In despondency he fears that God has forsaken him. Several times he prays to God, a shocking procedure if God and he are identical. And when a young man addresses him as "Good Master" he rejects the title because there is only one good, that is God. Duality is everywhere assumed.

How, then, did Jesus become our Redeemer? Paul answers briefly: Jesus broke down the middle wall of partition between man and God. Or again, he was the first-born among many brethren. The word at-one-ment would beautifully express the same idea. But it does not occur in the New Testament. It is frequent in the Old Testament, signifying a substitutive sacrifice. But this idea passed away with the Gospel. Each child of God is there called to be united with the Father as Jesus was and to be a vicarious helper of his still alienated brothers. The Synoptists, therefore, and even John himself, carefully avoid the outgrown word. Unhappily it was brought back by the early theologians, who found the Old Testament easier to comprehend than the New. Under their influence the King James translators accepted the word atonement in a single passage, offering, however, the alternative reading, reconciliation. The Oxford revisers employ reconciliation with no alternative.

Recognizing us all as children of God and made in his image, Jesus shows us, by his own example, that the difference between God and man is only one of degree. There is no such being as "mere man," nor is Jesus himself mere God. Were he so he would cease to be an example or ideal for me. A stone bridge may be a model of firmness and of faithfulness in work; but it is no example, for between it and me there is a radical difference of kind. My exemplar must be in some respects my superior, but the more closely he is akin, the more influential he becomes. Jesus undertakes to show us in himself a way of living. Now, if through possessing a nature unlike our own he is partially immune from our temptations, he would not be for us a genuine way, truth, and life. He would be merely playing a part. I cannot accept so degraded a view. I have experienced too deeply his strength-bringing companionship. Undoubtedly there are mysteries in him which carry him beyond my full understanding. There always are in proportion as one becomes great, i.e. approximates God. And how does Jesus approximate him? Has he made any clear statement of the central principle of his life?

XIX

He certainly has. As I search his sayings, trying to draw from them for myself what made him strong, I find a sacred word to which he returns in almost every utterance. It is the word Father. "God is my Father" is a summary of his whole teaching. The very words he speaks have no value as his, but only as they are the words of his Father.

Here I seem to lay hold of something which illuminates all life and brings me strength continually. For what is a father's aim? If he is a true father, if he is working out to the full the functions of a father, he endeavours to educate his child, to bring out its powers on every side, to lead it into abundance of life. He does not, if he is a good father, make the child subservient to his own needs. He makes himself subservient to the needs of the child. He adjusts and limits himself so that the child may understand him. He makes it his first business to endear the child to him and himself to the child. He shows how under all circumstances the child may resort to him with assurance of supporting strength. Where there is such a true father, the union of the two is in spirit complete.

Jesus teaches, then, that God can only be thought of rightly as a father. Divine relations, he would seem to hold, are only human relations carried to a degree of development impossible here. This Jesus proclaims as a Gospel, good news to the world. Let us consider it a moment and see if it is not truly good news. There is no such thing as blind fate. God is our friend. Everything he allows to happen is intended for our good, not good in itself—whatever that may mean —but always an opportunity which, if heartily accepted, will yield good for ourselves and others.

It may be objected that this interpretation of divine relations by human is anthropomorphic, and we all remember the denunciation of anthropomorphism extending from Xenophanes in the seventh century before Christ to Matthew Arnold in our own. Xenophanes urged that if horses and oxen were to represent gods they would figure them as horses and oxen. Men are doing the same thing, and why should they not? Certainly a horse-god would fall far short of what we know. But how could a horse come nearer than by seeing something divine in his own power, patience, loyalty, and love? Those parts of him that depend on physical conditions here—legs, lungs, mane, hoofs—he might wisely omit, since he knows nothing about the conditions of life elsewhere. Those found of value in all living things he might more safely trust. In short, what he would need would be discrimination in kind. The Psalmist is soberer. He lets his god say: "Thou thoughtest that I was *altogether* such an one as thyself." Jesus frankly treats fatherhood anthropomorphically. This fact should be borne in mind when we read the two ascetic passages in which the father's act is treated as pollution and a long train of disasters is launched on the modern world. There is no evidence that this attack on the family, called the Virgin Birth, was known to Jesus himself, to his mother, his disciples, or to Paul.

The Good News of the Fatherhood of God I accept and find in it daily strength. Two inferior forms of hardihood have often appeared. One of them is Stoicism, the refusal to be crushed, the sense of an inner dignity which enables me to stand on my own feet, no matter what happens. A second of milder aspect is the habit of looking on the bright side. In everything one side is brighter than another. Let me turn my face in that direction. Before Jesus revealed the strength available through the Fatherhood of God, these palliatives had value. But they are superficial and do not touch the sources of inner peace as do the words of Jesus. Not that he was the first to utter them. They are rooted too deeply in reality for that. Ζεύσπατής, Jupiter, had been heard of for centuries, but like θεός had gone on deepening its meaning till on the lips of Jesus it became capacious enough to hold love.

XX

That God was his Father was then the central teaching of Jesus. That tremendous truth fixedly embodied in his life made him not only the King of the Jews, but of mankind. I want to summarize briefly some of the varieties of power that came to him through this understanding. They are open to us all. In my own small way I have experienced them and know the support they offer.

Chief among them is companionship. I am never left alone. Whatever happens brings me God's kind voice and an opportunity for growth coupled with bounteous outgo. This immediate intercourse with a loved companion is the feature of the gospel of Jesus dearest to the mystic in every age, and justly so. It was constant in the mind of the Master, turning seemingly severe experiences into occasions of joy and blessing. But many mystics overlook the conjunct self and seek to come into intimacy with God by removing themselves from men, going into a cloister, stripping off fleshly powers, and making themselves as miserable as possible. They fancy they commend themselves to their Father when reduced to a minimum. This negative path turns men away from him who came to bring us the abounding life of his Father.

Fears cease. The only thing worth being afraid of is now seen to be fear. That is disloyalty. It assumes that our Father has evil in store for us. But anyone who has tried will find that his constant care can be trusted. Even death prepared by him becomes a deeply interesting, but not appalling adventure. "Father into thy hands I commend my spirit."

Regret, fear of our erroneous past is banished too. No sin is truly repented until through comp ehension and counter-activity we are actually bettered by its occurrence. Sitting in gloom and dwelling on our foulness will not commend us to God.

Faith in fatherhood removes harshness from duty. Love transforms it. It becomes a kind indication of what had better be done to secure the largest ultimate freedom. Or if I fail at once to feel that kindness, I at least know the blessings I have been receiving from my Father; and here is an indication of what he will gladly receive in return; gladly I give it.

A foolish father, still more frequently a foolish mother, lets a child grow up in indulgent ease. A wise father develops his child by frequent hardships. He counts it no unkindness to send his son out on a wintry morning to buy food for the family. To most of us, our Heavenly Father assigns severities in gaining food, clothing, and shelter. Even if such severities are not in themselves goods ready made, they are—better still—opportunities for developing alertness, resource, and natural continuance of useful work.

Nor are such disciplinary difficulties physical only. We are offered abundant mental perplexities. Our Father might originally have supplied us with all needful scientific knowledge, instead of leaving it for agelong search. And what a petty universe we should have had, and what elementary minds!

What takes long in the training of a child, and what our Heavenly Father is especially careful to train us in, is the overcoming of time. Very gradually we acquire patience and learn to prefer a future good to an immediate. Our Father has arranged that the rush for immediate good shall usually defeat itself and in the long run bring injury. He generally suggests the direction we should take. But the most frequent of his prescriptions, is to wait.

Perhaps the most important training a father ever gives his child is an understanding of self-sacrifice, so-called, that is, the putting away of the separate self and learning how important the conjunctive elements are, far more so than anything attainable in our isolated capacity. The call to regard mankind as my brothers is only another form of the call to regard God as my Father. According to Jesus, the two together fulfil all righteousness. How closely he knitted them in his own case! Open-eyed he accepted death that others might have life, and though he felt the pang, he had no wish to escape it. "For this cause came I into the world."

XXI

Such acceptance of the guidance of a Heavenly Father is neither Fatalism nor Pessimism. Fatalism lives in a locked-up world where personality has no place. Everything happens because of a central unintentional "it." Jesus and his followers change "it" to "he" and so make room for selective action on the part of God and ourselves. Nor is it optimism. It does not assert that all that happens is good. On the contrary it is steadily contending with Evil and will no longer employ such phrases as good events and bad events. Events become good or bad according as they are used. Our Father furnishes us opportunities only. Out of whatever he sends good can be drawn, but so can evil. Optimism seems to me more immoral than Pessimism, for Pessimism warns us of danger, while Optimism lulls into false security.

But a serious problem remains. How explain a loving God's government of an evil world? There can be no doubt that evil abounds. We encounter it every day, particularly in ourselves. Is, then, God limited in will or in power? In will, I maintain, and in that fact I find no aspersion on the being of such a God as I have described. Jesus interprets divine relationships by human. Now I have said that a wise father limits himself. He does not take his son and force him to go through certain acts. He does not impose himself on his child. He tries to develop the child's own desires and powers. He assists him, he shows him how he himself lives, he offers him every opportunity. But he expects the child to grow by experience, even experience of error. We might think that an infinite God would be able to stop all evil at once. The Heavenly Father of Jesus is too loving for that. Perhaps his limitation of himself for the sake of his children will be best understood by watching the same principle at work in modern education. At Harvard we must confess there are many loafers, men squandering time and opportunity and forming habits pretty sure to unfit them later for grappling successfully with the world. How shocking to tolerate such a mass of unintelligent evil? Are the officials here men of limited ability, or do they care nothing for their charges? Why do they not put a stop to this waste? The answer would be that their ability is limited, self-limited. They know that a student forced, as the routine education of the past attempted to force him, is no student at all. They therefore limit themselves to offering opportunities, to making those opportunities attractive, and letting the ultimate guidance, even if erroneous, be in the student's own hands. Men of independent intelligence are therefore trained here to-day to a degree unknown of old. Our Father in heaven had been using the elective system long before we discovered it.

Though Jesus announces his gospel as a universal one, several passages in the New Testament have an exclusive sound. Matthew says that Jesus shall save his people from their sins; John, that the world through Jesus might be saved; and Peter in the Acts that there is no other name given among men whereby we must be saved. But it should be noticed that wherever salvation is spoken of, salvation from sin is meant, not merely salvation from its future consequences. Yet even so, what becomes of the numberless tribes of men who never heard of Jesus? If we accept the teaching of Jesus and agree to see in human fatherhood a revelation of God, I think we shall consider the case of the heathen less forlorn than is often assumed. Each family has within it an outline representative of the Most High. Let this be studied and lived up to and Jesus' only way of redemption will be adopted. However superior our advantage is in beholding the great exemplar, no home has been left altogether desolate.

XXII

Such is my religious faith. In the midst of a perplexing world it leaves me peacefully at home in my Father's house with plenty of work still to do, but with the inspiration of knowing myself a fellow-worker with God and with the multitude of his other children.

And since I have written at such length upon religion, only a few words need be added on the relation of religion and ethics. So far as their contents are concerned the two do not differ. There is no act which is an essentially religious act. Its religious character depends on how it is approached. When we view it as it would be viewed by our Father in heaven, it is religious. Athletics is the opportunity for my obtaining a sound physical body and learning the care of my health. It is then as religious an act as going to a prayer meeting. There is, in short, no act which belongs peculiarly to religion. The Psalmist expresses this unqualifiedly:

"Lord, who shall abide in thy tabernacle? Who shall dwell in thy holy hill?

"He that walketh uprightly and worketh righteousness and speaketh the truth in his heart.

"He that backbiteth not with his tongue nor doeth evil to his neighbour nor taketh up a reproach against his neighbour.

"In whose eyes a vile person is contemned, but he honoureth them that fear the Lord. He that sweareth to his own hurt and changeth not.

"He that putteth not out his money to usury nor taketh reward against the innocent. He that doeth these things shall never be moved."

Such a sketch of the simplest moral acts is a code of religion also. Only the mental attitudes differ. In religion I face my father; in morals, my fellow-man, and each is supplemental to the other.

XXIII

It remains to state my belief about conscience and the objective ground of morals. Have we, as the Quakers say, an oracle within the breast which, if we only listen, will tell us infallibly in every situation what is the right course? I do not think so. Such extreme individualism disintegrates society and leaves no room to profit by experience. In this matter I am a follower of Jesus and of Kant.

Jesus held that the ten commandments were the best code of conduct then known, that we should not let our acts conflict with their precepts, nor even with their deeper implications. But he warns his hearers not to imagine that there are here ten pieces of righteousness laid side by side, each with an independent claim. On the contrary, they are merely varied announcements, predominantly negative, of the fundamental command to love God and our neighbour, the seemingly double precept resolving itself on reflection into a single mental attitude. The lifelong contention of Jesus with the Pharisees turns on precisely this point. The Pharisees were not the hypocrites we picture. They were the holy men of their age, insistent that there is an objective righteousness for each occasion which should be searched out by the wise and followed authoritatively by the common folk. This casuistry Jesus denounces. Let each man be impassioned with a love of righteousness and then become instructed about its diverse workings through his own daily experience. Jesus did not deny that it is well to wash before eating, or that it is wise to consecrate certain days to other than secular uses. But he did object to having these acts standardized, determined once for all by some authority. To be significant they should be kept fresh and flexible. Undoubtedly the Pharisees were right in calling the method of Jesus dangerous. We can only answer that it is less dangerous to the higher life than leaning on any authority without or within. By stopping criticism and individual initiative Pharisaism prevents growth, and with it that abundance of life which Jesus came to proclaim. The Catholic Church in its sagacious instructions for the confessional has followed the moral method of the Pharisees. Protestants have preferred the opposite dangers, and they have been large. Nevertheless, I am a Protestant!

Briefly stated, the doctrine of Kant is that "ought," the imperative of duty, is ordinarily a hypothetical imperative, i.e. a command involving conditions. It is therefore of no effect when the condition fails. "You ought not to smoke. It weakens the heart." "But I do not care whether my heart is weak or strong." Then for you there is no command. Such are imperatives in general. They turn on some covert hypothesis, which is not present in every case. Is there, however, any unconditional, objective, or Categorical Imperative which underlies all others and is unaffected by circumstances? There is, but there is only one. It may be stated thus: Act as if the maxim of your action were to become by your will a universal law. There are other formulations of this but all amount to the same thing, viz. the only universal duty is the duty of respecting duty. Royce, holding that loyalty comes nearest to a complete expression of moral obligation, was asked "Loyalty to what?" and answered "Loyalty to loyalty." That was his Categorical Imperative, the only command of conscience. I, too, am a strenuous believer in a Categorical Imperative, but I phrase mine a little more simply. I call it the law that there shall be law. Conscience warns us that acting from mere impulse, non-permanent desire, or reaction from stimulus, has no moral quality. A person is capable of something more than this. His will should express respect for law as law. It is true this is only a part of the story, the philosophic or a priori part. Kant calls it the form of ethics. The supplemental matter must be drawn from the special circumstances of the case. Just so when we are told to love our neighbour, we are not informed whether we should buy him stockings or gloves, or, indeed, whether we should buy him anything. This will vary with the state of the needy one's hands and feet. The precept of love is a categorical Imperative which applies regardless of circumstances. But these variable conditions are ethically as meaningless when parted from the imperative of love as is love when parted from them. The two belong together. Kant has been foolishly blamed for failing to see the partial character of his Categorical Imperative. But he intended it to be partial. He took upon himself the task of exploring the Metaphysic of Morals and never dreamed of superseding experience in the actual conduct of life. This latter he has treated with much subtlety of observation in a separate paper. But I think he has made it plain that taken by itself conscience is no compendium of diverse instructions as to how we should act in all sorts of cases. I know only one indwelling law, the law that there shall be law. Moral perplexity is possible and not infrequent. We encounter conflicting claims, and are obliged to say I would gladly do right if I only could discover what is right. In such cases, our only resource is to study the conjunct experience of ourselves and the race, and learn what has in the long run proved most favourable for fullness of life. As I have previously remarked, nothing outside life can justify living.

XXIV

Since in Part I I have described the great philosophic changes which have come about in my time, it may be interesting to note briefly the political transformations which have attended them. Every age is called a transitional time; and rightly, for change never ceases. But at certain periods changes are so rapid, and affect such large tracts of life, that they deserve pre-eminently the name of transitional. It is hardly an exaggeration to say that I shall die in a different world from that in which I was born. At my birth in 1842 there were twenty-two fewer states in our country than at present. We had not begun to acquire foreign possessions, like the Sandwich Islands, Alaska, the Philippines, and islands in the Gulf of Mexico. Two sudden shiftings of population deserve mention, one in Texas in

1848 at the close of the Mexican War, another in 1849 on the discovery of gold in California. The regular connection with the Pacific
Coast was by sailing vessel around Cape Horn. The Middle West was
thinly settled, Chicago having less than five thousand inhabitants.
The first considerable Steam Railroad, that between Baltimore and
Washington, was built in 1844. Of course, telegraphs, telephones,
electricity, and radio were not in use. For our knowledge of events
in Europe we were dependent on foreign correspondents. The first
regular steamer, that from Liverpool to Boston, arrived in 1840,
taking more than fourteen days for the voyage. As late as 1867,
when I crossed, there were only small paddle-wheel steamers, and
mine, a Cunarder, took thirteen days.

Few countries in Europe have remained unchanged. Victoria was,
at my birth, in only the fifth year of her long and eventful reign.
In France, Bourbons were the rulers. In most of my visits to Paris
Napoleon III was the Emperor. Two of three revolutions there I
have witnessed. Germany was a collection of petty states. In one of
them, Würtemberg, my University years were spent. Austria was
a huge and straggling empire, the over-lord of most of Italy. Her
quarrels with Hungary drove Kossuth into exile, and I saw him
received in Boston in 1852. The Crimean War of 1856, with the
later Russo-Turkish wars, profoundly altered the whole East of
Europe. Egypt first detached itself from Turkey and then, after the
rebellion of Arabi Pasha, came under the control of England. Italy,
which throughout my early life had been a collection of states,
was united in 1860 by Garibaldi, Cavour, and Victor Emmanuel.
France was overrun by Germany in 1870, and then gradually built
up the vast French colonies of Algeria and Morocco. Spain went
through many transformations, during the nineteenth century
losing all her American possessions. The year of my birth saw foreign
trade allowed for the first time in half a dozen cities of China. Japan
was opened to foreigners in 1854, following the visit of Admiral
Perry and the American fleet. India was a private possession of the
East India Company till 1858. The Suez Canal was constructed by
De Lesseps in 1860; the Panama Canal by the United States in 1914.
South Africa was transformed by the Boer War. But it would be
tedious to chronicle the changes in the many small countries, particu-
larly those of Africa, Australia, and South America. Since the Great
War, little remains of what was familiar twenty-five years ago.

XXV

This final section of my paper shall be an anatomy of myself.
An autobiographer, by his very title, announces that he is willing to

have strangers draw near and inspect his inward parts. They cannot do so merely by becoming acquainted with the events of his life, for the same events may spring from a wide variety of personal origins. Only the man himself, if self-conscious, frank, and disinterested, can rightly interpret them. This now becomes my interesting and difficult task. I will try to describe the way I am made as I see it.

From childhood I was curious about the significance of that strange creature, a human being, so like, so unlike a machine. Puritanism saved me from any simple solution. It saw depravity and high aspiration living side by side. Fortunately modern study of character has turned in the same direction. Before Boswell, biography was for the most part written either to record occurrences in the life of a king or statesman, or else it had a moral aim, and sought through the presentation of some saintly figure to stimulate virtue in others. Boswell for the first time painted a full-length portrait with no other aim than portraiture. Johnson's defects are as manifest as his excellences. In our day Lytton Strachey in England and Gamaliel Bradford in America have taught us that the first step in understanding a character is to note its limitations and see what colour they impart to the entire person. President Tucker said to me long ago, "Don't let your defects bother you. Make yourself strong enough to carry them off." To the same purport is the warning of Jesus against pulling up tares in a wheat-field. The different roots are too closely intertwined to be lightly torn asunder.

Early I learned that because of an exceptionally bad memory I could never be a great scholar. To no avail were my many attempts at improvement, especially after the reading of themes and examination papers had made the matter every year worse. Encyclopædic learning I must leave to Germans. I regretted still more to find that continuous constructive thinking was forbidden me. Whether I was cut off from this by the general physical weakness of the first half of my life or by special brain conditions I cannot say. The result was the same, I was not designed for a system-builder.

Now it is foolish to sit lamenting over what one has not. The wisdom of life is to accept whatever comes and extract power from it. Accordingly I turned to criticism. Criticism became my sacred word. Readers of this paper must have been struck with the frequency of its occurrence here. Its simplest definition is the sense of inadequacy. Slightly modified as the "Glory of the Imperfect," it appeared as the title of one of my earliest papers. Combined with appreciation of beauty—beauty in poetry, pictures, architecture, or landscape—it becomes a mighty engine, successively revealing what is adequate or harmonious and teasing us to bring this perfection to birth. It has been my guiding principle in many fields. I have altered successfully five houses. I never planned one from the ground up. I need something to begin with and improve. This ethical sense of a better in alliance with its twin sister, the æsthetic, trains practical judgment and makes one a generally useful person, resorted to by many for advice. Such advisory work has brought me much happiness and has enabled me to find situations for a large number of teachers. My recommendations are accepted because they are not generalities, but indicate just the work of which a candidate is capable.

Knowing that I was not a genius, was indeed in most respects less clever than other young men of my years, yet had my own way to make with little assistance, I was early led to feel the importance of work. All I have done has been costly in labour. Nothing in it is spontaneous. I have often thought I was planned for a loafer; but being born in New England was somewhat spoiled in the making. Sometimes I wonder that so many sons of the rich become men of power. They might have lived at ease and have rotted, if they had not had, a goodly number of them, a sense of moral responsibility to themselves and society. I have needed steady pressure, and have had it, thank Heaven.

The greatest longing of my youth was for literary fame. At that time this was a common desire. To-day the desire for wealth has taken its place. But I was badly hampered as a writer. Essentially a solitary, feeble in frame and ill at ease among strangers, I wrote few letters, talked little, and had no promptings to self-expression. Writing has always remained extremely difficult. The blank sheet of paper lying before me waiting to be filled has never ceased to be an object of horror. Yet I have printed seventeen independent volumes and am on the whole glad of the pains they have cost. The lack of fluency has saved me from writing nonsense. Style wins a certain dignity when one feels that the subject has been seen clean through and is meant to be stated just so. Easy writing is usually hard reading. Hard writing, if right methods are employed, makes a reader's work easy. As my modes of writing are the result of a good deal of study, I will sketch some of them here.

The peculiar feature of my writing for publication is the double copy, one for me, one for my reader. Whatever I write to-day is written with the aim of truth and fullness. Into it goes everything which might at this point have a bearing on the argument. But as this draft is merely a gathering of material it would be hardly intelligible to anyone but myself. To-morrow I rewrite this, discharging from my mind all consideration of truth, and studying simply ease of apprehension on the reader's part. The order of the sentences will frequently require revision. Some word or sentence will "stick out" and attract undue notice. The sentences may have too little variety of pattern. I shall come upon hitches which will oblige a reader to pause an instant. Unnecessary words will be discovered, even repetitions. But everywhere ease should be the one thing sought, the test of its attainment being: Does the page, on being read, seem short? These two aims, of truth and ease, are apt to be confused by many writers. When they come to their second writing, they are still thinking of accuracy. They remember something which had not occurred to them before, perhaps some qualifying clause which would add a fresh shade of truth, and in it goes, checking the smooth flow of the page and compelling slow reading. This is no time for additions, but for dropping everything that can be spared. Of course, some repetition will be useful to save the reader from being forced onward more rapidly than his mind can travel. But it should come in the guise of humour, illustration, or simplification.

One of the commonest hindrances to easy reading is the long sentence. I went through a paper last year which averaged four sentences to a page. It was dismal reading. I had almost forgotten the beginning of the sentences when I reached their ends. The writer was evidently merely clearing his own mind, with no thought of a reader. Yet I must acknowledge that a long and well-built sentence sometimes adds weight to an argument, while too many short sentences become choppy and annoy the reader with a perpetually fresh start. I am afraid my writing has often this fault. A judicious mixture of longs and shorts is best. The short sentence, too, should have importance, like a headline, unless it is the three or four words which come as a relief at the close of a complicated exposition. In any case the principle is plain: the reader is the important person; devices to engage him will always be in order; the architecture of style must never be forgotten; and ease must be an object of effort.

My procedure in speaking or teaching is different. Most of what I have to say can be found in some book. The only valuable element I can add is myself. Evidently, then, the minute methods I have been prescribing for a writer will be of little use to a speaker. Indeed, if I have a complete draft behind me of what I am going to say, I am wrecked. For the two processes of remembrance and live personal thinking are antagonistic. When I am trying to recall a phrase, I cannot think, and while I am thinking words must take care of themselves. Before speaking I must fill myself freshly with my subject, no matter how familiar it is. I may have spoken on it before, but I must have at hand only so much memoranda as will keep me from sprawling. After some hours of study and reflection, I draw up on a quarter sheet of paper an outline of the topics I propose to discuss, with special attention to their order. Whatever is simplest and easiest to comprehend should, of course, come first, whatever is more complicated later. I even assign the amount of time the different portions of my programme will require, but no sentences are written. Then with a mind stuffed with my subject, an orderly path visible through it, my outline and watch on the table, I stand before my class and begin to think aloud, as for myself, in the plainest language, letting the thought summon its own vocabulary. Somehow or other, the personality goes across. It is an untraceable and vitalizing influence, easily catching, though you can't vaccinate with it. Observe, or try to place it, and it disappears. Yet, while anything already written ruins me, I find that I speak better on a ground I have travelled previously. Perhaps while personality demands freedom, it is emboldened by exercise. Fear is its subtlest foe. Until a speaker is entirely at ease, his hearers will not be.

But there is more in teaching than this: there is moral discipline. In it one gets his best training in Imagination, which once gained— yes, gained in any considerable degree—invigorates every power of him who gains it and makes all the world around the better. For by imagination I mean the ability to put myself in another's place, think his thoughts, and state strongly his convictions even when they are not my own. Many a worthy man I have known who was altogether willing to do his share of the world's work, but was quite shut off from his fellows by lack of imagination. Men called him selfish, but he was not exactly that, only constitutionally incapable of seeing anything beyond his own horizon. On the other hand a man of imagination is welcomed everywhere, for he is a better father, friend, minister, lawyer, doctor, author, shopkeeper, or member of society, being able swiftly to perceive the diverse minds of these people and to adapt himself tactfully to each. Why people are willing to face the frictions of life without imagination is a mystery.

A few years of teaching will convince anyone of the need, the possibility, and the attraction of acquiring it. Each pupil differs from every other, and all stand at a long remove of development from their teacher. To be able to meet them all helpfully has been the fascinating passion of my life. It is a piece of Fine Art in which I have been enabled to meet with some success. Of course, I have fallen far short of a perfect teacher. No such being was ever known. But by perpetual criticism I have brought myself to circumvent a new batch of errors almost every year. Before my mind began to fail under my last surgical operation, I think I had attained much of what I sought. To meet everyone with considerate tact was becoming almost habitual, and the habit bred a dispassionate mind. I do not so often mix desires with my judgments as I see many around me doing.

Professor Shaler once remarked that there were two sets of Professors at Harvard. One was absorbed in private study, another observed also the general course of the University, noted its defects and was ingenious in proposals for their removal. I have always belonged to this second group. It fits in with my dominant method of criticism, i.e. with making my start in a given defect and aiming at betterment. This leaning toward administration has brought me many calls elsewhere. But I have found more interest in the further advancement of what is here. There has been no lack of variety. I have been connected with five departments—Greek, Philosophy, Divinity, Fine Arts, English—in two of these, taking the place of absent Professors. At six of our affiliated Western Colleges I was Exchange Professor, and many years before the Great War I was offered the Exchange Professorship in Berlin. This I declined because I was unwilling to meet the Kaiser, whom I regarded as the most dangerous man in Europe. As regards offices, I have been Tutor, Instructor, Curator, Assistant Professor, Professor, Professor Emeritus, Overseer, pretty fully a Harvard man. Harvard and six other universities have given me honorary degrees.

I remember how Dr. Andrew Peabody warned us students one morning at Prayers: "Young men, be careful what you dream. Dreams are apt to come true." I dreamed of happy marriage, of a large library, of foreign travel, of clearing my mind of philosophic and religious perplexities, of teaching in some great university, of being widely loved, of strenuous middle life with an old age of health and financial ease, of winning fame, especially as a writer. Looking back I can say I have little more to wish. The years have brought substantially what I asked—opportunity to do useful work as an organizer of one of the most distinguished departments of our foremost university, with more than fifteen thousand students in my classes, and kind faces meeting me wherever I go. Three of my books may live for half a century—my books of affection and gratitude— *George Herbert, Homer,* and the *Life of Mrs. Palmer.* The first was not intended for wide circulation, but was an appeal to scholars in behalf of a much misunderstood poet. The London *Times* gave it two strongly commendatory articles, and declared that whoever dealt with Herbert hereafter must take this book into account. The second I tried to restore to nature and redeem from artificial "Classicism." The sales of my translation of the *Odyssey* have increased in each of the thirty odd years since it was published, during the last three being over forty thousand a year. More than fifty thousand copies of Mrs. Palmer's *Life* have been sold. She herself has become a kind of patron saint of college girls and has been elected to the Hall of Fame. As I see these things rising behind me they do not seem of my doing. Some greater power than I has been using me as its glad instrument.

NOTE

Perhaps I should say that this Anatomy of myself is not intended as a complete autobiography. Being addressed to those who, for the most part, are teachers and writers, I sketch only those traits which directly concern their work. Several, even more fundamental, I have not mentioned. For example, I have inherited the Puritan distaste for ornament and prize simplicity. With this goes a passion for order that almost amounts to a disease. If anything is a little out of adjustment, I am as uncomfortable as a musical ear that hears a wrong note struck. While these traits have their worthy side, they sometimes lead me to harsh judgments.

NATURALISM OR IDEALISM

By GEORGE P. ADAMS

Born Northboro, Mass., 1882. Professor of Philosophy, University of California.

IN MEMORIAM

NATURALISM OR IDEALISM

PROBLEMS and ideas which promise to yield some measure of partial insight into their solution constitute the stock-in-trade of the philosopher. Hence I may best respond to the invitation to set forth my present philosophical beliefs by trying to formulate, not any framework of a completed system, but rather a single crucial issue. It is central in the sense that it arises—so it appears to me—in each of the major provinces of human experience. It is one important point of convergence of fundamental questions in Ethics and Logic, Epistemology and Metaphysics.

It is the *problem*, and not any final or facile solution upon which I would lay stress. It will, indeed, prepare the way to an understanding of our problem if I observe that the very enterprise of philosophy itself appears to be problematic from the outset. I am not referring primarily to the historical divergence of philosophical theories, nor to the apparent contrast between *der sichere Gang der Wissenschaft* and the fluctuations and diversities of theories of knowledge, of cosmology, and of metaphysical systems. Whatever may be the nature and import of this contrast it does not express the deeper paradox of the venture of philosophy. For the contrast just noted arises merely from the fact that the philosopher is trying to do on a larger scale and for a vastly wider range of 'facts' essentially the same sort of thing that the scientist so well succeeds in doing for a more restricted and specialized area. What is really going on when a muscle contracts, when water boils, when a meteor falls? From specific questions such as these—questions for scientific investigation—to the widest field of cosmological speculation and hypothesis, to the question as to what is going on in nature as a whole, where 'nature' includes human brains and the events of history, there is complete continuity of theoretical interest and of method. To be sure, the wider the area under investigation, the more hypothetical and speculative are our results, the less certain and empirical are our conclusions. But throughout *this* realm, from the most specialized problem of specific laboratory research to the widest survey of nature as a whole, the investigator, whether scientist or philosopher, is confronted by 'facts' which he seeks to explain, to grasp intellectually by means of an adequate theoretical insight.

This is never, I think, either the whole or even the major task of philosophical study and reflection. To state the matter quite boldly, without apology or subterfuge, the driving force behind philosophy is the desire to know what meaning and what value, or what lack of meaning and value, may be ascribed to human life and experience and to the setting in which they occur. Susceptibility to meanings and values may be the ear-mark of the 'tender-minded,' whereas the 'tough-minded' soul is content with 'hard facts,' the hardness of which is gained only when the film of meaning and value is scraped away. If we choose to state it thus, then I should say, quite categorically, that there is no such thing as a tough-minded philosopher or philosophy. Science is as tough-minded in this sense as you please. But by no sheer quantitative extension of the area of hard facts which come within the sweep of our survey does a scientific hypothesis grow into the stature of a philosophical theory. It does not do so unless, rightly or wrongly, such an area of facts is made the occasion and the basis for a comprehensive judgment upon the meaning of things.

Just here lies the initial paradox of philosophy. Philosophy is the desire for, and the love of, knowledge. It is *theoria*, understanding, contemplation, insight. In this it is not different from pure science. Yet the range of that into which it inquires and about which it seeks understanding and knowledge seems most intractable and opaque to theoretical appraisal. *Facts* may be thus known and in some measure, perhaps, understood, even very wide ranges of facts and events spread out afar in space and time. But the meaning or value which any fact or series of facts is said to have seems not to belong to the fact in the same 'objective' and describable way in which those aspects of fact do which elicit and which (in part) satisfy our theoretical curiosity. Meaning and value are felt or appreciated, they are correlated with those of our interests which are not primarily theoretical and disinterested, with sentiments and loyalties, hopes and fears, desires and aversions. Yet the driving force of philosophy, as distinct from science, is the desire to reach intellectual clarity with respect to just those meanings and values whose very nature seems to preclude them from the domain of what can be known and understood.

It follows that the enterprise of philosophy is—for us—threatened at the very start from two opposite sides. The philosopher may be tempted to renounce, as does apparently the scientist, any hope of rendering an intellectual judgment upon the meaning of things. This renunciation may, on the one hand, lead him to extend the categories of scientific description and explanation beyond the specific and restricted regions with which the scientist, as such, is concerned. He will in this case seek to embrace the whole of nature and life and mind within the framework of generalized scientific conceptions. In being thus extended and generalized, in being applied to such large areas, these conceptions may seem to the scientist to have lost their rigour and their precision. They become less verifiable and more hazardous. For this reason the scientist will dub them speculative and philosophical. But in truth they are prolongations of scientific effort and achievement; like the science which we know, such extensions, whether called philosophical or scientific, are never primarily concerned with meanings. They seize upon some one prevailing and dominant scientific concept of the age—matter and motion, evolution, stimulus and response, relativity—and read everything concerning which we may be intellectually curious in its terms. But that which, as philosophers, we most want to know, the meaning of life and of reality, of the search for truth itself, is either passed over in silence or it is taken as an easy corollary of such quasi-scientific generalizations.

On the other hand, impressed by the inability of scientific description and explanation—even when extended and generalized to render intelligible meanings and values—the philosopher may be led to distrust the competence of theoretical insight with respect to all those regions of experience in which something of meaning and value, something other than brute fact, presents itself. Romanticism and intuitionism, mysticism and irrationalism spring from a disbelief in the possibility of reaching any theoretical clarity with respect to meanings and values. They thus show themselves to be twin sisters of a naturalism which, with this same disbelief as a premise, restricts philosophy to the task of describing everything as a natural and neutral substance or event determined to be the thing it is by causes and energies which are wholly factual and 'natural.' The venture of a philosophy which declines wholly to merge itself either with such scientific pursuits as disregard of necessity, the meanings and values of things, or with the immediate, practical, and unreflective activities of living, is thus itself something deeply problematic if not paradoxical. Philosophy is not science because it interests itself in meanings and values; and science, as we know it in modern life, is bent solely upon a descriptive and theoretical insight into what things are and how they behave, irrespective of any meaning or value which they may have for our non-theoretical interests. And philosophy is not art nor religion, neither poetry nor life. Meanings are present here in abundance, but they are not made the deliberate objects of study and reflection. They are lived and are had rather than known and understood. Philosophy is indeed problematic from the outset, threatened with the danger of being overwhelmed both from the side of science and from the side of practical life and immediate experience. The most enduring and the deepest worth of the main current of the European tradition of philosophy lies in the conviction that there is something here for philosophy to do, and which it alone can achieve. This conviction, and the analysis of human experience and the scene within which experience goes on, in the light of this belief is the enduring worth of the great historical systems of philosophy. There is nothing for philosophy to do which science and practical life cannot achieve with greater success, unless there are meanings embedded within experience which require reflection and theory for their apprehension and their clarification. This is, as it were, the initial if tacit postulate of philosophical reflection. A 'scientific' philosophy is a misnomer and a hybrid, and equally so is a 'mystical' or 'intuitive' philosophy.

The presupposition of philosophical reflection is thus the belief that there are meanings embedded within experience and that their nature may be apprehended by thought. But any such statement as this at once imposes the demand that the concept of experience be clarified and in some way circumscribed. What right have we to say that meanings are integral to experience, and what status may we ascribe to such meanings? It is just here that our central and crucial problem comes into view. But before we attempt to formulate this, something must be said about the use of this most ambiguous and problem-breeding term 'experience.' The use and the connotation of this term, on the part of any philosopher, supply a touchstone for his entire philosophical edifice.

There are certain widely current uses of the term 'experience' in contemporary philosophy which appear to me quite unsatisfactory and positively misleading, and an enumeration of the more important of these will clear the ground for a more adequate analysis of the concept and a formulation of our main question.

Experience is no inclusive and self-contained domain or process, the boundaries of which (if there be such) are co-terminous with the boundaries of that realm with which life and knowledge, science and the arts are concerned. Experience may not be equated with reality, nor with the absolute. In so far as the post-Kantian (Hegelian and Fichtean) rejection of the *Ding-an-sich* committed philosophy to this identification, it rightly laid itself open to the charge of subjectivism, and prepared the way for the realistic revolt of the last generation. With the initial spirit and motive of this revolt I am in sympathy. Experience as that which we live through, as an *Erlebnis*, lies within a setting and environment which itself is not a literal part of the process or matrix of experience. But, on the other hand, the sole remaining alternative is not the reaffirmation of Substance and Things-in-Themselves, in a Kantian or pre-Kantian sense. We are not necessarily constrained by this alternative—either a philosophy of experience which denies the existence of anything which is not definable in terms of some experience or a realism (of a critical or sceptical tenor) which affirms a gulf between that which is real and that which is experienced. There are, at least, other alternatives whose fruitfulness as philosophical hypothesis deserve the most careful consideration.

The central difficulty and ambiguity which I find in contempory Pragmatism springs from the neglect of that environment or setting of experience, similar to the neglect which mars so much of post-Hegelian philosophy. Pragmatism did not share in the realistic revolt against the identification of experience and reality, and the consequent tendency to neglect the environment of experience. It was Absolutism and not Subjectivism which bred the pragmatic revolt. The temper of abolutism was to be curtailed and chastened by stressing the temporal flux of the stream of experience, the perpetual alternation within the life of experience of moments of precarious stability and satisfaction and periods of stress, difficulty, and readjustment. All reflection and thought, science and philosophy, even consciousness itself had its sole function in resolving the strains and problematic situations within the stream of experience; all thought was pertinent only to its temporal antecedents and consequences within this stream, and not to anything outside and beyond. The stream of experience was not thought of as having any banks which were not part of the stream itself. How else could absolutism be avoided? Hence the persistent rejection, on the part of Pragmatism, of any metaphysics, and the judgment that the central issues of traditional epistemology are otiose because they refer to a reality other than the temporal events within the flux of experience and life. When Pragmatism—as was inevitable—was in consequence charged with being subjectivistic, it took refuge in the biological presuppositions from which it took its point of departure. Organisms, which undergo life and experience, of course exist within an environment which provides the stimuli and the objects of their responses and their adjustments. What more of realism is wanted than this biological framework of environment and organism, stimulus and response, nature and life? But in its theory of knowledge and logic and in its (implied) metaphysics, this realistic reference to a real, which is no constituent of the temporal process of experience, is—so it seems to its critics—strangely enough, missing. Were it not absent, Pragmatism would be more kindly disposed to regard as legitimate a metaphysical interpretation of the nature of the real—of the banks within which the stream of experience flows.

Experience is, then, neither inclusive of the whole of existence nor is it self-contained; every pulse of experience bears upon and makes reference to a somewhat which is not any existent constituent of the stream of experience itself. The import and truth of this statement are obscured when it is said that experience itself is bi-polar, that it contains a subjective and an objective aspect, as if the banks between which a stream flows were a part of the stream itself. The duality in question is not internal to a substantive course of events which is existentially aloof from things, from nature, from reality. If nature is closed to 'mind,' it is not closed to experience. Experience is the meeting-place of organism and environment, of selves and the world. In this sense experience is incorrigibly metaphysical. There is no description of any experience which can dispense with terms having their locus in the one common and real world. To judge that any 'experience' is wholly illusory, false, private, and subjective, and hence cut off from that one common and real world, presupposes a prior reference to, and knowledge of, that objective world as a standard of reference. Were experience but a dream we would never know or judge it to be such. Nor is such a judgment wholly extraneous to the illusory or dream experience, itself a subsequent act of reflection. The very experience itself contains, however implicitly, that reflection and that knowledge. The only possible type or instance of experience which might seem to provide an exception to this objective and metaphysical character of experience would seem to be a pure, momentary, and wholly immediate feeling which is entirely *zuständlich*, and not in any degree *gegenständlich*. But were such feelings to be found—and I am not convinced that they ever are—they would be the most rudimentary and least typical types of experience, where experience has nearly vanished or is barely beginning.

It will be seen that 'experience,' as the term is here used, is not synonymous with 'consciousness' or 'mind' in the sense with which these terms are loaded in the modern psychological,

Cartesian, and Lockian tradition. The stream of experience, of living, of doing, of striving, and of thinking, is no series of states or events existentially unique and isolated from the common environing world of nature and of reality, of fellow-men and historical structures. Such isolation and detachment, such subjectivism as has coloured so much of modern philosophy and psychology, are nothing indubitable and self-evident. They are the residua and corollaries of historical and social forces—in politics and economics, religion and morals—which have fashioned modern civilization and which have left us with nothing final, but rather with tasks and problems. The identification of experience with consciousness, and the consequent absorption of metaphysics, morals, and epistemology in psychology, is a partial and abstract point of view, useful and necessary for certain purposes whose complete achievement would require the complimentary redintegration of psychology with science and metaphysics, history and ethics.

The chief witness, in modern philosophy, to the problematic identification of experience and consciousness and the resultant isolation of experience from reality, is the dominant position of the problem of knowledge. That problem is insoluble and consequently, I should say, meaningless if it be supposed that from a state of affairs entirely subjective, mental, and immediate, a reference to, and knowledge of, an independent real has somehow to be generated. There is no road from an initial substantive isolation of ideas to any subsequent cognitive intercourse with real things. It is the isolation which stands in need of explanation and justification, not the objective reference and cognitive intercourse. Once assured of an integral relation to reality, the 'new way of ideas' may yield fresh and significant results. Deprived of that relation *ab initio*, it is barren.

This vital concourse of what we call self and world (though as yet the words 'self' and 'world' are but symbols of the two somewhats which meet in every pulse of experience) is exhibited not solely in cognitive experience. Buying and selling, sowing and reaping, planning and doing, loving and hating, as well as seeing, hearing, and thinking—all such and countless other experiences show the same typical structure and relation. There is in each of these, on the one hand, an attitude—a stretching out toward something, an interest; and on the other hand an object—that at which the attitude is aimed and directed. We use things, we know and contemplate things, we enjoy and appreciate things, we seek and we shun things, and of such doings and sufferings are our experiences comprised. In each of these there is the same typical compresence of act and object, attitude and thing, self and world.

This literal and vital compresence of two factors is clearly present in such experiences as petting a dog, looking at the starry heavens, or driving a nail. Yet there seem to be experiences in which this compresence is absent, in which there are no things or objects belonging to the one world of nature in space and time, but only internal processes whose objects (if they have any) find no lodgment in nature at all. Such are the experiences of dreaming and revery, imagining and thinking, longing and planning for that which is not real and not in one's possession. The objects which form the complements of such acts and attitudes as these (for *some* 'object' there is in every dream, illusion, and desire) appear to be unreal and ideal. They are objects because they are what we dream and think of and not our acts or processes of dreaming and thinking. Yet they differ so, are so multiform and mutually inconsistent with one another and with 'real' things that some habitat, it seems, must be provided for them apart from the realm of natural, particular existences in space and time. They then comprise an ideal realm—'ideal' in no eulogistic sense, but rather in the negative sense of objects which are excluded from the world of natural existences. This is one genesis of the bifurcation of existence and essence, a motive and a conviction that, at any rate, bear witness to the fact that experience is not in all cases the simple compresence and meeting of two natural existences—physical stimulus and bodily response, or natural thing (in space-time) and a psychological or biological process equally restricted to the dimensions of natural existence.

There are, so far as I see, two alternative and divergent paths which open before us at this point, and the problem to which we have been leading begins to open out. The issue which arises is

not that of Realism or Idealism as commonly depicted. If we are
to use conventional shibboleths at all we shall have to describe
the issue as lying between Naturalism and Idealism, both of
which are realistic—committed equally, that is, to the conviction
that experience is not a substantive, isolated stream of events,
subjective and internal, but is the meeting-place of an independent
and objective world and of acts, attitudes, and interests.

The question at stake is the central problem of metaphysics.
What is the real world, the independent and enduring environment within which our experiences transpire, within which we
live and do, enjoy and suffer, achieve and fail? That there is
a world—or, if you chose, many worlds—of objects which are
experienced in the manifold acts of experiencing, seeing, thinking,
desiring, loving, and the like, this is indubitable. All experience is
objective in this minimal and neutral sense—neutral because the
metaphysical status of such objects has still to be determined.
Are these objects real or illusory? Do they exist within the spatio-
temporal order of nature or do they merely subsist in the more
shadowy realm of essence? All that we are as yet sure of is that
they are the objects upon which our acts of experiencing are
directed, and that they cannot, with fairness and impunity, be
identified with our experiencings themselves. The alternatives
confronting us now are these: (1) The real, independent world
shall be identified with a restricted or selected class of such objects.
All the other objects which fail to conform to the standard set by
this privileged type shall be judged to be unreal; they will be
said to be subjective or psychic additions, or merely human
interpretations and elaborations of simple natural stimuli, or
they will inhabit a non-human domain of subsistent and ideal
essences, as objective as you please, but not by any right of their
own clothed with real existence. In any such framework of
thought, reality is made amenable to the demand for simplicity
and a kind of absoluteness; it is identified with a central core or
nucleus whose complex apparent wrappings are lent to it through
a medium not of its own stuff. Material atoms characterized
solely by size, mass, and motion impinge upon sense organs and
nerve tissue and generate a rich world of secondary qualities far

outstripping in their content and texture the simple spatio-temporal processes in which they—mysteriously—originate. Such relatively simple and absolute physical processes are alone real and objective. The complexly variegated world which issues from their impact upon bodily organisms bears no resemblance and holds out no clue to that which exists and transpires within objective nature. Likewise from the side of men's practical life and experience. Relatively simple and permanent natural interests, impulses, wants, and instincts, generate in the medium of history and men's minds ideal ends and purposes whose scope and whose content are wholly human and subjective.

Such is the framework of Naturalism, and it provides one great metaphysical alternative. Is it possible to place our finger upon any one central and underlying motive which yields the formative, logical drive in the direction of the various types of Naturalism? I think that it is. And, strangely enough, it is a logical doctrine and scheme of thought which was fastened upon men's minds in the classical period of Greek philosophy. It lies in the presupposition and belief that in anything whatever there can be discovered a central, nuclear, essential, and substantial core—that which the thing *really* is—and in comparison with which most of the thing's seeming qualities are accidental, non-essential, and contingent. These are to be simply disregarded in any successful attempt to know what the thing in truth is. They depend for their appearance upon the extrinsic relation of the thing in question to other things; *they* are not intrinsic to its essential nature. If they exhibit themselves variously in different contexts, the essential or substantial thing itself is simple and unchanging. It is likewise absolute, unspoilt by any of the relations which lend to it the appearance of complexity. Thus simplicity, unchangeableness, absoluteness are the marks of anything's essential nature, while complexity, variety, and relatedness characterize its attributes and accidents. What we perceive—the objects and events of our direct experience—touch only the extrinsic and contingent and merely apparent qualities of things whose essential, unchanging, and simple nature can be grasped only by thought, by concepts, which are reached through a process of abstracting away these irrelevant and inessential qualities. The hold which this intellectual framework has had upon the European tradition of philosophy and science can scarcely be exaggerated, from the inception of the Aristotelian Logic to, say, the eighteenth-century doctrine of individualism.[1] This doctrine implied the twin beliefs (1) that each individual possessed an essential nature (the 'natural' ingredients, rights, etc.) surrounded by contingent and historical, positive and relational qualities external to his 'real' being, and (2) the belief that this essential core was present in all individuals, resulting in their essential equality. The significance of the historical and romantic movement of the nineteenth century (as well as that of Hegel's Logic) lay in its criticism and implied rejection of this logical presupposition, in its attempt (however unsuccessful the outcome) to bridge the gap between the essential nature of individuals and their contingent, historical accidents.

The philosophy of Hume exhibits, I think, in the clearest and most rigorous way, the results of applying this logical motive and framework to the analysis of human experience. For, as Hume sees, the direct objects of human experience—the world within which we act and plan and live—are characterized by pervasive relational complexities and not by simplicity, isolation, and absoluteness. The relation which was seized upon by Hume as central was that of causality. We live and act in a world in which things and events hang together and imply one another. Yet the real world, once it is known for what it is, is composed of atomic and isolated simple 'impressions.' Each impression is a little absolute. Hence the complexities and relations which characterize the objects of *our* world do not really belong to it—in itself—but are artificially woven upon impressions. They owe their apparent existence to 'custom' and 'imagination.' They are human and instinctive interpretations of impressions, of the given and real, fashioned ultimately in the interests of action and of life. Knowledge must discount them and terminate in impressions. The result is that the world which is known to be real is a world in which

[1] The Platonic philosophy appears to me, above all, as a struggle between this logical motive and the desire to find lodgment *within* reality, for all the objects of experience, 'to save appearances.'

life and action and experience are impossible. And the world in which alone we can purpose and act is an artificial world—a world of fictitious relations and complexities. Never has this logical motive, the definition of the real as that which is simple rather than complex, absolute rather than relational, substance rather than life and things experienced, led to so final a divorce between the requirements of theory and those of practice. This divorce it was which awoke Kant from his dogmatic slumber and set the problem for a genuinely critical analysis of human experience, untrammelled by this logical presupposition of the old tradition.

There is the other great alternative of metaphysical interpretation to which one would like to give the name 'Idealism.' It is no less 'realistic' than Naturalism. It, too, recognizes the conditioned, historical, and even sporadic character of every experiencing of things—things and structures which cannot be drawn within the processes of experiencing themselves. Things experienced are objective, in spite of, or even because of, their relational complexities, and the meanings—theoretical or practical—which they have within the human perspective.

This interpretation of our human experience lays stress upon certain pervasive traits which characterize experience at all levels, in every mode—non-cognitive as well as cognitive. I shall restrict myself here to a statement of these essential traits as they hold within experience, in so far as it is theoretic and cognitive. There is in every experience something given; but no experience is restricted to, nor does it coincide with, the bare presence of such an immediate datum in such wise that the world is narrowed down to just that datum, within the perspective of that unitary experience. I should reject any theory of knowledge in which the only indubitable elements which we possess wherewith to construct our world and our knowledge are definite data sharply bounded and self-contained in such wise that we are certain with respect to that which falls within its boundaries, and are compelled to resort to precarious inference or 'animal faith' with respect to anything which lies beyond. Neither percepts nor feelings, sense data nor essences, conceived as immediately given entities whose nature is fully disclosed in the experiencing of them, are the building-stones of the edifice of knowledge or experience. The elements or units of our knowledge exhibit a complexity which transcends any such simplicity. Neither knowledge nor any mode of experience are the loci of pure givenness and immediacy. There is a spread and a depth in all conscious experience of objects which thins down to the bare presence of a datum and nothing besides only at an ideal lower limit, which is the vanishing-point of experience itself.

The transcendence of the given, characteristic of all experience, appears in two different ways, and the relation between these two forms of transcendence constitutes our major metaphysical problem. There are instances in which the given is interpreted and invested with meanings which *appear* to be derived, not from the given nor from anything continuous with the given, but from the structure, interests, and previous experiences of the subject. The subject or self *apperceives* the given in accordance with its own disposition and training. The given supplies only the neutral nucleus, which is invested with various meanings imputed adventitiously to the datum. The criterion as to which interpretation is better or worse, true or false, lies in such cases, not in the nature of any objective world spreading out from the given focus, but in the structure, needs, and interests of the subject. Meanings, relations, classifications, and categories are in this case imposed upon and imputed to the objectively given, which does not own them in its own right. The world *as known*, as ordered and classified, as amenable to the requirements of the human spirit, is the world which has been fashioned out of raw given material (which is alone objective) and subjective forms and vehicles of meaning.

The second kind of transcendence of the given is that in which the elements which yield the means of interpreting the given are supplied from the side of the objective. The given is experienced as incomplete, but that which fills it out and supplements it is continuous with its own nature. The means of interpreting the given are not here, as in the first type, lodged in a self or subject which imposes *its* interpretation upon an external stimulus or material. The 'given' yields its own interpretation, or is capable of doing so if the proper and adequate medium for that development is provided. The apprehension of space and time, for instance, is neither merely the awareness of data of duration and extensity nor is it the reading into such data of supplementary extensions foreign to their own nature and imposed upon them. It is the awareness and recognition of what the data themselves are, not as immediately given, but as continuously supplementing and completing the given. This supplementing and interpretation of the given comes from the side of the object. Space and time are indeed 'ideal constructions,' but they are not for that reason arbitrary and subjective. The same considerations apply, in principle, to the problem of perception. Objects perceived do not coincide with given sensa, nor with immediately present data of any sort. They are saturated and drenched with meanings which transcend the given. But these meanings are not arbitrarily imputed to sense data. They are completions and supplements of the immediately given material itself, whatever that may be. They are as objective and real as the irrefragible, hard core of the immediately given.

The most familiar instance of a given which carries with it its own completion and interpretation is that of valid inference. Premises—data—impose their own conclusions, which are but their own meanings, supplementing (objectively) the nature of the original data. The process of drawing inferences, of reasoning, —a process occurring only in minds—is throughout constrained by data which are given as incomplete and which sustain and develop themselves. Mind, ideas and reason, are the scene of such objective development. Nor is such objective constraint limited solely to knowledge, to reason in its theoretical function. Right conduct is that conduct which is implied and demanded by the objective situation in which the agent finds himself. Its possibility and achievement rest upon the discovery of the objective meaning which inheres in the given situation. Morality is both an ideal construction and *also* objective, no less so than are perception and inference. The same medium of reason, in which an incomplete given develops its own nature, is present in both instances. In valid inference and in right conduct the constraint imposed upon our thinking and our doing is equally objective.

But what becomes, then, of our first type of transcending the given, of interpreting it in accordance with needs and experiences which arise, not from the side of the objectively given, but from the subject, self, or mind? There is here, apparently, the possibility of wider and wider departure from the objective, of the building up of structures which are wholly ideal and subjective, having no counterpart either in the given or in anything continuous with it. If, now, we assume the simplicity and absoluteness of the given and of the real, all ideal constructions, every transcendence of the given in thought, knowledge, and conduct, would indeed be 'ideal' in the sense of subjective and unreal. This assumption has, we have seen, profoundly influenced modern philosophy, and especially the traditional modern conception of mind and consciousness as a detached medium, isolated from all that is objective and real. Such a dualism renders error and illusion explicable and natural, but it renders knowledge correspondingly precarious and dubious. It generates a representative theory of perception, of knowledge and of truth. It yields the belief that the whole of human experience, cognitive no less than practical, is confined to sensations, impressions, and ideas cut off from objective existence. Such ideas may represent or duplicate the objectively real, though such cognitive success or practical solidarity with the real can never itself be experienced or verified.

The resulting problem as I see it is this. To what extent may we say that instances of our first type—the apparently subjective and merely internal elaboration of the given—are in truth cases of the second type, in which contact with something objective is never at any point broken off? Crucial here are the problems of perception and imagery. Are we to say that the content of perception is not objective because it is the result of processes of elaboration and interpretation within a specific perspective of sense organs and previous experience recorded in some way within the brain? Are we also to say that images and ideas are still further removed from the real and the objective because here the attachment to something given or something independent of the subject is still more tenuous? If, indeed, the objective realm is conceived in terms of what is simple and absolute, this is what we shall be compelled to say. Upon such a premise, percepts and images will be driven out of the objective realm and into a detached, subjective area. If, on the other hand, we recognize how unsimple and relational the given and the objective are, the situation may become radically altered. It no longer follows, of necessity, that because the given is always presented within a specific perspective, it is cut off from the objective world and condemned to some sort of unreality. Most promising and sound in principle seem to me the attempts to concede to the content of every perception—secondary as well as primary qualities—a real and objective status. I see no way of cutting across the content of perception, making portions of it objective and relinquishing the remainder to a less real domain. Yet some distinction there is between the worth and adequacy of different perceptions. This implies a criterion. What supplies the standard for the value, cognitive or otherwise, not only of things perceived, but of things experienced in any type or domain of experience? This is the final question. Before stating, in barest outline, in what direction I look for an answer, what of that region of experience, so closely allied to perception yet so apparently far from anything objective—imagery and thought? It is just this continuity with perception and this seeming freedom from constraint by objects which makes the problem of images and ideas so crucial. The one principle which we have here to maintain is this. An image, the content of imaging, may be said to be mental or non-mental. But in any case an image is some real *object* which is imaged. And it *is* the object rather than any subjective or shadowy duplicate of it. Just as a percept or perception is a 'real' object *as perceived*, so an image is an equally real object *as imaged*. The basic consideration in both instances is that of a specific perspective which may *not* be condemned to unreality because it is a perspective, hence relational and complex. And I should say the same thing about a concept, an idea, a theory. Because a theory, a judgment, or an idea is *about* something other than itself, and because the process in which the *existence* of the theory or judgment is displayed goes on in my body or mind or body-mind, it does not follow that the judgment or idea is a series of events disparate from the objective events to which they refer, and somehow duplicating them or corresponding with them.

If in elementary sensation or perception anything whatever of the organism's environment is known (and if it is not known there is no basis whatever for successful behaviour), then more of that environment may become disclosed in the more complex and more highly developed levels of mind. Memory and idea need not be representative rather than presentative because they are farther removed from their sensory and perceptual foundations. There are dimensions, characteristics, and relational aspects of the real world which can be presented and apprehended only by thought, by judgment and theory. A scientific theory grasps more of the world than any possible sensation or perception, yet its grasp, once consummated, is no less direct.

But is any such thesis as this able, when carried through, to do justice to those motives, those ingredients of experience and thought, which so deeply colour modern life and philosophy? Individualism, subjectivism, activism, responsibility for transforming our world in the light of man's needs and wants, the recognition of ideals and essences not lodged in existence—how can these motives be fitted into a framework of thought in which the controlling factors of mind and experience, ideas and judgment come from objects, from nature, from the world in which mind and experience live—from reality?

That there is here an antinomy it were idle to deny. Experience oscillates between two contrasted attitudes, that of recognizing, discovering, contemplating, and that of making and remaking, controlling and achieving. The relation between these two attitudes, and the two contrasting ways in which the environment enters into them, has always seemed to me the ultimate problem. In my *Idealism and the Modern Age* I tried to assert the primacy of the attitude of *Theoria*, in which the mind is ever—even in its practical intercourse with things—confronted by objective, significant structures, in whose apprehension *all* experience has its being and its life. Nor have I yet broken, in principle, with this belief. I still think that you cannot describe any of the major provinces of experience without recognizing the controlling influence of objective systems and worlds, constraining thought, feeling and will. Behaviourism and neo-realism are not wholly wrong; but they conceive in too simple a way the nature of those structures which constrain the life of the mind and which give it its filling and its content. The categories neither of physics nor of biology are fully adequate to this task, and their inadequacy springs, at bottom, from this. They interpret mind and experience as the residue of processes from which all objective meaning and value have been removed, as barely factual and causal, mechanical and natural.

Experience is never, I have said, the bare presence of a datum, save, perhaps, at its lower ideal limit where it is on the point of vanishing. Every datum announces itself as incomplete and, in so far, problematic. Corresponding to this characteristic of the datum is the fact that the experiencing, the awareness of the datum, is always more than simple acquiescence in what is given. Mind does more than record the immediately present. Its characteristic act is to claim for the datum a meaning which no datum within its own boundaries possesses. Hence the question of validity arises with respect to every pulse and moment of conscious experience. Given any bit of experience, and you have to ask, not only what it is and what its causal antecedents are, but also what measure of validity does it possess? This holds not only of each item of cognitive experience, perception, concept, and judgment, but of experience as practical and appreciative as well. This constitutes the ideal aspect of experience, 'ideal' in no eulogistic sense, but merely descriptive of this claim-making trait. All that is experienced—perceived, willed, and felt—is amenable, not only to the categories of description and causal explanation, but to normative criteria as well.

This is most simply to be seen in the case of judgment, which I take to be typical. A judgment is an event which occurs. This event has its causal antecedents. So far a judgment is like any natural occurrence whatever. But one has not exhausted all that one wants to know about a judgment when one has thus described

and explained it. One has still to ascertain the degree of validity which it possesses. That some judgments, at least, possess
validity is indubitable. The question now is this: Are the factors
which are responsible for the existence of the judgment, the
situation in nature from which the judgment as an event arises,
wholly factual, untainted by meaning and value, entirely *wertfrei*?
Three alternative positions are open to us: (1) That which determines a judgment to exist has in it no ingredient of worth at all—
judgment is a moment within a series of events which occur at
random or mechanically. Nor is any account here to be taken
of a subsistent, ideal realm which, while it exercises no constraint
upon the *existence* of judgment, yet provides an ideal criterion
wherewith to measure its worth. Such a position is naturalistic
monism. (2) The *existence* of judgment, as a natural event, is to
be understood as before, solely in terms of its causal and 'mechanical' antecedents. But there is also an ideal realm of normative
principles which determine a judgment's validity, though they
are otiose and inert with respect to its existence. Such a position
is that of a radical dualism. It stresses the divorce between
psychology and logic, between existence and essence, between
fact and norm.

It is difficult for me to see what validity could attach to
a judgment upon the premises of naturalistic monism and
determinism. Even if the existence of any judgment could be
rendered intelligible, its validity in the sense of its truth of
falsity would remain an empty word. It would be as meaningless
to ascribe truth to a judgment as to the fall of a meteor, if both
are wholly the outcome of matter-of-fact occurrences. Nor do I
think we are in any better position if we take refuge in a dualism
of determining, causal factors and validating grounds, of the sort
developed in the neo-Kantian schools. For here, too, the grounds
which determine a judgment's validity are kept entirely aloof
from the factors which render intelligible the judgment's existence.
If a judgment happens to be true, it is through no merit or worth
of the situation whence it has emerged.

There is a third alternative. It results from the recognition
that the principles which determine the validity of a judgment

are of no avail unless they belong to, and are continuous with, the factors which are responsible for the judgment's existence. The situation out of which the judgment is generated cannot be indifferent to the meaning and worth of the judgment, nor can the grounds of its validity be severed from the agencies which produce it. This implies that in some manner meanings and values are integral to existence and to reality. A judgment, *as an occurrence*, is occasioned by some sort of mind-body mechanism. A judgment *as true* is constrained by logical criteria which serve as a norm. What have these to do with each other? Here is, in miniature, the whole problem of the relation between descriptive and normative, 'is' and 'ought,' facts and ideals, events and their significance and value. The difference between a true and a false judgment (with respect to the occasions which breed them) cannot be that while a false judgment is caused by merely psychological processes, a true judgment is constrained by logical norms which belong to a totally different dimension. The true judgment must equally occur because of the psychological (or biological) mechanism which generates it. That 'mechanism' must be continuous with the structures and processes out of which a true judgment arises. The only principle which I can formulate is this: what we call logical principles are of the same stuff as merely psychological principles, but they are more inclusive, they have a wider range and embody more of the real world. Psychology is more abstract and partial than is logic. They are not hostile, nor do they inhabit incommensurable areas.

The growth of experience and of mind is the development of systems and of structures which incorporate and come under the constraint of more inclusive stretches of reality. This is the story of the history from touch to vision, from percept to concept. The more 'ideal' experience is, the more inclusive is the area of reality which it recognizes and to which it responds. Mind is ever the scene of control by a general scheme, by the outlying, absent and distant, rather than by the immediately surrounding and antecedent particulars. In this sense the order of physical events (as traditionally conceived) is the home of immediacy, or of the constraint, the push and pull of the directly contiguous in space and time. But even in the physical order of nature such immediacy has proven to be inadequate. How much more inadequate is it in the domains of living structures, of historic achievements and the worlds which are disclosed to and which sustain the career of mind!

Do such statements as these prepare the way for the acceptance of philosophical Absolutism? I do not see, as yet, that they do. An experience to which *all* the wealth of structure and meaning which belong to reality would be fully presented is a contradiction, since the ideal aspect of experience, corresponding to the fragmentary character of everything given and experienced, cannot be thought away. But it need not follow that such ideal meanings are deprived of lodgment in reality because they do not and cannot coincide with 'given' facts. They are not thereby arbitrary human accretions, imposed upon, and imputed to, a neutral and wholly factual, meaningless world.

This, then, is the philosophical framework—or some rafters thereof—the erection and completion of which seems to me most worth while attempting. Yet 'completion' is no term to be applied to a philosophical structure. Every philosophical hypothesis and organized framework of ideas has its surds and problems peculiar to its own genus. Within which type of structure, naturalism or idealism, do such recalcitrant elements plague us the least, when the widest sweep of nature and life, experience and history, are kept steadily in view? This alone can supply the means whereby the success of any philosophical venture is to be tested.

PRINCIPAL PUBLICATIONS

Idealism and the Modern Age (Yale University Press, 1919).
Contributions to University of California publications in philosophy (annual volumes, 1923–29).

THE GREAT ART WHICH IS PHILOSOPHY

By HARTLEY BURR ALEXANDER

Born 1873; Professor of Philosophy, Scripps College, California.

THE GREAT ART WHICH IS PHILOSOPHY

I

HAVING but the conviction that philosophy is an art—the Great Art—I can only speak as one for whom the interpretation of this art is worthily the task of a lifetime. In naming philosophy art rather than science I have no notion that I am in any wise detracting from its dignity as a quest for truth, but am adding thereto, for I conceive that I am ascribing to it a range and subtlety of expression such as no science may be found to possess, yet without which all communication of truth must be feeble and mutilated. Historically science is the offspring of philosophy, and is participant with it in the pursuit of understanding; yet science is not a capable heir in the sense in which philosophy inherits power from its own parent, which is the whole of that art whereby mankind has sought, and still seeks, to create intelligible images of the meaning of our human life, upwelling from chaos. Such imaged meanings are truth, and for truth no measures may suffice that employ less than the total resources of our intelligence, which richness of resource is the mark of art, and it is also the mark of philosophy, for where truth is the stake philosophy is of all modes of understanding the subtlest and the most penetrating. Therefore it is first of all with reference to the gift of truth-speaking that I name philosophy an art, although surely it is an art also with respect to its purpose and its wisdom, as I shall maintain.

An illustration which pleases me indicates after this fashion the distinction of science and art. Let one stand at his window and upon the pane etch the outlines of the houses and streets or the gardens and hills there to be seen. Let, then, the pane be removed to become the foundation of a study, in either of two modes. By the appropriate projection it may be made over into a map or plat of the area seen, such that one may comparatively measure the structures indicated and may, indeed, employ the whole design as a chart of locomotions, serving as guide and pathfinder, even though it would in no way resemble what one might see were he to follow the indicated paths. This, it appears to me, is exactly the method and the achievement of that form of knowledge which we call science; it gives us paths of motion, practical guides, whereby we may proceed with expedition and economy to those places where we wish to be; but why we should wish to go thither or what we are to perceive when we are arrived, these matters our chart does not reveal. And it is just these which are to be indicated by the other mode in which our study may be pursued; for the artist may take the etching as the beginning of a picture, to be filled in with colour and light, and so create for us the similitude of perception in all its living actuality, or perhaps, by his own imaginative correc- tions, indicate details which we may alter for the sake of gardening our domain more to our taste. Here the end is the moment of contemplation, or indeed of humanization, which we willingly recognize as of itself the satisfaction of our activity and the completion of our understanding. In each of these studies we have begun with an abstraction and have returned to its object with knowledge not previously possessed; but of the two the one has yielded us means and the other reasons, and it is the latter which most resemble the wisdom of philosophy.

Now I find a certain corroboration of the meaning conveyed by this image when I ask after what metaphors most nourish the roots of our expression and best carry the messages of human intelligence. Quite certainly these metaphors cluster about our body, about its parts and its functions and its suffused sensibility of its own growing life; the categories of all logics are to be found in respiration and heartbeat, in the extensions and pre- hensions of our limbs, in eyesight and ear-hearing, in mouth- speech and gesture-speech, in food-taking and in life-bringing, and in all the metamorphoses which dramatically construe the norm and the sense of the life of man. Such things, without addition conveying from mind to mind the colour and intimacy of what- ever is sensitive within us, constitute the priorities of under- standing and the root-meanings of discourse, and they establish for us effortlessly a milieu of unchallenged comprehensions which is the possibility of a society of minds and is the beginning of reason. To realize how structure-giving is this fact one need but reflect upon what difficulties would lie in our coming to an understanding with a mind-endowed octopus or squid, and, indeed, do lie between us and any illuminating communication with even those domestic animals that are most eager for our companionship; or obversely, one might note how among ourselves, when associated by kinds, we acquire a swift-mindedness which puts child at ease with child, youth with youth, elderman with elderman, or gives to men among men, women in the company of women, a conscious relief from the sense of artifice that goes with the conventions whereby we endeavour to facilitate association of the sexes. There are barriers to comprehension even within our human measures of the intelligible.

Of these measures a certain limited set, readily to be characterized, constitute the especial intelligibility of science. Primarily they are skeletal and muscular and locomotive, and assembled they yield us that image of the understood machine which is named by us scientific rationality. Its elements are distinguishable within the body. First, the rigidities of our bones, which give us space. The upright body of man is the gnomon of his circumscribing universe, in its plane foursquare with his right and left and before and behind, in its pole trine with the underfoot nadir, the overhead zenith, and the navel which is the symbolic *pou stō* of his spatial world. Again, the stature of man is our world's metre, analysed by our bones into thumb and palm and foot, into yard and pace (of which the platinum metre itself is no more than the refined generalization), and through the geomancy of our decadic digits subdivided into points and millimetres, or repeated out into *mille passus*, kilometric earth-girth, starsphere, light-year of space. Second, the flexions of our muscles, which give us motion and thence generate metric time. Each movement is a moment, an event, an accent; and the sequences of our motions throw these into rhythmic cycles, trinal with the movements of our tripartite limbs, dual with those of our bisymmetric bodies, and all underlain with the tempos of eternity given by pulse and breath. Clocks and dials and figurate years mean time only with reference to such measures. Third is number.

Quanta are *res*, things taken, taken first by physical and second by imaginative prehension; and these yield us the initials of mathematics. Metric number joins to fingering only breath-count, to space-unit a time-unit, in order to tell out the whole arithmetic of creation; while the frame of cosmos is bequeathed by the torsions and angulations of our joints, and the dimensions of space are given in the spheroids which circumscribe our axial spine, in the rests and postures which define point and plane, and by the index which adds sense-order to our locomotions. Such quanta and metres are wholly described by the real numbers; where mathematics passes beyond these it moves into the realm of the metaphysical and the ultra-scientific.

Space, time, and number are the ultimates of scientific reason (as nowadays science is understood), but they are themselves abstractions of our skeletal and muscular life—last abstractions if, indeed, we may not have arrived at one farther generalization which is making of space and time the supernumeraries of number, and of number the only cosmos. Yet space, time, and number, after all, are but elements. Of themselves they do not give us the conviction of understanding, which alone can confirm to the functioning machine its sufficiency as reason. To them we must add the unifying trait that to be genuinely a machine is to do something; to them we must add work and force. Our limbs not only move, they push and pull and lift and release; they are mallets and levers and screws; and in their directed motions they are multifariously in contact with a resistant encasement which only effort can shape anew. Most of our active consciousness, and the very root of our conception of activity, lives in our sense of muscular effort; it forms about our expending energies and the fatigues of work, of which the reciprocal is our sense of contactual resistances and recumbancies, generalized first into gravitational weight, and beyond into mechanical mass. It is true that in our more abstracted physics this mass tends to fade out into number (along with time and space), yet even if but as a ghost it lingers on in the polarities alike of the electromagnetic atom and of the hypergalactic universe; and it is only this ghostly reflection of our own puny exertion of effort that gives convincing reality either to atom or to universe. The machine, then, functioning, working, is genuinely this mechanical body of ours; and whether its forthfigurings be the magnifications of astronomical speculation, the comminutions of atomic systems, or the arcs and nodes of neural patterns, always its reason is the living body, motive and locomotive. In the structures and actions of this living body are the images and logic of all knowledge, which we call, in strict mode, science.

I have but one addition. Surreptitious and unnoted, light also is there. It is a light without colour or focus and it yields no perspectives, but none the less its presence alone is what gives us our imaginative readings of dials and graphs, visualizes our charts of motion, and renders legible those minute punctualities without which the machine could be only blind and blundering power. It gives, too, a morphology of the real and the possible; for where the sight falls, there the world is bounded and possibility ends; and where arm-reach and eyesight confirm their objects for one another, there reality is at its maximum of trustworthiness—these, at least, in the mechanical world. It is true enough that mechanistic science is unconscious of the presence of this colourless illumination, and offers for it no place in its logic; yet without it the machine could be only a chaotic Titan fumbling in the gloom of the abyss. All that truly makes of science a chart and a guide, cartographic for life, is the unrecognized presence of a reader and of a light which in more than a metaphorical sense is the light of reason.

Such are the measures which have created for us scientific intelligence, and which, in shaping the foundation, set also the boundaries of scientific wisdom. But there is another set of metaphors, clinging close to our bodily life, to which science has never allowed more than inadvertent admission into its systems, yet which has yielded us the keenest and most convincing of our understandings. In this set fall all those structural perceptions which are mediated by delicately adjusted sense-organs and are not concerned with locomotion; and in it also fall the organic thrills and responses which weave the pattern of bodily consciousness and fuse into one life the metamorphoses of our years.

One can distinguish this set from that which has given reason to science by calling its metaphors 'secondaries,' whereas the other is the set of 'primaries'; but this is only to repeat the rote of an old theory. It is much better to point out that the so-called 'secondaries' are the character-giving, as distinct from the motion-charting, metaphors of the understanding, and that in place of blurring into continua or reduplicating into automata they yield to us the intelligibilities of art, perhaps most of all of dramatic art. Certainly, as does the reason which gives science, they begin with abstraction, but they do not, like scientific thinking, pursue this initial abstraction into any realm of remote and universal law; rather, their end is an image, and an image having all the vividness and verisimilitude of the foundational experience, only now the experience is shown as significant and as lighted by its own truth. The mode is the mode of art.

Eyesight and ear-hearing are two of the fountains of this æsthetic understanding. Of light I have already said that its unnoted presence is all that rescues science from the chaos of unreason; yet the colourless and diffuse illumination which scientific reason utilizes is but the frail spectre of the full understanding which is eyesight's gift. Conceive what loss were one to expurgate from the world's letters all the meaning that vision and light convey! Not alone would the symbolism of colour vanish, but eloquence would fade from poetry and its glory from every apocalypse. And beyond letters lie painting and sculpture and intelligible form, all giving their interpretations of man's understandings of himself and of nature; and again beyond is the whole spectacle of the world, colour and form and motion combining, throughout seen and named and understood in reflection. For eyesight-seeing, even as to its root metaphors, is very much more than optical sensation. It is absurd to suppose that sense-organs and sensory tracts give an account of sense-perception; actual perception is as much emotion and idea as sense, and it is actual perception that is taken up in the metaphorical reasoning whose expression is art. Light and dark are rich in sentiment, while colour is almost an entire language of the feelings: drab and gay, turgid and lucent, depressing and inspiring, crass and refined——these are all meanings that are immediate in our colour world, and they are moral and intellectual and emotional meanings as well as significations of sense. It is with such resource that the metaphors of vision put understanding into art and make of the cosmic spectacle one of the pillars of metaphysics. I have often paused in considering the behest of some arch-astronomer, that I join in his admiration of the mechanic stars, to wonder if, indeed, his conviction would be so glorified were the object of his contemplation not celestial luminaries but some vast obscenity opaquing the abyss? Clearly, science itself borrows from art, and æsthetic emotion is one of the stays of its rationality.

If eyesight gives us a space which is vastly richer and truer than any which physics knows, so hearing leads into a time which is more real than any chronometry. The time to which I refer is musical; it is not to be understood in any technical sense, although musical art is its symbol, but it is musical in that broader mode which would make music to include the whole phrase-form of thought and the varied progressions of life, music as that curious discarnation which distinguishes time from space, spirit from matter, and gives to the ideal its unassailable empire over every provincial now. To musical time there is beginning and middle and end, or at least there is melodic direction, irreversible, and the symphonic interplaying of vital themes, which alone can give us some comprehension of the interpenetrations of cosmical times—such that we of to-day, for example, look upon light that may have departed its nebula when earth was carboniferous, or such that past, present, and future gather into one meaning in the conformation of the stars or the structure of a flower. The visible heavens and the world of organic forms are meshes of such temporal interpenetrations, but so also are our lives, with infancy and youth and our whole mind-echoed past and mind-foreseen future living within us, to be, in the one true sense, time.

Thus space and time have æsthetic modes richer in wisdom than ever can be the pale formularies of the space and time which physical science knows. Doubtless, also, there is an æsthetic of number which is more than formulary, and is metric in another than any quantitative sense. Such we find at hand wherever number shapes itself into structures and systems, wherever numbers are architectural or architectonic. Odd and even is surely an example; so also such descriptions as triadic, quinary, decimal, or, if one choose, surd and rational and transcendental. These are but simple types of numeral characters that in physical nature represent only accidents, but in mathematics create art; they do not originate with quantity nor are they employed for any primitive measure, and if they are subject to formula they are themselves underived. Mathematical perfection belongs to the ideas which numbers are rather than to physical things, and all appreciation of perfection is æsthetic. When Pythagoras, having discovered the theorem of the three squares, sacrificed an ox to Zeus, his devotion was that of an artist, not of a surveyor.

Contributory to this æsthetic of number (as likewise it is contributory to the æsthetic of musical time) is the rhythm of motion. For just as scientific reason utilizes light and sight without exhausting the significance of vision, so of motion the fuller meaning is abandoned to art. Our limbs are not only trinal, they are dactyllic and anapæstic; our bodies are not only duo-motor, they are iambic, trochaic, spondaic; and the combinations, diminuendos, and crescendos of these units yield that infinite poetry of pattern which is the dance of life and the movement of reason, whether logos or arithmos. Whoever has heard the insistent drum-beat taming wild men to its rhythms can understand, at least in spirit, both the music of the spheres and the transcendentalities of the mathematicians.

Reason, then, for art is in all its elements a more significant thing than is reason for science; and as this is true with respect to the elements, so also is it true with respect to the principle of sufficiency. For the finality of æsthetic rationality is a much more intimate thing even than light, and a more subtle and a more intelligible, being, in fact, no less than the life-form of the body itself, the Vita of man. Within the Vita are included the elemental functions of bodily existence—food-taking, for example, which is the most universally communicable of all meanings and gives us our first and surest comprehensions of the mouthing and chap-licking world of our animal comrades. Certainly, tongue and tooth and breast and heart are the very thrones of metaphor; it is these that form prime categories of reasoning and the last kennings of poetry; for through these and their kindred terms are conveyed, not only the simple modes of physical life, such as breath and nourishment, birth and death, but also, and with more intensity, the whole range of values which inspire our world with meaning: its glut and emptiness, courage and recoil, the gamut of love and the discords of hate, or again that sympathy and antipathy with which a Greek would give centre and periphery to his moving sphere, or which lingers on in our own ghost-haunted physics as attraction and repulsion, polarity, chemotropy. All such values are conveyed as the first intentions of the metaphors of the Vita; but second intentions are present also, and these penetrate even more deeply into metaphysical understanding. Among them none is more searching than is the image of metamorphosis. For within our lives each living moment leaps flame-like, illuminating past and future, so that we know the bodily Vita as one arc of being, bounded by birth and death and defined by its cycle of metamorphic change. The movement is that of transformation, but the outline is the outline of drama, wherein falls all that play of meaning through which the spectacle given in æsthetic space, the music which is the order of æsthetic time, and the modalities of rhythmic numbers shape the significance of our worlds. And so far as we men can discover it, the full reasonableness of Nature is just such a drama; it is the Vita Mundi, of which the measures cannot be less than the height of complexity that we may discover in our own lives.

Therefore I say that philosophy, which is the quest of wisdom and of wisdom's truth, is an art, and the Great Art, seeking its finalities, not in some unoccupied scaffolding of jointed generalizations, standardized for the trade, but in the self-understandings of a spirit that knows itself commanded by the god to make music, and having for its instrument a mind multifariously endowed. Such a philosophy will start with the miracle which each man knows himself to be and knows his world to be; it will begin in wonder, and it will be content with no conclusion which does not return to the philosopher an image as instant and vivid as is his own life. Its measures will be man's own complexities, the fullness of the Vita Humana, and it will regard with incomprehension that curious attempt, characteristic of the methods of the science called empirical, to build up complex things out of simplicities, knowing that the fate of such an attempt can never be anything but lost wanderings into the wilderness of destitute and unattached abstractions. Hypothesis, it is true, can give us some image of our world as one among the possible worlds, but that ours is just this world from among all those, and that I am just this man in the now and here of this life—this is a miracle which hypothesis can never entertain, and which only art can familiarize with reason. Nay, hypothesis itself can have no meaning except as directed to the future, and that a living future; there are no hypothetical pasts in a direction-made temporal world; life knows no possibilities save in what is to be. Therefore we shall define reality, not as some anatomized existent, but as the significant; and the only form of significance which we shall know is that which shall invest the miracle with the habiliment of our familiar life and make of it our parable. Truth *is* just this parable, and to discover truth is the Great Art.

II

Owning such a conception of philosophy as I have sketched, holding it to be more art than science, and an art in which the pattern of highest significance is the whole Vita of Man, there can be no misplacement of emphasis when I assert that philosophy is biographical in its mode, and in its method autobiographical. Biographical, too, I would say, of more than the thinker's moments, for every thinker and every thought is set, not in a point, but in a direction that is significant, tangential to the curve of life, and it is the nature of thought to define direction rather than situation; philosophy, therefore, is biographical of an age and of a civilization, in so far as these have discoverable patterns, and it is biographical of the world, also, for the life that each man lives is inseparably the world's life. And the philosopher, in his own biography, must necessarily discover the clues to whatever wisdom is to be his. I do not mean that he will examine with indifferent zest each and every leap and sting of experience, or that he will assemble the accidents of his days in some muddied reflection of the whole; but I do mean that whatever truth he finds must be in the nature of a self-discovery, some illumination of the alien by the familiar, intimately revealed. His perception of order may extend no farther than to images given by his bones and muscles in mechanic movement, ghost-haunted; it may grope helplessly within the twilights of personal and hapless things; it may, again, move spiritedly out, mind-winged, into understandings that reconstrue the life that book-learning makes possible as an expansion of his own; or it may open into clarities of theory that read in the hieroglyphics of nature the flown vitalities of the past or the auspices of a generative future. But in each case what the man's life is, what his powers are, in these are set the measures of his world.

Common to mankind is some myth of the Emergence. Self-discovery is unpremised; birth is without antecedents; each life is its own miracle—and the world's life, we suppose, must be its miracle, too. To be sure, after having lived awhile, we begin to recount memories; we speak mythically of anamnesis and metempsychosis, or with much service of calculation we assort heredities into genealogical traits whose marriages and adventurous unions have evoked us gradually from some Empedoclean flux, some chaos of monstrosities in which alone, we fondly suppose, could have been our anticipation. But when, abandoning tales, we come home to life, then our single assurance is that the goddess Matuta first created light. The curtain is raised; the stage, puzzlingly, is set. At the outset all the conversation is in the middle voice, and hauntedly in the aorist; but as the action progresses, the grammar takes on tense and structure; persons are distinguished; and the protagonist, who is to be the philosopher's self, discovers himself with the whole meaning of the drama for his rôle. It is in this fashion that life emerges and philosophy is born.

For myself, from early childhood and from out the oblivions

which lie beyond memory, I have been beset with the consciousness that things and moments are but the hieroglyphs of reality, that physical nature is tell-tale with scars (geology became my passion), and that metaphysical nature, if it be not void, must be spiritual in the one sense in which spirit may have meaning, and that is as an engrossment of values—which for me, from the first, included horrors along with beatitudes. For all this I needed no teaching; indeed, it could not be taught. The solitudes of childhood are incommunicably remote—tears and laughters alike incalculable—but this, at least, is their commonplace, that every unsayable perception is a message-bringer and a banner militant with meaning: all the *heres* are portals and all the *nows* dramatic vistas. This is the particularism of 'just this world,' which is the only world that childhood knows and the only world that can ever be real; it is a particularism in which all the objects are symbols, 'play-things' in a literal sense, not dead counters of abstractive commodities, but personal opportunities magical with promise. In so far as I have been able to penetrate the mind called primitive I find that there also this same symbolic particularism is the commonplace of life; nature for the fresh intelligence is wit-challenging heraldry, blazoned with local bearings, not some vast fortification to be breached and mined by the slow campaigns of theory. And if we ourselves will but lay aside the garment of our sophistication, we shall perceive that within our own lives the sense of symbolism is the nude actuality. As to myself, certainly, I cannot find that conviction of the symbolic character of the perceptual or of the vital moment has any origin or source; it is, and has been, omnipresent in the occurrence of such moments. Therefore, for me, no set of mechanic points can combine into the metaphysical image.

On the other hand, I concede no absence of a concern for structure. The allurement of universals is earlier even than the magic of numbers, taking childish form in dramatic rotes and in the airy pretence of mimetic play. The idea of a world, stellar and moral, was one of my excitements before books gave it form; and I was already in sport dubbed 'the philosopher' when what appeared to my elders to be danger lurking in my speculative curiosity led to the forbidding of certain books (Swedenborg among them), to admonitions and prayers, and on my part, after a certain bitterness of undeception, to a concentrated privacy as to things of the mind, maintained throughout the more growing years of youth. For mine is, I think, the second of the generations which are experiencing between parent and child the hostility of incomprehension, where the issue is the world of the spirit. For me, as for many another, the forms of religion fell broken, and it is only after the estrangement of a lifetime that I am beginning to read back into them a meaning not less richly symbolic than in those days was evoked by the fascinations of the new naturalism. Yet religion itself is far other than a set of forms; and he who would shape within his life its philosophy cannot, if he would, ignore what his experiences of religion (grateful or adverse) have made vitally his.

Three things I can distinctly see, traits now of my thought, the understanding of which was surely facilitated by an early background of religion. The first of these I can hardly better describe than as the intensified perception of the symbolic moments of life. Our Protestant stress upon the profound significance of 'inner experience' is surely just this; and while the thing itself antedates and survives religious imagery—being but the clarified appreciation of the double intentions that give us a world in giving us sense—nevertheless the images of religion make conscious their double intentions from the very nature of the truths they would convey. In this particular Protestantism is a more effective teacher than the ritual Church, for Protestantism relies almost desperately upon intuition for its understanding; so that one reared under its guidance, even while rejecting its particular parables, will none the less not escape his own discovery that the parable alone is the vehicle of communicable life. It all amounts, I suppose, to saying that religion is a form of evocation of our native idealism.

But with this comes a second and not less significant self-discovery. Values are the unmetred realities of things, out of time, out of space; and it is precisely value that is emphasized as 'inner experience'; any extension of a physical fact into a

meaning is such an experience, and all perception of cosmos is
in essence evaluation. No religion has ever more emphasized this
than has Christianity, holding with a kind of implacable integrity
to the good and evil, fair and foul, true and false of its dualisms.
For my own part its findings are frankly verified in my life.
I see nothing that is indifferent, except chaos, and nothing that
can be called true that is not either good or bad in its honest
essence. Therefore I have schooled myself to face even shudder-
ingly the black realities of cruelty and bestiality and senseless
monstrosity and pitiful affliction and the leprous destruction of
innocence and beauty; I have looked down into the reek of hell
as well as upwards towards the Bow of Promise; and I have
refused to praise God or to idolize Nature for the presence in
their world of what I abhor. I believe this to be Christian truth,
though it is perhaps beyond the pale of accredited theology.
Certainly it is taught by the Drama, which is so vastly more
convincing than any dogma can be; but even if the Drama were
peculiarly *my* image of its revelation, still I should believe it to
be the truth. Dualism is the old name for this belief, and metaphysically dualism means war at the core of being. I assent
to this.

The third trait is not unrelated to the symbolism and the
dualism which I am describing, being, as it were, their temporal
exegesis. It is the sharp sense of the reality of history and of
possibility with the constructed past and the destined future
seen as the perspective shifts of intelligible truth. As in no other
images of human thought Biblical literature portrays the past
as a brooding and the future as an inspiring presence, the one
a retrospect, the other an omen, but both immanent in the
symbolic now—lightnings of the Lord bridging the abysses of
before and after with a single flare. To me nothing seems more
difficult than the linear notion of time, as if its infinities could be
cut into finite strands or the thread of it sheared into oblivions.
Living time is totally different from this, with multitudinous
interpenetrations, like the combinations of duples and triples
in musical rhythms or like the possession within a single architectural perception of plane and perspective and empathetic

spaces. As our own bodies figure it, time is always fulfilled, memory and anticipation as vividly its substance as can be sense; and, indeed, ourselves moving are more keenly aware of recession and advance than of any station. Historic sense is no more than the recognition of the reality of such time beyond the border lines of our bodily being, yet at the same time not beyond the confines of personal significance. History elevates the fact into a symbol, the material into a spiritual reality, which becomes the more capable in proportion to the tenuity of its bodily hold. Greek consciousness cast this sense into the mode of tragedy—conceived not as gloom but as the life of drama; Christian faith has named it the indwelling of the Eternal; but in each description is indicated the serious truth that man's and the world's past and future are caught in the imaging present, and that only the most laden image can assess cosmic reality.

With this avowal I presume that I should accept the name of idealist, yet I must draw back from assuming it in any but a Platonic sense. For while I am convinced that the Vita of the body is bodily reality, and the Vita of human cultures is man's reality, and the Vita of all nature is the world's reality; and while I cannot but perceive that these realities are significantly involved, the one in the other, nevertheless I am still unable to evade the old perception of conflicting and broken and unfulfilled lives; and the certainty of these makes it impossible for me to discover as the heart of all some triumphant or playful One, master of the legerdemain of appearance, giver of the prizes of consolation. The grandiosities of stellar and organic evolution, when they seemed to be sweeping my generation into skies of elation, were for me hollow and reasonless; for I could see in the pictured progress, not one single imperious course, but only stumblings and gropings and blind explorations, pursued always in the shadow of imminent disaster. I should not have been a man of my time had naturalism not fascinated me; but neither should I have been true to the forms of understanding grained into my own life had I found in it either rest or reason. My truth lay elsewhere, and after the first flush of youthful curiosity its pages fell unillumining.

Whence illumination did seem to come was from the minds of men who directed their gaze, not to mechanic chance, but to the miracle of human intelligence. The distance from earth to sky is the measure, not of the stature of the Titan, but of Homer himself, says Longinus; and my own query ran, Who would study an amoeba when he might be studying the mind of Socrates? Greek philosophy, at its height, proclaimed the humanism first of reason and second of whatever is the parent of reason in this mind-gifted world: that, at least, I could see, and seeing it know that truth has no existence save in the white light of humane understanding—of imagination and of sympathy and of perception of good and evil; the moral fact is fundamental metaphysically, for it is the only fact that has meaning. If I saw, too, that the expression of truth must always at the last be in the language of myth, I owe something of this surely to Plato, though most, I venture, to that besetting conviction, with me up from infancy and confirmed by every significant moment of living, that the blaze of sense and the leap of emotion and the wrack of physical pain—all that springs focal into the nows and heres—is but the fiery hand inscribing the meaning of the world.

From another source came confirmation. Greek philosophy, sober, attempered, clean within its measures, set the model of self-controlled intelligence. Logic, we have come to call it, and reason and theory and wisdom; and it is the shaper of all of these in Occidental thought. But there are other shapes in which intelligence has been begot, and I have studied how the centuries have seasoned in the minds of another race of men, the ancient natives of America, a symbolic wisdom which imparts with symbols the Platonic and Christian understanding that nature is an image, that creation is groping and experimental, that human life is an ordeal with virtues for its flags and ensigns, and that some sense-transcending beauty is its only, but sufficient, glory. Remote from one another in time and tribe, men come to this one sanity, which having found they make over into a heraldry and a rite, and this they call their humanity.

Or, indeed, their God. For my third illumination is to look again at history and at hope, and to see the surge of human culture achieving race after race and period upon period its rituals of civilization in each of which some image of intelligible life takes on the form of letters and art and wisdom, collectively our treasure and in honour our enterprise. As an art of discourse philosophy is a Greek thing, and beautiful with intellect; but as the Great Art it is more than Greek and more than intellectual: it is æsthetic and religious, and it is a maker of the music for which even Socrates feared God's question, and despair of which was Dante's swoon from Paradise. The great fact of human history is its resurgent quest of the Good Life, to be the measure of the Good World and the Good God. And this is the metric truth of reality also, beside which the infinities of trans-stellar spaces and the infinitesimals of material atomies are as children's thumbsticks; for of this we can be convinced, that not less than the full span, not alone of man's achievement, but of his dream, must be his measure of the Vita Mundi.

Should you ask me if even this can be sufficient, I shall deny it. For who am I that I should know God? And who are all men and all lives that they should know Him? The circuit of my life is brief, and the circuit of my understandings is but its fraction. About me are many other lives, and some I guess dimly and most not at all; yet within each is its waste of perplexity and its islet of understanding, and only a feeble beacon is its communicable meaning. No, the deeps of being are not to be charted by the lanterns, few and intermittent, that mark the frail coasts of human understandings, and the sum of all lights that men have found them is as a spark, kindled to fail. Only arrogance or fatuity could make of man's life, or of man's life conjoined with all the varied lives of the animals, existent and extinct, or of these and together with them the unguessed life that is in dumb things—could make of these combined that which should plumb the Life of the World, or discover a metaphysics which should abolish mystery.

Nevertheless should you ask me what is precious in our natures I shall answer that it is this same spark of understanding. It is a frail thing, and it may be a vanishing; but it is our reality, and it is our participance in the world's meaning. I think, too, that it is something more even than this: it is our intimacy with God, and token of our love of him—for God, though he be but a lamp uplifted over chaos, I hold to be the Truth-bearer, and our love of him is our yearning after truth's illumination. Love of him also is the zest of life, when the search for truth is his service. In our day earth's measures have been fully taken, pole to pole, ocean deep to mountain height, and we know our bodily domain; and in our day, too, the measures of physical nature, in all its proportionality to our bodily stature and structure, have at least been brought within the purview of their completed record, the sciences equipped and their tasks assigned. No such momentous happenings have ever before in human affairs been brought to near completion; mankind has passed its youth and is facing its majority. And throughout the world is a wistfulness and unrest, where men are seeking a compensation for the flown joy and high elations of their physical adventure, which if it come will surely be in another than the physical dimensions either of geography or of science, and will surely take form in soundings of the possibilities that are within us of a new and more spiritual intelligence, and will shape out of maturer lives yet more penetrating images of wisdom.

III

Have I made clear the contour of a metaphysics? It could, I suppose, be distorted into propositions, more or less indicative of my meaning. Which would be: first, that the image of the machine and the physics which it has created represents little more than the fleshless bones of a world, articulate, macabresque. And second, that metaphysics which represents all that can be discovered by more than metric number can give no better definition of the real than that it is the significant. And third, that never the simplicities but only the height of the complexities of life can describe significance and represent truth, and that understanding proceeds always from the greater unit to the less, from intuition to analysis. And for a fourth, that life yields in the pattern of its own Vita—time and destiny imaged in one being—our securest and fullest depiction; and that within that Vita better and worse are alike real and are implacably inimical. With these propositions I should have intimated my theory of knowledge and have arrived at a position where I could go on with its implications as to nature and to human nature and to divine nature. And of nature I should say that it is only mistily shown to us as a being hovering ever upon the margins of chaos, a spectre out of the deep. And of human nature that it is a militant thing, hero-creating and devil-pursued, faithful and pugnacious and haunted, capable of ineffable loves and unspeakable torments, and gifted with a genius of artistic understanding. While of the nature which is divine I can only add, with Plato, that what the sun is to the eye and light to seeing, such is the Image of the Good and the countenance of God. Nor is this merely a figure, for I have already proclaimed that only in the language of parable can men and the races of men communicate to one another the findings of their lives.

But philosophy is a poor thing if it end its task with a proposition, and above all ignoble would be such an end of a philosophy which makes of life its image. For within life imperatives are as naked blades forbidding soft repose; it is for the mechanic men, caught by hypnotic glitters, wheel and shaft, to surrender to make-naught speculation—strange Nemesis of a philosophy which founds reason upon motion! None who recognizes good and evil as metaphysical and real can deem just any name of wisdom which bespeaks the relinquishment of fealty to the good or of war upon the evil; our highest grace is that we may love nobility and beauty and serve them, and that we may confess shame of what is ugly and base and rejoice to destroy them. Let us repeat it, out of the past: that philosophy is vain by which no man's life is illumined.

For myself, therefore, speaking as one living and as comrade of the living and as teacher, I profess that philosophy is a way of life which, whether or not mine own way be as any other's, is still a deed done in this world, and one among its measures. I and my thought may be of infinitesimal significance, but as a life lived my thinking self is an irreducible certainty, with which the truth of the universe can never be incommensurate. There may be, I own, numberless lost worlds separated by gaps unbridged by any measure, and numberless lives that are only guideless lanterns vanishing in the black. And it may be that my world and my life are among these. Nevertheless what it is that am I; and its truth must be my faith.

The command of this truth has ever been that I build, becoming after my fashion an architect and uprearing my city over the hill Utopia. Its foundations are fathomless and its skies are fathomless, but the place itself is illumined, for I have sworn that there shall be set therein no stone without measure and substance and no house without humanity and no temple without its shrine to beauty—and these are the lamps that give it light. It is fortified with a wall which I call reason, but I know well that beyond the wall it is girt about with unreason and a great night, incommunicable, though once and again there is tossed up out of the night a thing formed or a broken inscription or a far voice carrying a music across the waste, and I guess that other cities have been and are on many a Utopia. This is my faith; so I turn back into mine own town and build with a better heart. There I erect the seats of my Areopagites and enthrone upon them Courage and Temperance and Justice and Magnanimity and all the greatnesses of things human, before whom come the gods to plead their own causes and to be adjudged by men; and it is they who take their fates, whether they are to live or not, from the minds of mortals. And within my city also I design a freemen's Agora, to be an assembly-place and a market, where stout merchants bring shrewd common sense and rich observations out of other times and lives, and youths from their gymnasia enter to enliven the place with skills and humours and the graces of fancy, and philosophers come to discourse gravely of the affairs of State, and rhapsodes and musicians sing of heroes and loves and of all things glorious to man. But the loftiest place in my city is Acropolis, holding within its precinct the treasury and the principal temple. The treasure within the treasury is writings; there are found book-writings and writings of metal and of marble and of musical sound and of all wherewith men have shaped and inscribed their thoughts, and there also are the writings of nature, some in stone and some in star-dust and some in the spoors of the life that was before man's and in the sign-language of the life that is companionable with his. But before the door of the treasury stands the form of the goddess of Wisdom, for she alone can be the oracle of all that is written. Moreover, there are ascents that lead yet higher. There, upon the steps of the temple, at sport with laughing children, I behold one who had been disdainful of a deity, and though I perceive that he has understood tears, yet his face is shining with the smile that children love. And upon the stylobate are raised altars to noble minds, and these I recognize by the tokens that are over them: here is a cock and an image of Asclepias, and here is inscribed 'Remember the children of Metrodorus,' and upon another is lettered a sermon that was preached to the birds, and upon yet another, beneath an upright and inextinguishable flame, is deep engraved 'Yet more to be feared is Truth'—these there are and many more. But within the temple, which is named by me the Temple of the Pattern Man, there is only a wooden emblem, simple and geometrical.

Very likely it is due to the fact that I am a man of the Occident and a man of this day and hour that my image of what is beautiful and divine in the Vita Humana should be just this that it is. A boy at work with his carpenter's tools, amid the fragrance of seasoning wood; a young man eager about the souls of fisherfolk; a teacher quite simple in his certainty that the parable only can convey wisdom; tenderness toward babes, a whimsy for wild flowers, sunniness and gentle gaiety, but black wrath, too, against lies and cheats. To me life has not given his confidence, so superbly serene save for one torture-made moment, in the protective vigilance and sustaining power of an Allfather. But when, nakedly self-confessing, I ask myself what is most lovely in our human being, I do not find that supreme loveliness in other qualities than his; and these I can acknowledge as measures, though it be but to show me my own abasement. Moreover, when I watch at my accustomed post, which is far out on the rampart, full-conscious of the gulfs of chaos, my courage is little from myself, but much from the sign upreared on a hill loftier than Acropolis, where through suffering came not the wisdom of the Greeks but the Hope of all mankind.

Answer it! This fact, also: that the World which breeds bone and muscle and bodily motion to be the metres of its brute dimension, likewise creates love of beauty and nobility and the hope of life, and in spiritual wisdom discovers its embodied realities!

I have expressed myself in images which are not of the schools. Nor, I think, are my meanings greatly those of the schoolmen of mine or of another generation, though as I read their works I seem to see in them also imagists and poets and the makers of an art, which is surely to their fame, and a proof of what I am desirous of saying: that only as thought is established with thought is there structure and only as mind speaks to mind is a world evoked. Living, then, as mind is living, must be all that of which any can say that it exists or that it is truth or that it is real. And each such saying can only be by a lifting into eminence of some vicarious moment of life, chosen from among the many to bear the meaning of the many. Such living moments are images, images incarnate and vestured with reality. Therefore, with the more confidence and the higher hope, I send forth my own image-adventurers, asking that their destiny be a living understanding in comrade minds. For the World, also, is an image, whose other name is Life.

PRINCIPAL PUBLICATIONS

Poetry and the Individual: an Analysis of the Imaginative Life in Relation to the Creative Spirit in Man and Nature. New York, 1906. (G. P. Putnam's Sons.)

Liberty and Democracy: and Other Essays in War-time. Boston, 1918. (Marshall Jones Co.)

Letters to Teachers. Chicago, 1919. (Open Court Co.)

Nature and Human Nature: Essays Metaphysical and Historical. Chicago, 1923. (Open Court Co.)

Truth and the Faith: An Interpretation of Christianity. New York, 1929. (Henry Holt & Co.)

L'Art et la Philosophie des Indiens de l'Amérique du Nord: Série de Conférences faites à la Sorbonne aux mois d'avril et de mai, 1925. Paris, 1926. (Éditions Ernest Leroux.)

Mythology of All Races, vol. x, *North American*, Boston, 1916; vol. xi, *Latin American*, Boston, 1920. (Marshall Jones Co.)

PHILOSOPHY AND ITS HISTORY

By A. C. ARMSTRONG

Born 1860; Professor of Philosophy in Wesleyan University,
Middletown, Connecticut.

PHILOSOPHY AND ITS HISTORY

THE influences that have moulded an intellectual history are not always recoverable by the subject of that history. It becomes difficult, therefore, to comply with the request of the Committee to set forth "the psychological causes as well as the logical reasons" for philosophical conclusions. In the present instance the writer finds it quite impossible to identify the primary source of his abiding interest in the history of opinion. A like devotion to the historical point of view has been shared by others of his group—graduate students and young *Docenten*—in the university and professional school. But they also are unable to explain the origin of their preference. In the teaching of the place and time there was little to awaken interest in historical study in any field of inquiry. Was the impulse then due to the influence of that factor in thought—intangible, yet most real—which is called "the spirit of the time"? If this was the case, through what channels, by what means did the time-spirit exert its influence on scholars beginning their intellectual careers? For themselves the question remains without an answer, although they realize the fact to be explained.

He who expresses a preference for the historical approach to the problems of philosophy may reasonably be expected to define the sense in which the phrase is used. Certain interpretations may be excluded from the start. In the ebb-tide of speculative endeavour in the second and third quarters of the century gone, not a few, despairing of the issue, substituted the records of philosophical opinion for philosophy itself. Even then more courageous, if it should not be rather said profounder thinkers felt able to prophesy the reflux as sure to come, although it was not revealed to them all that the empirical forms of inquiry, in whose name philosophy was discarding, would by their own achievements motive the re-establishment of thought. A second type of historical investigation aims at the formulation of exact interpretations of the systems of the past. This—"philological"—history has its evident value in itself and as a basis for constructive effort. But if it is taken as the only form and goal of historical philosophy, it too is marked by a lack of content which narrowly restricts its value. Nor is the opposite extreme, tempting though it may be, defensible in the face of experience and critical analysis. The theory that the actual evolution of philosophy reproduces its logical articulation, that the historical process is identical with the rational development and represents *den Gang der sache selbst*, gave a powerful impetus to historical reflection and promoted much fruitful inquiry. Construed, however, in the literal sense, it cannot stand examination, and, like the analyses which it contradicts, it must be relegated to the category of rejected views.

In contrast to such interpretations, the history of philosophy may be conceived in a different way. This method is grounded in exact investigation, but it does not end with the establishment of historical data. Nor does it offer its results as a substitute for reasoned conclusions, although it recognizes the singular importance of its history for a discipline in which the area of demonstrative inference is so restricted, where so much remains matter of opinion, and wherein, for some at least, systematic construction presents so difficult a task. In the other direction, this view stops short of the interpretation of philosophical history as an *a priori* form of speculative activity: it conceives it rather as engaged in tracing out the origin, the affiliation, and the evolution of philosophical ideas. So history becomes an instrument of constructive endeavour, although it cannot supply the latter's place. It furnishes one of the most useful types of philosophical propædeutic. It registers the classical alternatives of thought as these have been wrought out by the masters of philosophical reflection. And to this advantage it adds a kindred benefit, as it guards against the revival of outworn theories or the repetition of discussions from the past. To the historian, for example, recent debates concerning biological evolution in its bearing on ethics and religion often sound like echoes of the years when Darwinism had just broken on the notice of the world. At times fundamentalists and naturalists alike approach the problem from the point of view of Wilberforce or Huxley, forgetful, as it seems, of the work of reflection which has been accomplished since 1859 or 1860. And "emergent evolution" is not of itself free from similar dangers. As it was found necessary in the appraisal of the earlier doctrine, so in the interpretation of the new, there will be need to distinguish between the natural laws of the phenomenal order and principles of speculative interpretation, to avoid the uncritical identification of "evolution" and "development," to question the confusion of genesis with nature and value, no less than to consider the data from which ultimate explanations must take their departure.

Historical philosophy makes further contribution still to philosophical progress as well as to its interpretation and to the understanding of the action and reaction between philosophy and general thought and culture. In particular, it brings out the rhythms of reflection, now in connection with specific forms of opinion, now as it considers the ebb and flow of thought in the movement of an era. If we return to the theory of evolution for a moment, who can overlook the analogy with other instances in which an outstanding discovery or principle has dominated the thinking of an age? The significance of evolution, like its validity, cannot reasonably be questioned. But when note is taken of its universal, at times uncritical application to problems of every type, or when it is commended as the unique principle of all explanation, the historical student is reminded of similar phenomena in other periods: the prominence, for example, of mathematics and astronomy in early modern times and the endeavour to make the mathematical method the organon of philosophy proper, or at least to approximate the two. Among rhythms of a broader scope, the movements of transition which close a period of construction and precede a second age have especial interest and meaning.[1] These movements involve not philosophy alone, nor even the activity of thought considered in its wider reaches: they affect individual and social living and the institutions on which these depend, as in themselves they are in no small part conditioned by the course of events at large. They display, moreover, regularities of development—negative and positive—which by some have been denominated laws, although,

[1] Cf. the writer's *Transitional Eras in Thought*, New York, 1904.

if it is used at all, the term must be understood in a looser and less definite sense than that which it bears in the sciences of physical nature. Thus the study of their history throws light on the problems of philosophical construction, especially for those reflective thinkers who, like men to-day, live in an age which is disturbed by many of the tendencies which are typical of eras of transition. The historian, indeed, will learn lessons of humility as well as gain suggestions for constructive work. He will find it impossible to ignore the difficulty for any thinker of making a just appraisal of the age in which he lives or the movements in which he takes a part. On the other hand, the sense of limitation will have a certain negative value, for he will be less inclined, or he should be less inclined, than those who neglect historical conclusions to indulge in unreasonable prophecies or exaggerated estimates of progress. More than these he will hesitate to proclaim the coming of a "new age," as, with a recent distinguished historian of modern philosophy, he recognizes the truth that "the advent of a new historical era is not accompanied by an audible click like the beginning of a new piece on a music-box, but is gradually effected."

Appreciation of the history of opinion, therefore, implies no exaggeration of its significance. And, as it has been remarked above, there were few incitements in the early training of the writer to historical reflection. The first introduction to philosophy was framed in terms of Scottish intuitionalism, conceived essentially in accordance with the formulation which had been given it by Reid. The dogmatic limitations of the doctrine were happily compensated by other factors: by the keen insight and broad outlook of the Master, by his regard for concrete fact and productive principles, at times even when the latter differed from his own, by his genuine interest in inductive science, fostered, perchance, by the "empirical rationalism" of his school. This final tendency was of notable advantage to his pupils in philosophy at the time. It cleared the way in general for the recognition of the close connection between philosophy and the particular sciences, and of its dependence on these for a large part of its initial data. In special, biological evolution had recently been established, the "new," "physiological and experimental" psychology was coming to America from Wundt's laboratory across the sea. It was a boon to the student to be spared the controversy over "science and religion," or "Darwinism and theology," although there was never a shadow of doubt concerning the positive character of the Master's own beliefs. And pupil after pupil was prepared to move forward to the newer psychological positions without hindrance from his training in the introspective method or the conviction which he carried with him from his student days of the reality and uniqueness of the mental life.

Intuitionalism of the type described included a realistic theory of perception, "natural realism," as the doctrine then was called, "direct" or "immediate realism," as it might be termed to-day. This was a function of the Master's insistence on positive conclusions, which was welcome to the pupil at the time, and for which he continues grateful, albeit later reflection has compelled divergence from many of the views that were then commended for acceptance. In the matter of realism, the physics and physiology of sense-perception, when more adequately studied, as well as the analyses of the epistemologists, render it singularly difficult to adhere to the theory in its "natural" or "immediate" form. Many of the distinctions which have been invoked in its support—the distinction between "original" and "acquired perceptions," that between "primary" and "secondary qualities," and the like—crumble before the test of critical examination or prove to be of relative, rather than of absolute significance. Concepts which the realist employs—substance, for one notable example—fare badly when they are tried by noëtical investigation, and this whether they are postulated by realists of the earlier or of recent schools. If realism, then, is to be retained and immediate realism has to be abandoned, the way is indicated toward a critical interpretation of the principle. This path has in essence been followed by the writer, under the influence especially of the modern epistemologists, in the event and markedly under the influence of Lotze. The result, it should be added, is not the same as the theory which has been advanced by the group of distinguished thinkers who term their view "critical realism" in the present and restricted meaning of the phrase. For the subtlety of the doctrine of "essence" can hardly be said to make good its deficiency in point of explanatory force or to mask its position of unstable equipoise between the two theories, immediacy and representationism, which it seeks to replace. In contrast to critical realism of this most recent type, the position which is here advocated may be termed symbolic realism or symbolism, the term being used to describe the relation of correspondence between perception and its objects. This interpretation is not believed to be complete or final, but is accepted as the best attainable in the present state of knowledge and opinion. It is possible that some day some Columbus of the mind will ground the solution of the epistemological problem by the discovery of some utterly simple, yet entirely successful principle of explanation. Meanwhile, it is necessary to be content with tentative and partial views. Among these critical or symbolic realism is held to be the best.

Critical or symbolic realism, once more, is broader than the earlier natural realism or, if the description be preferred, less inclusive in its content. The latter doctrine included a dualistic metaphysic. The former refrains from prejudging the nature of the objects of perception, or at least it reaches no formal answer to the question concerning it. The close interconnection of the question of knowledge and the question of the nature of the object is not denied; it is realized rather (and again with Lotze) that action and reaction between the two problems is so close and constant that it is impossible to discuss them in isolation. All that is intended is the freeing of the doctrine of perception from dependence on a fixed theory of the object and recognition of the fact that it is compatible with different theories. In another direction, the view adopted more nearly approximates the older principle. Many later thinkers tacitly restrict the inquiry to man's knowledge of a single class of objects, to "things" or the spatial objects which are perceived through the functioning of the bodily senses. This appears to be a view too narrowly limited. In addition to the objects which we call things, there are the mental objects of self-conscious reflection and the "social objects"

—as they may be termed for lack of a better name—which are functions or results of the collective and institutional life of men, and for the most part, also, in essence mental. The restriction is the more unfortunate because objects of these latter kinds are more directly known than things, and the processes by which we know them present fewer and less perplexing difficulties. The processes of knowledge and the objects of knowledge are here of the same order or of kindred orders. The initial crux of sense-perception, therefore, and not a few of the problems following from it, tend to disappear.

Finally, a philosopher's theory of perception leads to certain views concerning recent discussions of the nature of truth or tends to ally itself with certain positions in regard to them. The analysis of sense-perception in terms of symbolism, for example, facilitates the understanding of the pragmatist's contention that the major part of human knowledge is always indirect. And, in general, the contributions of pragmatism to the psychology and the philosophy of knowledge and belief are seen to deserve grateful recognition. Notably, their accentuation of the affective and conative factors in the processes of cognition and their defence of the legitimacy of these factors are of outstanding value. These conclusions, on the other hand, do not imply agreement with the resolution of knowledge into a function merely and always instrumental, or with the endeavour to equate truth and goodness or utility and truth. Thus the principle of critical or symbolic realism promotes appreciation of some elements of the pragmatic teaching, while it stands in the way of adherence to the analysis of the truth relation which is favoured by the school. In the event, the correspondence theory of truth, critically interpreted, appears to be more fully consonant with the facts and more nearly adequate to their explanation than either the coherence theory, long its principal competitor, or the pragmatic theory which is offered as a substitute for both the older views.

The early training emphasized—perhaps over-emphasized—a second antinomy of epistemology, the conflict between rationalism and empiricism, with rationalism construed by preference in terms of a direct analysis. Here again longer reflection, based on study of the modern systems, has modified the positions inculcated by the earlier teaching. For one later modern conclusion, indeed, the endeavour to combine rationalism and empiricism in a single doctrine, the pupil was prepared by the view which found the rational foundations of intelligence in axiomatic principles intuitively perceived. Quite apart from the question of the general validity of intuitionalism, it had the merit of forbidding any neglect of the particular, concrete elements in knowledge, although it resolutely insisted on the rejection of all theories exclusively empirical. To this comprehensive position the writer has consistently adhered. In connection with it, moreover, he has long accepted the view that Kant's celebrated endeavour to unite the two competing doctrines suffered under his initial separation of the lower and the higher faculties of knowledge. The theory of Leibnitz, which finds reason implicit in sense and continuity between them, is nearer to the psychological fact, despite the difficulty of giving "implicit" and "explicit" a determinate meaning, and more in harmony with a sound epistemological analysis. Later modern philosophy, metaphysics as well as noëtics, would have profited if this interpretation had never been abandoned. Sense and reason must both be recognized as constituent factors in the process of cognition, even though the rational element may need the greater emphasis. Likewise in the realm of existence, neither the concrete particulars nor the connective elements can reasonably be ignored. From the beginnings of reflective thinking, neglect of either phase of knowledge or of existence has led to defective or untenable conclusions. Systems which overlook one or the other of the two betray their error, now by their inability to construe the concrete world, now by their tacit assumption of that which they omit or, perchance, formally deny. The rationalist fails in his efforts to interpret by deduction the manifold of concrete experience: the greatest attempt of all, the Hegelian system, broke down when it was confronted with the attested results of inductive science and of history. An example of the second type is furnished by the sciences of physical nature. Their master idea is the concept of natural law. The imposing result to which they lead is the conception of the world as a system of laws of nature. But this method and this outcome, representing as they do the most successful cognitive enterprise so far carried out by man, may be contradicted by the assumptions in which they are grounded. If sensationalism and atomism are made the groundwork, it must be remembered that these, taken in the absolute sense, furnish no valid basis for systematic construction; while, in any sense, they stand in singular contrast with the principles of continuity, uniformity, regularity, interconnection, and the like, on which also science is based. The inconsistency is not essentially chargeable to science itself, for it is no necessary part of the latter's task to discuss its own epistemological foundations. None the less, the foundations which have been often assigned it are incompatible with the conclusions to which it comes.

In this union of principles, therefore, each of the conflicting epistemologies has its legitimate and substantive share. For philosophical reflection, however, in particular for the reflective thinking of later modern times, it is of importance to lay special stress on the rational phases of thought. The *a priori* interpretation of the rational foundations of knowledge raises a more doubtful issue. In respect of this, the writer has experienced a gradual weakening of affirmative conviction. It is difficult to abandon belief in the *a priori* analysis altogether: with the years this confidence grows steadily less firm. The history of the doctrine is suggestive of other issues, once prominent in speculative inquiry, but which have lost their foremost place, not because solutions, definite and complete, have been found for them, but because belief in their significance has waned. The problem under consideration may or may not prove to be an instance of this type. But the analogy is sufficiently pronounced to render pertinent the question whether it may not be so.

As epistemology passes over into metaphysics, the philosophy of mind assumes primary importance. It has been intimated above that the considered judgment of the writer recognizes the uniqueness of the mental life and the reality of mind as the subject of conscious experience. It cannot be denied, indeed, that powerful currents of opinion have in recent times run counter to such conclusions. The prevailing trend of thought has favoured the negative, rather than the constructive point of view. On the other hand, it is to be remarked that these destructive inferences have been neither fixed nor universally accepted. Among psychologists by profession the number of the defenders of the self is noticeably greater than it was a decade or so in the past. Concerning the problem of mind and brain, it was hardly considered in order in the United States a quarter of a century ago to advocate the theory of interaction. Yet it became evident shortly thereafter that the tide was on the turn, until a few years later the balance of opinion had greatly altered. And, in general, although the majority of recent thinkers have been negative or doubtful respecting the crucial issues of rational psychology, a succession of able leaders have steadfastly maintained positive views. So Lotze formulated his spiritualistic psychology and metaphysics at a time when mechanical naturalism was in the flush of its success. Followers of Lotze, or thinkers guided by a similar spirit, carried on the work in later decades. In France, and approaching the problem from a different direction, Bergson has defended mind in the individual by his incisive analysis of conscious personality. The over-individual manifestations of the life of spirit have been brought out by the students of the *Geisteswissenschaften* and by the idealistic philosophers, among the latter, for example, by Eucken, although in not a few other respects his system is vulnerable to criticism.

Thus the positive doctrine of mind has not lacked support from distinguished authorities, despite its rejection by important schools of recent opinion. And if it is valid, a further inference may be hazarded, one which ventures to look forward to the method to be followed by the reflection of the future. If the mental life is unique, if mind is real, the time must come when a realization of these truths shall enter as a substantive factor into our conceptions of the world at large. Hitherto it has often not been so, even on the part of those who in principle favour constructive conclusions, for their working ideas have been coloured by

popular notions half-consciously accepted. Too often the real
has been equated with the palpable, the tangible alone; the
equation forming the background of opinion, although the
philosopher's reasoned principles might contradict the narrowness
of his attitude. In order to reach a metaphysic commensurate
with the facts and leading to valid conclusions, the mistaken habit
must be eradicated. Until the readjustment is effected, philosophy
will continue crippled in its endeavour to frame a tenable theory
of existence.

These inferences, once more, lead on to larger questions. When
the theory of perception was under discussion, it was noted that
critical or symbolic realism does not prejudge the dualistic problem. But an affirmative view of mind, added to the doctrine of
perception, inevitably suggests metaphysical issues. There are,
in fact, several types of metaphysical analysis with which such a
system of rational psychology may be associated. It may be
articulated into an interpretation definitely dualistic. Or mind
may be given the primacy by a Berkeleyan disintegration of
matter. Or, thirdly, dissatisfaction with "empirical" idealism
may motive its replacement by idealism of the "metaphysical"
type. In regard to dualism, much will depend on the formulation
of the doctrine. The absolute separation of the world into two
entirely disconnected halves which bears the name of Descartes—
such an abstract diremption of existence is indefensible. As
William James remarked, the recognition of two varieties of
being in the world must not be allowed to obscure the numerous
characteristics which belong in common to both divisions of
reality. Nor is it reasonable to forget the connections which
subsist between them. Moreover, belief in some sort of a unity of
things is fostered by various kinds of reflective inquiry. The
longer philosophical study is pursued, the stronger the tendency
becomes to postulate a unitary system. The results of scientific
thinking point emphatically toward a similar conclusion, although,
like philosophy proper, they do not supply a demonstration of it.
Some degree of monistic interpretation, therefore, is hardly to be
avoided. The question remains whether such a monism of systematic connection necessarily excludes a dualistic analysis of the

objects related. On the whole, a negative answer to this question seems admissible. A moderate, or modified, dualistic theory not dogmatically promulgated, but in a tentative form, may be capable of defence unless one or the other of the idealistic theories can make good its claims.

Empirical idealism possesses unquestionable significance. As a counteractive of materialism, it is of especial value. It may be doubted, indeed, whether it furnishes so complete a refutation of mechanical naturalism as was held to be the case by Berkeley and as the argument has been renewed in recent times. For the destructive analysis of substantial matter may leave the problem of the mechanical order of the world still to be confronted. But over against all theories definitely materialistic, his immateralism had so much of force that it is allowable to echo Berkeley's own appraisal,that if his arguments are not found equal to demonstration, it is reasonable to wish they were. The principal weakness of the doctrine is conditioned by its empirical basis. The foundation impairs the superstructure until the whole is brought into a state of instability. If the denial of matter is maintained, it becomes difficult to defend the reality of mind without abandoning the underlying epistemology; if mind and the relations of things are rescued by a supplement to the definition of "ideas," why, in principle, may not "notions" be invoked by the advocates of the "materialistic hypothesis"? The pinch of this antinomy was felt by Berkeley himself, and increasingly as his work went on. *Siris* was anticipated in the changes made in the later editions of the earlier works. But *Siris*, for obvious reasons, has been a neglected book. The commendation of tar-water as a panacea, the amazing chemistry and the metaphysics associated with it, obscure the development of the philosophical doctrine. Moreover, it is the immaterialism of the philosopher's youth which forms his contribution to reflective thought. The rational idealism to which he was driven in the event, or toward which he moved in order to preserve his message to the world, was neither novel nor of unique importance. The significant fact is that he found the change of position necessary in order to save "the Principle," "the amazing truth," from dissolution, that his thinking which began empirically took refuge in elements of rational doctrine toward the close.

Is "rational" or "metaphysical" idealism then to be adopted, since idealism of the simpler type falls short of full success? It certainly has done the world great service in recent as in ancient times. With its confutation of sceptical or agnostic theories and, positively, with its stress on the connectedness of thought and of the world at large, it has repeatedly come forward to substitute a rational and affirmative philosophy for one decrepit or fundamentally unsound. It has promoted, moreover, the life of spirit, and the ideal disciplines which represent this in the field of formal inquiry. The debt to Idealism, therefore, is a great one, alike on the part of those who cannot see their way clear to accept it in its entirety, and for its convinced adherents who find in it the sure solution of all the problems of the mind. There are, however, considerations on the other side of the balance-sheet, of which certain may be mentioned here. It is grounded in the nature of the case that Idealism encounters difficulties in its construction of empirical existence. These have markedly embarrassed the systems which have included *a priori* constructions of the factual world. They persist even for the later and more moderate exponents of the doctrine whose appreciation of inductive science and its results has been genuine and hearty. Such issues give trouble in connection with the philosophical consideration of particular things: they become especially refractory with the endeavour to interpret personality and the life of persons. Idealism, once more, takes its departure predominantly from the problem of knowledge. For this reason it is constantly in danger of over-emphasizing the analysis of cognition as furnishing the clue to the explanation of the world, even though some of its later representatives seek to give the factors of activity and volition their due weight. In fine, the uncertainty concerning "thought," not to say the ambiguity of the concept, when thought is invoked as the principle of the world-order; the relation to consciousness and personality, on the one hand, the need to defend a necessary rational order on the other, produce an oscillation of interpretation which, historically, has baffled

members of the school itself. To those without, the crux appears
to show even in the terms which are employed to explain the
principle. So one of the finest of recent Idealists described it as
"that of which the designation as 'mind,' as 'human,' as 'personal,' is of secondary importance, but which is eternal, self-
determined, and thinks."[1]

On account of difficulties of this kind, the complete ontological
validity of metaphysical idealism continues to be open to debate.
Independently of the decision favoured, recognition should be
given to the service which it renders by its furtherance of the
Geisteswissenschaften, or of a considerable part of these. In the
philosophy of nature its failure has been conspicuous. To the
historical, the political, and the social sciences it has contributed
a vigorous forward impetus, compensating in many cases, also,
the one-sidedness of opposing doctrines by insistence on complementary phases of the truth. The influence of Hegel on historical
study, for example, is well understood. Less familiar, though it
deserves equal if not greater appreciation, is the record that,
completing the movement which his predecessors had begun, he
impressed the principle of genetic explanation on nineteenth-
century opinion a full generation before Darwin and biological
evolution accomplished their epoch-making work. In politics and
sociology, Idealism has counterbalanced the individualism and
atomism which have marked so much of modern thinking, in
particular the favour which these tendencies have enjoyed among
philosophers who in virtue of their birthright use the English
tongue. Individualism, in fact, has been characteristic of the
majority of Anglo-Saxon thinkers on both sides of the Atlantic.
That Locke should favour it was inevitable. It is intelligible,
also, that, as Leslie Stephen noted, the Utilitarians, though they
often spoke of "man," always meant by man the individual
human unit. Hobbes in the early years of English philosophy,
on the contrary, and Spencer in later times carried through
extraordinary feats of doctrinal construction. The former effected
a combination of individualism and absolutism with the aid of

[1] T. H. Green, *General Introduction to Hume's Treatise of Human Nature*,
§ 346.

his artificial analysis of the body politic and social. Spencer's achievement was almost more remarkable. A great evolutionist, a great sociologist, he yet succeeded in remaining loyal to his inherited traditions. He praises the earlier Liberalism not because its measures lessened human suffering, but because "they diminished the range of governmental authority and increased the area within which each citizen may act unchecked." Factory legislation, food and house inspection, poor relief, free compulsory education, make for "social slavery." In fine, "the undeniable truth" results "that there are no phenomena which a society presents but which have their origins in the phenomena of individual life, which again have their roots in vital phenomena at large." [1]

Extremes of doctrine invite extremes of critical discussion. And though the impulse must be resisted, it is legitimate to point out that, however persistent their influence may be, views like those which have just been described present but half the truth. The conclusion holds, moreover, despite the demonstrable fact that incomplete and partial theories may condition practical good. Error for error, a one-sided individualism may lead to nobler results than an absolutism equally one-sided. Historically, the individualism of the English-speaking peoples has been a source of benefit to themselves and to mankind. Under its guidance they have led the way in the promotion of civil liberty, in the establishment of democracy, in the founding of a chain of free commonwealths around the world. For although their principle is certainly defective, it implies appreciation of the most significant factor in the relation of the individual to the social group, to wit, the supreme importance of personal existence. Whatever be the case with groups of other orders, society exists not for itself, but for the sake of the members which compose it. Alike in the order of fact and according to the scale of values, the collective life finds its end in the lives of the individual units.

At the same time, the defects of the traditional individualism are unmistakable. It misconceives at once the nature of the individual and the nature of the group. Concerning the former,

[1] *The Man* versus *the State*, I, p. 285, III, p. 373.

it assumes that man can exist, or even attain to his mature development, in a state of isolation. It forgets that the individual is dependent on his relations to his fellows, and further, that at least a major portion of the specifically human functions are in part or whole social functions also. Language, science, art, morals, law, faith, the impulses from which they spring and the institutions to which they lead—are not these things, and others like them, the distinctive characteristics of human nature? And are they not grounded, also, of necessity grounded, in man's social life? In the other direction, since social organization is intangible and non-substantial, the tendency results to deny its reality, openly or by implication; to infer that the group amounts to nothing more than an aggregate of the individuals who compose it, to conclude in sum that its characteristics can all be deduced from the characteristics of the individual members, because the two are held to be in literal fact identical. Idealism, old and new, has repeatedly furnished the corrective for these deficiencies. That it incurs risks implicit in its own analysis, and which empiricism and individualism escape, is also proven. It may lead to absolutism, for example, or be associated with absolutistic tendencies, even though the extreme criticism to which in this respect the Idealists have been subjected in recent years was in part engendered by the bitterness of the crisis through which Western civilization has been passing. It may conceivably be the case, moreover, that no single school will find it possible to combine in exact balance the two complementary phases of the truth. In its simpler field, empirical psychology has so far not succeeded in reaching this ideal; and philosophy is certain to encounter greater difficulty still as it searches out the ultimate principles which lie at the basis of the political and social order. Nevertheless, the endeavour to approximate to a comprehensive theory is enjoined by practical, as well as by abstract considerations. The aberration of opinion due to the spirit of war has been pointed out. The end of the conflict and the beginning of the new order impose the obligation not merely to correct such errors, but to attempt a restatement, more accurate and inclusive, of the integral truth. The issue concerns, in fact, larger interests than those which the groupings of the past have represented. The world-community is visibly in process of formation. The work of establishing its foundations deep and broad has become of paramount importance. To this philosophy and philosophical inquirers must contribute their full share.

Up to this point little has been said explicitly of the realm of values, although from time to time it has been implicitly referred to. In particular, evaluation in the philosophy of religion has gone without discussion. For a period considerably prolonged the tendency of the writer was to favour the method of intellectualism in the determination of religious questions. The direct appeal to faith in support of the principles of religion he considered illegitimate, especially when it was interpreted in the arbitrary and exclusive way favoured by many of its advocates. In time this attitude of rejection underwent substantial alteration. Throughout, as at the first, there has been no recognition of the purely sentimental analysis of faith, least of all of emotionalism in combination with individualistic tendencies. Gradually, however, there grew up a disposition to accept a formulation of the doctrine which is believed to be moderate and tenable. The change resulted from a variety of causes. On the negative side, influence was exerted by experience of the need for a reinforcement of theoretical intelligence if the ethical values, above all if the religious values were to be conserved. Positively, the content and the significance of practical faith gained increasing appreciation as the conviction strengthened that, while it constitutes a supplement to theoretical intelligence, it can be logically articulated into the system of rational principles. At the same time, facts which tended to throw doubt on these conclusions were not overlooked. Among them one demanded special consideration. The appeal to faith in Western thinking has accompanied in a converse sense the rhythm of thought in general. In periods of constructive activity the recourse to practical reason has been limited. The doctrine develops to its maxima in eras when the old is shaken, when the new is not yet established, and men grope in hesitation about the foundations on which their spiritual life in the past has rested. Even the prominence of the philosophy of values in the reflection of the nineteenth century must in no small measure be ascribed to the influence of such forms of motivation.

The inference lies near that the fluctuations in its history prove the doctrine a phase of reflective thinking rather than a classical type possessing permanent significance. Against this conclusion, on the other hand, certain factors combine in effective rebuttal. The rhythmical recurrence of the movement suggests an analysis in terms of mere expediency. But its persistent reappearance in periods separated by long intervals of time, even though they be analogous, implies a content of principiant value, and this implication is confirmed when the issue is tried by closer examination. The significant content of practical faith is found to derive from its character as a coëfficient of ideal aspiration. Not the "cash value" of belief, nor its emotional effects in the stilling of doubt, the removal of fear, the assurance of peace and hope over against the losses and the apprehensions of life—when the principle is stated in such wise, its exponents either are beguiled into unhappy accounts of their own position or conceive it in defective forms. On the contrary, it is the significance, the ideal meaning, the value of practical principles which endow them with evidential force.

Much depends, in fine, on the way in which the principle of faith is formulated. Here the work of Kant has been preëminent, and greater attention should be given than is sometimes done to the safeguards which he threw around his doctrine. It is not suggested that his example should be followed in assigning a merely relative validity to theoretical intelligence, for Kant's negative conclusions concerning the scope of intellectual cognition widened the gap between the pure and the practical reason rather than facilitated the indispensable welding of the two into a single system. Nor does the *a priori* analysis of practical principles command assent after the acceptance of theoretical *a-priorism* has weakened. But the interpretation of evaluation in terms of reason; Kant's steadfast conviction that faith as well as knowledge is a function of reason, of reason functioning in its practical form; the subordination of desire and feeling in favour of a rational faith—these positions, coupled with his central recognition of the principle of values, prepared the way not only for the belief of later times, but also for a progressive development of the doctrine's inner meaning. On such foundations it is possible to build more comprehensive and more accurate formulations of the philosophy of values, as these are brought out by the progress of reflective inquiry. As the advance goes on, it becomes easier to construe the principle apart from earlier misapprehensions as well as from the accretions which always tend to gather round it. The tendency to urge it as a substitute for the intellect, or even to inculcate it in contravention of the latter, is seen to be an aberrant impulse arising from temporary practical need or from inadequate understanding. On the positive side, the complementary character of the two processes of the spirit comes more clearly into view, and with this the resultant ideal of their concurrent action. Toward the realization of this goal speculation and evaluation should alike press onward. In point of content, faith, so construed and grounded, supports the theistic view of the world and leads toward the acceptance of the Christian system.

PRINCIPAL PUBLICATIONS

Transitional Eras in Thought, 1904.

Translation of Falckenberg's *Geschichte der neueren Philosophie*, 1893. Contributions on English and American Philosophy to later editions of the same.

NATURE AND REASON

By JOHN ELOF BOODIN

Born in Sweden, 1869; Professor of Philosophy, University of California at Los Angeles.

BIOGRAPHICAL

WHAT is a life? No one knows. It emerges from the darkness like a meteor, makes a transient trail and disappears into the darkness again. What has philosophy to do with life? Sometimes philosophy is an expression of life, but more often it is make-belief, a compensation for the failure of life. An autobiography of spirit must at best be an after-thought and is of doubtful value. If I could point to a master, or masters, as the source of my philosophy, the task would be simple. But I can call no man master, though I have learned from many masters. What I have done is the result of a lifetime of meditation with its significant moments now and then, for the most part too fleeting and too much a part of the texture of life to receive a date.

I was born on a farm in the parish of Pjetteryd in the picturesque highlands of Southern Sweden. My ancestors had lived in that neighbourhood for generations and had been leading citizens, but their education had not extended beyond the parish schools. The clergyman's children were the only ones who went away to college. My father owned a considerable estate with a large pine forest, and would have been prosperous had his family not been so large. He married a second time in middle life, and I was the child of a young mother and a father advanced in years. I was nurtured on the Bible and the legends of the place. There were the groves and altars of the old Stone Age and there was the much older background of the trolls that lived once in the hills and in the bordering lake. My father told me the folklore of the place as his mother had told it to him, leaving my child's fancy free. Thus I learned respect for time.

I helped in the work on the farm until I was fourteen, and learned to love nature and respect the processes of nature, with its seasons of seed-time and harvest. There was not much machinery and the contact with nature was intimate. Through this training I became an empirical realist. I also learned the law of mutual aid. My parents were a sort of Providence to the neighbourhood, looking after the poor, the sick, and the dying, and I was the messenger boy. They were people of simple piety who believed that nature and man are included in a beneficent personal order in which there were evil forces as well as good, but the good prevailed. In this way I probably laid the unconscious foundation of a cosmic idealism. I came to love poetry and write verse, and acquired a feeling for the beauty of language. I roamed much in the woods, where I rounded up the cattle at night and knew all the wild-strawberry patches. I was given to day-dreaming about theological things, which occupied a large part in my education. This day-dreaming eventually became philosophy, which has sustained me in the vicissitudes of my career.

I graduated from the parish schools at the age of twelve. This might have been the end of my schooling, but a young curate, Pastor Bomgren, who conducted the examination, became very much interested in me and told my father that I had a better mind than he (the curate) and that it would be a pity to make a farmer out of me. He offered to take me into his family to tutor me for the gymnasium. He died before his plan could be put into effect. But he had changed my life. He seemed so grand to me that I could not believe what he said, but I knew that somehow I must have an education. His successor, Pastor Sjöfors, with his kind wife, carried out his intention, and after some tutoring I entered the second year of Fjellstedt gynmasium in Upsala, of which Kjerfstedt was the kind and masterful rector. I was the leader of my class, but the second year I fell ill and was sent home. Shortly afterwards my father died; and I decided to emigrate to America.

In the summer of 1887 I came over in the steerage and landed in a mining town in Illinois, where I worked in a blacksmith's shop for two years, getting what schooling I could on the side. The realism of wielding the sledge was added to the realism of the farm. I also learned a great deal about human nature in its rough, though honest and kindly, form. I graduated from a Normal school and taught for a year before I found my way back to college. I entered the University of Colorado as a sophomore in 1892. My most significant contact there was a course in Comparative Literature with Raymond Brackett, in which I was encouraged in interpretative writing and recommended to the editorship of the literary magazine as "the best writer of English in college." But I had spent my earnings. I was called to Minneapolis to help in the work of the Episcopal Church among the Swedish immigrants, and so found myself in the University of Minnesota in 1893–94. This was an important year because I was introduced to the social sciences by the beloved W. W. Folwell, to the psychology of William James by James Rowland Angell, and to Greek philosophy, both in survey and in the original. I wanted to go east, if possible to William James. An opportunity offered itself to go to Brown University in 1894. I became a student of James Seth for two years and discovered philosophy. I found that it was what I had always wanted. Really, it was my own philosophy of which I began to become conscious and which I tried to express in opposition to my beloved teacher and the great masters. It is characteristic of my mind that it has developed chiefly by opposition. The first masters with whom I wrestled were Kant and Hegel, whose works we took up for detailed study in seminars. I was fortunate in receiving my early training under so fair-minded and objective a teacher as James Seth. Seth taught me the importance of sympathetic understanding of those with whom I disagreed, and later G. H. Palmer pointed out that every philosophy means a great deal to the man who creates it. My earliest meeting with William James, whom I had wanted to know for years, was on the occasion of my presenting a criticism of his essay "Is Life Worth Living?" at our Philosophical Society at Brown in 1896. I succeeded in rousing him to an animated reply. When he returned at the end of the school year to give the annual address before the Philosophical Society, he introduced his paper, "The Will to Believe," by saying that it was written to meet objections which had been raised on his previous visit. He was my friend for life.

In 1897 my dream to enter Harvard was fulfilled, in part through the interest of C. C. Everett, who secured me a Hopkins Scholarship and followed my course throughout with paternal solicitude. William James greeted me affectionately and was most sympathetic to my venture into philosophy. It was the heyday of philosophy at Harvard, the day of James, Royce, Everett, Palmer, Münsterberg, Santayana. Among graduate students I was contemporary with Bush, Lovejoy, Montague, Holt, Perry, Sheldon, Savery, Rieber, Horne. Strangely enough I lived mostly with my own thoughts and took little advantage of this brilliant array of philosophers. The only course I had with William James was a seminar in psychology. I attended seminars of the other men, except Santayana, whom I met only occasionally and with whom I had only one heart-to-heart talk on philosophy. William James kept in kindly touch with me, inviting me to his home to talk over my incipient ideas. But Josiah Royce was the master with whom I wrestled for the salvation of my soul from 1897 to 1900. It was in his seminar especially that I developed and expressed the beginnings of my metaphysics. It was in opposition to absolute idealism that I developed my theory of a real non-serial time which I first advanced in Royce's Hegel Seminar in the spring of 1898. Royce had invited James to be present on the occasion. James, of course, was warmly sympathetic. I had expected to be caught in the coils of Royce's dialectic. No man at Harvard could stand up against Royce in argument. Instead of attacking me, however, Royce devoted himself to a sympathetic exposition of my idea and paid me the high compliment that I had discovered a new concept. I worked on it the following year and presented part of my material as my doctor's thesis in 1899. Royce was good enough to say before the seminar that in his Gifford lectures he had modified his exposition of time to meet my criticisms. I was appointed Walker Fellow and Lecturer for the following year, being given the opportunity to present my material to Royce's seminar while he delivered the second series of his Gifford lectures in Scotland. In 1900 I was awarded the Austin Teaching Fellowship, but on the insistence of G. H. Palmer, who was chairman of the department, I gave that up and accepted a professorship at Grinnel College in Iowa.

It is impossible to measure the influences that act on our minds and determine our course. The greatest contribution that Harvard— James and Royce in particular—made to my development was the faith which they so generously manifested. On a visit to me in the West, some time after I had left Harvard, Royce, in the kindness of his heart and fearing, no doubt, that I might be discouraged in my isolation, said in an awkward, bashful way that he felt he owed it to me to let me know that at the time I took my degree it was the opinion of the department that I was the best metaphysical mind that had come to Harvard so far, and that he thought it still true, but that he could not vouch for the future. This to me was the verification of the prophecy of the young curate, and has been to me what the oracle of Delphi was to Socrates. Whether I have proved or disproved the oracle, it has given me courage to keep on with my search for truth through years of neglect. It may seem frank to say this, but I am trying to write as honest an autobiography as I am able.

My active teaching career has been spent in the West, with rare leaves of absence—four years at Grinnell College, nine years at the University of Kansas, fifteen years at Carleton College (including the year 1927–28 when I was visiting professor at the University of Southern California), and from 1928 at the University of California at Los Angeles. My philosophy has thus taken form on the prairies of the great Middle West—the heart of old America—with its strong common sense and conservative social philosophy. The expansiveness of nature, with its unimpeded vistas and yet its sense of homely friendliness, must, it would seem, in the course of years get into a man's spiritual outlook. So far as my social relations are concerned, they have been mostly with the Western students whose hearts and minds have been as expansive as the prairies. I have never felt consciously restricted in my thought. What the unconscious effect of the massive conservatism of the West has been, I cannot say. The fundamental postulates of my mind were probably formed unconsciously in the earlier period of my life, and the West has been a continuation of my early life. Individual genius follows its own course, and if the environment is not congenial to its fundamental traits it will express itself in violent antagonism rather than agreement. I have always tried to be honest with myself and others, and my students have responded with honesty and affection.

I ought, perhaps, to say something about my relation to pragmatism; but I own that I feel a strong repugnance to doing so. For I meant to do a generous thing and received only misunderstanding as my reward. The thing to have done would have been to attack pragmatism, and then I should have received some recognition. But pragmatism was attacked on all sides and the debate only led to more confusion, so I thought I would try the method of sympathetic interpretation. Pragmatism certainly claimed to be a rediscovery of everything that is sane, and I tried to view it in that light. The method of C. S. Peirce aimed at clarification of meanings and might be used on pragmatism. I felt a deep friendship for William James. He was not well and was very much depressed at what seemed to him wilful misunderstanding of "us," meaning Schiller, Dewey, and himself, He wrote me rather pathetically that he wished I could see my "way clear to join the movement." I had a sporting interest in fair play, and felt that I ought to do what I could to help in clarifying the issue. So I wrote some papers in which I tried to interpret pragmatism in a realistic and objective manner. One of these papers: "What Pragmatism Is and Is Not," I submitted to William James. He replied enthusiastically, and said that I had "played all the variations and hit it right on every point," and that I was "one of the very few who have understood what we meant." I published the paper in the *Journal of Philosophy*, 1909. Schiller, though not enthusiastic, thought that I had defined pragmatism fairly, but that humanism means something more. Other pragmatists seemed to resent my interpretation. It appears that in attempting to clear pragmatism of misunderstandings I had "evaporated the richness of its meaning" for them. There was, I think, the further feeling that pragmatism—like the protective tariff—should be revised by its friends and not by an outsider. Many years later, in his *Reconstruction of Philosophy*, Dewey made many of the restrictions which I had made with an "of course," which was characteristic of pragmatism. I have at any rate the satisfaction that if I did not please the pragmatists I did not sacrifice truth as I saw it. Whether I had any influence in turning pragmatism into a more realistic direction, I do not know. The papers on pragmatism were included in *Truth and Reality*, 1911. But my interest has always been metaphysical rather than epistemological, and I returned to my main purpose.

Pragmatism is now dead, and it is not seemly to speak ill of the dead. No one seems to want to own it now, except writers of French doctor's theses. Schiller is a "humanist" and Dewey a "naturalistic empiricist." William James exists in glory in spite of pragmatism. But pragmatism, though dead as a movement, has left us an adjective which is used a great deal by men of science—the adjective "pragmatic." Intellectualism has emphasized too exclusively the æsthetic aspect of truth as coherence and simplicity. "Pragmatic" emphasizes the other aspect, the convenience of an hypothesis in dealing with the emergencies of experience. Truth as we have it is never an exact picture of the nature of things, but it enables us to proceed in the direction of further acquaintance with reality. Pragmatism is America's most characteristic contribution to philosophy; and its effects have been felt, not only in philosophy, but still more in such practical fields as education, religion, and law. Long live pragmatism!

There has been, I believe, a continuous and consistent development in my philosophy during the last thirty years, though I have made no conscious effort toward consistency. My ideas have come to my mind as a result of an inner and mostly unconscious dialectic. But sometimes some precipitating circumstance is evident. It was the reading in 1897 of Royce's *Conception of God*, especially the Supplementary Essay, which called forth my first paper on the reality of time as against absolutism—Hegel, T. H. Green, and Royce. My reading of Alexander's *Space, Time, and Deity*, in 1920, called forth my paper "Cosmic Evolution," upholding cosmic interaction as against mere emergence. My critical reaction to pragmatism made me conscious of the importance of recognizing the structure of truth as well as its function. Contemporary movements have been chiefly useful as irritants, when I have been conscious of them. If my development in retrospect seems consistent, the consciousness of this development has been decidedly discontinuous. The first idea comes as an overpowering intuition with great emotional vividness. I seize upon a piece of paper and write it down. Then through weeks, perhaps years, I build a scaffolding for it. And then perhaps the reader wonders why the idea should impress me so much when it has such a natural place in history. But the setting is all an after-thought.

The first expression of my philosophy took the form of temporal realism in my papers before Royce's Seminar and in my doctor's thesis on "The Concept of Time," 1899. These remain unpublished, but the fundamental idea was developed in the monograph, *Time and Reality*, published in 1904. (The idea was afterwards restated in Part IV of *A Realistic Universe*.) My first published paper, "The Reality of Religious Ideals" in the Grinnel *Unit*, 1900, indicates the main trend of my realism. The paper was afterwards enlarged and became the last chapter in *Truth and Reality*. My empirical realism and metaphysical energism, with the functional conception of qualities and values, found provisional expression in a series of papers in various journals. These papers were subsequently revised or rewritten and issued in *Truth and Reality*, 1911, and, more especially, *A Realistic Universe*, 1916. (The preface in each case indicates the previous publication.) My cosmic idealism found expression in *Cosmic Evolution*, 1925. The date of the books is no indication of the birth of the ideas or even their publication. Thus Chapters I, IV, and

IX, which indicate the main trend of *Cosmic Evolution*, were published in 1921, while the manuscript of the book went to the publishers the latter part of 1924.

In the main, twentieth-century science has furnished the content of my philosophy, but this has been assimilated to the other types of human experience and to the historic structure of philosophy. Though thought is a living process and must be tested by its actual success in systematizing present evidence, it is a matter of surprise how much of what seems original is foreshadowed by the geniuses of the past. Philosophy is akin to poetry in its divination of the future.

NATURE AND REASON

NATURE AND HUMAN NATURE

It is because we live within the matrix of nature that we can hope to understand nature. We must take account of nature as it is from our frame of reference, including our human organization, biological and social. There has been a tendency of late to emphasize nature as it appears at the level of electrons. But nature is not any more real at the level of electrons than it is at the level of human personalities. In any case we know nature only functionally, i.e. through its reactions. If there is anything that science teaches clearly at present, it is that nature is energy. It is not some sort of stuff, and certainly not neutral stuff. Nature is what it does. To understand the activities in nature we must take account of the whole relevant situation in nature. Human organisms are structures in nature and of nature. They are reagents in the matrix of nature. The appearances of nature in relation to human nature are real appearances. But the appearances vary at different levels of nature owing to the character of the reagent. Nature appears with a variety, definiteness, and objectivity to an organism, with specialized sense organs and a highly developed nervous system, that it cannot have to a jelly-fish. Pathological evidence shows that cerebral structure with its patterns makes possible an epicritic reaction to stimuli, i.e. a reaction to the location, intensity, and rhythm of stimuli, in contrast to the protopathic all-or-none reaction when the cerebrum fails to function. When we talk about nature, we generally mean nature as it appears to a normal, developed human individual. The baby does not react to nature as a mature individual does, partly because its brain is still undeveloped, partly because it lacks the social schema which the mature person brings to nature. The appearances of nature vary with the duration and structure of the reacting individual in the matrix of nature. At each level of nature the individual might say to nature: "that art thou."

As our attempt to know nature is primarily a relation of

nature to a human organism with its physiological and mental patterns, the trail of human nature is, indeed, over all our knowledge. This is no reason for agnosticism in regard to our knowledge of nature, since human nature is part of nature, and the reactions to human nature are real relations within nature. Difficulties arise only when we try to imagine what nature is to a reagent which is not human. Our categories and judgments, so far as they prove relevant to nature in its relations to us, are true of nature—in those relations. We try also to know nature in its relation to other reagents. But we must bear in mind that we are observing the appearance to a human agent of these reactions in other contexts. Our faith in knowledge implies that nature in its totality has a constitution akin to the human mind, and that our thinking of nature is relevant to nature in that sense. But there still remain the part-relations within nature on simpler levels of nature which we try to describe as best we can. At best our knowledge of nature on the lower levels is pragmatic, i.e. useful for prediction and perhaps control. We cannot have direct acquaintance with nature at these levels. In humanizing these levels, as we do in taking them into our schemes of knowledge, we are dealing with their character for us. What we must be careful to avoid is to discredit the relations of nature within the level in which we live and think in favour of the simpler relations. The epicritic reactions to nature are not less real than the protopathic. The former are the true appearances of nature at the level on which they appear, and they are the more adequate appearances.

The mechanical theory made it appear that the individual reactions in nature become more definite and predictable the lower down in the scale we go, but that was because mechanism is an intellectual transcript which we put into nature. The mechanistic interpretation of nature is as anthropomorphic as the romantic interpretation. Recent physics has shown that on the simplest level of nature the individual reactions are diffuse and uncertain, and that it is only because we deal with mass reactions in our treatment of matter that the reactions have for us the definiteness and predictability which they appear to have. The determinateness is statistical. It is, of course, absurd to speak of this indefiniteness of nature at the simplest level as freedom. Freedom can come only with organization, and choice based upon organization. But it is a gain to have destroyed the fetich of mechanism in nature.

We must bear in mind that we live on a macroscopic plane in nature, and our adjustments are to this plane. Electrons can be experimented with only in relatively abstract conditions in nature—a relative vacuum, shot through with enormous potentials of energy. At the temperature of the hot stars, structure and determinateness may be impossible. The physicist's findings seem at present contradictory and confused. Perhaps that is because the physicist has tried to interpret the lowest level in terms of categories borrowed from higher levels. Electrons figure in our living only in mass organizations with their unique properties. On this plane our convictions as regards temporal and spatial relations, of causal determinations, of the community of minds have relevance, whatever the results of physics may be within the elementary plane of nature. It is on the plane of human organization that we have science and philosophy. Electrons or jelly-fish, or even chimpanzees, cannot make the reactions of science and philosophy. Science does not question the primary convictions which have been born out of our life in nature. It deals with specific problems. Philosophies must be criticized on the basis of their success in weaving into as simple, coherent, and adequate a scheme as possible our beliefs and judgments about the world in which we live. It is not the business of philosophy to make absurd the convictions by which we live on the level of human nature, but to make them explicit. Obviously it must do so from the point of view of our human intelligence since we have recourse to no other.

PHILOSOPHERS' RATIONALIZATIONS

In order that philosophy may clarify nature it must place itself in the midst of the living continuities of nature, and not separate itself from nature. It is the glory of ancient Greek thought that it never separated man from his environment, nor thought from nature. Its conviction, that reality must be taken in its integrity in order to be understood, is sound, however crude the results. Even Parmenides, in spite of his scepticism as regards the senses, is clear that thought must not be separated from the world it is to know. And Protagoras, in spite of his emphasis on human nature, is confident that nature is as it appears to human nature. The great rationalists, Socrates, Plato, and Aristotle, while they emphasized that knowledge means an insight into structure, and not a mere heaping up of perceptions, held to the conviction that it is the structure of reality which we strive to know, and not something inside our heads. But here the Golden Age of philosophy closes. Neoplatonism sought refuge from the problems of a complex and perplexing world in a mystical trance without distinctions. And scholastic philosophy was preoccupied with setting in order dogmatic theological beliefs. But neither of them separated intelligence from the world it strives to know.

Modern philosophy got on the wrong track at the outset on account of a false psychology. Descartes was a great physiologist, and discovered a great deal about the nervous system. He also had a good intention, viz. to place the soul in nature. But his conception of the soul as a point-entity situated in the centre of the brain made the relation absurd. That he made the mistake of making the pineal gland the centre of the brain is of little importance. Aristotle thought of the brain as a refrigerator for cooling off the blood, and supposed that the heart is the centre of the soul, but he had the right psychology, viz. that the soul is the dominance of a certain form or structure which makes the organism function at a new level. Plotinus was more nearly right than Descartes when he located the body within the soul, for mental activity includes the whole organism with a plus quality which distinguishes mental activity from merely automatic activity, which mental activity uses. Mind is a structure in nature involving, not merely the physiological mechanisms, but the social environment and the cosmic environment. It is reality functioning in a unique way in a

milieu of unique structure. Descartes' conception of the soul
as an inextended thinking substance in an extended inert body
made any commerce of the soul with its environment impossible,
and therefore made knowledge impossible. And the absurdity
was not lessened by the parallelism of Spinoza or the pre-
established harmony of Leibniz. It is safe to say that the
mechanistic physiology of Descartes has been and remains the
greatest obstacle to a sound psychology and a sound philosophy.
By isolating mind from its environment, it has been the source
of the false subjectivism that has dominated modern philosophy.
The remedy proposed by behaviourism, viz. to eliminate mind
altogether, is not likely to lead to an intelligent appraisal of
reality. The only hope is that physiology may in the course
of time follow the lead of the new physics instead of the old,
and discard mechanism as a scientific concept altogether.

Descartes' isolation of the soul from its *milieu* in nature led
to Locke's spurious distinction of primary and secondary
qualities. The former are supposed to be duplicated in external
nature, and to be constant and invariable in things, independently
of the organism; the latter are supposed to exist only in consciousness, and to be the result of the action of the qualities
of nature upon the organism. Both primary and secondary
qualities for Locke serve to characterize things, and are the
only pragmatic basis of our consciousness of things. But both
are events or "ideas" in consciousness. Locke's conception of
knowledge as nothing but the agreement or repugnancy of our
ideas insulates knowledge from the world which it is to know
and makes it unreal. Experience becomes a container instead
of a relation as it really is. While Locke still believes in the
correspondence of the primary qualities and their arrangement
with their archetypes in nature, it is obvious that this external
world cannot enter the field of knowledge which is concerned
only with "ideas." Berkeley draws the inevitable conclusion,
and the external world becomes only a set of sense qualities.
Since these are conceived as "ideas" or psychological events,
Berkeley thinks they must exist in a mind and have a mind
as a cause; and since this cause cannot be our private mind,

it must be the divine mind which causes the "ideas" in us with the regularity and objectivity which we observe. Hume returns to the naturalism of Locke as regards sense qualities. But for Hume they are just "impressions," while mind resolves itself into a string of distinct psychological events, the only difference between psychological events and sensible events being a difference in vividness, i.e. a functional difference. Nature figures merely as assumptions of unknown powers. The order of nature is not in the events of experience, for these are distinct and separate. Our feeling of causality is due to "unknown qualities" or "a natural instinct" of human nature, and is added to the constant conjunction of events in experience. The conjunction of events is contingent and may surprise us at any time. Psychology has usurped the place of metaphysics; and Hume's psychology does not rise beyond animal instinct, and the conditioning effect of habit. We cannot speak of structure, either in the human mind or in nature. The world is a meaningless show. It is true that we retain an animal faith in the show, but that is due to irrational instinct. Hume exposed the futility of the intellectualistic assumptions of his day and made philosophy a huge joke. We shall have to ask Hume to consign his own philosophy to the flames with other useless knowledge. What a pity that Hume could not have made his sound instinct for reality the starting-point of his philosophy instead of a refuge from it!

Kant added *Gestalt* psychology to Hume's psychology of habit. But unfortunately he accepts Hume's conception of experience as a succession of separate and distinct events, and the separation of these from reality. Hence the forms must be superimposed arbitrarily upon the events. Kant was right when he maintained that nature exists for us as determined by the structure of human nature. But Kant commits two errors in his account of the forms which human nature contributes to nature. One is a mistake in analysis. He confuses the contribution which is due to tradition—in his case the Newtonian tradition—with reflex action. The other mistake is in supposing that the structure of the human organism must be irrelevant to nature-as-it-really-is. This artificial separation of human nature from nature results in Kant's regarding the particular appearances of nature as "faked" by human nature in being "given" to human nature, and it results in his regarding the structure of human nature as arbitrarily imposed upon the data of nature. Hence the world as experienced, and as investigated by science, becomes a show world. The unity of apperception becomes a magic circle, separating the cognitive process from reality. But human nature is part of nature, and the appearances to human nature are true appearances. Nature is not "given" to human nature in the cognitive process; but the cognitive process is nature functioning at a certain level. Mind is the crest of the wave of nature, or rather the dominant chord in a matrix of waves having a unique organization and quality. It is the whole-situation in nature which has form, not something in our heads. Kant's spurious invention of an intelligence which should create its own data as well as its forms was intended to get rid of the artificial separation. But it was a purely gratuitous invention of which Kant himself made no further use. We can conceive of no such intelligence. But his suggestion led the romanticists, who felt no restraint of fact, to put themselves in the place of the Almighty and by the "omnipotence of thought" create their own world *a priori* with supreme contempt for experimental science.

Present philosophy is a whited sepulchre, calcimined with a coating of science and mathematics, but within are the dead bones of the past, and the ghosts walk abroad. The Cartesian dualism and the artificial empiricism which was based upon it form the background of "critical realism." There is no agreement among "critical realists" as to what we know. Some seem to think that we know certain primary qualities, such as shape, size, and position. Some think that we do not know the properties of nature at all, but know their order. The percepts, the ultimate data of knowledge, are mere "patches in the brain," in the picturesque language of Bertrand Russell. How we get out of our heads to perceive the structure in nature is a mystery. Perhaps it is just certain philosophers who are out of their heads. Some think we know reality only under the guise of certain essences which, though they emerge somehow in the reaction of the organism to nature, do not exist in nature, but in some eternal realm of their own, wherever that may be (evidently in the head of some philosophers). The "direct" or "naïve" or "new" realists, on the other hand, insist that they intuit the properties as they are in nature, independently of human nature. For them the percipient organism is a neutral medium. All relations are external relations, i.e. make no difference to the terms related. The Cartesian substances have become neutral stuff—mere transparent ghosts. But the ghosts remain. In the meantime romanticism, with a philosophy based upon wish-psychology, lingers on. But the almightiness of thought is not so impressive as it was in the nineteenth century. None of the current philosophies have really connected with the energistic theory of the science of to-day. Meanwhile, a crude behaviouristic psychology is inoculating the popular mind with a crass nineteenth-century materialism. It might be well for academic philosophers to take a holiday and go into retirement, until the dialectic of scientific and social advance shall produce an appropriate philosophy as in the days of ancient Greece. But as the chief end of academic philosophy is to furnish a living for professors of philosophy, such a renunciation is scarcely to be hoped for. In any case it would not avail unless we could muzzle certain popularizers of science who are corrupting their science with the old subjectivistic traditions.

PROLEGOMENA TO FUTURE PHILOSOPHY [1]

If we are to philosophize we must recover the sense of reality of the plain man and the unsophisticated scientist. We must place ourselves in our theory where we live in fact, viz. in the energy *milieux* of nature. Our psychological organism responds with its duration and organization within nature. It is not neutral. There is nothing neutral in nature. Everything is more

[1] For a fuller statement see *A Realistic Universe* (Macmillan), 1916, and *Cosmic Evolution* (Macmillan), 1925.

or less determinate activity. Nature is what it appears to be in its various *milieux*, including those of which a percipient organism is an aspect. It does not hide behind its appearances. But the real appears. In this Hegel had the true insight. The perceptual appearances of nature are not patches in a brain. They are characteristics of a total situation in nature in which we distinguish stimuli, sense organs, nerves, brain, and a mental structure with its tradition. But these are not separate entities. The psychological organism, with its individual duration, structure, and initiative, is for science a "bulge" in a cosmic field of energy. The soul expresses nature in a certain *milieu* of nature. It is not a rank outsider. It is not a string of psychological events in a brain, but a dynamic structure of an organic situation in nature. Even an imaginative event is not a patch in a brain, but an aspect of the activity of the entire organism, including the sense organs, as well as the nervous system and the brain.[1] Mental continuities in social communication exist in nature as truly as electro-magnetic continuities. We have been misled by mechanical metaphors to discredit mental communication and to imagine minds as patches in brains, interrupted by the mechanical nexus in nature. But our recognition of the immediacy of mental continuities is as irresistible as that of sense continuities when they exist. Language is not the essence of mental continuities but the code, which must, of course, be built up by a conditioning process. But it is the quality of mental continuities which enables us to distinguish them from one another, and from mere wind for which we also have language. This does not mean ghost communication. It is the specific situation in nature which has a mental quality just as another situation has the quality of colour. In either case we must interpolate a medium which will help us to explain the experience, not one which will make the experience impossible.

We must distinguish our primary convictions, which are born out of the matrices of nature (including society) in which we live and act, from our rationalization of these convictions.

[1] *Cosmic Evolution*, pp. 147–154.

Folklore is encrusted with rationalizations which we assimilate so early in our experience that they seem primitive to us. Such encrusted rationalizations require criticism. The primitive convictions no one doubts in his heart nor ceases to act upon them. Among these convictions are the following: that we live in a world of interacting things, some of which are social, that we know these things through creative insight into their behaviour, that these things are changing things, but with such constancy that we can in a measure learn to anticipate their behaviour in specific situations, and that they are spread out with reference to one another and ourselves at various distances. The rationalizations of these convictions have been various. There have been different theories about the nature of things, about the agency of things, about their flux and constancy, about their temporal and spatial relations. Rationalizing philosophers have professed to doubt the reality of the physical world with its apparent properties and its temporal and spatial characters. But their conduct has corresponded to their primitive convictions. I have found that my noble friends among the epistemological idealists live very much as I do, in spite of their theories that matter, space, and time are mere appearances. They require food and shelter like other men. They buy coal to keep warm, and they do not treat coal as spirit. They use various means of locomotion to get to places, in spite of their theoretical disbelief in the reality of space. They worry about the passing years and about getting old, in spite of the supposed ideality of time. Worst of all they die and deprive me of their companionship, at least in the familiar way. Their faith in an eternal order of meaning and value is sublime and inspiring. But their conception of it does not seem to explain the world in which we live. Their philosophy is more of a compensation than an explanation. What men live by is their real metaphysics. Their rationalizations must be treated critically.

It is the province of science and philosophy to rationalize the matrix of nature in which we exist and act. But we must not forget that our rationalizations grow out of the tradition in which we live. We are prone to find that reasonable which is congenial to our prejudices. Throughout the process of rationalization, certain primitive convictions persist. They are the real *a priori* element in the cognitive process. But man cannot live by primitive convictions alone. He must attempt to understand his relation to the world. To this end he must try to re-create the structure of nature by imaginative hypotheses. These in turn must be criticized both from the point of view of their coherence and from the point of view of their suitableness to predict the behaviour of nature. In the limited state of our knowledge, the latter criterion is more important. We may have to work with inconsistent hypotheses for the time being. This is illustrated in present physical theory. Both the electron, the unit of material energy, and the photon, which is the unit of radiant energy, may be regarded for some purposes as waves and for other purposes as corpuscles. It has been suggested that they travel as waves and react as corpuscles. We have at present no satisfactory theory of either material or radiant energy. To be satisfactory our hypotheses must be both coherent and serviceable. The more successful our rationalization is in these two respects, the more we feel that we have imitated, in our conceptual structure, the structure of nature.

The knowledge relation is a momentous and unique relation among the relations in nature. To say that the cognitive relation is neutral and makes no difference to nature is absurd. Nature as it manifests itself in the cognitive situation has a clearness, definiteness, organization, and value which it cannot have in other *milieux*. One cannot over-estimate the effect that conception and language have in articulating the distinctions in nature, though they have, in the sophisticated mind, given rise to false separations. What we must bear in mind is that nature is pluralistic, that it exists in an indefinite number of other *milieux* besides the cognitive, and that the other *milieux* have their own conditions and characteristics of which we must take account indirectly, i.e. because of the differences they make to the cognitive *milieux*. The wood burns to ashes whether we watch the process or not; and we must try *a posteriori* to understand the conditions of the *milieu* in which wood burns. How difficult this is can be appreciated only by one who is familiar with the present problems of the physical sciences. So far as knowledge is true, in the sense of the above criteria, it deals with reality as it is. Since knowledge involves a creative element, an imaginative venture, it is liable to error, and must be corrected in terms of the primary experiences. In this sense it is instrumental. But the love of knowledge is an end in itself, and has its own value. The relation of philosophy to common sense and scientific knowledge should be to criticize the partial knowledge with a view to wholeness of knowledge. But in its effort to attain complete insight into reality, philosophy is concerned, not merely with science, but with art and mystical experience and their contribution to the meaning of life.

The fundamental conception of reality in the science of to-day is that of individual systems of activity in action, reaction, and interaction with one another. An activity system is the ultimate unit of existence, but activity systems are complex to thought, and can be analysed into certain attributes. These are our conceptual abstractions for the purposes of description and cannot give us the uniqueness of the individual reality. This uniqueness can be grasped only in æsthetic and practical realization. It is an insight gained through appreciation, not mere analysis. But if conceptual thought is unable to reproduce the individual synthesis, it can describe and predict the behaviour of things. In analysing an activity system, we find we must take account of three types of variables—energy, time, and space. Henri Poincaré threw out the fruitful suggestion that energy means constancy. Einstein has shown that inertia or mass is energy of the opposite sign, thus getting rid of the dualism of matter and energy. In describing any activity, such as a falling body, a chemical composition, a type of radiant energy, we find that there is a variable or a set of variables (which are constant under determinate conditions), such as gravity, chemical elements, quanta of radiant energy. But these empirical constants by themselves do not constitute activity.

We must also take account of its spatial and temporal aspects. It is fashionable now to hyphenate the latter into space-time in describing translations in space. We have then four co-ordinates in terms of which we describe motion. Our mathematical picture is a purely descriptive device and, as Einstein says, has "no physical significance." Suffice it to say that in order to have description we must have certain identifiable constants which we can track through space and time. Such factors do not exist in isolation. They are aspects of activity systems, i.e. they always involve time and space. In material systems, electrons are the units for description. We must remember that constancy is here used in a relative sense. According to the theory of relativity there are no absolute constants. The units of mass, length, and duration vary with the perspective in a world of relative motion. They also vary with the field. We cannot regard our variables in isolation from the structure of the field in which the activity takes place.

The analysis by science is pragmatic and does not pretend to give the full implications of the postulates involved. It is an edge, as William James would have said, by means of which we lay hold of reality, but it is a thin edge. The spatial and temporal aspects, as dealt with by the physical sciences, are especially thin and all but obscured in the artificial conventions which have been substituted for them in the interest of description. There is particularly a tendency to spatialize time, and thus lose sight of its metaphysical significance, as Bergson has so well pointed out. The merit of science is that it has recognized that, in some sense, space and time are essential aspects of activity systems. The relations in the real world are never a complete close-up as in the being of Parmenides. The action in activity systems is always over space, and always involves the passage of events. That is the intuitive basis of scientific description. The mathematical conventions which it uses are instrumental towards predicting occurrences whether within an individual system or between systems. I can now claim the support of Einstein in holding that in order to describe dynamic relations in nature, we must postulate a medium of space as well as matter. Without spatial distance, there could be no metric concepts. The nature of space must be ascertained empirically. What science requires is a metaphysical continuum in which (to use Einstein's language) there are "no parts that can be tracked through time." Space has "no mechanical or kinematical properties," no inertia. It has absolute conductivity. It lends itself to three dimensional location. Einstein adds a peculiar property of his own, viz. that space or space-ether is capable of having its geometrical structure altered in the neighbourhood of matter. But whether this is true of space or of a physical medium in space remains to be established. We must, I think, accept the physicist's and astronomer's finding as to the nature of space. The measurement of space in terms of conventional units is secondary, and presupposes the objective reality of space. The extensive units of measurement are derived from bodies in space and not from space, which has no units.

Time is the passage of energy whether quanta of material energy or quanta of radiant energy. If we view nature merely on the simplest level the passage has no direction. It is only when we view nature from the whole-point-of-view as entropy and history that the passage has measure and direction. The units of energy which the physicist postulates for descriptive purposes are not apparently affected (barring the relativity effect) by their passage. They may enter into compounds in which new characteristics emerge, but their own character is not affected permanently, at any rate, by the combinations into which they enter. Real duration, in the organic and psychological sense of cumulative growth of the past into the present, is unknown in the physicist's world. Cumulative duration depends upon the peculiar structure of living things, especially the highly organized living things. It is here that we have the duration of habit and memory. Time, as the real passage of events, is bound up with change, whether it be the emergence of something new or the dissolution of the old. The quality of the passage of events depends, not merely upon time and space, but upon the energy structure of the system involved. It is clear that the passage of events is prior to the spatializing of this passage in terms of chronological systems. The confusion of the temporal attribute of passage with the quantitative measurements of this passage has been one of the outstanding errors of philosophy.

In analysing an activity system we must take account, not merely of the variables, but of the structure of the activity. It is this structure which gives meaning to the activity and which we try to state in a formula. In a world without structure, there could be no thought, and therefore no science. Without cosmic control there would be no measure, no quanta, no patterned activity. It is true, as Kant pointed out so impressively, that if the mind had no structure we could not have knowledge. But it is equally true that if nature had no structure we could have no knowledge. Mind is an individual activity system in nature, and therefore can express nature. From the point of view of evolution, mental structure is a creative adaptation of life to the cosmos.

In activity systems the parts are sensitive, in determinate ways, to one another's presence in temporal and spatial relations. Otherwise there could be no community, but only isolated monads. This sensitiveness of the parts to one another and their mutual determination does not constitute an organism. An organism is a characteristic type of organization and assimilates, grows, reproduces, and interacts with the environment as only an organic type can do. But every system of activity is sensitive to the presence of other systems in determinate ways. Sensitiveness or awareness is always an attribute of activity systems; and since activity is universal, awareness must be universal. There is nothing inert in nature. Sensitiveness characterizes nature at all the levels of organization of energy. This is not animism. We must distinguish between awareness and mind. Mind is one type of activity system, bound up in this existence with a highly complex organism through which it functions. Mental activity systems also possess awareness; but, as with other activity systems, the awareness varies with the situations in nature. Awareness plays about the zone of activity, to borrow a metaphor from Bergson, and gets its colour and significance from the activity system. We have now defined the five attributes of activity systems, viz. energy, space, time, awareness, and structure.

Qualities are functions or aspects of activity systems in their various actions, reactions, and interactions. There is no sense in speaking of a thing by itself as having properties, for properties are functional adjustments. There is no such entity as a thing in itself. Everything that exists is interrelated in activity systems, and every activity system is sensitive to changes in its field, and every field is interrelated in a determinate way with other fields. The universe is itself a system of interrelated activities controlled by a total cosmic field. Qualities are the ways of things or the appearances of things in various contexts and under varying conditions. By thing I mean an individual activity system. The only clue we have to the nature of things is their way of acting. It is clear that the properties or qualities must vary with the situations in nature, since they are aspects or functions of determinate situations. Sense qualities involve certain organic specializations as part of the situation. But the organic specializations of end-organs and nervous system are as much part of the situation in nature as the stimulus. Sense qualities are physical emergents. But the discrimination of qualities, their abstraction as aspects of things, their meaning in the order of nature is due to mind and the social tradition. Not all properties are sense-properties. There is the immense variety of properties in the various contexts of nature where organisms do not figure—chemical properties, magnetic properties, etc., which are conditioned by the simpler systems involved and their interaction. These various functional relations in nature make a difference indirectly to our sense perception, i.e. we can watch the changes taking place in nature, or they may be noticeable only in their duration over periods of time, but in any case they are inferred to account for nature as we sense it.

Similarity and difference are not properties of nature except as we include mental reactions as part of nature. They belong

to the second order, not the first order, of reality. They are
the result of our conscious operations on the appearances of
nature. Identity can have precise meaning only in the operations
of measurement. Grouping things into classes on the basis of
similarity is due to our subjective interest, though the result
must be relevant to nature. The relevance has reference to the
particular level of perception. Compare, for example, the discrimination of the expert with that of the novice or the discrimination through the microscope with that of the unaided
senses. We may group various hues of red into one class or
series on the basis of the subjective affinity of our responses
to these incommensurable qualities. We may further group
into a class of classes all disparate hues of colour to distinguish
them from the various qualities of grey; and we may group all
the hues and greys into a more complex scheme because they
all refer to the causal relations of certain energies in nature
to the organ of sight. Clearly such grouping is a subjective affair
and secondary to the primary appearances in the causal nexus
of nature. Philosophers may hypostasize the classifications
into essences or eternal objects, and talk about the participation
of the individual appearances in the essences or the ingression
of eternal objects into the individual events. Surely this is a
trick of language. So-called essences like colour do, indeed,
subsist as abstractions in the realm of spirit and enjoy a dubious
eternity there, for they are linguistic fictions, the artifacts of
mind. They do not exist in nature in the sense that properties
do. They are affective responses, while properties are qualifications of certain causal situations in nature (including, in sense
appearances, our organism). It is indifferent to the appearances
in nature that they strike us as identical, similar, or different,
though this may help us to sort them in convenient ways and
so improve our adjustment to nature. This function of essences
was first made clear by Locke. There is, however, objective
structure in nature which mind must recognize; else there could
be no approximation in the process of discovery. Between the
energy systems of nature there are determinate exchanges. In
these exchanges we try to discover constants which we can

track through the exchanges. But the recent history of physics shows too clearly that these constants are pragmatic constants. The real structure of nature is for us a limit which we can at best hope to approximate. Even functional recurrence in the infra-microscopic realm of physics is probably statistical. Our reaction to nature, not nature, is stereotyped.

According to my own empirical realism we take account of reality as it is in our primary relations within nature. In our secondary or cognitive relations, we often err in our interpretations of appearances, but the appearances of which we take account are real. All the appearances of nature in various contexts are on a par, so far as existence is concerned. Our emphasis on some appearances as more important than others is due to our interests. For practical purposes our selection is different from our emphasis for æsthetic purposes. The spatial and temporal appearances, i.e. the appearances of distribution at various distances from us and the appearance of motion with reference to us, are as real as the appearances which we call qualities. Values are real appearances. But they exist only in contexts where desires are involved, for values are satisfactions. We rank values according to importance or worth, but this does not affect their existence. Spiritual qualities are as real as material qualities, and in human life are more important. By spiritual qualities I mean those which we recognize in our social intercourse, including the intercourse with the divine, wherever it is an experience and not just words. We recognize human selves as having an intrinsic meaning and value which we must respect, and which we demand that others respect in us. In other words, we regard selves as ends, and not merely as means. We recognize the striving for truth, morality, and beauty as the unique activity of rational beings. In other words, it is their function to create in accordance with conscious ideals, and not merely to enter blindly into the creative situations of nature. Ideals are creative energies in nature. The distinction between material qualities and spiritual qualities is primary, and not dependent upon our rationalization. We may rationalize the human individual into an organization of electricity, or we may regard him, as Aristotle did, as having an influx of cosmic creative reason, but the properties which we must recognize in social relations are in any case the same. The activities are real, and they are for us *the* reality. We must deal differently with selves from the way we deal with material things. This conviction cannot be set aside by rationalization. On the contrary, reason, if it is fair, must take account of this difference in trying to piece together its experiences into a consistent whole.

If we conceive reality as activity systems, the great problem is the problem of organization. The organizations of activity, as we observe them, exist in various kinds, degrees, and ranks. These types are not absolute in the local evolution of which we are a part. They emerge in the process. The problem is: Why do they emerge? My belief is that they do not emerge by accident, but by virtue of the relation of our local field to the structure of the larger cosmic field and the genius of the whole. Activity systems maintain themselves by exchange with the environment. Matter cannot give rise to radiations of a certain type unless it is first charged by the patterned activity which it gives out. Hence in a self-maintaining cosmos there must be a constant process of give and take. This means that the types of organization are eternally incarnate in the cosmos, though the bearers vary, and, "like runners, hand over the torch of life."

In any local history, whether individual, social, or cosmic, the cycle runs its course because it is charged by patterned energy from the larger whole. But the response is not a mere repetition of the pattern communicated. The particular history responds to the stimulus in terms of its own structure and duration. The individual emerges as an act of cosmic genius in the appropriate conditions in nature. In the inorganic world there seems to be exact reproduction of patterns. Witness the similarity of the spectra of matter everywhere. But where there is cumulative duration, i.e. where the past is taken up into the history of the individual, the variation of response increases. The living organism becomes less and less dependent upon the immediate stimulus, and lives more and more with reference to the past and the future. This is evident wherever there is learning from experience, but especially so where there is imaginative memory and anticipation on the basis of memory. The unit of reality at any level is not the instant, but the dynamic whole-pattern of the individual with its duration. It is this whole-pattern which determines selection, assimilation, and response, whether on the chemical plane or the psychological plane.

If evolution is statable in terms of the organization of energy into greater complexity, there will always be a certain amount of relativity about what we call levels or critical steps in local evolution. The origin of living compounds marks for us a critical step of fundamental importance, though if we could have followed the stages in the evolution of nature we should probably have found it difficult to fix upon the critical moment. In some respects the evolution of the multicellular organism with its co-operative parts and forward-looking pattern is a more significant crisis than the simplest beginnings of life. What strikes me as the most momentous crisis is the appearance of creative reason, with its reflective analysis and synthesis. For this cannot be accounted for in terms of mere duration, however complicated. Creative reason cuts across the past and the present alike. It substitutes ideals or limits for custom. It marks the beginning of true freedom. Sensation, habit, memory, even the response to similars and kinds, may be routine. Creative thought marks a radical change in our response to nature and to man. It reconstructs experience in accordance with its own demands. Aristotle is right that here we connect with another order of reality, a spiritual order, the creative reason in the cosmos.

When we take the emergent point of view and follow the successive organizations of matter, through ever more beautiful complexities, it seems as though each later step in the series followed naturally from the preceding. We are especially inclined to invest matter, the lowliest emergent organization of energy, with greater and greater potencies. Mind itself becomes a function of matter, or at most a speculative hypothetical limit. Everything seems part of nature's routine. How different when we view the process from the point of view of creative spirit! In the communion of mind with mind, in language, art, and institutions, matter has merely instrumental significance. The supreme reality is the meeting of spirit with spirit in a unique synthesis with its emergent properties and values. As we view nature from the point of view of spirit, the process of evolution, i.e. the process of organization, is seen as a process of spiritualization. As we follow the beauty of each stage of organization down to the atom and electron, the problem becomes to find matter. It is now matter which becomes a limit, the only significance of which is that it is the potential stuff for organization or spiritualization. The realm of matter and the realm of spirit are the two great realms, and it is the realm of spirit which overlaps. Here we have the great contrast. Matter spends its energy in radiation, spirit grows rich by expression. The more it spends the more it has. If it spends nothing, it dies. Therefore, it is more blessed to give than to receive. Matter is the realm of routine as contrasted with the free creativeness of spirit.

Matter is essentially a medium of exchange. It must become charged with patterned energy to give out patterned energy. Eventually, when the local expenditure exceeds the supply, the local matter goes the downward course. This does not mean absolute loss of energy. The energy which is expended here finds elsewhere a centre of reaction where the process of integration may start anew. This is implied in the conception of the cosmos as a going concern. The material energy is constant, but its distribution varies. In this redistribution, energy is communicated as patterns or whole forms; and these, in the adventures in space-time, give rise, in accordance with the local conditions, to a new cycle—as the communication of patterned energy in biological conception gives rise to a new generation of the type of the preceding or nearly so, and as the patterned energy of society produces, in successive generations, greater or less conformity to the established type.

The cosmos, viewed as a whole, does not come into being or pass away. It is self-sustaining. It has a constant structure. Not only is its energy, viewed in the abstract, constant, but its levels or types of organization are constant, since energy is communicated as patterned energy. Evolution is a local process in which the material cycle runs its course, in unique response to the patterned energies communicated from part to part within the whole, under the guidance of the spirit of the whole. The patterned energies, which are communicated from more advanced systems, furnish the impetus to advance. The individual response, however, is due to the character of the individual system, and not merely to the impetus from outside. Hence there need not be individual repetition. This becomes increasingly true with the emergence of life and its unique duration. Over and above the routine of nature there is creative spirit, ever present in its own right and in its own kind—a unique realm of energy which exists, not by division but by unity, not by dissipation but by expression. This creative spirit gives meaning and order to nature's routine, and in the fullness of time incarnates itself into the flesh of mother earth to produce a new kingdom of order and value. Matter and spirit remain the two fundamentals. Of these, spirit gives organization, life, purpose, meaning, worth to the process. Matter furnishes the raw material and inertia. Transformed by spirit its random motion is standardized into patterns, and becomes meaningful and beautiful so far as its inertia permits. Without spirit, it is mere weather.

It is the tendency in present thought to emphasize science as the exclusive method of apprehending reality. Far be it from me to minimize science. It has vastly enlarged our conception of reality. But we have seen that at best science leaves us with abstract systems. It cannot, as science, give us back the unique reality of individual activity. Science must be rooted in the primitive convictions which furnish the background of thought and be supplemented by, and integrated into, the intuitions of concrete reason in moral, æsthetic, and religious activity. These intuitions must furnish the goal of scientific activity itself. It is in our moral, æsthetic, and religious experience that we grasp the individual significance of things and selves and the spirit of the whole. The world of values has its place in the scheme of the whole as well as the world of existence, and in the final analysis the two are inseparable. This must be true if we accept a spiritual control as the guiding field of activity. The world of values has its structure as well as the world of facts; and in our view of evolution the structure of value is the structure of fact. The structure of beauty is the structure of the cosmos, and science is really a pursuit of beauty, if the cosmos is dominated by spirit. In a broad sense the cosmic process is an æsthetic process, for the realization of pattern is an æsthetic realization. Spirit increasingly dominates matter and gives soul to matter, until emergent spirit wins its freedom and uses matter as its instrument in its expression of the ideal—the ultimate cosmic pattern, which in the imperfect process figures as a limit. There is, however, always the inertia of any level to the charge of a higher dominant pattern, and so we have the problem of maladjustment and evil.

The love of form, which is the individual inspiration of the scientist, the moralist, and the artist, points to the same objective order which in religion reveals itself as the great companion and enters into vital communion with those who are devoutly disposed. The genius of the cosmos creates in love and inspires the reciprocity of creative love. Being a free creator it seeks to bring to birth free creators. Its service is perfect freedom. It does not despise matter, but uses matter affectionately as the instrument of creativeness. But matter at best is a transient and imperfect embodiment of spirit. The creative genius which spiritualizes nature does not emerge in nature's cycles. It has its own individual life of infinite richness and value. It has its eternity in the life of spirit—in the ever-present cosmic spirit, which incarnates itself afresh, as the individual permits, in the cycles of matter, and in the continuity of emergent spirit within the economy of cosmic spirit. Here worth is the test of survival, and that survives which has sufficient prospective realization, in other words, which can enter into the freedom of creative spirit.

In a world in which spirit lives and works, the free realization of the category of worth, as set by the spirit of the whole, is immortality. But in a pluralistic world of interaction and freedom there may be damnation as well as salvation. We determine what the world shall be for us in the world of values. Whether our individual life is worth living or not, whether the pessimistic or optimistic outlook is justified, whether we are free creators or creatures of circumstance, whether damnation or salvation shall be a fact, as far as we individually are concerned, is a venture of faith. The structure of value is eternal, but our participation in it lies in our own control. To choose freely to realize, in our individual lives, the beauty of spirit is the great affirmation; to refuse to do so is the great negation.

PRINCIPAL PUBLICATIONS

Time and Reality, Psychological Review Monograph Series, 1904.
Truth and Reality (Macmillan). 1911.
A Realistic Universe (Macmillan). 1916.
Cosmic Evolution (Macmillan). 1925.
Studies in Social Theory in the American Journal of Sociology, 1913, 1914, 1915, 1917, 1921, and in the *International Journal of Ethics*, 1914, 1919, besides articles in various journals, which have been incorporated in part or in a revised form in the above books. These have been indicated in the prefaces.

A PHILOSOPHIC MIND IN THE MAKING

By HAROLD CHAPMAN BROWN

Born 1879; Professor of Philosophy, Stanford University, California.

A PHILOSOPHIC MIND IN THE MAKING

IT is difficult to decide with what age an intellectual auto-biography should begin. As the twig is bent so the tree grows and mental habits and directions of interest acquired at a very early age distinctively condition later development. My father and mother were omnivorous readers and both delighted in reading aloud, so that before the age of twelve I was familiar with far more literature than is generally required for college entrance, an overweighted portion of it poetry. They had something of a passion for complete editions. To read Scott, Dickens, Carlisle, or Macaulay meant to read their complete works. This "all or none" law of reading got its hold on me early and is still manifest in my behaviour, for I am still distinctly uncomfortable when I have to read some but not all of a philosopher's writings and frequently prefer to read none when time forbids reading all rather than face the mental uneasiness omissions entail.

In reading, everything was grist that came to my mill and philosophy happened along a few months before my fifteenth birthday. Rummaging in the garret among some old books of my grandfather's on a snowy February afternoon a copy of Sir William Hamilton's *Metaphysics* fell into my hands. As an old school lawyer and judge, grandfather believed firmly in Metaphysics as the best intellectual training for a lawyer. Hamilton had been his standby and the thorn in the flesh of all young men who entered his office, of whom my father, after Williams College and the Harvard Law School, had been one. The word "metaphysics" was wholly strange and with adolescent imagination I suspected it might be so because of some socially disapproved connotation. It might even be something naughty and taboo. The only way to know was to find out for myself, so the book was conveyed with much stealth to my room below and secreted amongst the paraphernalia of a toy theatre not yet put off with other childish things.

Leisure time for the next few months, and there was much of it, for I was not a sociable youngster, was spent poring over Sir William Hamilton. It did not take long to discover that

Metaphysics was something eminently respectable, at least as far as pornographic standards might be applied, but whatever disappointment lay in that attribute of it was atoned for by the fact that it was almost unintelligible and totally different from anything I had ever read. My difficulties were enhanced by the fact that I had acquired the meaning of 'prodigy' for 'phenomenon,' I think from Nicholas Nickelby, an interpretation that gave Sir William some weird turns. Much of what was understandable, at least partially, seemed obviously untrue, so I approached father at the end of my task with the question, why people wrote meaningless and untrue things in books. His answer led to a confession, and much amusement on his part, but the amusement was kindly and the upshot was the suggestion that I have a try at the more modern Herbert Spencer.

Neither my father nor my mother was philosophically minded, and I think both their philosophical and religious beliefs could be fairly well covered by Socrates' utterance "that no evil can happen to a good man, either in life or after death." Nevertheless, the volumes of Spencer's *Synthetic Philosophy* were provided for me in due order and I got through them after my fashion before entering college at eighteen. Also, true to the all or none law, I completed Hamilton's *Logic*, which still stands before my mind as an almost perfect form for lectures unaccompanied by text, and his *Discussions of Philosophy and Literature*. Some zest was added to my reading of Spencer by conversations with the family dentist, Dr. C. T. Stockwell, himself the author of a little philosophical booklet, *New Modes of Thought*. Indeed, for a time I developed quite a flair for the dentist's chair. Alas, it has not survived! But Dr. Stockwell was very kind and spared me much time in helpful talk.

A few months after my father's sudden death, Williams College claimed me by family tradition, and the Harvard Law School loomed vaguely in the future. In anticipation college meant three things: the opportunity to study French literature, about which I had somehow become curious; to find out more about philosophy; and to explore mathematics, a love for which had been inculcated in me by a very remarkable high-school teacher. Of course there was a stated curriculum to be followed that only permitted increased freedom of electives as the years went by. The curriculum never bothered me very much, however, for it was possible then, as now, to pass most courses by a few hours' application before examinations, and the library had been provided by some thoughtful alumnus with large, comfortable, leather-covered Morris chairs from which the bookshelves were easily accessible to him who would seek solace there. That library was my home for the next four years. I was still, and perhaps more than ever, a social misfit. The required curriculum did teach me the genius of Homer in collecting irregular verbs that I can still conjugate, although I have mostly forgotten their meanings, and I acquired some skill in the application of my room mate's motto καταψευδεῖν καλῶς, which we translated "a good bluff well swung availeth much." Unconsciously I followed James's dictum that one should do something every day that he does not want to, sufficiently to "get off" requirements without too much pain to myself or contumely from my teachers, but I hardly won their admiration.

For two years a student could take no philosophy, but I read whatever came to hand in not too big sets and pestered the noble seniors and juniors of my fraternity with questions and discussions usually aimed at setting them against their class work. I remember Flint's Theism, taught with due piety by the President, Dr. Carter, was a pet aversion. When in the junior year I could first elect philosophy, Professor Perry was the *locum tenens*, omniscient in my eyes with his new Ph.D. from Harvard. I then and there decided I'd try some day to know as much as he did—if I did not decide to become a mathematician or devote myself to the writing of French poetry. Bad habits stick, however, and I'm afraid I was not an impressive student even in philosophy, for my business at hand was then a reconstruction of Leibniz in a more satisfactory form, and course requirements only occupied the interstices of my time. Professor Russell returned the next year and I laid the great Leibnizian achievement before him, a rather unsatisfactory effort as I remember it, but very kindly received. From that time Professor Russell never failed to aid and abet me in following my own interests in spite of the limitations of courses, at a cost to his time and strength that I appreciate now far more than I did then.

In French and mathematics, the gods were with me. When the offerings of the college's limited mathematical curriculum were completed, Professor Ferry let me go on by myself and be credited with work on Burckhardt's *Functionen-theorie*, the German, of which I then knew nothing, learned incidentally, and Reye's *Geometry of Position*. From time to time written reports were turned in as the spirit moved, and when puzzled, there were evening discussions in Ferry's rooms beginning with mathematics and ending about 2 a.m. It is a wonder he could stand it, but those evenings were among the brightest spots of my college career; and somehow Ferry had the gift of teaching everything else along with mathematics. Incidentally I read Appell's *Éléments d'Analyse Mathématique*. It connected somehow with Leibniz, or seemed to.

French fell under Professor Morton, a supremely conscientious teacher of grammar but a cultured gentleman with fine æsthetic sensibilities, a philosopher, and a student of cultural history. It did not take long to see that he hated grammar and composition as much as any of us, but I got from him such a strong sense of a great beyond that it was not impossible to grasp inclination by the scruff of the neck and master the elementary nuisances for the sake of the future. The reward was the entrée of his home, much interest in the interplay of philosophy, literature, and art, and an awakened interest in cultural history.

College evoked two special interests not incorporated in my anticipations. A sophomore requirement in physics effected a consuming interest in the theory of light, not as complicated a matter in '99 as now. For a semester I did little but study light, and I think I read everything on the subject in the not too extensive library. Physics was then the thing, and light in particular. However, the rest of the course suffered somewhat from this preoccupation with a single part, and after somewhat curt advice to stick to assignments, physics began to go the way of Novalis's Sophie, the career of a physicist to the realm of Platonic

Ideas. However, the fascination of the subject has never quite vanished, although it is becoming desperately difficult to keep in touch with its modern developments.

The other interest that unexpectedly emerged during college days grew out of an intense longing for companionship. The American college is not ideal for a boy who is really enthusiastic for books. He is a misfit and herded with other misfits. This led me to an intense interest in human behaviour and to devour psychology, both normal and abnormal, but with comparatively little resultant light for my real problems. Why were individuality and personal initiative dreaded unless devoted to socially sanctified ends? Why do men gain popularity by being a little more like the crowd than the rest of the crowd? What is the source of the power in catch-phrases and college spirit? I tried to solve these problems, even in those pre-Freudian days, by a sort of psycho-analytic method and kept elaborate note-books, now, perhaps fortunately, lost. Prior to this time books had been a means of escape from life, but now they took on a new value as means to an understanding of life. Ever since, I have been impatient with those theories of philosophy, or anything else, that pose as mere gratification of curiosity for curiosity's sake.

It was a relief to escape from the fetters of college custom and collegiate types to the independence of the graduate school at Harvard. Chesterton, I believe it is, says there is more affectation in eating corned beef and cabbage on principle than caviare from taste. The joy in not being obliged to pretend interest in football games or simulate enthusiasm at rallies! Perry had wiped from me, quite unconsciously on his part, the last whisperings of the call to carry on the family legal tradition, but I was not quite sure whether mathematics or philosophy would take its place. The first year of graduate work shows a divided course. Mathematics fell under James Mills Peirce, a fine old man, who taught me a great deal about the stage and the drama, but whose great days as a teacher of mathematics were over. The second-year philosophy was wholly in the ascendant.

It is impossible to recount all the influences of a great graduate school and this was almost the heyday of Harvard's. Still I was not a good course man, and I am sure I never evoked much interest from Santayana and was a distinct disappointment to Palmer. Charming as were Palmer's lectures, I was not ready for ethics and my work was very superficial. James was then ill and taught only one year during my sojourn at Harvard, an elementary course that, as a graduate student, I attended but did not take for credit. He was accessible to us, friendly, and I felt his personality and believed in him but I knew his ideas better from his writings than from personal contacts.

My range of interests was still somewhat narrow. The philosophy of mathematics, philosophy of science, logic, algebra of logic, history of logic, and metaphysics, were my choices of subjects. The others were necessary evils. And there was always that impulse to try to understand why human beings behave as they do, but the psychology of the laboratory, like that of the books read at college, had little to do with this. Harvard came to mean primarily three men, Josiah Royce, E. V. Huntington, and E. B. Holt. Huntington, whom I had known and admired during his short sojourn at Williams, was then engaged in his studies of systems of postulates for mathematical systems and he helped me over many bumps on my road. Holt gave me perhaps the greatest thing I got from Harvard, a sense of the importance of grasping the specific meanings of statements. He is almost the only man I have ever known who has never let me get away with a statement not quite understood, and whom I think I always understood until he wrote the *Concept of Consciousness*, a book I have never been able completely to master. From Holt also came the first insight that there is a psychology or physiological psychology that can actually contribute to an understanding of human nature. How many of my philosophical ideas were derived from him then and in later years I do not know, for we have discussed all subjects, and he has the faculty of making ideas appear in me so that I cannot tell whether they are his or mine.

Of the Harvard years, the greatest direct influence was Josiah Royce, as much by opposition as by assent. The dialectic method always put me on my guard. As I should now formulate my conviction, it is that words get their primary meanings from experience with the things they denote. The connotative definition is an attempt to formulate the results of this experiencing. When the defined word is made an element in a dialectic development, there is always the danger that some neglected aspect of the facts may become relevant to the situation under discussion and falsify the conclusion. I feel safer now, as I did then, when I can maintain some sort of contact with the conditions that give rise to terms and check conclusions by them. Royce's "world of description" was very much to my mind, but his "world of appreciation" seemed to be a cover for something that needed further analysis. From Royce also came the notion that however much a philosopher might know about philosophy, it was also of extraordinary importance for him to know other things as well. It was under his influence that I began a broad course of scientific reading that has been continued to this day. The very method of his seminar in which men of the most diverse interests were gathered together gave a sense that nothing could be alien to philosophy, although sometimes his linkage of subjects, while always clever, was a bit forced.

Royce—and I think this grieved him a little—sent me out from Harvard well started on the road to pragmatism. This resulted from trying to clear up for myself the problems of the new mathematics of number theory and the problems of Russell's Principles of Mathematics which had just appeared. A year of my work, taken in Germany just after my marriage, and prior to my Ph.D., did little but get me acquainted with another type of life, give me some mastery over German, introduce me to a few philosophers of a different sort, and let me read Prantl's Geschichte der Logik and Shroeder's Algebra der Logik, in toto.

From Harvard I passed to my first position at Columbia and to the most strenuous seven years of my life. The problems of a young instructor with a growing family, no great financial sense, and illness were upon me and led to a program of teaching that mounted during my career to twenty-four hours a week. I think I hold a record in giving the standard course in elementary deductive logic seventeen times in one year. It was not great teaching nor was any of my work there such as I should now be proud of. However, there did come a certain facility of speech and a partial mastery of a characteristic timidity that still annoys me in speaking before a strange audience or a class I have not met before, and sometimes holds me tongue-tied at association meetings, especially when a little tired.

Nevertheless, the Columbia days were great days and I cannot begin to trace the ideas that germinated there in my conversations with my colleagues and friends. Woodbridge's lectures impressed me by their sanity of view-point and excellence of style, even when a little oracular. From him came a gentle but continuous pressure to write which was partly resented, for I had almost persuaded myself that I should get my ideas thoroughly matured before laying them before the world, and yet greatly appreciated, for I knew half-consciously that if I did not keep writing I would never get to writing. Bush was an omnivorous reader and was always presenting me with something I should have read and discussing it with great common sense. Montague's dialectic skill awed me a bit and I must confess to being often a little frightened by an impassioned fierceness with which he conducted an argument. However, it was not long before I knew him too well to fear that a bite would follow the bark, and I owe much to the pressure of meeting his vigorous criticisms. Also Montague gave me my first vital interest in social philosophy.

The really great intellectual influences of my Columbia days, however, were Professor and Mrs. Dewey. Beset by personal and practical problems, it was Mrs. Dewey who, although so far as I know she never set up to be a philosopher, made me see that these problems could be looked at with profit from a philosophical view-point, and it was Professor Dewey who engendered in me the belief that such problems were not a mere dissipation of time but a precious source of knowledge. From him I got a new vision of bridging the gap between abstract scientific problems and living, a bridging that is of infinite value to me in teaching and will, if anything, lend vitality to such philosophy as I may produce. Poincaré was a favourite author, and it was very impressive to me that the psychological insight of James, the mathematical learning of Poincaré, and the educational experience of Dewey had all led to philosophies that have so much in common. What was lacking in all was a sort of metaphysical background. It could not be metaphysics in the Idealists' sense, nor a direct transcription of science, but an attempt to get at, through scientific knowledge, a conception of a universe that would sanction that knowledge and furnish some sort of perspective for approaching normative problems. The desire to attain some such metaphysics has guided almost every study I have undertaken since that day.

The vicissitudes of my career as a pedagogue put often in mind a remark of Professor Perry's, made back in the Williams days, or perhaps at Harvard: The best way to learn a subject is to try to teach it. To this I added my own emendation: Never voluntarily put anything into a course that a student can read just as well in a book. The first real plunge was a course in Æsthetics that fell to my lot through the unexpected resignation of Dr. Pitkin. At the time my only idea of the subject was the somewhat vague one derived incidentally by studying the history of philosophy, and a remark of Royce's that somehow had stuck in my mind, that he never could see there was much of philosophic value in æsthetics anyway. However, Pitkin turned over his notes to me, and I went at it. The notes were chiefly concerned with techical analyses of the arts and I stalled a bit with the history of æsthetics. Gradually, since I have always kept the course, there began to take shape in my mind a special formulation and development of the problem. The guiding influence was Tolstoi's question, what is there about art that makes it worth the time and money expended on it, and Guyau's very suggestive title, "L'art au pointe de vue sociologique."

Unconsciously a Deweyan method seems to have dictated its development. First the inquiry, what were primitive peoples trying to do when their activities resulted in something we call art. Then the search for a point of transition when some valued resultant not primarily premeditated should appear from such activities that had sufficient importance when seen, to lead to modification of the procedure in order to conserve and enhance it. Here the clue came from Miss Harrison's *Ancient Art and Ritual*. From this point my problem was easily formulated: What features of a work of art are capable of affecting the observer, and how? What is the nature of the observer that he can be so affected and brought to the state of mind intended? What prompts the artist to create? And what is the social significance of the fact that observers are so affected by works of art. The search for answers to these questions was the first broadly synthetic philosophic task I ever undertook.

The æsthetics has been of major importance for the rest of my philosophical development. In the first place it confirmed me in the use of a sort of historico-genetic method that I had already employed in an effort to discover what mathematical statements really meant, how we get from simple counting to abstract number theory and from land measuring to geometry. Secondly, it led me to look upon all specialized human activities, religious, moral, political, and intellectual, as specializations of more general ones due to the chance discovery of some value in a phase of them that led to that phase being isolated and perfected for the realization of that value. This is, of course, Westermarck's and Dewey's approach to ethics. Lévy-Bruhl, and this does not mean assent to all his theses, generated the suggestion that normative thinking, logic itself, might also have emerged as a result of similar discoveries in the use of natural psychological capacities. For some years I have been struggling with the problem of the discovery or invention of intelligence and believe I have met with some slight success. The problem solved would furnish a much needed prolegomenon to Robinson's *Mind in the Making*.

In the third place, the æsthetics compelled an approach to the study of human nature from the emotional rather than from the intellectual side. Indeed, the psychology of thinking never really gripped me until the question arose of understanding the significance for the individual and for society of human lives emotionally enriched through æsthetic experience. The most unsatisfactory aspect of Professor Dewey's *Experience and Nature* is that he had first formulated in his mind an independent theory of knowing, then discovered the importance of affective life, and tried to bring them together as the flour and shortening of the bread. In general, the neglect or the sentimentalization of the feeling life seems to me the greatest weakness of our scientific age and its philosophies.

My psychological materials have largely been derived from behaviourism, the Watson with whom one talks rather than the sometimes irritating Watson of the Press, from the physiologists, and from Freud, who gave me some important clues as to the nature of the drive of creative imagination. This does not mean that I am ready to stand for behaviourism or Freudianism as systems, but is merely to indicate that I have found more true and useful materials for my purposes in writings of these schools than in others; but I have no prejudice against utilizing genuine discoveries by anyone, introspectionist, behaviourist, structuralist, functionalist, Gestaltist, or Eidetiker, if they serve my turn.

Another unexpected result of interest in æsthetics was a renewed interest in the history of philosophy. From Cornford's dangerously brilliant book, *From Religion to Philosophy*, came the suggestion of an anthropological genetic approach to the subject that took root in the soil prepared by the Æsthetics. The history of philosophy ceased to be a story of the errors of the human mind, perhaps occasionally salted with true insights, but the history of individual men elaborating their attitudes toward the world about them in intellectual interpretations restricted by available knowledge and shaped by some socially transmitted thought model. The term *model* is due to Rignano, the conception of the influence of socially transmitted models to Cornford.

At about this period of my development a sneeze wafted me from Columbia to Stanford. Not to be cryptic, an attack of scarlet fever, caught from a sneezing student, kept me for a summer in New York and led to my meeting Professor Stuart, who invited me to Stanford. This move led me to continue the teaching of the history of philosophy with a growing conviction of the importance of the approach that I had conceived. Probably, by the way, the idea of this approach could have been gotten from Dewey, but while I can hear of such things from others, and approve them, for them to take on real vitality for me, I must arrive at them by my own road. The course has never pleased me, for it did not take long to discover that the scholarship necessary to carry out the task in the desired fashion was the work of a lifetime, and not an avocation for a pedagogue whose most vital interests were in other problems. Also, all current histories and texts are woefully inadequate for such an approach.

Stanford also gave an opportunity to continue working on æsthetics, and best of all the opportunity to institute a course on the philosophy of science along such lines as pleased my fancy. The initial idea was to review the basic conceptions of sciences: physics, chemistry, biology, psychology, and anthropology, from the point of view of asking the metaphysical question, What sort of a reality would sanction such scientific interpretations? From the first the materials were wholly readings in science, with no attention to the extant philosophies of science. My own philosophical development, and most of what I have since written, has been the outgrowth of problems that appeared in connection with this course.

The development into a philosophy has been slow. In the first place the astounding and unexpected development of physical-chemistry that was just taking shape at the time of my removal to Stanford in 1914, and the wealth of new material that has appeared almost in monthly *quanta*, has furnished a challenge that demanded a retention of flexibility in conclusions. It is only recently that I have begun to feel the inception of a position that can both comprehend actual findings and leave room for further inevitable modifications and corrections. But, like Russell, I am still hesitant about the significance of the *quanta* theories and their results. In the last few years I have been trying my conclusions out against such books as C. D. Broad's, Bertrand Russell's, Whitehead's, and Alexander's, but until I was pretty sure where I was going I never looked into any of these, except Russell's and Whitehead's mathematical philosophy, and I was pretty well advanced in the interpretation of mathematics in the early Columbia days.

These remarks are not to be understood as preparatory to claiming any originality or priority of ideas. Such questions have never had the least interest for me. Civilization depends upon the free offering and acceptance of truths whatever their sources. It can permit no patents. Obviously acknowledgments, when possible, are pleasant courtesies, but in philosophy especially the form of the assimilation of an idea is almost as important as the idea itself. Frequently both idea and its use are suggested by the difficulties of other philosophers who have missed out somehow. Our chief acknowledgments should probably be to the errors of others, but perhaps the most subtle form of flattery is to have our ideas ascribed to distinguished philosophers, whom, to our shame, we have never read. However, the thrill of such flattery is usually short-lived, for attention to the ascribed source usually shows that we, or it, have been completely misunderstood.

Retournons à nos moutons. The concept of levels early suggested itself as a way to link together the fields of the different sciences. I think the idea came while reading Auguste Comte, and I first heard the term used in a lecture by Spaulding at Columbia. It has been a useful and illuminating conception, but its newer forms, in connection with the doctrine of emergence, are utterly foreign to me. The current popular attempt to view cosmic history under a disguised version of Herbert Spencer's ponderous formula, a progress from an incoherent, unstable homogeneity to a coherent, stable heterogeneity, always recalls Royce's demonstration that the reverse process is equally characteristic of reality. There can be no doubt that, whatever we mean by the term entity, where certain structural features occur, certain characteristics of the entity are present, and that the structure of some entities can be expressed in terms involving simpler orders of entities in such fashion that the characteristics of the more complex can be seen as consequences of the characteristics of the simpler when structurally combined but not identical with them. In this sense these latter characteristics may be said to have emerged, but they can also demerge if the structure characterized by them is disintegrated. This is quite in accord with Professor Woodbridge's contention that matter means structure.

Emergence becoming cosmology is a typical example of philosophical emotional perversity, the use of emotion as a substitute for thinking instead of as a stimulus to thinking. In the light of our present knowledge it is as easy to think of the universe as statistically identical as to think of it as having a directional course—that is, some stars are becoming hotter and their atoms disintegrating; others are becoming cooler and heavier atoms are being formed. There seem to be limits in both directions, for the heavy atoms become radioactive and disruptive to their neighbours also, and the limits of disintegration seem to be in proto-hydrogen. Solar systems and stars may both be generated and destroyed as appendages to processes taking place in different parts of the cosmos. All objects, as Broad says, are strands of history; but the cosmos, as we now know it, may be either a history or a statistical identity—that is, may contain at each moment samples of approximately all potentialities. The almost Spinozistic trend of modern physics suggests the latter. In our ignorance we can do little more than follow Aristotle in the belief that each thing is at its best when it is doing most fully that of which it is capable and busy ourselves with seeking more light. Mind is certainly a specialized detail within the complex whole and not an object of cosmic striving.

The biological and physiological aspects of nature have also been difficult to interpret in a satisfactory philosophical fashion, but the difficulty has been not so much from changes in data as from a certain poverty, or better, a one-sidedness of them that neglected aspects of problems concerning which a philosopher needs information. Bergson's *L'Évolution Creatrice* gave me a real thrill, although I could never sympathize with the neo-vitalistic movement. It seemed essentially a mystical development, and mysticism is for me the imaginative satisfaction of an emotional urge replacing empirically sanctioned observation. Nor was his stressing of the term *intuition* congenial, for that word usually covers poverty of analysis. Yet mechanistic biology of the older type, such as Jacques Loeb's, always appeared to be lacking in something. This discrepancy has been partially overcome in my opinion by the application of the principle of levels. This principle leads to the conception of organic sub-structures functioning as wholes according to descriptive laws that are foreign to mere physics and chemistry, but are rendered possible by physical and chemical processes binding together their elements.

For some time my biological reading was chiefly along the lines of T. H. Morgan's investigations, but the chromosomes and the genes persisted in explaining too much. It was impossible, as the theory used to stand, that the differences in individuals of the same stock that do occur could occur. Also it seemed to set the organism in too great opposition to its environment. It was not until the recent appearance of Child's *Physiological Foundations of Behavior*, with its conception of growth as a form of reaction to and partly determined by environmental interactions, that I began to grasp a philosophical conception of the organism that appears to me now to be in accord with observation, not contradictory to the discoveries of the scientist and harmonious with the conceptions of the physical world derivable from the other sciences.

Psychological conceptions are always a stumbling-block to philosophers. The greatest confusions I find in the contemporary British philosophers, Russell, Broad, Whitehead, and Alexander, result from a wholly inadequate psychology. I have always felt a certain irrational joy at Auguste Comte's omission of this subject from his list of the sciences on the ground that its problems belong partly to physiology and partly to sociology. Perhaps this is not wholly true, but at least the physiologists are beginning to tell us a good deal about those physiological structures that make human behaviour what it is, and the behaviourists are telling a good deal about the characteristics of that behaviour. Those who devote themselves to the description and classification of mental processes—the introspectionists—even if their methods are justifiable or justified, do not seem to have added greatly to the sum of knowledge. For a time Freud loomed large on my horizon. I tried very hard to get inside of the doctrine and look at the world through its eyes—the method Royce laid down as best fitted to give understanding; but the world so seen did not fit very well with the world as lived in, so I gradually emerged with about as much Freudianism left as is contained in Holt's *Freudian Wish and its Place in Ethics.* I owe part of my rescue to my colleague, Professor Stuart, who has hauled me back by penetrating criticism and kindly ridicule from more ill-considered acceptances of half-illuminating ideas than he probably realizes. He has often made me lots of trouble, for which I have been very thankful afterwards, and has frightened me out of many literary projects that I should have later bitterly repented.

The most difficult problem my philosophy of mind has had to face hangs upon the interpretation of sense qualities and imagery. For both, the whole position developed demands the discovery of specific physical or physiological structures that are "qualitied"— Mr. Alexander's term—by them. It is easy to make hypotheses, but difficult to get hold of crucial tests of their validity. Long before reading Alexander I had tried to think through his supposition that all sense qualities are characteristics of structures in the extra-organic physical world, but that hypothesis is difficult to reconcile with the facts of sensation. Also, I have tried the hypothesis that sense qualities pertain to qualitied structures within the organism, with consequent difficulties in understanding our sensing of an external physical world. The most satisfactory hypothesis seems to be that some sense qualities, probably colour and sounds, are qualitied states of extra-physiological structures that can be reproduced as a result of physical processes as qualitied states of certain organic structures; and others, temperature, taste, smell, and the like, are qualitied states of organic structures only, but may be produced under the influence of specific sorts of contacts with external matter.

Images also require some physical or physiological qualitied structures. I am sure that neither sense qualities nor images can be qualitied brain events. Only recently, in Hollingworth's *Psychology of Thought,* have I found a sanction for what I have for a long time speculatively held and suggested as an hypothesis to my students, that the image is nothing but a qualitied organic state, specifically located in a sense organ or muscle, that, by the mechanism of the conditioned reflex, has replaced natural conditions as the innervator of an action pattern formed under their influence. Such a qualitied structure may, as in the case of the visual image, be similar to a qualitied character of the situation represented, or, as in the case of "sub-vocal" speech, be wholly different. Such qualitied states become images through their acquired capacity or conditioning to represent something other than themselves in innervating engrams.

It is pleasant to agree with Mr. Alexander that our spatial and temporal perceptions are not derived from the characteristics of sense qualities, but it is disturbing, as in the case of Bergson, to find him taking refuge in intuition. Spatial and temporal perceptions are clearly related to the consequences of our experiences in acting. I cannot forget a chance remark of Dewey's, that experiencing means *trying out*. It seems to me their sense data are those intra-organic sensations that arise in the course of our innervations preparatory to seeking something far or near, to the right or left, above or below. They are closely analogous to those innervation sense data that lead us to expect an object to be light or heavy, wet or dry, hot or cold, on the basis of a mere visual distance contact.

Alexander's mental quality is a pure mystery to me. Perhaps it is lacking in my make-up, but when I approach a specific instance in which I am conscious of something, James's method of getting an understanding of abstract terms, I find nothing but, say, a clock ticking on my table, organic qualitied conditions as the ticking tends to produce movements contrary to those necessary for writing, and a slight unpleasantness, irritability, as a feeling tone. My content of consciousness is primarily a juxtaposition and partial fusion of these qualitative conditions. I wonder whether the so-called mental quality may not be suggested by a half-discerned recognition that sensory response is always accompanied by the qualities due to empathic responses that Langfeld so well interprets in the case of contacts with works of art? The total qualitative condition characteristic of the organism in such a situation is a composite, like the taste of a beefsteak in which taste, tactile, temperature, and olfactory qualities are fused, a fact that justifies us in speaking of a pleasant day, a fearful storm, or a horrible monster. I do not understand the neglect of the consideration of empathic conditions and their significances by both psychologists and philosophers who are concerned with the problem of the nature of mind.

This is no place for a full presentation of a philosophy of mind, but there is one point I cannot willingly pass over. Psychology is much too preoccupied with the stimulus-response concept. At any moment there are myriads of stimuli and only certain of them motivate the dominating patterns. This fact is too readily brushed aside as due to intensity, habit-shifting interest, or something of the sort. As Bergson pointed out, the animal organism is an accumulator of stored-up energy that it releases more or less explosively. It is driven to find outlets, and "stimuli" in actual practice, as opposed to laboratory conditions, do little more than provide opportunities for release. The direction of the release is determined generally, not by the nature of the acquired engrams, but by some state of metabolic unbalance, involving an energy level that we call mood. We can be too buoyant for a book to exert appeal, too depressed to respond to humour. We may go out of our way to find trouble. In one state I quietly watch a fly crawling over my hand, in another I gently brush him off, and in another I attempt a vicious attack. It was Kempf's *Autonomic Functions and the Personality*—and Kempf is quite aware of the peculative character of many of his theses—that gave me the first suggestion of the importance of autonomic functions. I believe now that all spontaneous and all deliberated action is motivated by problems of autonomic adjustment under conditions imposed by the demands for action in a given environment. My main argument for stressing the social importance of art is that our empathic responses to works of art have their immediate effect in effecting autonomic readjustments, that result both in modifying the direction of our thinking and the persistency of our endeavours. There is more than a little truth for me in Poincaré's rhapsody, in which he makes the effects of contact with the beautiful the basis of the impulsion to scientific advance and the source of the triumph of the Greek civilization in Europe.

As sufficiently behaviouristic to see truth in the statement that thinking is sub-vocal speech, at least in so far as it implies that words are the chief images used in thinking, language takes on a special philosophic importance. I am ready to "enjoy" the irony of Mr. Russell by casting my lot with the Patagonians and others for whom the sentence is the psychological unit, always remembering that a child may treat a word as a sentence where his elders would not. Jespersen appears to be the most thoughtful of the philologians, and his suggestion is that sentence structure arose out of the disintegration of a holophrastic speech. I have been greatly influenced in my conception of language by him and by inferences drawn from Boas's *Handbook of American Indian Languages*. If the relation between speech and thinking suggested by the behaviourists has truth, there ought to be some relation between the structure of a language and the mentality of its habitual users. I like to think that I can see some such relations in the case of the French and the Germans, but the relation should be far more manifest if one could get in contact with the thought of those using some language outside of the European group and based on a quite different structural plan. It must be confessed that I have as yet failed to get assurance as to such differences, although I have sought for them from Chinese, Japanese, and Hindu students with whom I have been thrown in contact. Anthropologist friends, although they approve the principle, fail to produce satisfactory materials for evidence.

My social, moral, and religious philosophy is still at its infantile stage. It is still anthropological—that is, still seeking to find out what human practices have been in these fields and what men believed they were getting out of them. I think I can see fairly clearly the emerging aims of differentiating moral and religious striving, as I have that of æsthetic striving, but I am as yet far too ignorant of the details of the processes involved to place them in their proper perspective in human life. Hence I cannot yet claim any general social philosophy, unless it be a philosophy of education, and here I am so much under the influence of

Professor Dewey that I doubt if my ideas are more than a repetition, with possibly some elaboration, of his.

I am quite sure that our schools and universities are on the wrong track in their efforts to teach. If I were a Mussolini of the state of education, my first decree would be a death-sentence on anyone using the verb "to educate" in any other than a reflexive usage; I educate myself, you educate yourself, etc. It seems to me that the school and the university should merely be environments peculiarly adapted to the arousal of curiosities and providing means whereby a satisfaction of them can be found. This is, of course, the program of the "Schools of To-morrow." The university, and all higher education, differ only in the fact that the curiosities there aroused must be evoked largely through books and be satisfied through books, always provided students have been taught to read.

The lack of ability to read is the greatest handicap under which those of the present generation that come to the university are placed. They have, of course, learned to repeat words; to give definitions of them, sometimes; but to use words as a medium to direct thought to real situations, and to live those situations in imagination through the help of words, is generally beyond their powers. The textbook that can be memorized and the formal definition are the curses that hold them down. I do not mean there is nothing that needs to be remembered or defined. The situation that a problem defines discloses many features to be remembered and taken account of, and a definition may help to clarify it; but to one who succeeds "in walking around the idea and looking at it on all sides" the formulation of the definition or of the facts seen can be made in many different word groups. The student who can use only one of them does not usually know what he is talking about. This is as true in philosophy as in science, and I think the philosopher, especially the dialectician, is rather extraordinarily prone to play with such word groups, taking definitions as rules of the game, with the result that he often attains a sort of very beautiful and complicated analogue of a chess problem solution rather than a vital philosophy.

If teaching is impossible, what becomes of the professor?

Ideally the university becomes a dwelling-place of scholars, each so vitally interested in the problems of his field that he inspires others with his interests and shares with them his labours. Under actual conditions there must be lectures in which he talks about his field and tries to communicate a feeling for its significance and interest. To my mind such "courses" might well be required, but should carry little or no credit. Unsolved problems lying in the offing need not be concealed or tentatively solved. Those deriving interest from such lectures may then enter upon a more intimate relation with the lecturer, in which they see how he is working at his materials, and be encouraged to try their own hands at the work. Then with growing experience they can be entrusted with their own problems and irregular consultations and opportunities to discuss difficulties or results. Under present conditions, unfortunately, something of the task-master attitude is still demanded.

Discipline is not without value, but occurs in its best form when it becomes necessary to perform an uncongenial task for the sake of succeeding in a congenial one, as the study of German grammar may be essential to getting information that may help to solve a problem in literature, philosophy, or science. Our wretched habit of letting a textbook or a teacher(!) tell a student everything he is expected to know (say again) is utterly subversive of attaining this sort of discipline. I have no patience with the full pitcher and empty glasses theory of education, nor with the artificial discipline of enforced cramming. My friends in departments of education tell me that the inferiority of those who are willing to become teachers and of most of those who seek education makes any such programme as is suggested above unworkable. I do not believe them. Is this the dogmatist overriding the empiricist? I do not think so, for the plan is justified by what I know about human nature, although the principle of selectivity involved might alter somewhat the groups seeking higher education, perhaps even diminish them; but I suspect in the long run, if thoroughly developed, it would have quite the opposite effect.

Philosophy, as I have written in published papers, justifies itself as supplementary to science by developing an integration of knowledge that can lend coherence and confidence to human aspirations and ideals. A metaphysics is merely the set of basic principles on which it rests. As such it is essentially a product of maturity, but its actual articulation may proceed in either of two directions. The philosopher may first formulate his metaphysics and rationalize his views of life accordingly, or may first develop his practical philosophy and elaborate his metaphysic as needed. In each case there is probably a partly conscious foreshadowing of the other part. Even when the metaphysics takes precedence in the *opera*, there seems to be throughout it a foreshadowing of the attitude towards life involved; and when, as seems to be the more modern fashion, an integration of the attitude towards life precedes, as with Dewey or James, the metaphysic is always hovering in the offing. These two elements should mature together in the mind.

Academically this need generates difficulties, for our scientific predilections demand early published research. In philosophy such research is likely to lack perspective and so exhibit an academic character and lack of vitality that may be noted in much contemporary philosophy in America and indeed in the whole modern world. The scientist can take his problems piecemeal, the philosopher must solve his synthetically. The scientific spirit now dominates, and philosophy suffers accordingly. The young philosopher must imitate scientific procedure, so unless he has a happy faculty of forgetting his formulations of conclusions and a sufficiently courageous ego not to fear charges of inconsistency, his synthesis either never arrives or is a mere formalism in which his heart is not present. Professor James used to say that ideas came to him as the charcoal sketches of pictures and that the detailed filling in arrived gradually. Certainly no picture could be produced by dividing the canvas into square inches and completing each one as a special problem. Perhaps our young philosophers should be encouraged to try their hand at broad general essays and mature their early work through specialized studies later.

Our educational system also tends to foster a distinction between the scholar and the teacher. There have been discussions as to the advisability of classifying professors as teachers or research men, and schools of education seem to be gradually adopting a new form of the Ph.D. to distinguish those who merely wish to know the meaning of what they drill their victims to say from those who want to be able to handle the facts with which they deal and perhaps find out something more about them. I think the distinction is wholly vicious. There is, of course, a difference in the ability of men in getting others to share their interests, and some extraordinarily able investigators should never try to give popular lectures or elementary courses. Comparatively few of us have the intellectual power and the emotional drive to really produce significant advances of knowledge; but unless a man has the thrill from the subject-matter with which he deals that makes him feel it all important and fills him with personal ideas about it, he has no place in an educational institution, even the most elementary. The attempt to grasp the importance of a subject to the progress of civilization is itself a sort of research that concerns even the most elementary instruction. In so far as valid, the distinction between the teacher and the investigator is the distinction between those who are thinking about the social significance of their subject and those concerned with the increasing discoveries in its field. Both are researchers, for all thinking about a subject is research, unless we narrow the term to include only the attainment of notably successful results, a thing not necessary for all fruitful educational contacts. Hence every scholar must believe that his subject is *the* indispensable element of a curriculum, as, of course, philosophy is.

With this view of the teacher and the life within a university, it is obvious that my philosophical development cannot be disentangled from my classroom work. To my elementary students I owe the pressure to keep my thought in touch with the problems that confront all men in their adjustments to the demands of life, to hold my abstractions to the outgrowths of concrete needs, and to avoid unclearness. To those more advanced, there is a debt for criticism and for raising difficulties overlooked that have to be met. There is little that I have written that has not first been inflicted on some group of students with enough care to produce at least a good semblance of understanding. Thinking before an audience is easier for me than before a typewriter, and the too carefully prepared lecture almost always fizzles. To be interested in my subject and intent on making a few points usually leads to success and an extension of the thought, whether utilized on the spot or matured in private afterwards.

Prejudices? Yes. Sully Prudhomme says somewhere: "Un homme n'est pas un artist si, chez lui, aucun sens n'est particulièrement délicat, si certaines couleurs, certaines lignes, certains sons ne l'affectent pas comme des caresses ou des blessures." If I might parody him, I should say, no man can be a philosopher if, for him, no outlook on life is particularly dear, if certain ways of thinking, attitudes toward facts and beliefs, do not affect him like caresses or wounds. For myself, I believe "citius emergit veritas ex errore quam ex confusione," and I should prefer to be proven wrong and acknowledge my error rather than be praised for the profundity of ineffable insights. The concrete particular instance as a check to generalization gives me a glow of comfort. Yet I fear dialectic and the preeminence frequently accorded to logic. The purely intellectualistic philosopher turns me to ice, for our intellectual processes are only instruments used by our organisms in maintaining or recovering vital intra-organic correlations that are ever and anon threatened by the vicissitudes of the world to which it belongs—that is, our problems arise as emotional conflicts and are practically solved when we recover the peace that passeth understanding, the σωφροσύνη of the Charmides. Mere intellectualism, could it exist, would have the horror of a Frankenstein.

I am also prejudiced against the anthropocentric perspective in metaphysics. Man is essentially a part of nature, and his peculiarity is, as Pascal saw, that he thinks; but I am prejudiced against the prejudice that mind is the master work of cosmic process. As was indicated above, the earth with its living organisms appears in cosmic events as a mere by-product. In the evolution of living forms, man is one specific occurrence. In his acquired capacity to anticipate the future and to modify environment to suit his needs rather than suit himself to environment, he seems to excel all living creatures. But for all we know the natural processes of evolution may produce some organism with more numerous or more subtile senses and with a more delicately balanced nature that may acquire a mind vastly superior to his, or, on the other hand, his present organic balance may be too delicate to persist and he may become extinct through disease or more directly by his own acts. I cannot see why the universe should be deeply stirred in either event. The absence of man with his mind, or an electron with its field of force, would undoubtedly make the universe different; but to assume that that difference is of importance to the universe is to endow the universe with thought and feeling—a truly primitive anthropomorphism.

Yet in another sense philosophy must be anthropocentric. The philosopher himself is a man, and to man the potentialities of his mentality are of prime importance. He must make himself at home in the cosmos. But he is not what he would be, nor is his environment as he would have it. Even the Faust who hails the fleeting moment: "Oh, still delay—thou art so fair," is a prey to the living discontent inherent in the possessor of mind. Contentment lies only in change, and human changes involve the kind of participation called mental action. Mentality demands knowledge that futures may be anticipated. It creates art that its emotional problems may be adjusted and their solutions shared. It weaves moral codes so that men can extend their achievements through co-operation. It invents gods as a spur to its aspirations. The philosopher is mentality engaged in evaluating the forms these achievements have attained and remoulding them for the better articulation of the impulses inherent in the human variety of the living organism.

A philosophy is, therefore, in its core a program for a way of living from which emanate specific directional tendencies of thinking, feeling, and willing. In a measure Fichte was right in challenging men to acknowledge their philosophy and show the sort of men they were. We demand consistency and truth of philosophies merely because inconsistencies and untruths seem to be obstacles to the realization of what is peculiarly human in our potentialities as living beings. A science that is true and consistent would be wholly adequate, but a philosophy that is merely this and nothing more may be insignificant. Indeed, historically, where truth or consistency have been in a measure lacking, significance has often cast its halo on a philosophy and raised it to a place of high esteem. If it is true that there is no great contemporary philosophy, it is perhaps because philosophers, in a scientific zeal to be accurate in their dealings with data—a wholly commendable effort in itself—have neglected to develop the significance of their results. Philosophies far more acceptable to scientists than Bergson's have far less philosophic weight.

This is the story of the making of a philosophic mind, although to one who reveres philosophy as I it is almost unbearably arrogant to characterize myself as such. May it be understood as Saint Paul's "earnest of the Spirit in our hearts." What has been given is but the outline of a philosophy, a sketch that the future may see transferred to canvas, for it is now sufficiently matured to be entrusted on that journey toward life or toward oblivion that is the great adventure of any articulated philosophy. What that chapter will hold only "the Law that abides and changes not" will disclose.

> For strangely graven
> Is the orb of life . . . .
> And men in their millions float and flow
> And seethe with a million hopes as leaven;
> And they win their Will, or they miss their Will,
> And hopes are dead or are pined for still;
> But whoe'er can know,
> As the long days go,
> That to Live is happy, hath found his Heaven!

PRINCIPAL PUBLICATIONS

Intelligence and Mathematics: Creative Intelligence, 1917.

Problem of Method in Mathematics and Philosophy: Essays in Honour of William James, 1908.

"Infinity and the Generalization of the Number Concept," *Journal of Philosophy*, 1909.

"Problem of the Infinite in Space and Time," *Journal of Philosophy*, 1910.

"Structural Levels in the Scientist's World," *Journal of Philosophy*, 1917.

"Social Psychology and the Problem of a Higher Nationality," *International Journal of Ethics*, 1917.

American Philosophy: Civilization in the U.S., 1922.

"The Problem of Philosophy," *Journal of Philosophy*, 1924.

"The Materialist's World," *Journal of Philosophy*, 1925.

"Scientific Thought and Reality," *Journal of Philosophy*, 1926.

"The Milesian Background of Scientific Ontology," *Journal of Philosophy*, 1927.

"Why the Sensa?" *Proceedings, 6th International Congress of Philosophy*, 1926.

THE PHILOSOPHICAL *CREDO* OF AN ABSOLUTISTIC PERSONALIST

By MARY WHITON CALKINS

Born 1863; Professor of Philosophy and Psychology, Wellesley College, Wellesley, Mass.

THE PHILOSOPHICAL *CREDO* OF AN ABSOLUTISTIC PERSONALIST

By way of preface to this formulation of my philosophical *credo*, I must state unambiguously that by 'philosophy' I mean 'metaphysics'; and that I use 'metaphysics' in roughly the following sense: the attempt, by reasoning, to know what is ultimately real. It will be observed that the words 'by reasoning' mark off philosophy, thus conceived, from mysticism; and that the phrase 'the attempt' admits the possible failure of any metaphysician in his quest.

This use of the term 'philosophy' does not, of course, interfere with my unconcerned acceptance of that academic convention which turns over, to supposedly competent members of departments of philosophy, instruction in ethics, logic, and æsthetics. Primarily, however, ethics and æsthetics and old-fashioned formal logic seem to me to be divisions of psychology, mainly distinguished from rigidly descriptive psychology first as explicitly normative, as demanding the valuation of the objects of their study, and second as practical, as demanding the application of psychology to conduct, to artistic production, and to scientific method. It follows, to my mind, that if philosophy were merely a covering term for ethics, æsthetics, and logic, one or all, there would be no faintest justification for a specific department of philosophy or for an association of philosophers as such: rather, we philosophers should be sorted out and assigned, some of us to general psychology, some to history, government, and economics, some to this or the other of the arts, some to the physical sciences or to mathematics.

Obviously, this conception of philosophy as metaphysics sharply opposes two other conceptions greatly in vogue to-day. The first of these is logical atomism of the Bertrand Russell type, the theory that "logic is what is fundamental in philosophy."[1] The second is the doctrine brilliantly set forth by John Dewey that philosophy is the enlightener of "the moral forces which move mankind" and that the "task of philosophy is to clarify men's

[1] Cf. *Contemporary British Philosophy*, vol. i, p. 359.

ideas as to the social and moral strifes of their own day." Thus conceived the history of philosophy is as Dewey points out "a chapter in the development of civilization and culture . . . a living picture of the choice of thoughtful men about what they would have life to be and to what ends they would have men shape their intelligent activities."[1] I cannot too unequivocally state my conviction that Dewey here proposes not the reconstruction, but the abandonment of philosophy. He may be right or he may be wrong about the value of metaphysics, but he is not justified in the identification of philosophy with a socialized ethics.

<h2 style="text-align:center">I</h2>

My philosophic *credo* is made up of four articles. The first of these may thus be stated: The universe contains distinctively mental realities; it may or may not also contain non-mental entities, but in any case irreducibly mental realities exist. I am eager to point out that by this conviction I associate myself with metaphysicians of many points of view, not merely with out-and-out idealists, such as Berkeley, Hume, Hegel, Royce, and Pearson, but with dualists, classic and contemporary, of many sorts, with Descartes and Locke, with Pratt and Sheldon, for example—in a word, with philosophers of every type who assert or admit the existence of mental entities or qualities. I call special attention to the fact that the group includes upholders of the contemporary doctrine of emergent evolution. For these writers hold that though mind has emerged from a "lower level of existence, . . . it does not belong to that lower level," but is rather a "new order of existent with special laws of behaviour."[2]

There is evidently only one metaphysical doctrine inconsistent with this basal conviction that mental realities exist. This is materialism in the broad old-fashioned sense of the term—what

---

[1] *Reconstruction in Philosophy*, 1920, chapter i, pp. 25–7.

[2] S. Alexander, *Space, Time and Deity*, vol. ii, p. 46[2]. Cf. A. O. Lovejoy, "The Meanings of Emergence and Its Modes," *Proceedings of the Sixth International Congress of Philosophy*, 1927, p. 30 (reprinted in the *Journal of Philosophical Studies*, 1926, ii, p. 176[2]); and C. Lloyd Morgan, *Emergent Evolution*, especially Lectures I, II.

is nowadays often called naturalism, or behaviourism, or monistic realism. Anti-mentalism would be an unambiguous term to cover all forms of this doctrine that so-called mental realities are reducible to non-mental; the theory that consciousness is a function of a non-mental organ, the brain; the doctrine that thinking is, like golf-playing, a material bodily reaction[1]; or finally the teaching that consciousness, like physical qualities, reduces ultimately to a non-mental 'neutral stuff.'[2] I, however, ally myself with the great majority of philosophers in asserting the existence of mental realities and in consequent opposition to the materialistic reduction of mental to non-mental. My frankly empirical reason for this conviction is that I directly experience mental phenomena. I know immediately what perceiving, imagining, feeling, and willing *are*; and I know as immediately that the subvocal contraction of throat-muscles in pronouncing a word, say 'justice,' is a phenomenon distinct from that of 'thinking' justice, though the two phenomena are closely correlated. Because I encounter mental reality, directly experience it, realize it as somehow significantly different from what I observe as bodily process or physical reality, I assert its existence.

II

The second article of my philosophic creed carries me a step further and separates me from a few of my former companions—from Hume, from Karl Pearson, from Ernst Mach. It embodies the conviction that mental realities are ultimately personal, that the mental phenomena which I directly observe are not percepts, thoughts, emotions, and volitions, in unending succession, but rather perceiving, thinking, feeling, and willing self or selves.

[1] For an example of contemporary materialism, cf. Alexander's doctrine that reality, categories included, is spatio-temporal (*op. cit.* i, 183, 189 ff, 246[1] *et al.*). Note the inconsistency of Alexander's repeated statement that every existent is "expressible *without residue*" in terms of a lower order of existence, with his emergence-conception (*op. cit.* ii, pp. 45 ff. Italics mine).

For statements of the behaviouristic position, cf. J. B. Watson, *Psychology from the Standpoint of a Behaviorist.*

[2] Cf. E. B. Holt, *The Concept of Consciousness*, pp. 103, 106, 110. Cf. also Bertrand Russell, *Analysis of Mind*, pp. 25[2], 121[2].

With William McDougall, I hold that it is impossible to "find . . . 'an idea' or 'a sensation' lying about loose in the world. . . ." One might as well "expect to find 'a falling' or 'a movement' without something that falls or moves as 'a perceiving' or 'a remembering' detached and isolated from the subject who perceives or remembers."[1] And this conviction once more is based upon the appeal to immediate experience. Even Hume has implicitly admitted the existence of the self whom he overtly denies, by such expressions as his famous, "I enter most intimately into what I call myself," and even more significantly by his teaching that both 'necessary connection' and 'identity' are cases of the 'transition of the mind.' For obviously 'transition' can be attributed only to a continuous being and is an utterly meaningless term as applied to a string of momentary 'mental phenomena'—to mere impressions or ideas.

Through direct observation I have thus gained two convictions: first that mental realities exist; second, that every mental existent is either a self or a part, phase, aspect, or process of a self. Obviously, this experienced self must be studied, analysed, scientifically described. The outcome of such study may very briefly be summarized: it is the conception of the self as a complex, unique, more-than-momentary (or persistent), yet changing entity, conscious of (and so related to) an environment. These characters, it must emphatically be restated, I directly experience and do not merely infer. In recognition, for example, I am conscious of myself as persisting, as the same self who earlier perceived this same object; in rebellious volition I individualize myself, set myself up against other selves, realize myself as unique. In feeling and perceiving I am conscious of myself as passively related to my environment, whereas in willing and in affirming I am aware of myself as in active, creative relation to surrounding objects.[2]

[1] *Outline of Psychology,* 1923, p. 40.
[2] I cannot date with precision my adoption of the personalistic point of view; but I feel sure that it is the outcome of my study and teaching of psychology during the 'nineties. A particularly influential text was the famous ninth chapter of James's *Principles of Psychology,* in which he declares that "the universal conscious fact is not 'feelings and thoughts

III

With my next step forward, I break fellowship with many who, up to this point, have been my companions. For my philosophy is, in the third place, unambiguously idealistic, that is mentalistic.[1] I hold, in other words, not only that the universe whatever else it contains includes mental realities, but that the universe is through and through mental in character, that all that is real is ultimately mental, and accordingly personal, in nature.[2]

i. It will be expedient to elaborate this conception before considering the arguments against and for it. The chief question at issue is evidently that of the nature of the physical world. How is it possible to conceive of comets, and rocks and dandelions as mental? And, if we so conceive them, how can we account for the empirically realized distinction—a distinction sharply stressed by our argument against materialism—between brains and bodies and indeed all physical objects, on the one hand, and experiencing conscious selves on the other. Idealism offers two solutions of these problems: first, that of Berkeley, followed in our own day by Pearson[3] and Mach[4], which reduces the physical

exist' but 'I think' and 'I feel' " (p. 226[2]). An article, "Psychology as Science of Selves" in the September 1900 issue of the *Philosophical Review* is my earliest published avowal of the personalistic standpoint in psychology. For later statements of it I may refer to my "A First Book in Psychology," to a series of papers in the *Journal of Philosophy*, 1908–9, and to two later papers, "The Self in Scientific Psychology, *American Journal of Psychology*, 1915, xxvi, pp. 495–524, and "Converging Lines of Contemporary Psychology," *British Journal of Psychology*, 1926, General Section, xvi, pp. 171–9.

[1] I use this barbarous term in the interest of clearness, for the term 'idealism' is nowadays sometimes narrowed in meaning to designate first one, then another, form of idealism in the wide sense—to refer to Berkeleian idealism, for example, or else to absolute idealism; and again 'idealism' is used to cover an essentially dualistic conception of a world of persons and things regarded as alike ideal because significant parts of a significant world order (cf. J. E. Creighton, "Two Types of Idealism," *Philosophical Review*, 1917, xxvi, p. 515[2]).

[2] My first teacher in philosophy, Professor Charles E. Garman, started and guided me in the line of thought which culminates in an idealistic philosophy.

[3] Karl Pearson, *The Grammar of Science*, chapter ii, § 12, pp. 65–6.

[4] Ernst Mach, *Analysis of Sensations*, Open Court edition, 1914, p. 22[2].

world to a system of ideas; second, that of Leibniz, Royce, and Ward, which conceives the physical world as made up of selves of an extra-human type. Either doctrine is theoretically possible; but I adopt a form of the Leibnizian conception chiefly because the results, speculative and experimental, of modern science seem to me more readily translatable into its terms. Accordingly, I think of the physical world as an extension, downward, of the obviously social world made up of human beings and of the 'higher' animals. I conceive the conscious selves who constitute the infra-human world as like myself in my inattentive, dazed, inactive, sleepy states. And the sharp contrast which unquestionably I observe between so-called physical and psychical reality I conceive, after Royce's fashion, as the significant distinction between uncommunicative and communicative selves. In other words, I contrast selves, or persons, with physical objects not on the ground that the selves, and not the things, are conscious, but on the ground that the selves, and not the things, are in actual or possible intercourse with me. In Royce's phrase once more, I conceive of physical nature not as 'unconscious,' but as 'uncommunicative.'[1]

Against two misconceptions of this personalistic nature philosophy I must briefly guard. It is not, in the first place, a return to pre-scientific animism, for it does not interpret every recurring sense-complex as sign of an individual self: I do not, for example, assert the existence of a specific leaf-self indicated by that complex sense experience described, ordinarily, as perception of a leaf. Rather, I hold that this experience may indicate merely one part or aspect of an infra-human self, or again a whole group of such selves—in other words, that one part of a leaf or else a cluster of leaves, and not the single leaf, may constitute the 'bodily sign' of a self.

A personalistic nature philosophy is not, in the second place, as is often implied, incompatible with the conception of scientific law. For the old mythical view of natural law as inexorably compelling, non-mental power has long since given place to the conception of scientific law as the statement of a repeatedly

[1] *World and the Individual*, vol. ii, p. 225[2].

observed, generalized, and justifiably predicted sequence of phenomena. The phenomena in question may at least as well be mental as non-mental. In fact, Herbert Jennings—a biologist, be it noted, not an idealistic metaphysician—says explicitly that scientific laws consist in predictions of the following type: "When you have such and such experiences, you will have such and such other experiences."[1] Obviously, scientific laws, thus conceived, have a place in a personalistic nature philosophy.[2]

ii. From this rough sketch of the personalistic conception of the universe, I turn to the argumentative support for the doctrine. I base my idealism squarely on Berkeley's fundamental position: the insistence that what any man unchallengeably knows— what he knows, in other words, without any element of hypothesis—is himself and his experiencing, clearly a mental reality. But contemporary realists, in so far as they do not cavalierly ignore Berkeleian idealism, persist in 'refuting' it—not by a criticism of this consideration but by an attack on two subsidiary arguments, Berkeley's relativity argument and his demonstration that if the secondary qualities are mental, so also are the primary qualities.

The realistic 'refutations' of these arguments vary in conclusiveness. As regards the second of them: Nunn and Whitehead and others certainly show without difficulty that Berkeley proves merely that 'all our sense perceptions are in the same boat and must be treated on the same principle,'[3] and that accordingly Berkeley's argument, effective as it is, in opposition to Descartes and to Locke, does not avail against the conception of the secondary qualitites as themselves non-mental. Against Berkeley's relativity argument—his contention that an 'external' object must be mental, not material, because it is immediately per-

---

[1] "Doctrines Held as Vitalism," *The American Naturalist*, 1913, xlvii, pp. 392–3.
[2] On all this, cf. Leibniz, "Monadology" and "The Principle of Nature and Grace"; James Ward, "The Realm of Ends," Lectures III and X; Royce, "The World and the Individual," vol. ii, Lecture V; and my paper on "The Personalistic Conception of Nature," *Philosophical Review*, 1919, xxviii. pp. 130 ff.
[3] A. N. Whitehead, *Concept of Nature*, p. 44².

ceived as possessed of opposite qualities (of heat and cold or of sweetness and bitterness, for example), contemporary realists counter as follows: they simply abandon the conception, fundamental to Berkeley's destructive argument, of material things as stable objects of perception and teach instead that external things have no fixed and permanent characters.[1] Thus, bluish green, bluish grey and blue are, in Pitkin's phrase, at one and the same time and place the "real physical colours" of a given hillside.[2] The usual mentalistic criticism of this realistic doctrine points out the precariousness of those theories of perception advanced by the realists, in place of the conventional view which they abandon. But although I believe these criticisms to be amply justified, I shall not take them up in detail.[3] For the truth is that the realistic opposition to these two Berkeleian arguments is entirely irrelevant precisely because no thoughtful idealist, from Berkeley down, rests his case upon them. One sometimes indeed suspects that many contemporary realists take their Berkeley at second hand, else they could not overlook his whole-hearted admissions of this point. A good example is his comment on the relativity argument: "It must be confessed," he says, "this method of arguing does not so much prove that there is no extension or colour in an outward object as that we do not know by *sense* which is the *true* extension or colour of the object."[4] In truth, Berkeley invariably puts "the whole upon this issue": the fact, already stressed, that the external object, as known by any man is always an experience of his own. "If," says Philonous to Hylas, "you can conceive it possible for . . . any sensible object whatever . . . to exist without the mind, then I will grant it actually to be so."[5] And to Hylas's eager reply: "What more easy than to conceive a tree or house existing by itself

---

[1] It is only fair to add that the self-styled "critical realists" oppose this doctrine.

[2] "Implications of Biology" in *The New Realism*, p. 463[3].

[3] For statement and criticism of these different theories, cf. Durant Drake, "The Approach to Critical Realism," in *Essays in Critical Realism*, pp. 15 ff; May Sinclair, *The New Idealism*, pp. 71 ff; and my *Persistent Problems of Philosophy*, fifth edition, 1925, pp. 413 ff, 423 ff.

[4] *Principles of Philosophy*, xv.

[5] *Dialogues between Hylas and Philonous*, i, Everyman Edition, pp. 232 ff.

independent of, and unperceived by, any mind whatsoever," Philonous responds by insisting that it is a "contradiction to talk of *conceiving* a thing which is *unconceived*." In the end, Hylas, the realist, admits that he has been making "a pleasant mistake enough. As I was thinking of a tree in a solitary place," he concedes, "where no one was present to see it, methought that was to conceive a tree as existing unperceived or unthought of, not considering that I myself conceived it all the while . . . And this is far from proving that I can conceive [it] *existing out of the minds of all spirits*." To be sure, Hylas, closely followed by the neo-realists of our own day, goes on to urge that, despite this fact that known trees and houses turn out to be percepts, images, or concepts, it is none the less impossible categorically to deny the existence of unknown objects; but Philonous, who represents not only Berkeley but modern idealists, shows without difficulty that such alleged unknown realities are utterly negligible, mere nothings, no more to be asserted than denied.[1]

I have postponed to the end the consideration of what seems to me the crucially important difficulty in idealism. As has already appeared, I discount most realistic criticisms. Either they assume the existence of extra-mental reality; or they attack only the subsidiary arguments for idealism; or they ignore the fundamental idealistic position; or they are guilty on all these counts. But contemporary realism has sent one pointed shaft into the very heart of idealistic doctrine. This is Moore's contention that according to the fundamental idealistic argument (by which the idealist "discovers" every alleged non-mental reality to be one of his own experiencings) other selves as truly as material things reduce to the thoughts or imaginings of the idealist, losing all independent reality of their own. In other words: Moore argues that the idealist, on his own principles, directly knows only himself and his own experiences and has no right to infer from the latter the existence of any person save himself.[2]

[1] *Dialogues between Hylas and Philonous*, ii, Everyman Edition, pp. 256 ff. Cf. my *Persistent Problems of Philosophy*, p. 418.

[2] Cf. G. E. Moore, "The Nature and Reality of Objects of Perception," in *Proceedings of the Aristotelian Society*, 1905–6, vi. Moore's position is summarized in *The New Realism*, pp. 6[2] f, 146[2]. It is of interest to note

In my opinion only three rejoinders to this serious argument lie open to the idealist. (*a*) He may, in the first place, accept solipsism as the only arguable metaphysical position. But as a matter of fact no philosopher seems ever definitely to have grasped this horn of the dilemma. (*b*) The idealist may, in the second place, adopt the standpoint of the pluralistic personalist—of Leibniz and Ward, of Richardson and Burns. He may hold that he directly knows himself as a responsive, not a solitary, mental being, and that he justifiably conceives his environment as like-natured with himself. With Ward, he may believe that "Man only knows the world as he . . . interacts with it and . . . finds it intelligible. And finding it intelligible, he can only conclude that it is not, after all, an alien Other, but has its ground and meaning either in another self or in a community of selves."[1] (*c*) This uncritically pluralistic type of idealism I am, however, unable to accept, since it is, by Ward's own admission, without 'philosophical justification,'[2] or, in Richardson's phrase, a mere 'hypothesis.'[3] And yet I believe that idealism, of a third sort, may escape solipsism by the doctrine of the Including Self. The argument of this absolutistic type of idealism runs thus: In that direct experience of myself which is, as yet, the only immediate certainty I have admitted, I am aware of myself as, at many points, involuntarily limited, thwarted, and hampered. But this direct awareness of myself as involuntarily limited involves and includes the direct consciousness of something-which-is-in-some-sense-outside-me. The two assertions seemingly contradictory,

that Berkeley himself recognizes a difficulty for the idealist in that knowledge of other selves which everyone believes himself to possess. For Berkeley lets Hylas exclaim: "If you can conceive the mind of God without having an idea of it, why may not I be allowed to conceive the existence of matter notwithstanding that I have no idea of it?" (*Dialogues between Hylas and Philonous*, iii, Everyman Edition, p. 267). Unquestionably, Berkeley evades the consequences of this criticism by his quibbling distinction between 'notion' and 'idea.'

My conviction of the significance of this argument I owe once more to Professor Garman, who, by his vivid setting forth of the position, made me for many months a firm, though unhappy, solipsist.

[1] *The Realm of Ends*, Lecture II, p. 28.
[2] *Ibid.*, Lecture IX, p. 200[2].
[3] C. A. Richardson, *Spiritual Pluralism*, p. 63[2].

yet each made with immediate certainty, that I am conscious (1) of limit but also (2) of somewhat-beyond-the-limit are reconcilable only if this somewhat-other is conceived as a greater self of which I constitute an identical part. In fully knowing myself I therefore know the nature of that including self which is, from one point of view, other than I, because greater, but which, since I am actual part of it, also is a greater myself.

IV

(1) The culminating article of my philosophical *credo* is embodied in the assertion that the universe literally is one all-including (and accordingly complete) self of which all the lesser selves are genuine and identical parts, or members. To this conclusion, I am driven by varying considerations. The first of these has just been disclosed in the defence of my personalism. As I have tried to show, to account consistently for my own experience I must regard myself as included in a greater self. And this Greater Self, unless all-including, must (by a similar argument) itself be included in a still-greater self. In a word, only the conception of myself as identically part of an all-including self can reconcile the two experienced facts: (1) all that I know is myself in my own experiencing yet, (2) I know myself as limited by somewhat-in-a-sense-beyond-me.[1]

Another road to the acknowledgment of Absolute Self has two distinct stretches. (*a*) Of these the first is the inference from the occurrence of relations to the existence of Absolute Being. This argument starts from the fact of the experienced relatedness of events and things. On this point, like every absolutist, I am at one with my pluralistic critics. But whereas the latter accept without further metaphysical probing the fact of relatedness, with other absolutists I insist on explaining 'relation,' on pressing

---

[1] Royce's arguments from the implications of ignorance and of error to the existence of Absolute Self, may be regarded as specific cases of this argument from the awareness of involuntary limits. For statement of these arguments, cf. "The Conception of God," *Address by Dr. Royce*, edition of 1897, pp. 18 ff, 46 ff; and *The Religious Aspect of Philosophy*, chapter xi; and my *Persistent Problems of Philosophy*, pp. 451^2–2^1.

the question: precisely what is the nature of the alleged relation between any two terms? I find that only three theories of relation are advanced. (1) By the first a relation, R, is a part, a character, of one or both the related terms. But this, the pluralistic 'internal relation' conception, has only to be stated to be instantly rejected. For if R is from the start contained within a term-to-be-related, m, obviously R cannot also play the rôle of relating, or linking, m with another term, n, external to it. In a word, nothing can relate or link two terms which is itself part of either of the terms.

(2) The second of the pluralistic theories, the so-called external relation theory, does not encounter this difficulty. It is the doctrine of contemporary pluralists which conceives the relation, R, not as itself a part of the unrelated term or terms but as distinct from, external to, the terms to be related. Thus, the pen is one thing, my hand is another, and the spatial relation which connects them is a third entity. It follows, according to the pluralists, from this externality of the relations to the terms related, that things are now related and again unrelated. (The pen, for example, is not always in the grasp of the hand.)[1] But there is certainly a difficulty in this everyday conception of relation. For the alleged relation, R, which is conceived as external link between the terms m and n, is itself a third entity and, far from relating m and n, it has itself to be related to each of them. In Bradley's phrase, a so-called relation, external to given terms, can be 'nothing' to them.[2] It is simply another reality, a *tertium quid*, itself implying an unexplained relatedness to each of the terms m and n which it supposedly relates. And accordingly the search for relations involves us in an infinite and hopeless regress.[3]

(3) In the face of the failure of these pluralistic theories of relation, I find no resource save in the absolutist doctrine that the ultimately real relations are those of whole and part, of

[1] Contemporary realists, as everybody knows, conceiving knowledge as a kind of relation, teach that things are sometimes known and again unknown.

[2] *Appearance and Reality*, p. 32.

[3] Absolutists and pluralists alike too often overstress the infinite-regress consideration. Really, it is a mere corollary from the basal difficulty: the fact that a truly 'external' relation is inherently incapable of relating.

including and being included. The beings of the universe are, from this point of view, all of them parts of some including entity, and are thus related to each other only indirectly. The apparently external relations between things, people, and events are useful fictions based on the conception, contrary to reality, that such things, events, and people exist in ultimate independence and not rather as included parts.[1]

And now that I have come so far I inevitably go the last mile with the absolutist, agreeing with him that, however many the wholes or including entities, each must constitute a part of an ultimately all-including being, the Absolute. For any lesser including entities must themselves be related, seeing that they are (to say the least) alike and different; and thus, by the very argument just outlined, they must be parts of an all-including and self-related being.

I am well aware that most present-day philosophers, urged on by William James, L. P. Jacks, F. C. S. Schiller, and others, cry down this absolutistic argument as abstract speculation or futile 'logic-chopping.' But contemporary *Gestalt*-theory seems to have made this cavalier dismissal of the doctrine impossible by its experimentally grounded conception alike of thoughts and percepts and of physical objects as *Gestalten*, or configurations, unified wholes of subordinate parts, not mechanically added sums of independent units. A melody, for example, is, according to this view, a *Gestalt*. It includes a series of successive tones but it is not constituted by these tones, is not a mere aggregate of them, as is proved by the possibility of transposing the melody, thus losing all the specific tones but retaining the individual structure of the melody. In a word, the *Gestalt* is precisely the 'including whole' of the absolutist; and the Absolute is no more nor less than the supreme *Gestalt*.[2]

(*b*) This argument from relatedness, it must at once be admitted, leads me to the acknowledgment not of Absolute Self but merely

---

[1] On all this, cf. W. Stern, *Person und Sache*, pp. 147 ff, 165 ff, 256 ff.

[2] For a brief exposition of the *Gestalt-Theorie*, with references to the literature, cf. my "Critical Comments on the *Gestalt-Theorie*," *Psychological Review*, 1926, 33, 135–58.

of Absolute Being. In other words, through this argument I gain
no knowledge of the nature, mental or non-mental, of Absolute
Being. When, however, I combine the outcome of this relation-
argument, for the conception of the universe as absolute, with the
argument already outlined[1] for the universe as mental and therefore personal, then there emerges the well-grounded doctrine of
the absolutistic personalist. The fusion of the two conclusions,
the universe is personal and the universe is Absolute Being,
precipitates the doctrine that the universe is Absolute Self.[2]

ii. In the remainder of this paper I shall try first, to tell what
I mean by Absolute Self and second, to consider some at least of
the difficulties involved in the conception. (a) By Absolute Self
as absolute I understand, in the first place (1) all-including self:
no shred of reality however trivial, however futile, however base,
can be outside it. There can be no lazy motion of a moth's wing,
no whirl of dust along the highway, no stab of joy, or throb of pain,
or groping question which can fall outside the Absolute, the all-
including being. A corollary from this doctrine is that the Absolute is ultimately changeless. A changing being, Bergson's life
current for example, may indeed be conceived monistically as
including all lesser entities, but as changing it has an irrevocable
past, which is no longer, and a genuine future, which is not yet,
and it cannot therefore be thought to be literally all-inclusive.[3]
By Absolute Self, as absolute, I mean also (2) a One or unique
Whole of parts, not a sum of ultimately independent entities; I
mean a *Gestalt*, not an aggregate. Somewhat as a circle defines

---

[1] Cf. Section II of this paper.

[2] It is possible, indeed, to reach this conclusion by starting from the
conception of the universe as both absolute and mental. For a universe
conceived as mental *but impersonal* would consist in an aggregate of mental
phenomena instead of constituting an individual whole. A consistent
idealistic absolutist must accordingly conceive the Absolute as person.

Hegel and Bradley and my great teacher, Josiah Royce, are the
personal absolutists who have influenced me most. Bradley denies to the
Absolute the name 'self,' but none the less means by 'Absolute Experience'
precisely what the personal absolutist means by 'experiencer,' or 'self.'
The reasons for counting Hegel a personal absolutist are set forth in
Chapter X of my *Persistent Problems of Philosophy*.

[3] Cf. *Persistent Problems of Philosophy*, fifth edition, p. 440[2].

its sectors and is not made up or put together of them, so the Absolute determines the nature of the many included within it.

(*b*) The Absolute Person *as self* I describe as a conscious being; and by 'conscious' I must mean essentially what I mean when I describe myself as conscious. In other words I must hold that the Absolute Self genuinely perceives, thinks, feels, and wills.

Tumultuous objections to this doctrine, so baldly stated, press upon each other. They fall into two groups: difficulties involved in conceiving the universe as Absolute and difficulties inherent in regarding the universe as Self which includes selves. (1) The fundamental difficulty of the first type is stated as follows: Personality involves limitation and accordingly the Absolute, which means the Unlimited, cannot be conceived as self. This objection, in this general statement of it, I very briefly dismiss. For, like Hegel and Royce and many besides, I mean by 'absolute' not 'unlimited' but 'self-limited,' that is, limited-by-nothing-external-to-oneself. But my critic urges more specific objections. It is impossible, he insists, to conceive of Absolute Self—that is, of changeless, all-including self, unhampered and unthwarted from without—as sharing in certain of our human experiences, sensational and emotional—in our hearing and our smelling, for example, and in our grieving and our yearning. Yet, as the critic rightly insists, the very core of personal absolutism is the doctrine that every human experience is identically a part of, constituted by, the absolute experience. The Absolute must indeed have sense experience, must feel regret and longing else, in Royce's unforgettable phrase, he will be "less and not more than we are."[1] Two difficulties seem to me to be here involved: in the case of the sense experiences, that of attributing to Absolute Self that functioning of bodily organs which accompanies our sense perception; in the case of both the sensational and the emotional consciousness, the apparent necessity of conceiving Absolute Self as either passive or as thwarted. The first of these objections I may at once dismiss as implying the essentially

[1] *World and Individual*, ii, p. 364.

dualistic position already rejected.[1] The second of them, as it applies to sensation, is also readily met. For I can attribute to Absolute Self the qualitatively various sense experience—the seeing, hearing, and the like—and yet regard Him as creating, not passively receiving, these experiences. I cannot, however, so easily dispose of the difficulties centring in what may be called the baffled emotions. It does indeed seem on the face of it impossible to attribute sorrow or disappointment, yearning or doubt, to Absolute Self, that is, to the literally All-knowing Person whose will is expressed in the existent universe.

This crucial difficulty I do not mean to evade. But I believe that it is met, and can only be met, by the Hegelian conception, stressed and illuminated by Professor Royce, of the Absolute Person's sharing yet transcending the experience of the included, partial selves. I find no lack of human analogies. The sympathetic parent or older friend may genuinely feel a child's grief, affective quality, organic sensations and all, and yet transcend it by the confident realization, impossible to the child in its inexperience, of the grievous happening as itself a factor in a genuinely satisfying situation. And the good teacher will realize the precise questionings of his puzzled pupil; but will experience not only the questioning but the answer—will, in other words, share yet transcend his pupil's experience.[2]

This Roycian conception of sharing and also transcending experiences offers a clue to the solution of still other problems which I shall barely suggest. It may serve in the first place to reconcile the conception of Absolute Self as changeless with the equally essential doctrine that Absolute Self, as all-knower, experiences change. The critic urges that personal absolutism (and indeed absolutism of any sort) is incompatible with the admission of the experienced reality of change: what I directly

---

[1] I have briefly treated, in *Persistent Problems of Philosophy*, fifth edition, pp. 456 f, the specific question: Can Absolute Self be conceived to have sense-perceptions without a body? Or, on the other hand, can a body be attributed to Absolute Self?

[2] The Freudian conception of sublimation may perhaps be affiliated with this doctrine of transcendence.

know, the critic insists, of change, of progress, of dissolution, gives the lie to the assertion of a changeless Absolute. In reply, I admit that the Absolute Self shares this finite consciousness of pastness and futurity, but I add that He also transcends this awareness of change by knowing past and future alike as parts of a more-than-temporal whole.[1]

When I face the even more difficult problem concerning the goodness of Absolute Self, this conception of sharing-yet-transcending offers me at least a formula, indicates how, conceivably, the problem may be solved: On the one hand, I must regard the Absolute Person, just because He wills the all-of-reality, as willing the good, in the sense of the self-sufficient, object of will. And, on the other hand I cannot, if I would, deny the stark reality of ugliness, of stupidity, of anguish, and of sin. I must then, it appears, conceive of Absolute Self as genuinely experiencing, and indeed willing, ugliness, stupidity, anguish, and sin as real though subordinated parts of a whole, which, in its totality, is good. To the question: how can these horrors and brutalities constitute parts of a good I have indeed no specific answer. But the truth that Absolute, and thus all-powerful, Self wills them not for finite selves existing apart from Him but for Himself, the sharer of all experience, gives me metaphysical assurance that the question has its answer.[2]

(2) I turn to the criticisms of the second type, those which stress the incompatibility of this doctrine of the all-including absolute self with the experience which every man has of his own individuality. A man is no longer himself, my critic urges, if he is simply one part, one bit, one ingredient of a Great, all-devouring Self; and, conversely no real, individual self, infinite or finite, can be supposed in a literal sense to contain real persons, genuine individuals, as parts of itself. In the face of these objections I appeal, as my critic appeals, to human experience, but I read it with a difference. The everyday self, I protest, does experience himself as a sort of hierarchy of many partial selves, as includer of a reasoning and an impulsive self, of a conscientious and a

[1] Cf. Royce, *World and Individual*, ii, Lecture III.
[2] Cf. Royce, *The Spirit of Modern Philosophy*, Lecture XIII.

reckless self, of a business-like and a speculative self. In the words
of the old rhyme:

> Within my earthly temple there's a crowd,
> There's one of us that's humble, one that's proud;
> There's one in eager search for earthly pelf,
> And one who loves his neighbour as himself.
> There's one who's broken-hearted for his sins,
> And one who, unrepentant, sits and grins.

And the concluding verses express the naïve perplexity:

> From much corroding care I should be free
> If once I could determine which is me.

The personal absolutist holds precisely that no one of these
conflicting selves but the articulating whole of which they are
parts constitutes the human *me*; and that similarly all the human
selves may be and are parts of the One Self.

There remains the question: is not this conception of the
included self utterly incompatible with the experience of self as
individual? My reply presupposes in the first place the conviction
that to be individual is to be unique, to stand in a class by oneself,
to be irreplaceable by anything else, however similar; and, in
the second place, the belief that the objects of volitional and
emotional consciousness are always individuated.[1] By way of
these conceptions I achieve the metaphysical assurance that every
human self though indeed part of the Absolute Person, is a unique
part, individuated by absolute will and inviolably distinct from
every other embodiment of absolute purpose.

In brief and arid outline I have indicated the outcome of my
metaphysical thinking.[2] I have devoted the greater number of

---

[1] Cf. Royce, *The Conception of God*, edition of 1897, Appendix, pp. 273 ff,
294, 304.

[2] I have throughout been hampered by the fact that I have recently,
in far greater detail and with more explicit reference to other systems,
attempted a similar statement. To this fuller discussion, in the last chapter
of the last edition (1925) of my *Persistent Problems of Philosophy*, I venture
to refer any reader of this paper who may find in it too summary a statement of personal absolutism.

my pages to the development, first, of the idealism and, next, of the absolutistic personalism which distinguish my conclusions from many systems of contemporary metaphysical doctrine. But I am eager at the end to stress once more the point to which at the start I called attention: the wide acceptance by modern philosophers of the first article of my philosophic creed: the doctrine that mental realities exist. In my opinion, philosophers nowadays greatly underestimate the significance alike of this doctrine and of the relative unanimity with which it is held. I urgently invite all such realists as assert the existence of mental beings to make common cause with idealists of every type against the materialism which, under different names, presumes to deny the experienced reality of the mental life.

PRINCIPAL PUBLICATIONS

Psychological

An Introduction to Psychology. (The Macmillan Co., 1901. Pp. xv +
509. Second edition, 1905.)

A First Book in Psychology. (The Macmillan Co., 1910. Fourth
revised edition, 1914. Pp. xxi + 428.)

"The Self in Scientific Psychology," *American Journal of Psychology,*
vol. xxvi, pp. 495–524. 1915.

"The Truly Psychological Behaviorism," *Psychological Review,* vol.
xxviii, pp. 1–18. 1921.

Philosophical

The Persistent Problems of Philosophy. (The Macmillan Co., 1907.
Fifth edition, with new chapter on Twentieth Century Philosophy, 1925. Pp. xxvi + 601.)

The Good Man and The Good. (The Macmillan Co., 1918. Pp. xx
+ 219.)

"The Order of the Hegelian Categories in the Hegelian Argument,"
Mind, vol. xii, N.S., pp. 317–40. 1903.

"The Idealist to the Realist," *Journal of Philosophy,* vol viii,
pp. 449–58. 1911.

"Henri Bergson: Personalist," *Philosophical Review,* vol. xxi,
pp. 666–75. 1912.

"The Foundation in Royce's Philosophy for Christian Theism,"
Philosophical Review, vol. xxv, pp. 282–98. 1916.

"The Personalistic Conception of Nature," *Philosophical Review,*
vol. xxviii, pp. 115–46. 1919.

"The New Rationalism and Objective Idealism," *Philosophical
Review,* vol. xxviii, pp. 598–605. 1919.

"The Dual Rôle of the Mind in the Philosophy of S. Alexander,"
Mind, vol. xxxii, N.S., pp. 197–210, 1923.

"On Certain Difficulties in the Modern Doctrine of Essence," *Journal
of Philosophy,* vol. xxiii, pp. 701–10. 1926.

"Value: Primarily a Psychological Conception," *The Journal of
Philosophical Studies,* vol. iii, pp. 413–26, 1928.

THE FAITH OF A LOGICIAN

By MORRIS R. COHEN

Born 1880; Professor of Philosophy, College of the City of New York.

THE FAITH OF A LOGICIAN

A. S. M. Amico delectissimo.

ALL autobiography, as Goethe realized, must inevitably contain a
mixture of fiction with its truth. Our views as to our past development cannot but be moulded by our present beliefs. But for that
very reason autobiography is one of the ways of exhibiting one's
fundamental beliefs. The assigning of motives is always a somewhat arbitrary procedure—many conflicting ones are equally
plausible. But when one has little space to develop adequately
the logical reasons which seem to support one's main positions,
it is convenient to fall back on the form of a personal confession
of faith with an indication of the motives which led to that faith.

EDUCATION AND THE SEARCH FOR A
FUNDAMENTAL PRINCIPLE

If philosophy is viewed broadly as the love of wisdom or general
knowledge, I may say that such a love was awakened in me between my seventh and tenth year by my grandfather, a poor
tailor in the Russian town of Nesviesh. Though he never learned
to write and had only a moderate reading knowledge of Hebrew,
he had become the master of an extraordinary amount of knowledge and wisdom. Walks and talks with him first stimulated my
imagination about the world at large and its history. From him,
also, I acquired a certain ineradicable admiration for the ascetic
virtues and a scorn for the life of wealth, ease, creature comforts,
and all that goes under the old name of worldliness.

For the rest I had a rather varied education. I began, like other
orthodox Hebrew boys, with the Bible, and then went on to the
Talmud. The first non-religious book which I read was a Hebrew
copy of Josephus. When, in 1890, I was sent back to live with my
mother in the larger city of Minsk, I began to read Yiddish books
on Hebrew history and soon drifted into very secular romances.
In 1892 I was brought to New York, and in 1895 I entered the
scientific course of its City College, where, in addition to mathe-

matics, physics, chemistry, and biology, I learned to appreciate French literature.

Possibly the circumstances of my youth, which prevented me from participating in the usual boyish games, emphasized my inclination to indulge in idle or disinterested speculation. In any case, my own limited experience is in accord with the Aristotelian view that philosophy grows out of our native curiosity or wonder about the world at large. To philosophize has always seemed to me as natural and desirable in itself as to sing, to dance, to paint, or mould, or to commune with those we love.

Nevertheless the specific occasion which led me into technical philosophy was my interest in the Socialist Labour Party. Wishing to prepare ourselves for more active and intelligent propaganda, a small group of us, young college students, read Marx's *Das Kapital* and other socialist classics. The references in Marx and Engels to Hegel's dialectic method gripped me most emphatically. My courses in logic and economics at college had led me to J. S. Mill, and I felt that the fundamental issue between individualism and socialism was inextricably bound up with the difference between the psychologic and inductive method represented by Mill and the dialectic and historical method of Marx and Engels. Not having any competent guide to philosophy, I naïvely turned to Hegel himself and tried to get enlightenment from an English translation of the third part of the *Logic*. This, of course, was too tough a diet for a philosophic babe. Yet I could not abandon the quest. I had a vague conviction that there was something radically wrong with Mill's doctrine of induction and his attempt to build up a world out of independent things, facts, or "states of mind." After all, somehow or other, things *are* intimately connected in the same universe, and, indeed, they often fuse their very being. Though I could not grasp the exact force of Hegel's argument, it became associated in my mind with Shelley's lines:

> Nothing in this world is single,
> All things by a law divine
> In each other's being mingle . . .

My search for more definite enlightenment along this line led me to the neo-Hegelian school; and the books which afforded me most food for reflection were Watson's *Comte, Mill and Spencer*, and Dewey's *Psychology*. They confirmed my aversion for the positivists and for their superficial efforts to dispose of the problems of reality. Yet I could not accept the constructive claims of the neo-Hegelian philosophy. I had a strong repugnance to a certain vague, supernatural element in it that is incompatible with the spirit of the natural sciences, which have always seemed to me man's supreme achievement in the way of solid knowledge. The intellectual world was thus divided for me into two camps, and I could not be at peace in either. I therefore fell into a slough of philosophic despond from which desultory reading and agonized efforts at original thought could not extricate me.

In the spring of 1899 I gained the friendship of Thomas Davidson. His personal affection and his touchingly unrestrained faith in my abilities increased my zest in life and in philosophic study. He aroused in me the great dream of a group of congenial spirits co-operating to create a philosophic encyclopedia that should do for the culture of the twentieth century what the Brothers of Sincerity did for the Saracen culture of the 10th or what Bayle, D'Alembert, and Diderot did for the culture of the eighteenth century. My heart was thus set on the systematic and comprehensive aspect of philosophy and I was led to read generally along diverse lines. With the poverty of time and energy at my disposal then, and for many years after, the distension of my interests filled my intellectual life with many enterprises that just fell short of completion. Davidson himself, at that time, held to an extreme subjectivism and individualism which neither gratitude nor personal admiration could induce me to accept. At his suggestion I turned from the problems of socialism and metaphysics to the problem of knowledge as dealt with by Hume and Kant. The reading of Hume left me with a profound admiration for the clarity and honesty of his scepticism as to various metaphysical and religious dogmas; but in addition to being a little irritated by that genial Tory's attitude to the rational principles of moral and political reform, his fundamental position seemed to me to involve flat contradictions. If the mind is assumed to know its own impressions only, it cannot logically know that there is an external world that produces or causes these impressions. The relation between such an external world and the impressions of the mind certainly does not conform to Hume's own description of causality as the habitual succession of impressions *in* our mind. The contradiction between the practical certainty and the theoretic scepticism as to the existence of the external world (expressed at the end of the first book of Hume's Treatise) seemed to me to arise only because he had assumed both that the mind knows nothing but its own impressions and that we also know that our individual mind is only one among other objects in the universe. Obviously, if the second assumption is true, the first is false; and as the assumption of the existence of the larger world is involved in our very discussion, the mind cannot be limited to a knowledge of its own impressions only. That which is known is always more than the mere (subjective) knowing activity itself, else there could be no present recognition of past thoughts.

The effort to understand Kant's solution to Hume's problem was interrupted at that time by the necessity of helping to organize and, after Davidson's death in 1900, to continue the practical educational work which he hoped to develop into a Breadwinners' College. For a number of years I thus conducted classes in cultural history, in which I tried to apply the evolutionary philosophy to the history of industry, of the family, of religion, and of Greek and Hebrew literature. The reading of some of Professor Boas's anthropologic writings, however, soon raised doubts as to the adequacy of any formula of universal evolution, whether Hegelian or Spencerian. The discovery that our histories always depend upon our assumption as to the nature of the things studied, led me to reject the prevalent illusion that the history or temporal genesis of anything can enable us to dispense with the direct study or analysis of its present nature. The history of labour, marriage, and religion, while extending my vista, offered me no solution of their contemporary problems. Historicism, as well as psychologism, were thus ruled out for me as all-sufficient philosophic methods or as substitutes for direct rational and metaphysical analysis. In this I was strengthened by the study of Aristotle, begun in the Davidson Society and continued for two years under Professor Woodbridge. Studies in ethics under Professor Felix Adler also brought me back to my original conviction—to wit, that the problems of individual and social ethics were honeycombed with metaphysical assumptions.

It was the study of Russell's *Principles of Mathematics,* some months after I was appointed to teach mathematics at the City College, that finally liberated me from the feeling of helpless philosophic bewilderment and enabled me to undertake an independent journey. The demonstration that pure mathematics asserts only logical implications and that such logical implications or relations cannot be identified with either psychologic or physical events, but are involved as determinants of both, seemed to me to offer a well-grounded and fruitful starting-point for philosophy. For whatever the opinions of philosophers, they must rely on the validity of logical reasoning to establish their position; and at no time could I take seriously any attempt to question the fruitfulness of mathematical method in building up scientific knowledge. This renewed faith in logic and mathematics showed me how to avoid both the Scylla of Mill's inductive empiricism and the Charybdis of Hegelian absolutism. An inadequate view of the reality of relations or abstract universals still seems to me the common vice of both these influential philosophies. (1) Empiricism (the modern name for nominalism) never seemed to me to account for the real connections in the world. How can relations, if they exist in the mind only, connect things external to it? Moreover what can we say about any fact or thing that does not involve abstractions as determinations? (2) Similarly does the Hegelian denial of the reality of abstractions lead to the location of connections not in an objective nature but in an absolute totality that is beyond understanding. While such an absolute totality may be an ideal demand of thought, its content is always something of which we are most ignorant. Nothing is therefore really explained by it.

The doctrine that abstract logical or mathematical relations are real justified for me the hypothetico-deductive procedure of science in which we follow the implications or effects of one single aspect or factor of a situation. For not all things that occur together are relevant to each other. Scientific search is difficult just because of the exuberant multiplicity of existential coincidences, which are irrelevant to our inquiry as to the order of meaning. But if scientific inquiry is successful it discovers abstract relations which do characterize the world of phenomena. Thus instead of the alternative of either swallowing the whole universe or starving intellectually, the method of logical realism showed me how to bite into it.

In subsequent reflection this metaphor of "biting into the world" proved itself peculiarly apt in suggesting that opposing considerations must be taken into account in explaining anything, and indeed that nothing is definite apart from both of every pair of polar categories such as form and matter, identity and difference, mediacy and immediacy, etc. The reality of mathematical relations, and the principle of polarity, opened for me the path to systematic philosophy.

LOGICAL REALISM

The discovery of the logical or hypothetical character of pure mathematics showed me in a new and clear light the relation of scientific method to induction, to scepticism, and to a priori rationalism. This led me to a better understanding of the old and fundamental issue of conceptualism (or subjectivism) versus realism.

Mill's contention that the truths of mathematics were approximations or inductions from experience became impossible after the distinction had been drawn between physics as a science of existence and pure mathematics as the development of the logical implications of *all* kinds of assumptions. That there are no two rational numbers whose ratio is $\sqrt{2}$ or π, is not and cannot be an induction from experience. Experience alone cannot prove the absolute impossibility of things that have not as yet occurred.

This disposed of the absolutistic nihilism (which may call itself empiricism, relativism, or scepticism) that denies the existence of all necessary truths and tries to maintain that even propositions like "2 plus 2 equals 4" are contingent so that on some other planet the result might be different. One does not have to go to another planet to see that two pints of water and two pints of alcohol will not necessarily make four pints of the mixture. But the hypothetical truths of pure mathematics are not affected by empirical physical facts that do not conform to its postulated conditions. The truth of the proposition that "two and two equals four" (assuming the usual definition and postulates of arithmetic) is not a question of physical observation, nor of psychologic habit, but of logical proof. It can be demonstrated that its denial involves self-contradiction, and thus cannot maintain itself. It cannot, therefore, be true that all assertions are merely personal opinions; or if you call them opinions, it is certainly true that the opinion "2 plus 2 equals 5" is not as true as "2 plus 2 equals 4."

However, the same realization of the logical and hypothetical nature of pure mathematics also destroyed classical a priori rationalism. It destroyed the ground of any assertion that we know a priori and with apodeictic certainty that physical space must be Euclidean, just as the development of modern physics has rendered vain Kant's further argument that we know a priori that physical nature must follow Newtonian laws of mechananics. Indeed, renewed faith in formal logic showed me that since all proof rests on assumption, it is vain for any philosophy to pretend to prove all of its material propositions. It must make indemonstrable assumptions in regard to existence, value, or duty. This is particularly cogent against Kant's transcendental method, i.e. the attempt to prove certain propositions true because they explain how experience is possible. We cannot explain experience or anything else without assuming something; and it is a downright logical fallacy to assert that because our assumptions explain something they are therefore demonstrably true. Obviously Kant does not and cannot offer any cogent proof that there may not be some other set of assumptions which will also explain the facts of experience.

That an assumption is not proved is, of course, not an argument against its truth. So long, also, as assumptions differ there will be ground for preferring the one that best explains the assumed facts. But the recognition of possible alternative assumptions bankrupts the pretension that philosophic assertions are all necessary and not merely probable truths. Doctrines as to the material nature of the world or of our duties in it can thus never be more than merely probable.

The principles or laws of every science are the rules or constant relations which hold amidst all the changes in its field; and so the fundamental laws or postulates of pure mathematics or logic are the invariant forms or relations which hold of all possible objects.[1] Logical laws are thus neither physical nor mental, but the laws of all possible significant being. No material fact can be deduced from purely formal considerations, but formal relations are assumed in inferring any fact from any others, and indeed no fact can be formulated except in terms of the forms or universal relations embodied in it. The world which is the object of science (since all science involves logic) is thus a union of form and matter. It is rational in the sense that its phenomena do conform to the laws of possibility that are the objects of logic; but the element of chance or contingency can never be eliminated from it, since all proof must rest on unproved assumptions. The world may also be said to contain an irrational element in the sense that all form is the form of something which cannot be reduced to form alone. The duality or polarity of terms and relations cannot be eliminated by reducing everything to terms alone, or to relations alone. We may say that everything which is intelligible can be expressed in logical form; but that which is expressible has no valid claim to absolute totality. Nor is there any contradiction in speaking of the inexpressible, since it is of the essence of all expression to point to something beyond itself.

THE PRINCIPLE OF POLARITY

The principle of polarity is suggested by the phenomena of magnetism where north and south pole are always distinct,

[1] I have tried to show this in greater detail in the *Journal of Philosophy*, vol. 8 (1911), pp. 533 ff., and vol. 15 (1918).

opposed, yet inseparable. We can see it in general physics where
there is no action without reaction, no force or cause of change
without inertia or resistance. In biology the life of every organism
involves action and reaction with an environment. There is no
growth without decay, or as Huxley puts it, protoplasm manages
to live only by continually dying. This suggests a supplement to
the principle of causality. Not only must every natural event have
a cause which determines that it should happen, but the cause
must be opposed by some factor which prevents it from producing
any greater effect than it actually does. A physical or chemical
system has the precise rate of change that it has, an organism
attains its specific form at any moment, a social movement has
just the effect or influence which it in fact has, because of the
presence of certain opposing or balancing factors necessary to
produce the definite result.

From this point of view not only every static, but also every
kinetic system, involves a balance or equilibrium which makes
description in the form of equations applicable. Of course it is
only when the elements are measurable and thus numerically
formulated that equations can generally be employed in a fruitful
way. But it should be noted (1) that exact or mathematical
reasoning is not restricted to quantity, but is applicable in non-
quantitative realms like group theory or analysis situs, and (2)
that quantitative determination is but one way of eliminating the
indetermination of such descriptions as A is hot, A is cold, A is
large, A is small, etc. Statements such as A is 60° F. or 5 yds.
include the truth of opposite partial statements and assert
something definite and determinate in relation to all compar-
able objects.

The principle of polarity, of necessary opposition in all determinate effects, thus becomes a heuristic principle directing our
inquiry in the search for adequate explanations. Hence, if we pass
from the realm of natural events, where reigns the principle of
causality, to the wider realm of all possible objects of consideration governed by the principle of sufficient reason, our principle
of polarity becomes a supplement to the latter. It then asserts
that in all determination there are opposing elements or categories,

such as unity and plurality, identity and difference, activity and passivity.

The obvious value of the principle of polarity is in enabling us to avoid one-sided and interminable (because indeterminate) issues, and in making us more hospitable to the complexity of seemingly paradoxical facts, such as that we rest alternately on our feet while walking or that we remain the same while growing or changing. All this is of the utmost importance in metaphysics or general philosophy where we are subject to two great temptations: (1) to hasty generalization about objects like the universe, which are not as determinate as is commonly supposed; and (2) to deny the vision of others who see things from a different point of view.

(1) The question of the indeterminateness of the absolute or total universe will occupy us later. At present it is well to note that while reality has many elements and everything is held in place by opposite forces working at the same time, our thought and expression is linear, i.e. we think and write along one line at a time. (2) That the great philosophers are generally right in what they assert (of their own vision) and wrong in what they deny (of the vision of others) was recognized by Leibniz. In any case we must be both critical and sympathetic toward the philosophy of others, and avoid both the blindness of excessive partisanship and the mushiness of eclecticism typified by those soapy minds that, when confronted by the choice between heaven and hell, hope to combine the good points of each.

The effort to eliminate false alternatives or one-sided views is characteristic of the Hegelian philosophy. Yet the principle of polarity is not the same as that of the Hegelian dialectic. In the first place the distinction between the formal and the material, between logical categories and historical existences, removes the Hegelian confusion in which concrete things seem to be generated in time either by ghostly conflicts or by sublimated matings of abstract categories. Novelty in concrete being cannot be generated by the combination of pure abstract forms. This objection may be taking Hegel's metaphors too literally; but the confusion needs to be eliminated in any case. In the second place the principle of polarity leads to a more emphatic denial of identity between

opposite categories like being and non-being. The opposition
between contrary categories is neither absorbed nor in any way
transcended by their unity, any more than abstract unity can be
generated by abstract difference. The opposing considerations involved in all existences (like the north and south pole of a magnet)
are different aspects which never become identical though they
necessarily coexist. Nor does the fact that they are only phases of
concrete existences make them in any significant sense unreal.
(We can, of course, define the real as that which exists only as
concrete; but then the proposition that the abstract is not in this
sense real becomes a mere tautology.)

So long as significant wholes involve diverse parts, the latter
are to the scientific vision just as real or valid as the former. On
the other hand, since absolute totality is an ideal limit in some
respects never actually attained, the parts are psychologically
more real or vivid than the whole. If abstractions are parts of any
possibly existing world, statements about these parts need not be
false. Partial truths are not simply false; for in the effort to attain
truth, false statements must be eliminated, but partial truths
need only to be supplemented.

The principle of sufficient reason on which we rely doubtless
postulates a world in which different things are more or less
connected. But the ideal totality does not exist in nature at any
one time nor even as any actuality of knowledge. It is a necessary
ideal to indicate the direction of our scientific effort, but it cannot
serve as an explanation of any particular thing in it.

Under the head of polarities we may distinguish between
contradictions, antinomies, and aporias or difficulties. Strictly
speaking, contradictions are always dialectical, i.e. they hold
only in a logical universe. Thus if I say a house is thirty years old,
and someone else says it is thirty-one years old, the two statements are contradictory in the sense that both cannot possibly
be true at the same time and in the same respect. Both statements, however, can certainly be true if we draw a distinction,
e.g. thirty-one years since the beginning and thirty years since
the completion of its building.

Thus two statements which, taken abstractly, are contradictory may both be true of concrete existence provided they can be assigned to separate domains or aspects. A plurality of aspects is an essential trait of things in existence. Determinate existence thus continues free from self-contradiction because there is a distinction between the domains in which these opposing statements are each separately true. When opposing statements are completed by reference to the domains wherein they are true, there is no logical difficulty in combining them. In the purely logical or mathematical field, however, we deal not with complexes of existence, but with abstract determinations as such. Here two contradictory assertions always produce a resultant which is zero, i.e. the entity of which they are asserted is absolutely impossible.

Of incompletely determined existence—as in the case of the total universe—contradictory propositions do not annihilate each other (since they refer to a complex of existences); and yet they cannot always (because of the indefiniteness of the subject) be reconciled with each other. This gives rise to the antinomies of metaphysics.

In general, the opposite statements that are true in regard to existing things give rise to difficulties when we cannot see how to draw the proper distinction which will enable us to reconcile and combine these seeming contradictions. Thus we frequently find certain facts in a scientific realm calling for one theory, e.g. the corpuscular theory of light, and other facts calling for a diametrically opposite one, viz. the wave theory. Such difficulties are solved either by discovering new facts, which give one of these theories a preponderance, or else by discovering a way of combining the two theories. Sometimes an intellectual dilemma is avoided by rejecting both alternatives. This is illustrated by the old difficulty as to whether language was a human invention or a special revelation. The difficulty was avoided by introducing the concept of natural growth.

Nature also presents us with seeming impossibilities in the form of practical difficulties, e.g. how to live long without getting old, how to eat our cake and yet have it too, etc. Such contingent or physical impossibilities may baffle us for ever. Yet some of them may be solved by finding the proper distinction. Thus the invention of boats enabled us to eliminate a former impossibility —namely, how to cross a river without getting wet.

This analysis puts us on guard against two opposite evil intellectual habits: on the one hand to regard real difficulties as absolute impossibilities, and on the other to belittle such difficulties by calling them false alternatives. Thus it is not sufficient to say that the old controversy between the claims of the active and those of the contemplative life represents a false alternative and that we need both. It is, in fact, most frequently impossible to follow both, and the actual problem of how much of one we need to sacrifice to the other often requires more knowledge than is at our disposal.

The Universe as an Absolute Totality

The fact that we can speak of the Universe and can refer to *it* naturally inclines us to emphasize its unity. It is, however, possible to speak of a heap of things that have no bond except that of being together in a given space. Whether the universe, as the totality of all things actual and possible, has a greater unity than a merely spatial one, we are, in view of the fragmentary character of our knowledge, in no position to answer. We do not even know with certainty whether the universe includes a finite or an infinite number of material particles. Because of its essential incompleteness we can form no definite image of it.

The universe cannot be made definite by distinguishing it from something outside of it. Nor can it be made complete and definite by showing the order or pattern which prevails through it, since all sorts of incompatible patterns and lack of order are also found in it. The universe is obviously not completely or actually in existence at any one time. It contains many abstract possibilities which are not physically compossible, so that when some of them are realized, others become impossible. If the chaos of illusions and contradictory possibilities are said to exist in the mind only, they are not thereby banished from the universe, since the mind exists in it; and if we define existence in such a way that illusions are said not to exist, all illusions will not be thereby eliminated. The realm of existence may by definition be restricted to some orderly cosmos, but the universe will continue to include many other things besides.

This indefiniteness in what is denoted by the term universe, as an absolute totality without qualification, makes all sorts of contrary propositions true of it.

The universe is neither given in experience nor is it a mental construction; yet it is certainly in some sense given.

The totality of all things is obviously not given in sense perception. What is so given is always something occupying some part of time and space. Obviously the total universe includes more than we can ever perceive or form into an image. Our experiences taper off into the indefinite, but in any case no finite number of them can give us an absolute totality. Neither can the universe be a mental construction. The extent and complexity of the world is beyond our power of synthesis. We cannot think of all the possible relations of even a finite number of entities, and the number of possible qualifications of our world is endless.

Yet it is impossible to maintain that nothing at all exists, or to deny that there is a world in some some sense or other.

Out of this and similar dilemmas we can extricate ourselves only by recognizing that "the world" is a symbol for something not completely determinate. It is partly known, but also always involves the unknown. Any part of the latter may become known, but never the whole of it. Part of the universe exists, but many more parts do not. Many parts of the universe are determined, but so long as plurality, individuality, and novelty are not denied, contingency or indetermination is uneliminable. Part of the universe is material and part is mental. But any assertion that all is matter or that all is mind amounts to a violent resolution to use an old word in a new and confusing way to include its negative. For consider the difference between the house we live in and the house we dream of. Whether you say both are material or both are mental, the factual difference remains and is accounted for by neither of the monistic assertions about the universe.

Similar antinomies hold with regard to the assertion that the universe is changing and that it remains identical. Stated positively the universe is an ideal, in the sense that it indicates the direction in which the full nature of things is to be found. It is present formally not actually. As present it includes all unreality, illusion, etc., which in a certain sense do form the content of the world, even if we define existence to exclude them as unreal.

Philosophy of Nature

The two poles of philosophic interests are the macroscopic and the microscopic, the infinite totality of everything (*the* universe), and the ultimate elements which enter into anything. Logicians may be most passionately interested in the larger vistas, but a faith in truth similar to that of Browning's Grammarian makes them devote themselves to the minuter problems.

Is the world one or many? Both the continuity and discreteness of things stare us in the face; and monists and pluralists differ because they fail to do justice to both of these aspects of nature. Since every proposition (A is B) involves elements that are different and yet in some way identical, there is no hope for philosophy unless it recognizes that identity and difference while logically different are existentially inseparable in the nature of anything. The classical philosophers, impressed by the logic of identity, naturally belittled the importance of change which introduces diversity into the nature of the things that change. Modernistic philosophers stress the fact of change so as to ignore those elements of unity or identity without which things cannot be said to change. Common sense is shocked by the idea of change without anything that changes; and logic reconciles change and constancy by saying that the nature of anything is the group of invariant relations which remain the same through the change.

As a result of the progress of modern physics and biology many of the formerly assumed constancies of nature, like the eternity of the hills or the fixity of species, have disappeared. But science has also discovered invariable order in changes which formerly seemed chaotic and arbitrary.

If change is essential to the constitution of natural or temporal objects it follows that they cannot be adequately described in terms of what they actually or sensibly are at any moment. The actual dominates us sensibly and vitally, but it is only an infinitesimal part of the larger world of possibilities. The nature of anything must include its possibilities. The danger of taking possibilities seriously, however, is that of thinking of them as if they were thin copies or ghosts of actual things floating in space.

The fact that things change according to some order gives rise to the idea of determinism and causality. But if anything is to be affected by something else, it must be distinct from that other. It must, then, have a realm which is not due to, or affected by, that other. A genuinely pluralistic world cannot be completely determined in all respects. The general impression that the discovery of laws by the natural sciences rules out the element of chance or contingency from our world is shown to be erroneous by the following considerations:

(1) The most thoroughgoing mechanism necessarily involves contingent data. If you derive the present arrangement of particles in the universe from a previous one by assuming some law, you push back the contingency to the past arrangement. Mechanical forces cannot be supposed to operate except on a given distribution of material particles. The contingency of such distribution cannot be eliminated by an infinite regress.

(2) Every physical law asserts that a certain phenomenon or characteristic of it depends on a limited number of factors and on nothing else. There is no use in saying that temperature and pressure determine the freezing-point, if the latter depends upon everything else. Every law of dependence thus implies independence of all other things, which are thus irrelevant to the given effect.

(3) The ultimate laws of nature are themselves contingent. They just happen to be. Any one law or reason from which they might all be derived (which is logically impossible) would itself be contingent, without any proof that it might not have been different. The derivation of most of our laws cannot eliminate all contingency, and the existence of a different world is always a theoretically significant alternative.

The insistence that the search for scientific law presupposes elements of independence as well as dependence in nature, aids us against vicious forms of atomism, organicism, and mysticism. Atomism is vicious if it makes every entity a complete and independent universe, in disregard of its relations to other entities. We see much vicious atomism in individualistic anarchism and in pleas for irresponsible self-expression. Vicious organicism is the refusal to note any relative independence or externality of relations between things which happen to be juxtaposed in our universe. It shows itself in the persistent tendency to confuse every line of clear thought by appeal to a vague totality which is irrelevant to the point at issue. Mysticism is vicious or obscurantist if it denies the definite or determinate character of things in the interest of beliefs that cannot stand the light of reason.

Teleology and *Vitalism.* The belief that independence, contingency, and spontaneity in nature are not inconsistent with genuine laws or invariant relations (strengthened in me by the writings of C. S. Peirce) does not justify the use of final causes by vitalists to deny the scientific fruitfulness of physico-chemical explanations in biology. It is perfectly legitimate to describe organic and even inorganic phenomena from the point of view of the consequent so that the antecedent seems a means. But we must be on guard against attributing conscious effort and intention to nature when there is no adequate evidence for their actual existence. It is tempting to describe the behaviour of organisms in terms of self-preservation; but it is equally legitimate to describe the life of every individual as a successful effort to attain death. The circulation of the blood in the human body is one of the necessary conditions of its consciousness, but consciousness is not a necessary condition for the circulation of the blood. Most of the arguments used by Driesch, Bergson, and other vitalists against possible progress in the physical explanation of biologic facts seem to me demonstrably erroneous. But at best they would only prove that in regard to certain phases of life we must remain in ignorance. Bergson's attempts to explain specific biologic phenomenon (such as the supposed similarity of structure between the eye of the scallop and the vertebrate eye) by means of "life as a whole," conflicts with the rule of scientific method that specific effects must be explained by specific causes. Nor will the hypothetical "psychoids" and similar entities of Driesch and others stand the test of scientific verification. The phenomena of life are assuredly different from those of non-living nature; but there is no proof that life did not arise (or may not now be arising) out of non-living material. And there is no good reason why the scientific methods which have proved fruitful in the inorganic sciences should not be tried in the field of biology. Popular teleologic evolutionism, in which man appears at the top of a biologic ladder that all other organisms are trying to mount, seems to me romantic vanity. That many species—indeed all vertebrates—have originated in simpler forms seems historically clear. But there is no law of evolution that all organisms must change in a given direction. Protozoa and vast numbers of other "lower" forms do not seem to have changed since the beginning of geologic time. Indeed, experimental biology does not need the concept of evolution at all. When it clings to it, it is only out of verbal piety.

The study of biology should also impress us with the discontinuity of nature. For without such discontinuity we could not recognize different species.

Mind and Body

The rejection, in my youth, of the whole supernatural world-view left no room for the mind or soul as an entity existing apart from the body. I have never been able to imagine what mental life apart from any body can possibly be. All sensations, feelings, emotions, etc., seem to me to be events in a body, and to involve consciousness of that body. If, then, the rejection of the belief in ghosts or disembodied spirits be materialism, I should call myself a materialist like Democritus, Hobbes, and Spinoza. Such materialism makes me reject the fundamental assumption of Freud and others who talk of purely mental determinism. Mental life is spasmodic and interrupted so that it lacks the continuity for the direct application of the causal relation. It is doubtless true that worry and other emotions will have serious bodily effects. But the cause of these bodily effects can be found in the bodily accompaniments of the emotions. It is therefore only in a popular and practical, but not in a scientifically accurate, sense that we can speak of the mind as exerting efficient causality. The sense of mental efficiency is an indication of vitality. But the laws of causality operate just as truly when we are not mentally very efficient.

I must reject with some vehemence the view of those materialists or behaviourists who think that the existence of conscious phenomena can be denied or adequately described in purely physical terms. Consciousness, when it happens, is a real addition to the phenomena of nature. It is unlike anything else. How it originates and what sustains it seem to me to be empirical and not metaphysical questions.

The popular notion that materialism has been refuted by the theory that atoms are composed of electrons seems to me rather fatuous. Natural science must remain materialistic in the sense that it must always reject explanations of material phenomena in terms of disembodied spirits or other unverifiable entities.

The form of materialism that is objectionable to science and which has been refuted by philosophers since Plato is that of nominalism, which denies the reality of relations or logical connection between things. For purposes of certain analyses it is convenient to regard matter as entirely inert; but reflection shows that a material world must necessarily involve some spontaneity; and there is no a priori reason why life and mind may not develop in it. All we need to remember is that our conception of the material world must include the possibility of such development.

Mind is often considered, not as a natural existence or function of an individual organism, but abstractly as when we speak of the mind of an age or nation. We thus speak of science as a spiritual body to which different individuals contribute. As a natural existence, however, science appears as a complex of books, apparatus, the memories of individual organisms, etc.

ETHICS

From a naturalistic point of view the whole life of the human species is a minor episode in the history of a tiny speck of cosmic dust; and man's natural fate is determined by forces which visit death and destruction upon the just and the unjust. Yet logically the problem of ethics is just as legitimate as the problem of physics. In both cases we may be said to begin with a set of primitive judgments—in the first case that certain things exist and in the second case that they are good or ought to be. We deal with these judgments scientifically if we examine them critically and elaborate them in the form of a rational system determined by principles. The greater difficulties of a theory of ethics are due to the greater variability of man's moral judgments and their dependence on all sorts of conventions which differ according to time and place. Diverse peoples who agree in condemning murder, incest, theft, etc., as immoral do not necessarily mean the same thing by these terms. Christians who accept the command "thou shalt not kill," do not think it wrong to do it at the command of a military officer. Few see anything wrong in long-distance killing, e.g. in our starving other peoples like the Chinese by monopolizing the fertile lands that keep us in luxury. The Old Testament horror of incest does not touch Abraham's marrying his half-sister.

Moral feelings are very strong, but this does not prevent them from appearing as irrational taboos to those who do not share our conventions. This should warn us against the tendency to make ethical philosophy an apology or justification of the conventional customs that happen to be established. Suppose that someone were to offer our country a wonderfully convenient mechanism, but demand in return the privilege of killing thousands of our people every year. How many of those who would indignantly refuse such a request will condemn the use of the automobile now that it is already with us?

On the other hand, there can be no moral appeal except to some desire that persists. The most rabid amoralist like Nietzsche must appeal to his reader's sense as to what is desirable; and the followers of Karl Marx, who boasted that he never spoke of justice, would be dumb and ineffective if they could not appeal to a hatred for the injustice of our present economic order.

These reflections lead me to the rejection, not only of the

Hebrew idea of moral laws as commands of Yahveh, but also the Kantian view of specific moral rules (such as that against lying) as absolute or categorical imperatives. It leads me to the Aristotelian conception of ethical judgments as matters of wisdom in the conduct of life. Specific ethical rules are lessons as to what is good, illumined by past experience and therefore subject to correction and revision. This saves us from fanaticism and such hideous insensibility as is involved in Kant's condemnation of a lie told to save an innocent life from a foul murder. The naturalistic view of morals also carries with it a greater regard for natural desires. The moral life must, to be sure, be one of discipline and self-restraint, if like any other art it is to achieve anything. Restraints on natural impulses are, however, good only if, like the restraints on public traffic, they make possible a greater freedom and a maximum of natural satisfaction of our heart's desire. At the same time I cannot completely accept hedonism. The virtues of the hero and the martyr point to the incommensurability of certain moral values, and this offers insuperable difficulties to any calculus of pleasures. Nor can I accept indiscriminate altruism or love of humanity as an adequate principle of all moral life. It is neither possible to love all mankind—I cannot love my neighbour's wife and children as my own—nor would it be good to do so. We can only love what is lovable; and the philosopher must not forget that everything that is morally vile arises out of human nature. If all our natural impulses were good, all training and education would be needless restraint and evil. But the impulses of men and women to direct the conduct of their children and to train them in certain ways are themselves natural, and it is vain to try to suppress them in the interests of unrestrained naturalness.

The truth is that our nature is full of deadly tendencies and that the life of culture or civilization is wisdom organized to combat natural evil. Often, indeed, such organization misses its objective and adds to the burden of life so that some return to simplicity is necessary. But the life of reason is developed by civilization and is not compatible with a return to a purely animal status.

Philosophy of Law

Human beings cannot live together without restraints on their anarchic impulses. Yet, if laws are to be effective, these restraints must appeal to the community. This difficulty is solved by general obedience to a ruler or rule. In modern societies the rule of law is relied on more and more to eliminate the arbitrary personal bias of rulers and to make men more certain as to what are their rights and what they may safely undertake. But philosophic pluralism makes us distrust rules; for the latter are based on generalizations as to what takes place in a dominant number, but not in all cases, so that rules always work hardships in individual cases whose peculiarities are not anticipated by the rule. Many things must therefore be left to the intuition, tact, or good judgment of well-disposed and competent judges or other officials. There can be no government by law apart from men who will administer the law according to their ideas and feelings. How can we guard against the arbitrary and tyrannical abuse of such discretion? Yet, discretion or judgment, if it is sound, embodies some reason or rule which subsequent study may make clear.

My interest in this field was first stimulated by the course of judicial decisions in labour cases. The arbitrary (and often unenlightened) character of these decisions revealed to me the inadequacy of the dogma that judges declare but do not make the law. The rejection of the absoluteness of this distinction between making and finding threw light on the issue between realism and idealism, as to whether the mind makes or discovers the nature of the world.

The unsatisfactory character of American judicial decisions in labour cases led me to question the value and adequacy of the moral principles of the American Bills of Rights which form the justification of these decisions. "Equal protection of law" seems highly desirable in the abstract, but in its application to actual unequal individuals it turns out to be most vague and unsatisfactory. But my aversion to positivism, to the position of those who, like Duguit, claim to reject the strictly ethical or normative point of view, led me to see the truth in the old doctrine of natural law and natural rights. The moral demand that law should answer to man's interests cannot be ignored in the study or in the making of the law; and the evaluation of these interests is thus an integral part of any philosophy of law.

Law, and even the ethical ideal itself, may certainly be viewed as the historic resultant of various social forces. Yet the old problem of natural law, the problem as to what under given conditions the law ought to be, remains. Realism in the law can be combined with genuine idealism in the doctrine of the inherent limitations of legal idealism due to the conditions of human nature, habits, the legal machinery, and the limitations of man's desire for the moral good.

PHILOSOPHY OF ART

My general inclination to naturalistic rationalism was fortified by the discovery that it seemed to be the most satisfactory account of a field to which it is seldom applied—to wit, the field of art.

The ascetic and democratic ideas with which I began to philosophize predisposed me to view æstheticism as a form of snobbery. That which has its roots deep in human nature or answers to our fundamental needs cannot depend upon acquaintance with rare paintings or esoteric music. Reflection, however, on the fact that only a few who are highly trained understand the meaning of such scientific laws as that of gravitation, suggested that in the field of art, too, training may make clear what is otherwise vague and indistinct. This led to a distinction between taste which is immediate and vision which involves discrimination in the object seen. If taste denotes mere sensibility there seems little basis for saying that where two tastes differ one is necessarily superior to the other. A pluralistic philosophy finds plenty of anthropologic evidence for the view that talk about superior taste may mean a blindness to its natural diversity. The terms higher and lower have a meaning only in regard to things of the same kind that can be arranged in a linear series. But on what basis can one declare that a taste for Da Vinci's faces is superior to a taste for Turner's landscapes, or either to a taste for Japanese prints? If anyone is justified in saying that it is poor taste to prefer jazz to Beethoven, it can only be either on the ground that those who prefer the latter are "better" people or else because the objective content or structure of Beethoven's music shows greater art than does jazz. This means a consideration of art rather than mere taste.

If we look on the fine arts as a special group of arts we can see that the problem of creation which they involve is ultimately the rational one of adapting means to ends.[1] To be sure the end is not always clear at the beginning, but becomes clearer as we work towards it. But this is true also in scientific research and other activities. What distinguishes the fine arts from the other arts is the character of the resulting product (I reject the suggestion that what characterized all activity in the fine arts is its pleasantness. Some of it may be painful and not as pleasant as certain activities in the industrial arts or in business.) The artistic product does generally please the observer (with reservations as to the sublime), but not all things which please us are the products of fine art. The latter pleases us by producing things that have a certain structure characterized by rhythm, harmony, or, more generally, beauty.

Beauty is generally viewed as an immediate attribute; but reflection shows that it also elevates us above the actual or material object which embodies it. Aristotle's dictum that poetry is more true than history, means that the artistic representation of the essence of an object has more significance than the mere recital of brute historic facts. Liberation from the actual through a suggestion of possibilities beyond it is as characteristic of art as of theoretic science and religion.

PHILOSOPHY OF RELIGION

Having been brought up as an orthodox Hebrew, religion was first associated in my mind with cultus, with prayers and ritual

[1] This means that intelligent art criticism must be based on a knowledge of the problems which face the artist and the technique whereby they are solved. The true critic repeats in part the intellectual work of the artist himself.

observances. The history of Buddhism, Christianity, and Islam confirmed the view that ritual, what men do on certain occasions, is the primary fact, and that the beliefs and emotions associated with ritual are more variable. The same prayer or ritual may have quite different emotional effects. Also many a man like Chief Justice Marshall goes to church without bothering his head about any question of belief. Robertson Smith's observation that ritual is generally older than the myth which explains it, has always impressed me as the beginning of wisdom in a rational study of religion. It is certainly profusely exemplified in the succession of diverse mythical explanations of the Hebrew Sabbath, the Easter ceremony, the worship at Mecca, etc. A Christian saint may replace the local heathen god, but people continue to worship at the same shrine.

From this point of view recent discussions of religion initiated by William James's "Varieties of Religious Experience," seem to me singularly provincial and unilluminating. They throw no light on the main streams of human experience expressed in the great historic religions, such as Brahmanism, Buddhism, Zoro-astrianism, Confucianism, etc. James's remark that the religious experience of the great mass of people is secondary, and only that of the founders is important, is certainly superficial. The character of the founder of a religion is largely a product of tradition. Gautama, Moses, and Jesus influence the religion of their followers through the ideal personality that tradition has moulded. Tradition is the most powerful influence in religion. Of the hundreds of millions of people who follow the way of the Buddha, or invoke the name of Mohammed, how many do so because they were born and brought up in their respective communities? How many of those who are convinced that the supreme truth has been revealed to Moses or Jesus have examined the claims of other religions? Clearly the forces of social cohesion determine the main stream of religious phenomena. These considerations have destroyed for me the force of the argument that religion must be true because so many people believe it. As we learn more about diverse religions we find no substantial common core of dogma or belief. Neither the belief in a personal God, nor in personal immortality with moral retribution after death, is common to Old Testament Judaism, to Buddhism, and to Confucianism.

I confess that I have never been able to understand any theism that was not anthropomorphic; and I have not since my thirteenth year seen any logical force in the theistic argument that the entire universe must have a person (on the human model) as its cause, designer, or director. Any conception of personality which we can form is necessarily based upon such infinitesimal knowledge of the unimaginable whole wherein we move, that it seems to me blind arrogance to be confident of the personalistic explanation. Nor can I see how the author of our whole world can be called good, without blunting the edge of the distinction between good and evil. I do not like to call myself an atheist, because those who apply that term to themselves seem as a rule singularly blind to the limitations of our knowledge and to the infinite possibilities beyond us. As a pluralist I believe that the forces which control all things are ultimately many; and if I could use the term polytheism without implying that these forces are exclusively personal I should call myself a polytheist.

Though I am singularly sensitive to the literary charm of certain types of mysticism, such as that of St. Bernard or Tauler, it seems to me amazing that anyone should argue as James did that the mystic's ecstasy can prove any of the dogmas of religion. I can see no proof that the object of the mystic's experience has any more objective validity than the similar visions of one under the influence of drugs. Nor is the moral elevation of religious conviction beyond question. There is not a revolting feature of human life that has not at one time or another been an intimate part of religion. Sacred prostitution, the sacrifice of children to Moloch, thuggery, assassination, superstitious opposition to science. persecution and wars, the sanctification of slavery and other social abuses—these are but a few phases of religion that it is well not to forget. It may be urged that religion did not originate these practices, but only sanctioned them. But if so, why may not the moral and æsthetic goods often attributed to religion be similarly of independent origin? History does not support the view that the actual religions of mankind have been the source of good only.

Despite the darker side of religion, such as uncharitable beliefs in hell, I doubt not that it lifts men above mere brutish existence and saves them from the deadening absorptions of the market-place. Popular religions are doctrines of hope which sustain men's faith by assuring them that the world as a whole is not indifferent to their moral strivings. I for one cannot see in history or in nature any rational proof of "a power not ourselves making for righteousness." But surely the deeper religious consciousness recognizes that moral effort justifies itself apart from rewards or outer success. Rational naturalism and the great religions are at one in impressing us with the wisdom of humility and resignation. We are not gods, and cannot mould the entire world according to our heart's desire. But we can, by learning to face the truth, attain peace and freedom from vanity. God is not only an existent power but an ideal of holiness, which enables us to distinguish between the good and the evil in men and thus saves us from the idolatrous worship of a humanity that is full of fatal imperfections. Men need not live for ever or beyond the grave to attain true spirituality—to act with a view to the inherent quality of our acts and to see them as parts of the eternal web of the world.

. . . For to bear all naked truths,
And to envisage circumstance, all calm,
That is the top of sovereignty.

PRINCIPAL PUBLICATIONS

"The Philosophy of Mathematics," in the *Journal of Philosophy*, 1911.

"Qualities, Relations, and Things," *Ib.* 1914.

"History versus Value," *Ib.* 1914.

"Mechanism and Causality in Physics," *Ib.* 1918.

"Subject-matter of Formal Logic," *Ib.* 1918.

"Communal Ghosts," *Ib.* 1919.

"Concepts and Twilight Zones," *Ib.* 1927.

"Jus Naturale Redivivum," in the *Philosophical Review*, 1916.

"Amor Dei Intellectualis," in *Chronicon Spinozanum*, 1925

"The Natural and the Social Sciences," 1927 (Ch. XXIII of the *Social Sciences*, ed. by Ogburn and Goldenweiser).

"The Place of Logic in the Law," in *Harvard Law Review*, 1916.

"Later Philosophy," (Ch. XVII of the *Cambridge History of American Literature*, 1922).

Introduction to *Chance, Love, and Logic*, by C. S. Peirce, 1922.

A SEARCH FOR SYSTEM

By G. WATTS CUNNINGHAM

Born 1881; Professor of Philosophy, Cornell University.

A SEARCH FOR SYSTEM

WHAT are my philosophic beliefs? Why do I hold them? These are the questions I have been asked to answer in response to my acceptance of the invitation to contribute to this volume of essays. My answer must needs take the form of an account of a search whose positive results (such as they are) have issued largely through negations—a search originally motivated by two basal demands of my nature. Of course the story can here be given only in skeleton outline, and personal influences apart from which the story might have been very different cannot even be touched upon. The broad psychological causes out of which my need for philosophy arose, with which I begin, will be stated as briefly as is consistent with the purpose for which they are even mentioned. Then I shall pass on to a consideration of the beliefs themselves, together with the reasons on which they seem to me to rest.

I

I was reared in a pious family set in the midst of a pious community, piety by common consent being equated with a strict orthodoxy (as locally understood) of beliefs and practices. Needless to add, I was pious after the same fashion. On the other side, I was intellectually curious; and any subject that presented a challenge was from the first welcomed and eagerly pursued. My early scholastic training was got in the public schools of the community, and during my period of tutelage the instruction varied in efficiency from mediocrity to excellence. But, fortunately for me, the more competent instructors came at the time of my most compelling need of them; and I was finally able to go up to college with advanced standing in several subjects. When I entered college I was thus equipped with a dual heritage: a vivid religious sentiment—which, thanks to my parents, had the saving salt of a vital connection with the business of living— and an open mind. Even then these sat rather loose to each other, and there were not infrequent conflicts between them; to bring them together has been the burden of my later development.

My earlier attempts to achieve the synthesis were, as was inevitable, characterized by failure, since they took the form of mere negations. Whether or not my later efforts have been more successful, they have at least been more in the open; and the progressive negations through which they have advanced have left a precipitate of positive content that presumably cannot be wholly explained by psycho-analysis.

As a raw undergraduate I was carried through the ordinary courses in logic, psychology, ethics, and the history of philosophy. I was also exposed to the intricacies of B. P. Bowne's theistic metaphysics. These studies interested me greatly, though, as I now recall, none had any marked effect on my general attitude. At the time my main interests lay in other fields, particularly in mathematics and literary studies. Meanwhile the demands of my religious consciousness had been set aside in a compartment by themselves, where, for the nonce, they were fairly quiescent; "reason's colder part" did indeed now and again throw a chill breath into the sanctum, but the heart's "I have felt" was generally able to melt it away.

Mathematics appealed to me because of its precision and certainty; literature, because of the emotional satisfaction it gave. As I proceeded to the higher mathematics, however, my interest in the subject gradually waned. I began to tire of what then seemed to be its perverse tendency to depart from factual situations and its consequent abstractness; and naturally I soon found myself engulfed by hypothetical formulations, the significance of which I did not see or care seriously to investigate. This, I now of course realize, was for me very unfortunate; but such was my weakness. So I turned my attention primarily to literature, which continued to attract me; here at least my emotional nature found expression.

The three years immediately following my graduation were devoted to the teaching of English in a small college, and the more literary side of the work brought deep personal satisfaction. But it did not wholly satisfy. Though not insensitive to the niceties of form, I was much more interested in what my author had to say than in the way he said it; and I usually found him silent or speaking *ex cathedra* relative to my queries concerning justification of the position advanced. When confronted by the necessity of considering a poet's significance, for instance, or of comparing him with a fellow-poet and raising troublesome questions about relative merits, I invariably found my discussion very weak on the side of his 'literary form' and strong (after my own halting manner, of course) on the side of the content of his message. But when I asked concerning the truth of the message, I was left to seek alone. There was an uneasy feeling on my part that I was here entangled in a heresy, that "a thing of beauty is a joy forever," and ought to be a joy in its own right; but I remained bound in my sin. That other saying of Keats's,

> Beauty is truth, truth beauty—that is all
> Ye know on earth, and all ye need to know,

still had its appeal; and I even thought to save my soul through its repetition. But in my poor rendering of it there was always an emphasis which I did not seem to find either in Keats or in those who think with him on the point. As I understood it at least, that other emphasis now appeared certainly one-sided, and perhaps wrong; but how to modify the emphasis so as to remove my vague discontent remained for me an unsolved problem. And with this, my religious consciousness stirred again uneasily; if truth is imperious in beauty, why not also in good and God?

At this juncture I fell back upon philosophy, which I had never completely deserted. Attendance on the lectures of the late J. E. Creighton, of Cornell University, in the summer term of 1904 led me in the autumn of 1905 to enroll as a graduate student in the Sage School of Philosophy, where I found a group of scholarly and sympathetic instructors, to each of whom I owe much for whatever insights I may since have attained. In this fortunate environment I remained for three years, and it was during this period that my philosophic eyes were first really opened. The tradition of the Sage School in those days, as now, was to conduct the student along the historical avenue of approach. Under skilful guidance I was inducted into the major systems, with special emphasis upon Plato, Kant, and

Hegel. In these systems, particularly in the system of Hegel, I seemed to discern promise of what I had long vaguely and vainly sought. Henceforth my philosophic beliefs began to take shape with something of a reasoned foundation on which to stand.

II

From Plato I at the time learned little, though I hope I have later learned much. I was fascinated by his doctrine of Ideas, and especially by his treatment of the Good. Here I glimpsed a vista which seemed to open fruitful possibilities, but on the whole it remained for me a misty one. In later years I think I have seen more, and I am now inclined to attribute my first difficulties with the Platonic doctrine to a misconception of his two 'worlds' and their relation to each other. However that may be, I then derived little help from Plato with reference to my own special problem, though never did he send me away quite empty-handed.

With Kant the case was different. There was indeed much in him that I did not in the least understand; and not infrequently when face to face with him I was constrained to question whether it were not the part of wisdom for me to turn back and content myself with wallowing in the mire of inchoate or clamorous feelings. More than once he almost persuaded me that I could never be a philosopher. But in time I thought I could see through at least the outline of his analysis of experience. I was much impressed by his deduction of the categories—that is, by what of it I could understand, and this I naturally took to be fundamental; between the points I could not touch I made shift to swim as best I might. It was through Kant's eyes that I first saw the way past the withering atomism of Hume's "bundle of perceptions"; and, though the same conception has recently been presented in more compelling formulation, I see no reason to change my mind on the point—the answer to it that Kant gave seems to me in principle effective now. I thought, also, that I found in Kant the basis upon which could be built a satisfactory defence of the validity of scientific and philosophic thought against the logic of the *Treatise*.

But on this point I could not see that Kant himself had done more than lay the foundation; his superstructure of the *a priori* forms seemed even flimsy. Any position in support of which its author could argue, for instance, on the basis of the assumption that space or time could be imagined apart from phenomena I could not but feel is in a state of very unstable equilibrium. But there were other, and for me at the time still more serious, logical difficulties with which Kant confronted me. I chafed at the bit which he insisted on putting between my teeth. He seemed to make a great deal of things-in-themselves, and from time to time he spoke of them with something like affection; yet he was constantly reminding me that truth is of phenomena alone. Of what significance, then, his truth could be and how by it he imagined he had escaped the dangers of Hume's scepticism or of Berkeley's subjectivism I was at a loss to understand; and I thought I could in this connection see the structure of the *a priori* exhibiting one of its loosest joints. Why he should have deemed it necessary to raise this bogey, and what use he made of it once it was raised, remained troublesome questions until I had caught the sinister significance of his statement, "Macht zwar der Verstand die Natur, aber er schafft sie nicht." There seemed little difference here between 'making' and 'creating.' Likewise, the dualism between 'pure' and 'practical' reason was for me a stone of stumbling. Of course, it was a separation which in my own incoherent fashion I had long since made for myself and with which I had for a time lived content; but now, in the same incoherent manner, I was struggling to surmount it because it no longer satisfied. And just at this crucial point Kant failed me. Nor was I greatly encouraged by the meagre results of his passage from morals to religion. I was convinced that the bifurcation of experience had something to do with the debacle, and I grew increasingly suspicious that this bifurcation was intimately linked with the form-matter dualism of the other *Critique*. My suspicion on this score was greatly strengthened by Kant himself, or at least by Kant as I understood him; for in the transcendental deduction he had taught me that all such dualisms were justly to be held suspect. Thus, despite his explicit avowals to the contrary, he indirectly encouraged me to feel that my hopes were not in vain. What I wanted was a truth which was something more than mere 'validity' or abstract consistency, and a good which was something more than a blind and arbitrary feeling or an empty form; I was in search of a true which was also real and a good which was also rational. Kant led me to think that such was possible, and he even seemed to point the direction in which it might be found. But the synthesizing principle, so far as my understanding of Kant carried me, remained a desideratum only; and for a time I drifted rather helplessly and narrowly escaped a pretty thoroughgoing scepticism.

The Hegelian tradition, then dominant in the Sage School, came to my rescue. I entered upon the study of Hegel with avidity, and, as best I could, I followed his principles through their elaboration in his own writings and in those of later representatives of the movement. From Hegel himself I caught a glimpse of the synthesis I had long desired—a synthesis through which reality was brought to thought, and will and feeling were linked with reason. The enthusiasm with which I welcomed this insight is evident in the monograph[1] in which I set down the results of a rather assiduous study of Hegel's system.

Turning the pages of this essay, I find that from Hegel I then gathered the following views: (i) thought is genuinely objective, transcending the relativity of individual experiences through its inviolable contact with and determination by things-in-themselves; (ii) thought is not bare abstract cognition, but includes within itself so-called intuitive perception, feeling, volition, as well as cognition, and is adequately described only as the unifying principle within experience; (iii) thought is a process of mediation which proceeds from immediacy to immediacy through the power of the 'negative,' that is, through the removal of inconsistency within any given immediate and the

---

[1] *Thought and Reality in Hegel's System*, 1910. Though remaining by the main theses of this essay so far as its exposition goes, I am now inclined to think that some of its evaluations are perhaps more enthusiastic than true.

consequent subsumption of it within a 'higher' immediate—an immediate involving less of discrepancy and imperviousness to thought; (iv) this process is a progressive definition of reality, since every immediate to which thought is driven is an aspect of the real, and since reality functions throughout the process; (v) the final immediate of thought—the immediate in which thought at last rests—must be said to be the absolute real, and is neither an abstract particular nor a blank universal, but the universal filled, the particular completed by its own ideal construction, in a word, the individual; (vi) this final immediate of thought is one in the dual sense of being both systematic and all-inclusive, and perhaps may be termed self-conscious. So far as I understood them, all of these views I was at the time inclined to accept without criticism, with the possible exception of the monistic implications of the system, which troubled me largely because of their obstinacy with reference to the sort of individuality which I seemed to experience within myself and to find among my fellows.

In the writings of Bradley, Bosanquet, and Royce, as in the lectures of my instructors, I found much enrichment of the Hegelian principles. In their hands the dialectic method descended more obviously into the concrete whirl of factual situations, and, to my mind, gained immensely in power thereby. Their treatment of the immediate and its self-transcendence in thought, their insistence on the futility of the older epistemological controversies and their fortification of this position by masterly expositions of the various forms of knowledge in development, their opposition to associationism and atomism and their substitution therefor of the organic and systematic view of mind, their emphasis upon and elaboration of the psychological and social matrix of the self—all of this appealed strongly to me and added much wealth of detail to some at least of the principles which in Hegel had apparently received only skeleton treatment. Here I followed gladly.

But the new insistence on the Absolute gave me pause. Here I could follow only from afar and with progressively hesitant steps. The constantly repeated assertion that time is of phenomena only, that reality, though including time within itself, is nevertheless trans-temporal, deepened the suspicion already aroused by Hegel and raised questions which I nowhere found answered to my satisfaction by my guides. I was curious to know what, on such a view, one could say concerning the apparent inseparability of time and the 'individual' which all along I had supposed was in some sense to be equated with the real. It had been maintained (this I thought was the lesson) that the nisus of thought was towards the 'whole,' that the whole as experienced always implicates its own transcendence, and that reality is what thought, functioning within the given, compels us to affirm. But I now seemed to be confronted by the consideration that reality, real reality, is quite other than what seemed to be the implication of these principles—that it is a static whole in no sense involving a nisus, and even so ineffably perfect that the drive of thought itself pauses helplessly at its threshold. Why the impasse? Bradley's "happy suicide" of thought seemed to amount to little more than confession of failure. If it is thought's function to expand the real by ideal construction, why should reality suddenly grow so great as to pass beyond it? If, on the other hand, reality does at length negate thought, what boots it to add that thought foresees and acquiesces in its final humiliation and rejection? If thought is in indissoluble touch with the real anywhere, it ought apparently to be so everywhere. And if it finally fails us, there is little consolation to be had from the consideration that it at least carries us to the top of the mountain—unless, indeed, another guide is ready to hand to see us safely into the promised land.

> The little more and how much it is,
> The little less and what worlds away.

But I could not see, on the other side, that efforts to make the non-temporal Absolute intelligible were successful. Royce's appeal to the *totum simul* of the scholastics and his analogy of the span of consciousness plainly would not do, as Bosanquet himself observed. My main difficulty with Royce's position, however, was not that which Bosanquet points out. What is said in criticism of it seems indeed true. That in an all-inclusive consciousness events could not lie side by side precisely as they are in a finite span, but must necessarily suffer some subtle sea-change because of the inevitable modification of the earlier by the later—this seemed plausible. For surely it is hardly to be supposed that omniscience would "see in any lapse of successive events nothing more than a finite being would see so far as he followed that identical lapse." But my chief trouble was with the prior question whether, following the method on which we all seemed to be agreed, there was any logical necessity for positing such an all-inclusive and non-temporal reality by whatever name designated. So, while agreeing with Bosanquet that Royce had failed in making the Absolute intelligible, I was still forced to doubt that Bosanquet himself had succeeded any better, or that anyone could succeed starting from our common premises and following our common method.

This doubt on my part rapidly grew into a settled conviction, and the process was hastened by my study of the writings of Bergson.[1] James's oft-repeated criticisms of the "block universe" had, I think, very little influence on me. His criticisms were too intimately bound up with his peculiar view of the pragmatic theory of truth to take hold of my imagination; for, as formulated by him, the pragmatic theory of truth seemed to me either obvious or false and, as obvious, I could not see that it touched my problem in a very significant, certainly not in a definitive, manner. Nor did Dewey here render me any great assistance. His formulation of the pragmatic doctrine under the concept of instrumentalism and his consequent insistence upon the function of the factual situation in the process of thinking had all along appealed to me as in principle sound; but, having gone so far, I was at a loss to understand why he was not logically bound to go farther, and where he stopped (as I supposed, at least) I could not see that we were in touch with my own special difficulty. Very probably all of this was in error, and doubtless these two protagonists of pragmatism had much more to say to me than I, at the time and under the conditions, could hear. I now think

[1] *A Study in the Philosophy of Bergson,* 1916.

this was certainly true of Dewey. Be that as it may, it was rather the pattern of Bergson's thought which, on one important side, fitted into and supplemented my own. To be sure, my reaction to other aspects of his view was rather decidedly negative, and particularly on a point which I shall indicate below. But his conception (intuition?) of duration, in so far as that is to be identified with his view of the deeper self as distinguished from the other self which is the 'external projection' of it and his correlative view of time as a whole of mutually interpenetrating parts, was to me of the greatest assistance. Here I found a 'whole' which, so far from excluding time, was constituted by it and was also experienceable and (in my terminology) intelligible.[1] I found here also further confirmation of my feeling that existence is indissolubly linked with time, at least the sort of existence which we experience directly within ourselves and which to us is in the end alone intelligible. So it seemed to me a short step to the identification of this sort of 'whole' with reality—if, that is, we could take our own existence as a privileged instance. At any rate, there was (so at least it now seemed) no contradiction involved in the step. But it also seemed clear to me that this conclusion was not foreign to the tradition which hitherto I had followed; on the contrary, I thought I could see that it was necessarily implicated in the premises and method of that tradition. Thus I found myself confronted by a dilemma: "either the organizational theory, accepted with explicit avowal of its implications concerning the ontological value of time, or the admission of the final bankruptcy of the concept of a 'world'." [2] And I was committed to the first alternative.

But I could not follow Bergson in his conception of 'creative evolution.' My main difficulty here was linked with the other side of his view of duration. His very suggestive analysis of conscious experience I found incomplete and negligent of what I was compelled to regard as one of its basal features. He insisted upon describing it wholly in terms of the past overflowing into

---

[1] On Bergson's 'intuition' see *op. cit.*, Chapters III, IV.

[2] "Coherence as Organization," in *Philosophical Essays in Honour of James Edwin Creighton*, 1917.

the present, and so as purely heterogeneous; but I could envisage it only as fundamentally teleological and end-serving, and apart from the teleological dimension of experience I could not see that either past or present possessed meaning. This feature I thought became still more clear and significant when experience was considered at the level of inferential knowledge and moral endeavour. Now the notion of creative evolution appeared to be rooted in this basal error of analysis, and in the end to be meaningless. The view of the world-process as an aimless activity of a blind original impetus differentiating itself, for no assignable reason, into equally blind tendencies directed upon the impalpable void—this view seemed to be Bergson's creative evolution, and such a view I could only regard as factually groundless and in its own right even self-contradictory. So I was constrained to substitute for it another view which I ventured to call 'creative finalism.' According to the summary statement of this view I then gave, "creative finalism views reality as an organic process which is through and through teleological. Its fundamental nature is to create ends, to produce tendencies, and to govern itself according to its own creations. These ends are progressively defined and revised with the advancing process in which they operate; they never can be finally and completely defined, and the process is, therefore, unending. Its homogeneous nature is necessitated by the fact that within it there is always an ideal dimension by means of which its past and future are inextricably involved in each other; this ideal dimension, the dynamic imagination, functions in the present and binds past, present, and future into an organic whole. Though it can never be described as *just this* or *just now*, still it is always identical with itself and possesses a determinate content." And I thought this view to be in harmony with my tradition.

In very sketchy outline, such is the *Weltanschauung*, of which in 1916 I supposed myself to be in possession, and such are the broader influences instrumental in its formulation. Naturally my whole edifice had all along been blown upon by other winds of doctrine, though without very marked results. Latterly, however, some of these winds have mightily prevailed, and at least some parts of my superstructure have been rather seriously affected. A more intimate acquaintance with, and penetration of, pragmatic and realistic doctrines (through various media too numerous to mention here, but the writings of Dewey, Russell, Whitehead, and Alexander should be particularly noted) have forced modifications more or less profound—so profound, in fact, that the question now is, What remains? In undertaking to answer this question I can do little more than direct hasty glances at the foundations. And the discussion must be carried forward without further references to historical affiliations, though justice and gratitude alike impel me to acknowledge my great obligations to Viscount Haldane. My reformulations owe much to contact with especially his later views.

Taking stock of the present situation, I seem to find some of the older views which still stand and others which have more recently developed. I shall list them under the headings of (1) method and (2) problems and results.

(1) As to method, I hold the following views: (a) the method of philosophy is the method of reason; (b) the method of reason must be described through analysis of the problematic given, in which alone thought functions, and such analysis reveals that thought is the interpretation of system; (c) the problematic given controls (ideally) the process of thinking and is not made by it; (d) the criterion of truth is control by the given, which is equivalent to saying that system is the criterion. (2) As to problems and results, I seem to discern the following: (a) the difference between science and philosophy lies, not in method, but in the degree to which use is made of the common criterion; (b) in a sense we are all absolutists, though the assumption that in the end the absolute is self-sufficient as both all-inclusive and non-temporal is doubtful, and, in any event, must be settled by factual considerations and not by merely *a priori* argumentation; (c) the nature of thought is to assert truly, and there is no sheer error; (d) 'existence,' 'reality,' and 'object of thought' tend to fall together, but there are distinctions among them which in principle are important. In what follows I shall try to draw out these several points by more explicit statement, and I can only

hope that my necessarily dogmatic assertions will not in the end remain enigmatic.

(I) METHOD

(*a*) That the method of philosophy is the method of reason and not of some non-rational feeling or intuition I base mainly on the two following considerations. The method of reason is a method of which we do make use with some degree of success, and in science at least there is no question of any other; it should therefore be applied in philosophy as far as it will work and until it can be shown definitely to break down. Its incompetence in philosophy has not been proved by those philosophers who have most vigorously pushed the claims of another method; on the contrary, such philosophers have found themselves at the last forced either to fall back upon reason or to remain content with what logically is an unutterable mysticism. Beyond further elaboration of these points with an eye open to the precise use of terms I hardly know what more one could say on the matter, except to remark that the position here defended does not imply the denial that parts of the universe may fall beyond the reach of thought, but only the insistence that, if they do, they are of no concern to philosophy.

(*b*) The more important question concerns the nature of the rational method. Here fateful divergencies in philosophy have their origin, and I submit that the answer to the question is of basal significance. I have above asserted that the method of reason is in point of fact identical with the interpretation of the problematic given, and I now wish to develop this further.

I am, in the first place, confronted with the prior question of the given. And in this connection it seems important to note that there is a difference between the mere given and the problematic given. By the mere given I understand that which is presented as a self-contained fact without either inner discrepancy or outer implications. By the problematic given I understand that which, because of internal discrepancy or external reference or both, comes as a challenge. These two types of the given are quite distinct, and the distinction is for method important.

With reference to the mere given I must here content myself with the following observations. No such given is found in experience, and were it found there it could not be for thought a point of departure. Every datum within immediate experience is unstable; what seems to be fixed and hard turns out to be derived through a rather elaborate process of mediation—a process identical with that which Hobbes named 'resolutive'— as is illustrated from different angles by Bradley's primal feeling or Russell's logical atoms or Bergson's duration or Santayana's essences. Furthermore, such a mere given would necessarily fall in wholly non-reflective experience, and would consequently remain for thought intrinsically barren; this, I think, has actually been shown by Dewey, though I have no warrant for appealing in this connection to his authority, and I myself first learned it from Hegel. Thought takes root only within a problematic situation, no problem, no thinking; and what is taken as a non-problematic datum is precisely the outcome of the resolution of the problematic where analysis is supposed to rest, and which is then viewed in isolation from the process whereby it has been attained. A mere datum means nothing until it becomes problematic or emerges through the resolution of the problematic.

For me, then, the given which is a problem is alone the starting-point of thought, and the process called thinking is nothing more than the interpretation of such a given. And here are involved two basal considerations that must be dwelt upon for a moment. There is the problem and there is the problem-solution, and both are essential to a complete act of thinking; thought is at once a problem-raising and a problem-solving function. Of course there is no intention to hold that every problem raised by thought must be solved then and there, or even anywhen and anywhere; nor does the position here advanced involve such an absurdity. That not every act of thought is complete is clear, otherwise scepticism would never have been heard of; and the view that thought functions only within a problematic situation is open to admit this. The point is that within the situation in which thought functions there are both a problem and some-thing relevant to its solution, and if either of these conditions

were absent the situation would not be thought-provoking—
would, in short, not be problematic. I wish now to press this
matter further and ask why this is so.

The answer would seem to be that the problem and its relevant
material are inseparable, and either taken alone is an abstraction:
remove either, and the other disappears. Without the relevant
material there would be no problem, for the problem is precisely
conflict and discrepancy among the elements of the situation,
and cannot hang by itself unsupported. A problem in general
is meaningless, and a particular problem is just what the terms
connote—a conflict within a given situation. And, of course, where
there is no problem there can be no problematic stuff; there
relevancy would be meaningless.

From these considerations it follows that a problematic situation is *eo ipso* systematic. There is no clash without system, and
there is no relevancy without system; both alike involve identity.
There is no clash between Abracadabra and Socrates until
the two are conjoined in a synthesis and made elements of a
common whole; and then only does anything gain relevancy
with reference to them.

Furthermore (and here we pass to a very important matter)
there are two logical possibilities with reference to the system.
It may in fact be self-sufficient, or it may be self-transcendent.
If it were self-sufficient, two conditions would have to be met:
both (i) the problem itself and (ii) the solution or relevant
material would fall wholly within it. In other words, the problem
would emerge from the elements of the given situation, and from
them alone; and the solution would seek and find among these
elements all its relevant material. In this case we would have an
'absolute.' Were these conditions not met, the system would
not be self-sufficient. It would have to be transcended. The nisus
to its transcendence would lie within the situation itself, otherwise thought would have no ground for passing beyond. And the
transcendence might go in either, or both, of two directions.
On the one side, the problem might not be explicable in terms
of the situation itself—as happens when the problem grows out
of previous situations—and then the system is transcended in

the direction which I may here designate as backwards. On the other side, and forwards, the system would be transcended when relevancy leads beyond it. All of this could be put in another way by saying, more technically, that the system may be wholly immediate[1] or mediated beyond either from above or below, or from both directions at once, and in any event its transcendence would be a *self*-transcendence.

(c) Again, the system controls thought and determines its functioning. And this holds whether the system is of the 'real' or imaginative, the veridical or the illusory, the factual or the evaluative. The problem is nothing but a discrepancy among the elements of the system, whatever they may be; and the relevant material is precisely those same elements in relation to that discrepancy, so the solution must have its habitat there. This would be the case, ultimately, only where the situation is self-sufficing. But even where transcendence is present, it is the implications of the situation that lead beyond, and this self-transcendence of the system is still the guiding principle. So we may say broadly that thought is controlled by its system, either as self-sufficient (if such there be) or as self-transcendent.

(d) Finally, the criterion we are bound to follow by this method is the criterion of system—the criterion imposed by the situation in which thought functions. True thought solves its problem accurately; the accurate solution of the problem is attained when the conflict is finally removed, and this result is accomplished through the systematization of the conflicting elements. If the system is self-sufficient, the problem is finally solved and the truth absolute; if otherwise, the problem is partially solved and the truth hypothetical.

(2) PROBLEMS AND RESULTS

Bottoming myself on the preceding considerations of method, I go on to draw, among others, the following general conclusions:—

[1] That is, with reference to a beyond; for me it would, of course, involve mediation within itself.

(*a*) So far as method is concerned, I of course see no difference in principle between science and philosophy. Each follows essentially the same method, and each is controlled by a common criterion. This is not to deny that there are differences of detail in technique; there are such differences even among the sciences themselves. But, as among the sciences so between science and philosophy, these differences arise from variations in the material dealt with, not from variations in principles of method. In science as in philosophy, the situation is always a problematic situation, and the business of thought (scientific or philosophic) is to interpret the situation so as to remove discrepancies from it; and it is the situation which determines and directs.

The difference between science and philosophy lies partly in the types of system under consideration. But the more significant and definitive difference, I think, is to be found in the attitudes assumed with reference to system. Broadly speaking, and subject to correction within limits of the principle, science is concerned with systems which *ad hoc* are assumed to be self-sufficient, or at least it is not concerned to raise any question with reference to such self-sufficiency; while philosophy is primarily interested to inquire whether any system is self-sufficient and on what assumptions it may be held to be so. Otherwise expressed, the main problem of philosophy is precisely the problem of system; science ordinarily assumes (tacitly or explicitly) system and works within that assumption.

The scientist may grow wary of the self-sufficiency of his system and raise questions about the beyond; in so far he becomes philosophical, and precisely because his concern is now with the scope of his system. The philosopher (as ordinarily meant) may, on his side, become a specialist and limit his inquiries to a system assumed for the moment to be self-contained; in so far he is strictly scientific, and he is so because he is then working within the attitude of the scientist. When the scientist raises questions as to the extent of his system, he is engaged with the philosophy of his science. When the philosopher arbitrarily limits his inquiries to a given system and works wholly within it, he is not a philosopher in the sense in which one would be said to be who is primarily alert to the self-sufficiency or transcendence of systems. And I think at least clarity might be gained if we would make this distinction explicit in our technical terminology.

While on this point I may, in passing, state what seems to me involved with reference to the question of religion. Religion—meaning by it the attitude of what is commonly referred to as the 'religious consciousness'—is like science in that it assumes a self-sufficient system, but it is quite unlike science in that its system is not *prima facie* supposed to be amenable to thought. It is wholly unlike philosophy, which both follows reason and assumes no ultimate. When religion turns theological, its attitude may be said to be scientific, in that it now invokes reason, but only within set limits, though it may be very unlike science with reference to this assumption. On its side, however, science has at times been quite dogmatic, and it is not easy to say off-hand which is the narrower dogmatism. When religious thought becomes sufficiently open-minded to entertain, and even to push, serious inquiry into the self-sufficiency of its system, it has then become philosophical.

(b) If at this juncture the traditional absolutist were to interrogate me, I should be embarrassed. Under pressure, the best I could do, I presume, would be to call for some distinctions and answer accordingly.

In one sense of the word I certainly am an absolutist, and I do not see how any of us (whatever our method) escape from being so. We all seek for that which gives us final satisfaction; that we call the real, and that is what I understand the absolute in principle to be. Where we rest from our intellectual labours, there is the absolute. The question that really divides us is whether there is any justification for writing the word with an initial capital. For my part, I see no compelling reason for this; yet my principles seem to drive me farther, and the embarrassing question is, How far am I driven?

I am committed to the view that it is intellectual satisfaction in which alone we can finally rest, and nothing short of a self-contained system will give such satisfaction. This follows from my view of the nature of thought and the situation in which it functions. If, then, self-containedness is equivalent to all-inclusiveness, I am logically obliged to accept ontological monism. But are these equivalent? So far as I can see, *a priori* argument throws no special light on the question; from the controversy about terms and relations very little help is apparently to be gained. Relations actually do relate, I take it, and all terms are in some sense related. At least, I seem by my principles to be committed to this, nor am I able to understand on what grounds one can hold that terms are not modified by the relations which actually do relate them. But I do not see that this carries us very far with reference to the point at issue. The question, as I see it, is what terms are actually related and how. Now I should certainly contend that this question is to be answered (so far as it may be answered) through the activity of thought; but I am bound to hold that the activity of thought can do nothing more than disclose the terms as actually related. In other words, if ontological monism is true, then any problematic given must implicate all there is; but whether such is the case is a matter of fact to be revealed (if at all) through the activity of thought following the implications of its factual matrix under the control of which it functions. On the other hand, I do not find that the systems of thought speak unequivocally on the question. The self-encased entities that have been offered in evidence as supporting pluralism —the various 'simples' and finite 'wholes'—seem to involve implications beyond themselves; whatever else they may be, they certainly do not appear to be unmediated immediates. Nor am I able to discover any for myself. And yet there do seem to be systems that are quite loose each to the other; there is no clear implicative relation between the colour of my hair, for instance, and that of the ring on my finger, though it is not at all impossible that further clarification might reveal such a relation. And it is precisely this confusion and ignorance which is the source of my embarrassment in discussing this phase of the question. I see no reason why a self-sufficient system might not be one of many, but I find none such among the finite systems known to me.

With reference to the non-temporal aspect of the traditional absolutism the matter seems more clear. That a self-contained system may lie in time presents, so far as I can see, no very great difficulty. The argument that such a system involves a self-contradiction would appear to beg the question, since it rests upon the assumption that a dynamic system must necessarily depart from its own basal nature to become something other than itself, and this is just the point at issue. This assumption can be traced to another, which I must hold is false. That is the assumption that the identity in thought may be defined once for all in terms of judgment taken in bloodless isolation from its concrete setting. To this must be opposed the consideration (necessitated by my principles and, as I think, by the principles of those who in this connection disregard it) that the 'unity' of judgment is itself nothing more than the system judged about. Whether there is a self-contained dynamic system, then, is once more a question of fact. And, as I think Bergson has shown, our own conscious life furnishes us with an illustration of what such a system might be. Of course I do not suggest that the finite self is a self-contained system; but its incompleteness is not due to the fact that it is characterized by change. It is incomplete rather because it gets its filling from beyond the circle of its inner nature, from an environment which remains alien: expand it till all the material necessary for its expression were within it in the sense in which the content of ideal thought is its own object, and it would be a self-sufficient system, however much it might be featured by change. The complete is not necessarily the complete*ed*; a system may be unfinished, and yet all of its implications fall within itself. And I think the principle here would hold of a system which could be said to be 'all there is,' if there be such a system.

I may add by the way that it is precisely because of its bearing on the above problem that the problem of mind seems to me as significant for philosophy as it is for the social sciences. But I must turn to my third point.

(c) Thought is the interpretation of the problematic given which, on analysis, is seen to be system. The nature of thought is to disclose the elements of system in their implicative relations; or, to borrow Bosanquet's expressive phrase, thought is the

'active form' of system. This is what I understand by the trueness
of thought. Thus I hold with Bosanquet that the nature of thought
is to affirm truly. And yet more often than not thought is erroneous. But I do not see that there is any contradiction between these
two statements, unless one identifies error with sheer error. And
to do this is meaningless. That there is error arises from the fact
that thinking is a process in time, and therefore cannot take
everything at once and completely; the complex implications of
the problematic situation outreach thought's vision. Even so,
however, erroneous thought is in an important sense true—in the
sense, namely, that errors are always implications. In the realm
of thought there are no sheer errors, there are only mistakes—
actual implications linked with systems to which they do not
belong, self-transcendent systems taken as self-sufficient. Herein
lies the power of self-correction, which is a basal characteristic of
thought; a partial truth may be completed, and even demands
that it be. A sheer error, however, remains incorrigible, and can
be met only by a bare negation; but in the end both alike are
meaningless and fall, if anywhere, in the realm of the thoughtless.
And all of this, I suppose, is little more than a restatement of
Hegel's doctrine of 'negativity.'

(d) To ask, then, whether sheer error is non-existent raises
the larger question: How does the existent stand in relation
to the object of thought? And here definition is at once
imperative.

If we are to understand by the existent merely what in any
sense, intelligible or otherwise, is, or may be said to have being,
then *cadit quæstio*. The answer is both obvious and insignificant.
There is certainly no justification for supposing that what exists
in this sense must be an object of thought. Of course, every
object of thought would be an existent, but so might much else
besides, and there is no way of determining how much or what.
Here unbridled fancy is given free play, and any abstract possibility may be an actuality.

If, however, the existent is to mean what has being in a manner
such that the 'go' of it may be known, the situation becomes
different and the question intelligible. On this assumption the

existent must be said to be an object of thought. But here it is necessary to note certain important distinctions.

By an object of thought I understand broadly the system in which thought functions and which controls. But this system presents different aspects, and these should be distinguished. In the first place, it may be regarded as either actually or possibly controlling thought; that is, it may be the object of an actual or of a possible thinker. Again, the system may be taken *ad hoc* in immediate practical relation to an actual thinker, and only as thus related. And, finally, it may be taken as the entire set of implications of which thought (actual or possible) is the active form. When taken *ad hoc*, I shall call it a *psychological* object of thought; when taken as the total system of implications, I shall call it the *logical* object of thought. I regret using these terms, but at present I can think of no better; in any case, it is the distinction which is emphasized and which is important for the argument, not the terms used to indicate it.

Going back on our question with this distinction in mind, I should want to say that the existent may be a psychological object of thought, and that it must be a logical object of thought. It may, but need not, be an object for a thinker; but it must either be, or be within, a system. In other words, "to be" is not necessarily "to be perceived," but it is necessarily "to be implicated." And this conclusion follows from our preceding considerations, granting that existence is to be taken as a concept meaningful for philosophy.

Am I, then, to say that existence and reality are equivalent terms? Not precisely, and here another distinction remains to be noted. There are two aspects of the logical object of thought: it is (i) terms-as-related and (ii) terms and relations, a whole with separable elements. And there is a difference according as it is taken from one or the other angle—a difference in principle the same as that between Spinoza's *natura naturans* and *natura naturata*. This would appear to be a difference of importance, and words are needed to mark it. I should wish to limit the connotation of the word 'reality' to the logical object viewed in the first sense, and to use 'existence' to refer to the same object in either sense indifferently. The real, then, would mean the logical object as system; the existent would mean the same object either as system or as parts. The two terms thus are co-extensive in the sense that if X exists it is real, or if X is real it exists; but they are not identical, since an existent may not *per se* be real. This is to fall back, of course, upon the principle of the traditional doctrine of degrees; but I fail to see that we do, or can, escape the principle, however we choose to symbolize it.

Returning to the question with which the discussion of the point began, the intervening considerations would seem to lead us to hold that sheer error is both unreal and non-existent. And so, it would have to be added, is everything else which like it is to have no implications for thought—which, that is, is to have nothing to do with system. Round squares and golden mountains exist only in a universe of discourse wherein they have significance; and only if they can be subsumed in system may they be said to have reality.

If I am not shamelessly to transgress the limits of space allotted to me, I must in conclusion content myself with the barest reference (which is not at all indicative of my estimate of the subject's importance) to the recent epistemological controversy as carried forwards by the realists. At times it has seemed that the debate has gone on the assumption that the object of thought is the mere given; and, of course, in so far as this assumption is made the discussion is at once thrown beyond the reach of my method. Within my principles, however, and with suitable modification of details, there is room for both 'subsistences' and 'essences,' provided neither is so conceived as to push it outside of the real in my sense. If analysis would be aided by these further distinctions, I should be free in principle to accept them. But I should be forced to hold that analysis does not necessitate them, except in so far as they are merely distinctions among implications terminating in the object of thought; if left *in limbo*, they are from my point of view worse than useless. And I am especially fearful of essences in this regard. What I seem to miss in the dualist's account is a precise connection between essence and the situation from which it is resolved. What I should ask of him is that the linkage be made sufficiently strong to prevent essence from tumbling backwards into the abyss of sheer error. But, if this request be granted, it is not easy to see wherein his dualism lies. For then essence would appear to merge into an implicative relation and, so, to be something more than the *what* of the real thing "divorced from its *that*." If essence is relevant to the object of thought, it would seem *ipso facto* to be an aspect of system; if it is not so relevant, there would appear to be no need for further complicating the situation by the addition of an abstraction. But to argue this in detail is here impossible. And I will conclude by stating my general principle: if the subsistent and the essence are to be distinguished from the existent, the demand for such distinctions must have its locus and motive within the situation itself, and the meanings attributed to them must attach to the system from which they are resolved.

What in the above general observations is old and what new is a question which might legitimately be raised, and in reply I should certainly not be inclined to make any claims to novelty. To myself (if I may presume to adapt Bradley's statement to fit the case) all of them appear to have been mainly borrowed, and if I had only succeeded in borrowing more I probably in the future would have less to modify or retract.

PRINCIPAL PUBLICATIONS

Thought and Reality in Hegel's System (Longmans, Green & Co., 1910.)

A Study in the Philosophy of Bergson. (Longmans, Green & Co., 1916.)

Problems of Philosophy. (Henry Holt & Co., 1924.)

Five Lectures on the Problem of Mind (University of Texas Press, 1925.)

THE PHILOSOPHY OF A MELIORIST

By DURANT DRAKE

Born 1878; Professor of Philosophy, Vassar College.

THE PHILOSOPHY OF A MELIORIST

I. Personal

IF there is any keynote that has given a hint of unity to my thinking in diverse fields, it is a sense of the needless unhappiness from which men suffer, and a passionate longing to do my bit in formulating and diffusing a clearer intelligence concerning the art of living than I commonly find among my fellows, or have applied in my own life, as I have groped my way toward a greater *Lebensweisheit*.

The Philosophy of a Reformer, I thought of calling it. For I have the blood of the Crusaders in my veins, and I agree with Mr. Wells that "satisfaction with existing things is damnation." Surely we are called upon to spend ourselves without stint in the war against evil, and to lead the way, as the measure of our insight and power allows, toward that goal of rich and adventurous happiness which human life so pathetically seldom attains.

But I am keenly conscious that a reformer becomes a disagreeable and pernicious person when he thrusts his own particular nostrum down the throats of his fellows. The ways in which life may realize itself are manifold, the forms of possible happiness beyond the imaginative grasp of any one philosopher. We must guard against destroying needlessly any humble pleasure or any joy outside our own ken, in our zeal for the realization of that ideal, however lovely it be, which has captured our own imagination. To all zealous crusaders for a Cause, Santayana's words are a necessary warning: "Alas! Their propagandas! How they have filled the world with hatred, darkness, and blood! How they are still the eternal obstacle, in every home and in every heart, to a simple happiness! . . . I wish individuals, and races, and nations, to be themselves, and to multiply the forms of perfection and happiness, as nature prompts them."

But while the lover of human happiness should be catholic in his sympathies, quick to understand and slow to reprove, he cannot fail to see how needlessly mean are most men's lives; how crushed by a hard and ruthless industrial order; how cramped for lack of a liberalizing education; how blocked by a thousand stupid prejudices, superstitions, taboos. Without being so presumptuous as to suppose that he has found the ultimate truth, he will know that many of the ills from which men suffer are curable, and that philosophy, though worth cultivating for its own sake, will be judged in the end, as will every art and science, by the contribution which it has made to the welfare of sentient beings.

This at least has been the faith which has underlain my mental history. The particular events in that history are hardly worth retracing. I have come under many influences, of which the most important, perhaps, were my Christian (New England Puritan) upbringing and the philosophical atmosphere of Harvard at the turn of the century, when James, Santayana, Royce, Münsterberg, Palmer, and Dickinson Miller formed a galaxy whose like was not elsewhere to be found. My ardently religious bent was given the critical discipline it needed by the wise and scholarly teachers of the Harvard Divinity School. A later year at Columbia introduced me to Dewey, Woodbridge, and Montague, whose philosophy, in some respects alien to my earlier teaching, slowly but eventually penetrated to my consciousness. In the meantime I had been impressed by Mr. Strong's writings; and the correspondence and prolonged conversations which I have had with him during the past dozen years have been of the utmost value to me.

Like most students of philosophy I have crystallized my ideas through oral presentation before committing them to writing. My experience in teaching has been varied: first at a co-educational university, then at a college for men, and now for fourteen years at Vassar—the first college for girls to take rank by the side of the great men's colleges, and now, with its liberal curriculum, its magnificent plant, and its highly selective method of admission, more than ever in the forefront of agencies for women's education. This vocation has done what it must always do for an eager and devoted teacher—kept me in contact with growing minds and constantly at the business of questioning and reformulating my beliefs.

At Wesleyan (in Connecticut) I had to teach for three years courses in Bible; and during that period I made a careful study of the life of Jesus, my chapter on this subject in *Problems of Religion* embodying some conclusions then considered radical, but now becoming more familiar. At Vassar I have taught, in addition to my philosophical courses, the history and philosophy of education, and had some hand in educational conferences. For some years I was a member of the Council and of the Advisory Committee of the Religious Education Association, and have been (I am afraid) one of the most talkative members of the Theological Society, which we have lately made over into the American Theological Society, with Eastern and Western Divisions.

I have lived and travelled much in Europe, believing earnestly in the importance of international friendships and an international outlook. In accordance with this conviction I accepted invitations to lecture at a number of universities and clubs in Switzerland, Germany, and Italy in a sabbatical year, 1923-4, my aim being primarily to explain as well as I could in the various languages, of which I am none too proficient a master, the ideals of America. This subject I had already discussed in English in *America Faces the Future*. Needless to say, my interest was not in a complacent glorification of American life, but in summoning my countrymen to be true to the splendid visions of our forefathers, as yet very imperfectly realized in practice, and in asking sympathy from Europeans with our strivings. Conversely, I have tried to understand sympathetically the ideals of the leading European peoples and parties—including the Russian Communists, whose spirit and achievements have seemed to me, as they have to so many other impartial observers, of the utmost significance for the future of mankind.

Such, then, is the background of my thought. And now I will try to summarize the conclusions to which, through these years of study and teaching and lecturing, I have been led. Space does not permit me to show the grounds upon which I hold them; I must therefore present them with an appearance of dogmatism. But they are all, of course, tentative and subject to revision;

and my defence of them is, I hope, good-humoured and not without a sense that I may be, on any point, entirely mistaken.

II. METHODOLOGY

There is no work more important for the forwarding of human happiness than that of teaching people to love honest, fearless, open-minded, exact thinking, and to hate prejudice, dogmatism, and loose reasoning. But to think clearly and honestly demands self-restraint in belief, the habit of mental wariness, a keen scent for one's own unconscious prejudices, and, above all, a readiness to discard beliefs which it is comforting or inspiriting to hold. The average person shuns unpleasant facts as he shuns unpleasant people. Yet an unflinching facing of facts is our only road to salvation, since it is in the world of importunate facts that we have to live. So anything that fosters the habit of easy credulity is bad for us, and the "will to believe" is a dangerous self-indulgence. "The right to believe," James once told me (as he doubtless told many others) he wished he had called that famous essay. I loved the man—who did not!—but I felt then, and I feel still, that the doctrine has had a very demoralizing effect upon philosophy. If there is evidence of the truth of any hypothesis sufficient to convince the clear and unbiased mind, there is no need of any will to believe, and no question of any right; if there is not sufficient evidence, to believe because the belief "meets our needs " or "satisfies our religious natures " is an attempt to escape from reality, and is fundamentally dishonest. In the end, it will not pay. In the end, men must learn to adjust themselves to the world as it is, instead of imagining the world to be as they would like it to be. Our wills, our "needs," our "hearts," cannot tell us what exists; only empirical evidence, such as the trained scientist seeks, can do that. Philosophy must be as objective, as disinterested as science, if it is to be equally successful.

The history of philosophy, as too often taught and written up, glorifies that speculative originality, that pretentious completeness, that reverberation of moral and religious "needs," that disguised exercise of the will to believe, which characterize the systems of so many of the philosophers called great. Their grandiose vistas are far more alluring than the patient spade-work of the more critical, cautious, self-restrained thinkers. But to my mind a college teacher should beware of attracting young and impressionable minds to the fascinating dreams of the great irresponsible speculators, should expose their unconscious prejudices, their incaution and wilfulness, the futility of their attempts to find short-cuts to truth. After all, there is a technique of truth-seeking. Is it not time that philosophers developed a professional code, branding obviously specious reasoning, and what Mr. Overstreet calls "wish-thinking," as unprofessional?

With our best efforts a certain amount of subjective coloura-tion will remain. But much contemporary philosophizing seems to me needlessly subjective. For example, the use of the criterion of *inconceivability* to reject an unwelcome or puzzling hypothesis. *Anything* is conceivable; anything, that is, save what is self-contradictory, where one assertion cancels out another and leaves nothing *said*. We do not have to be able to visualize a state of affairs in order to entertain it as a supposition. And the fact that a given thinker's mind refuses to entertain a certain possi-bility is merely a bit of personal psychology. The only important question is: Is there evidence that the supposition is true or untrue?

Intuition is an equally subjective criterion. Different people have conflicting intuitions; and the belief in intuition really means belief in our own intuitions. These have a convincingness about them which is hard to resist. But it seems clear that intuition is either a rationalizing of instinct or an unanalysed residuum of experience. And either may be misleading. A summary of the results of trusting intuitions would show that while they do sometimes lead to truth they often lead to error. Only the patient use of the empirical method, as worked out by the sciences, can decide which is which.

In science, hypotheses are tested by observing how well they "work," i.e. how well they cover and explain the facts of experience. But in my own time I have seen the word "works" spoiled for serious thinkers by the intrusion of that sentimental usage which says that a belief "works" when it satisfies, or consoles, or inspires. A multitude of beliefs "work" in this sense, and most of these beliefs are untrue. A belief that "works" is said to be thereby "verified." But what is verified, in the cases to which I refer, is the inspiriting or consoling effect of believing, not the truth of the proposition believed. . . . Even the word "truth" itself is wellnigh ruined. We are told that a belief is "true" for me if it "works" for me, while another belief is true for you. A correct usage would say merely that the one belief *seems* true to me and the other to you. Or that this belief satisfies me and that belief satisfies you. The word "truth" in this "empirical" sense means merely "accepted belief," or "inspiring belief," or "working hypothesis." But to say that a given belief is a "truth" in one of these senses is merely to make a psychological observation, to describe the sort of experience someone is having at the moment, and to confuse us in our search for truth in the historic and legitimate sense of the term.

I understand that for "radical empiricism" this subjective sense of the term "truth" is the only legitimate sense. I have to-day one set of "truth-experiences", to-morrow I may have quite divergent experiences. To-day, for example, it may be "true" for me that you are dead; to-morrow, when I am better informed, it will be true for me that you are alive. . . . But what sort of "truth" was this which belonged to a proposition that declared you dead, when, as a matter of fact, you were alive! It is surely a flimsy sort of "truth"; in fact, it is precisely what a stricter usage calls "error." It did not *become* error at the moment when I learned that you were still alive. The proposition that you were dead was erroneous all the time—as you can testify; even though the supposition that you were dead had for me all the subjective earmarks of truth, and therefore, according to the radical empiricist, *was* true!

Strictly speaking, we can never know, beyond the shadow of doubt, when we have truth. We must content ourselves, when we go beyond the description of our experience of the passing moment, and beyond the dream-worlds of mathematics and logic, with various degrees of probability. But we know what

we *mean* by "truth." We mean, not a particular kind of experience, but a relation between a proposition, or a supposition, and
the objects to which it refers. Experience points beyond itself.
"Radical empiricism" is an anthropocentric philosophy in a far
profounder sense than the Ptolemaic. It is a myopic fixation upon
the flux of experience itself; noting, to be sure, its memories, its
anticipations, its outward reference, but never discounting its
subjective colouration, never penetrating beyond appearance to
existence.

III. Epistemology

This brings me to epistemology, which, in spite of considerable
current opinion to the contrary, I consider a necessary gateway
to any profound understanding of the world in which we live.
When in 1911 I published *The Problem of Things in Themselves*,
I reckoned myself an epistemological dualist, being impressed by
the duality between the cognitive state which is the vehicle of
knowledge, and the object known. Since then I have come to see
that the neo-realists are right in their contention that *what we
are aware of* is, not the cognitive state, but (in perception) outer
objects. There is much illusion mingled with our awareness of
outer reality; but *in so far as perception is accurate*, the data of
our experience are the very physical things that surround us. To
recognize this is important; and I therefore now call myself an
epistemological monist, though I still emphasize the duality of
which I have spoken, and realize that the terms "monist" and
"dualist" are too ambiguous to be of any real use.

In 1916 I conceived the idea of a co-operative volume which
should formulate a realistic epistemology more accurate (as I
thought, and still think) than that presented shortly before in
The New Realism. Six other American realists—Santayana,
Strong, Lovejoy, Pratt, Sellars, and Rogers—joined me in the
undertaking; and the volume, *Essays in Critical Realism*, was
published, after long and fruitful discussion, in 1920.

We were all convinced realists; that is, we all considered the
realistic hypothesis as overwhelmingly probable. *No* existential
proposition can be *proved*, for we have no indisputable existential

propositions to use as premises. An existential proposition is to be accepted if it covers the relevant facts of experience and explains them better than any rival hypothesis. This is surely the case with the realistic hypothesis. No scientific theory is, to my mind at least, better evidenced. In my doctor's thesis, in my essay in the co-operative volume, and again in chapter iii of *Mind and its Place in Nature*, I have set forth this evidence, as I see it, and I shall not even summarize it here.

Realism holds that physical things exist in their own right, prior to and independently of our awareness of them. But "neo-realism" had attempted too much. It had attempted to reduce the cognitive relation to two categories, the knower (or organism) and the object known. Critical realism insisted that any cognitive experience may conceivably be hallucinatory; the awareness of physical objects is not, in itself, evidence that such objects *exist*. Hence we need *three* categories to describe the cognitive situation, the knower (or self, or organism), the object of knowledge (which, in the case of knowledge of an existent, has its own independent existence), and the datum of experience, that of which we are aware. In accurate and literal knowledge the datum is identical with the object of knowledge. But whether knowledge *is* accurate and literal is a matter for inquiry in each case. Thus the three categories are always necessary for clear thinking. When they are used there is no difficulty in explaining the fact of *error*—except, of course, the metaphysical difficulty of how an erroneous datum could be "present to consciousness," could be "given." But of that later.

In the Preface to the co-operative volume I alluded to a difference of analysis between two groups within our group. That difference hinged upon the use or avoidance of the term "essence." Santayana had revived the term, and Strong, Rogers, and I adopted it in our analysis of knowledge. An essence is a "describable somewhat," a character or complex of characters; it is, in fact, anything mentionable, without regard to its existence or non-existence. Cognition consists, we said, in taking a certain essence, of which we are aware, as *existent*. Veridical perception consists in having as perceptual datum, and taking as existent, an essence which does actually exist as the object, or an aspect of the object, to which the body is reacting.

Now this use of the term "essence" seems harmless enough! Its sting lay in the fact that it enabled us to give a clear (and therefore disputable) statement of the status of the data of perception. These data seem so real that the plain man takes them to be necessarily actual components of the existing outer world. The neo-realists had attempted to return to this naïve view, but were blocked by the many difficulties which reflection interposes. Dualistic realists usually call them mental states, failing to distinguish between the essences which do exist *in us*, as our mental life, and the essences *given* in perception (such and such outer objects). It is these latter essences that *confront* us— blue skies and red sunsets, noise and music, dazzling sun and twinkling stars. But these terms all describe essences such as come under the third category of cognition; they are neither mental states nor physical existents, but data of experience. There is a physical atmosphere about our earth, but *it* is not blue; there are vibrating strings and air-waves, but they are not noise or music; there are vast globular masses of matter which we call sun and stars, but the dazzling disc and the twinkling points of light which we see are something quite different. Nor are these essences which confront us mental existents, unless in a strained and misleading use of the terms "mental" and "existence." For they are this or that "physical object out there." They are, in a word, supposititious physical objects, essences of physical aspect to which perception, whether rightly or wrongly, imputes existence.

My own belief is that these supposititious physical things take shape in our imagination through the "projection" of our mental states into the outer world. And I agree with the dualistic realists, that only the mental states and the independently existing physical things *exist*. But perception is largely illusory; the essences which confront us are, to a considerable extent, *not* components of the existent physical world. And because they are the products of "projection" they are not the essences which make up our mental life. What then? Well, they are just essences and nothing else, just items in our discourse, supposed existents. The status of being "given," being a "datum," is just this status of being imagined or supposed. And what is "given" is not existent at all—except in so far as these "given" essences *do* exist, *did* exist prior to our awareness of them.

The years since 1920 have shown how difficult it is to make a novel analysis of a familiar situation intelligible to thinkers whose minds have run in other grooves. In a number of articles, particularly in the *Philosophical Review* for January 1928 and the *Journal of Philosophy* for October 13, 1927 and March 29, 1928, I have to the best of my ability answered the critics of the doctrine; and I am not so innocent as to suppose that a page or two here will clarify for any one an analysis which, though simple enough, requires, apparently, for every one (as it required, I know, for me) a very considerable mental wrench. I have as yet seen no reason to modify the exposition which I worked out in *Mind and its Place in Nature* in 1924. And I am persuaded that the analysis of cognition presented there, or the closely similar analysis presented in several of Mr. Strong's recent writings, gives the correct solution of the difficult and baffling problem of epistemology.

IV. METAPHYSICS

The reason why the epistemological solution above outlined has not met with wider acceptance is, I suppose, because it is unintelligible without a backing in metaphysics. How can essences *appear, confront* us, be *given*, if they do not *exist*? If we read Santayana we find him distinguishing sharply between the realm of appearance (the essences brought before the mind by "intuition") and the realm of existence. But he fails to tell us how there can be a realm of appearance. How *can* an organism exercise "intuition"—or, as I should say, awareness? It may seem more mysterious that the organism can intuit essences which do not exist; but there is really just as much need of explaining how it can intuit essences which do exist.

It seems to me that to explain awareness we must suppose the organism to be something more than physical, as that term is commonly understood. It must have such a nature that the givenness of these essences is inevitable under the circumstances. Only, I submit, as we admit the existence of inner events (i.e. states of the organism) of a "psychic" character and a mechanism of "projection," can we explain our attribution to things outside our organism of the sensible qualities which we seem to perceive in them. In "introspection" we are focusing our attention upon this inner life of ours. But even here we are at arm's length, so to speak, from the events which we are introspecting; we cannot note the fine parts of our own inner events, we can cognize them only *en masse*. According to critical realism our data may be to any degree illusory. This I believe to be true of introspective data, as well as of perceptual data. But in both cases the fact that we *have* data, the fact that essences *appear*, requires for its explanation a realistic belief in mental states.

By elaborate arguments I have defended the view that this mental life of an organism is the very substance of what, if it could be perceived from without, would be called its cerebral processes. An identical set of events would in such a case be cognized in two ways; what we should know of it by introspection would be different from what we should know of it by perception, but the two sorts of knowledge, when scrutinized and corrected, would be compatible.

A perceiver would see, for example, grey matter. But the greyness would be illusory as referred to the cerebral process he was watching, as illusory as would be its apparent blueness if he were looking through blue glasses. So on correcting his physical knowledge of the cerebral processes he would finally have to admit that perception, as elaborated by science, could give him only a *structural* knowledge of these processes. Introspection, while misleading through the relative simplicity of its data, gives us a warmer, more intimate knowledge of these events, gives us their *feel*, their "psychic" character.

Now if cerebral processes have a "psychic" character, there are reasons for believing that matter everywhere has such a nature. Organic processes are indeed different from the events going on elsewhere in the world. But they have developed out of these simpler events. So, I hold, our mental life, the very substance of (some of) these organic events, has flowered out of the universal life, is of the same stuff, and differs only in *form*.

This difference, however, is profound. Consciousness is, precisely, a process of very complicated structure in space-time. I do not see how there could be perception, or memory, or any other conscious process, except as a phase of the life of complex organisms. If so, *consciousness* must not be attributed to anything of which we know except living organisms. By saying that all matter is "psychic" in nature I mean merely that it is of similar substance to that of which our mental life is composed.

This doctrine does not take us far in our knowledge of matter. Yet it is sharply set off from many contemporary views. It is existentially monistic; it postulates no "minds," or "souls," or "egos" of a substance alien to matter. Of course, physical science has not yet reduced its world to one substance; and I have no wish to be monistic in advance of science. But what I mean is that I see no good reason for an existential dualism of the traditional philosophical sort, mind *versus* body as two fundamentally different sorts of existent.

And on my view there is no need to postulate "emergent" evolution. New *forms* are, indeed, continually arising. But just as the various atoms are simply differing structures of protons and electrons, whose mass behaviour is probably the exact resultant of the behaviour of the component protons and electrons, so all existent events seem to me probably resultant from the behaviour of the ultimate units of existence. The conception of a "vital force," or "entelechy," is mysterious. No such entity has been discovered; and the argument that it is necessary to postulate such an entity to account for the behaviour of organisms is a mere argument from ignorance, based upon our present inability to explain their behaviour in detail in terms of their known components and the laws of their behaviour. In view of the extraordinary complexity, the delicate balance, and the ultra-microscopic structure of organic mechanisms, such ignorance is inevitable. But it creates no presumption against the supposition that there is a purely mechanistic explanation.

Consciousness seems to most thinkers something obviously not resultant from physical processes. But if my pan-psychic doctrine is true, it is a natural and inevitable result, granted such an initial collocation and such laws of behaviour as would produce appropriate combinations of atoms and a favourable environment. For on my monistic view no new substance appears on the scene when consciousness appears, but only more complex mechanisms, capable of receiving impressions from, and reacting to, the world about them in more and more complicated ways.

Mechanisms, I say; and I accept the deterministic implications of the term. But this is not to deny "free will," in the empirical and useful sense of the term. Choosing and willing are facts that certainly take place. We are free, in the sense in which freemen are free and slaves are not; our volitional impulses are causes of subsequent events. The empirical fact is that we are free to do as we will, within limits, if we exert our wills vigorously enough to overcome whatever inner and outer obstacles stand in our way.

There is, to be sure, another sense of the term "free will," in which it means the absence, or partial absence, of causes out of which our volitions grow. Why do some people want to believe in such uncaused volitions? I suppose it is because they like to believe that, whatever their past life, their inherited disposition, and their nurturing environment, they can at any moment, by merely exercising their wills, do what is right. This goes with the traditional notion that acts are rather obviously right or wrong, that right conduct is to be had for the choosing, and wrongdoing is the result of a perverse exercise of the will. A more sophisticated ethics shows us that right conduct is a matter of delicate adjustment to infinitely varying situations, requiring not only the will to do right, but sound instincts, wide sympathies, and keen intelligence. To improve human behaviour is an intricate art, which includes the guiding of inherited tendencies, the counteracting of bad environmental influences, and the bringing to bear of new and appropriate stimuli. Success in this task can only be expected to the degree in which causal relations can be discovered and utilized. That is why all clear-headed educators, social reformers, penologists, and the like, are working on the assumption that determinism is true.

In some cases, to be sure, what is most needful is to rouse the will to exert itself; for the one thing lacking to produce right conduct may be the will to adopt it. So praise, blame, the holding of people "responsible" for their acts, even punishment, at times, and the inciting of remorse, have their uses in determining conduct. But if there is no determinate way of developing a wholesome will, if the will is an untrainable, indeterminate variable, then there is no reason for expecting that the most skilful technique of education can make headway against the capriciousness of this elusive and mysterious entity. It will readily be seen that a philosopher who pins his faith, as I do, upon a future life for man on earth far wiser and happier than any he has yet achieved, must hope that determinism is true. Yet believing as I do that we should not let our hopes influence our beliefs, and realizing that the indeterministic hypothesis, though lacking positive evidence, cannot be disproved, I have to content myself with saying that even if there be a little loose play in the human organism, at least its behaviour can be *very largely* moulded by appropriate influences, and *in so far* man's future may be made better than his past.

V. Ethics

Some people fear that the acceptance of the deterministic hypothesis will lead men to a sense of personal irresponsibility, and so to folly and sin. But if this ever happens it is proof that such men have not learned the *worth* of morality. They would not prefer discordant to melodious music, or unpalatable to delicious food. Neither will they prefer foolish conduct if they have clearly seen its folly. The trouble is, traditional exhortation has led people to divide conduct into delightful behaviour which they really *want* to adopt, and drably righteous behaviour which they feel they *ought* to adopt. Once convince men that morality is simply the best way to live, and that to be virtuous is to be a virtuoso in life—once teach a morality that really *is* the best way to live, and normal people will espouse it gladly, because they will actually *prefer* it. They will be eager to find means of counteracting the tendencies to folly which they find in themselves; they will be on the side of morality instead of rebelling in their hearts against it.

Moreover, when this sensible attitude toward morality becomes commoner, we shall be able to make headway against the stupidities and superstitions of current moral standards and develop a better code than is yet anywhere generally accepted. We must, of course, go gingerly in these matters, adopting a scientific attitude and distrusting the overemphasis of our immediate desires. But traditional morality is not moral enough. It is haphazard, formalistic, dogmatic, and blind. It sustains manifold injustices, fails to rebuke some of the most callously anti-social forms of conduct, and, on the other hand, too often stifles the free and happy development of personality. We must apply the same open-minded, experimental attitude toward morality that has so strikingly improved the material aspects of our life. We must base our morals solidly upon observation of the results of conduct, and aim consciously to secure the maximum of attainable happiness for mankind.

This view, which I expressed in *Problems of Conduct*, I have applied even more explicitly in my latest volume (1928), *The New Morality*. Perhaps I should apologize for that catchy title; I do not mean, of course, that this conception of morality is original with me, or new in this twentieth century. But it is a conception held as yet by a very small minority; and its acceptance in widespread degree will be a phenomenon of the utmost importance.

There are always those who cannot distinguish between the conception of the general happiness as the *raison d'être* of morality and the preaching of a self-indulgent epicureanism. One of the primary lessons of experience is that pleasure-seeking, when more than incidental, is a poor way to forward the general happiness, and that selfishness is its greatest foe. But these practical decisions have nothing to do with the philosophical conclusion that the justification of moral rules lies in their value in conducing to human happiness. Certainly we must learn to think not in terms merely of our own little life, or even of the interests of the particular group, or party, or nation to which we happen to belong, but in terms of the welfare of mankind. But if sacrifices are to be made, they must be for a greater good. Any so-called "moral" code that does not make for the greatest attainable happiness is a cruel code, deserving our emphatic repudiation.

I have considerable sympathy with the current tendency to define good and bad in purely biological terms. According to this "behaviouristic" value-philosophy, values are simply "objects of interest"; whatever an organism seeks is *ipso facto* a good. Morality, then, consists in an organization or integration of "interests." . . . This is much better than supernaturalistic or mystical ethics. It is correct in making values relative to the needs and situations of organisms. But, I submit, the mere fact that an organism tends to react in this way or that does not create *value*, any more than the fact that water tends to a lower level makes a waterfall a good. If water *enjoyed* falling, a waterfall *would* be a good. It is the fact that organisms *enjoy* this and *suffer* from that, which brings good and evil into being. If they had no capacity for enjoyment or suffering there would be no point in calling one act *better* than another; we might describe organic tendencies, but it would not *matter* in the least which found expression in action. In their primary sense "good" and "bad" refer to qualities of conscious experience. The moral sense of these terms is derived from this primary denotation.

Objects and acts, then, are not "good" or "bad" because desired, but because, whether or not we happen to desire them or feel the urge toward them, they are, potentially, means for the enhancement or diminution of happiness. It is not a matter of any one's opinion, or approval, or interest, it is a matter of *fact*. There are desires and inner drives, the fulfilment of which would bring only pain. On the other hand, there are acts for which we have no desire, conscious or unconscious, which would bring happiness in their train. We must learn what to *desire*.

It is not true as an empirical fact that a complete integration of interests is always desirable. To some extent acts may remain miscellaneous; to exclude everything that does not "integrate" may be to lose much of the incidental worth of living. An integration of interests is *better* than a set of miscellaneous and independent interests only in so far as mutual independence brings conflict, and that, in turn, unhappiness. It is a matter for experimental observation to decide when it is best to curb impulses and when we should be tolerant of divergent purposes and diverse forms of happiness.

Certainly youth, and older folk, too, should be flaming and adventurous and gay, when the hard conditions of human life permit. Most people only half live. We should work to secure for men and women rich, varied, interesting experiences, so far as they can have them without hurting themselves or others. We should get out of our stupid individualism, cultivate *Mitfreude*, and count the joys of our fellows as our own. Our religion should concern itself with the technique of happiness—which otherwise people will take so little trouble to learn! It must, indeed, since human nature is so heedless and selfish, be admonitory and repressive. But through and beyond these necessary inhibitions it should keep before men the vision of a more loving and daring, and so more exciting and joyous, human life.

VI. PHILOSOPHY OF RELIGION

What, then, is religion? I have expressed my ideas on this important matter in several books, but perhaps most clearly and succinctly in an article on "The Definition of Religion" in the *Journal of Religion* for March 1927. As a matter of fact any definition of religion is arbitrary. No brief formula could cover all the confused and multitudinous phenomena of the historic religions; and our definitions are really formulations of what we consider most important and worth preserving.

Those who define religion in terms of emotional experience, a sense of mystery, of dependence, of gratitude, or of oneness with God, do so doubtless because such a "deepening of the inner life" seems to them of supreme value. And certainly some of these emotions and attitudes are intrinsically worth cultivating.

The mystic's ecstasy is at its best one of the most wonderful of human experiences. . . . But joyous and inspiriting as these emotions may be, they have their dangers. In particular they may cloud our thinking and they may paralyse our activity. Emotional attitudes do for most people take the place of *evidence*; they drug the mind into accepting pleasant beliefs, instead of prodding it to inquire whether or not the beliefs are true. They do for many take the place of a truly religious *life*; they lead to a glossing over of the maladjustments in human life, instead of prodding people into a serious effort to cure them. The satisfaction in a sense of mystery leads to contentment with ignorance. The mystic's rapture leads to an unjustified and inhuman optimism. The sense of dependence leads to a feeling of helplessness and resignation. Instead of this glorification of impotence, or the blindfolded and unsocial optimism of the mystic, man needs to realize his power, through study and effort, to understand and remake his world. We must get away from the lazy and selfish idea that religion exists primarily for personal consolation. There is something more important than that.

Many people think of religion as primarily a matter of beliefs— belief in a supernatural direction of events, in certain alleged historical events (such as the resurrection of Jesus), in the immortality of the soul, or, more vaguely, in the friendliness of the cosmos to man. But as to all this, the unanswerable objection is that religion has no special way of determining whether or not these beliefs are true; that is the task of science, including in that term a scientific history and philosophy. If there is sufficient evidence to convince the impartial mind that any of these infinitely varying beliefs is true, there is no need for religion to give such a belief artificial protection and erect it into a dogma. If there is not sufficient evidence, a Church has no moral right to teach the doctrine as ascertained truth. To do so is to encourage people to be prejudiced, i.e. to prejudge the issue, to answer momentous questions without going through the laborious task of examining the evidence impartially, weighing contrary hypotheses, keeping the judgment suspended, and revising ideas continually in accordance with new discoveries.

There will be many, of course, to argue that religious experience constitutes or contains evidence that certain of these cosmological or historical beliefs are true. These arguments are too numerous to deal with here. I can only record my conclusion that there is nothing to be learned about reality from these experiences, save only as to the laws of psychology. I am not inexperienced in such directions; but I can see no reason for supposing that mystical experiences, or conversion, or faith, have any *noetic* value. There are no discoverable organs by means of which we can get, through these experiences, into contact with a trans-subjective reality. And the hypothesis that we are in such contact explains nothing that cannot be explained in purely psychological terms.

We must be honest enough to say outright that the historical doctrines of traditional Christianity are based upon an historical method long since discarded by trained historians in other fields. And its traditional cosmological doctrines are based either upon loose reasoning or upon premises unwarrantably assumed. Happily, most of these doctrines concern matters of merely theoretic interest. Not that I wish to disparage theory, having spent a large part of my life in theorizing. But theorizing about the universe or the soul is philosophy, and theorizing about a Virgin Birth or Resurrection is historical speculation. Neither is religion. Men believe these doctrines because they have been taught to believe them, because their family and friends believe them, because they cannot bear to give them up. But two things are certain: first, we do not really know any of these doctrines to be true; and secondly, it does not make any fundamental difference in our duties, whether they are true or untrue.

One word in parenthesis. This intellectual honesty does not necessitate a rejection of the belief in God. For there are conceptions of God that necessitate no dubious arguments and no will to believe. Since I am here making a statement of my own beliefs, I will say that in a very real sense I believe in God, both transcendent and immanent. God as transcendent is an essence, the ideal Good, bearing much the same relation to specific goods as philosophy does to the sciences. God as immanent is the Power which is visibly in the world making for righteousness (as Matthew Arnold said) and all Good. God is the universal self in each of us, our good will and idealism and intelligence which binds us together and drives us on by inner compulsion toward that ideal life for which in our better moments we strive.

What is fundamentally important in religion, however, is not to have a clear and rational conception of God, but to live as brothers one with another. Religion on its best side is a continual rededication of the heart to ideals; it is moral idealism gladly espoused and devotedly wrought into life. The real enemies of religion are not freethinking and "unbelief," but selfishness, laziness, intolerance, divisiveness, callous individualism. In so far as religious emotions, theological beliefs, ceremonies, sacraments and church-going foster a really religious *life*, their usefulness may be gratefully acknowledged. But the worth of a heroic and radiant life depends upon none of these other things. To find the best way to live together is a matter for empirical study, and is not to be deduced from any theological belief. Nor, to adopt it, is it necessary to seek any supernatural help.

We do, however, individually need help. Traditional techniques of conversion and moral inspiration, as used by the churches, are hopelessly intertangled with theological ideas which men are increasingly unable to accept. It is imperative that we learn how to get equally good results, and to get them for a far greater number of people, without imposing upon their minds these often beautiful but ill-founded and inevitably passing beliefs. We need a great religious revival, the preaching of a religion which, without being at odds with our intelligence, will make us so in love with love as the way of life that social injustices will be wiped out and war become impossible. An important task for philosophy is to pave the way for such a religion by clearing the ground of the false ideas of religion which obsess men's minds, and bringing into relief the true function of religion in human society. That function is to lead us to identify ourselves individually with the Great Community of men and women of good will, and by thus lifting us above our personal fortunes and giving us something great and lasting to live for, to keep alive in each of us a sustaining faith and a steady underglow of joy.

This is the philosophy, not of an optimist who believes that all's right with the world, but of a meliorist, who holds that human life can and must be made far happier than it has ever yet, in any lasting way, become for any but a few fortunate souls; the philosophy of one who holds that the way to such a consummation is through a rigorously scientific training in fact and a parallel development of human affections and of religious ardour—in short, through the increase of intelligence and of love.

PRINCIPAL PUBLICATIONS

The Problem of Conduct (Houghton Mifflin & Co., 1914).
The Problem of Religion (Houghton Mifflin & Co., 1916).
Contribution to *Essays in Critical Realism* (The Macmillan Co., 1920).
Mind and its Place in Nature (The Macmillan Co., 1925).
The New Morality (The Macmillan Co., 1928).

PHILOSOPHICAL LIBERALISM

By C. J. DUCASSE

Born 1881; Professor of Philosophy, Brown University,
Providence, R.I.

PHILOSOPHICAL LIBERALISM

STRANGELY enough I reached the age of twenty-four without any suspicion that I harboured a latent interest in philosophy, indeed, without even adequately realizing that such a subject as philosophy existed. My early studies of Latin and Greek in a French *Lycée* would, in the course of time, have made me acquainted with some of the ancient philosophers; but after some years I abandoned the classical curriculum and turned to mathematics and science, with a view to preparing myself for the *École Centrale* and the career of a civil engineer. Illness, however, interrupted these plans and led to their eventual abandonment. I then spent a year in England, and within a few months of my return to France left for Mexico City to enter a business house in a minor position which had been opened to me there through connections.

As I look back upon these early years in France and England, a few things stand out which now seem to me to have been factors of some importance in my intellectual development. I still remember, for instance, the vivid impression of the moment when, in my study of Latin, I first realized in myself an appreciation of sentence structure. I also remember becoming clearly conscious some years later that the mathematical, and in particular the geometrical, modes of thought were to some extent colouring my reasoning processes on other subjects, inclining me to seek order, clearness, and objectivity. Again, I recall that the habit I eventually developed, of beginning every systematic inquiry with the most definite statement possible of the matter in doubt, had its origin in the constant question, "What are we trying to find out?" asked in class by one of my teachers in England, Dr. Cecil Reddie.

After two years in Mexico I came to New York. I had as yet discovered in myself no special interest in any one subject or liking for any one occupation. Only the need of making a living had led me into business offices, and I can well remember how puzzled as to my place in the general scheme of things I felt at times when not engrossed with the novelty of life in surroundings so different from those in which I had grown up. It was after a year or two in New York that a philosophical book for the first time came into my hands. It was called *The Science of Peace*, and written by a Hindu scholar named Bhagavan Das. The book dealt with the relation of the Individual to the Absolute, and contained a chapter, beyond which I think I did not go, in which the author brought into his discussion the thought of various European philosophers, and in particular of Fichte and Hegel. That I found such a book rather hard to understand goes without saying; but the reading of it at least made me realize the existence and the general nature of the questions that philosophy asks, and revealed to me at the same time the intense interest that such questions had for me. I was then able to perceive in my recollections of earlier years some incidents which, all unheeded at the time, had nevertheless pointed to philosophical leanings. I recall, for instance, something that occurred when, together with other young people preparing to make their first Communion, I was being instructed in the elements of Christian theology by the pastor of the French Protestant Church, to which my parents belonged. He had explained how the freedom of man's will and the omniscience of God were reconciled. When at the next meeting of the class I was called on to recite, I shocked the good man by giving quite a different account of the matter, which I had worked out for myself in the meantime. He spent much effort trying to make me "understand," and I almost as much trying to explain that I understood, but did not agree.

Not long after my discovery of philosophy through the book mentioned, I left New York for the Pacific Coast, and in a few months, finding my dislike of business pursuits growing at the same rate as my preoccupation with philosophical questions, I entered the University of Washington. The years I spent in business offices, where punctuality, diligence, and dependability are exacted of all, were without doubt salutary discipline for a temperament by nature prone to the laziness of an imaginative sort which often goes with artistic inclinations. Such inclinations in myself I trace to a German maternal grandfather, who in his day attained some success as a painter. To him, perhaps, I owe also a rather strong mystical bent, which somehow manages to thrive in peace side by side with what I may possess of the traits typical rather of the French strain, such as love of explicitness and clear logical articulation. Among other general factors of influence should, I think, also be reckoned the removal from my native environment to Mexico and the United States. The fact that I had to make my living there as I went forced me to adapt myself to the ways and institutions of my new surroundings in a far more thorough fashion than if I had come as a traveller. This has, I believe, tended to develop in me the possibility of sympathetic insight into diverse or even incompatible traditions, philosophic and otherwise, as well as a corresponding measure of freedom from the danger of imprisonment within any single one.

To my first teachers in philosophy and psychology at the University of Washington I am conscious of a heavy debt. Close contact from the outset with the active and keenly critical mind of Professor W. Savery acted, not only as an invaluable general stimulus, but also as a constant incentive to logical watchfulness of my own thoughts and those expressed by others. His merciless dismissal of the pretentious, empty words which so often would pass for philosophical thought, early placed before me the wholesome example of an exacting intellectual standard. My work with Professor H. C. Stevens in the psychological laboratory gave me my first concrete acquaintance with the nature and the practice of scientific method in empirical investigations. I had the privilege of working with him on a problem in which he was at the time interested, and the tireless patience, painstaking care, and scrupulous scientific honesty that characterized his procedure in research constituted a lesson to which I owe much. At Harvard, where I came three years later to study for the doctorate, most of my work was with Professor Royce. His unaffected and kindly but impressive personality, his powerful constructive intellect, the extraordinary range and thoroughness of his learning, and the genius which enabled him to find for even remotely abstract logical considerations the most concrete and living illustrations, all made upon me a profound and lasting impression, the effect of which, although not easy to analyse in detail, has been far-reaching.

However, among all the contacts, impressions, and experiences of my student days one event stands out above everything else in the effects it has had on my subsequent philosophical development. Up to the time of my coming to Harvard, the train of thought which had affected me most was the idealistic. The philosophy of Berkeley had disclosed to me a novel and fascinating point of view, which I had followed through Hume; Hume had led me to Kant, and from Kant I had come to rest in Schopenhauer, of the essential soundness of whose philosophical system I was thoroughly convinced. Realism had thus up to then made very little impression upon me. On the occasion of my first paper in Professor Perry's seminary at Harvard, however, the actuality and the nature of neo-realism were brought home to me suddenly and in the most living manner possible. On that, to me, memorable occasion I defended my idealistic positions fiercely, and remained unconvinced of any unsoundness in them. On the other hand, I could not at the time clearly perceive the defect which I believed existed in the position of Professor Perry, and I resolved to examine his published articles with care before the next meeting of the seminary. It was a few days after this that the event to which I have alluded above occurred. I was at home quietly reading some book unconnected with the matter when suddenly a most vivid and luminous insight came to me that neither idealism, nor realism, nor any other metaphysical position could, in the very nature of things, be either refuted or proved. Startling as were to me both the content of this insight and the abruptness of its irruption into my consciousness, it proved to be but the beginning of some forty-eight hours of the most extraordinary state of mind I have ever experienced. It was as if the key-log of a jam on some river had suddenly given way. All my previous philosophical ideas seemed to be loosed from their moorings, and to rearrange themselves in new relations together with countless others, unthought of before, that came tumbling in their train. For nearly two days, with hardly any sleep or food, and in a state of the highest exaltation, I wrote feverishly, yet not fast enough to put down anything more than bare reminders of the seemingly numberless ideas which kept crowding into my consciousness. But alas! these reminders mostly proved quite inadequate to recall the ideas they were meant to fix, when later in soberer mood I returned to them with that purpose. However, the original insight that had precipitated all the rest remained clear and unimpaired at the end, and radically altered my philosophical perspective. If the fundamental position of every ontology is incapable equally of proof or disproof, then it is logically arbitrary, and represents only the taste, whim, or temperament of its upholder. Once this conviction is attained, tolerance becomes the only rationally possible attitude, and a tolerance not of the subjective sort that we may develop towards the mistakes or the ignorance of others, but of the objective kind which is commanded by differences of sheer taste, such as exist, for example, in wines or in foods. The general standpoint is characterized by a conviction of the complete relativity to extra-logical factors, of the very bases of metaphysical systems; and it seems on the whole best labelled by the name which Professor Royce suggested to me at the time—namely, philosophical liberalism. Logically speaking, such a position stands to others in the relation which holds between a propositional function and the several propositions obtainable from it by assigning to its variables their several possible "values." Not in ontology only, but as the following pages will show in every other branch of philosophy also, an analogous, completely relativistic analysis has forced itself upon me, with its unavoidable implication that in each case the "values" which the variables receive depend wholly upon the constitution or the aims of the individual concerned, or, as some might prefer to put it, upon the free expression of the human spirit.

From this account of early experiences, influencing factors, and opinions, I now pass to an outline of the philosophical position to the development of which they seem to me to have contributed in various ways; and in this connection I must acknowledge the great debt which in more recent years I have come to owe to the appreciation and the encouragement generously given me by Professor Santayana and Professor Lovejoy, and by my mathematical friend, Professor E. T. Bell.

I begin with a brief statement of what I conceive to be the proper subject-matter and method of philosophy. The view often put forward that philosophy differs from the sciences in being more general, seems to me untenable. The scientist acknowledges no limits of generalization or abstraction, at which he would have to stop and call in the philosopher. On the contrary, the scientist goes just as far as he can, and when he stops it is because for the time being he lacks the facts or the insight needed to go farther. These the philosopher cannot supply; his generalizations are not more far-reaching than those of the scientist, but about other things. It is in respect of subject-matter, then, that philosophy does, I believe, essentially differ from natural science. The subject-matter which philosophy alone studies, and which seems to me its only proper subject-matter, is values. In saying this I do not mean that it is the task of the philosopher to apply value-predicates to facts. That is the task of the critic. The task of the philosopher is to supply exact knowledge of the meaning of the value-predicates that criticism must use. We employ constantly a vast number of critical predicates, the meaning of which we cannot be said to understand except in the vague, intuitive way which suffices for habit-covered situations. When such predicates are to serve, not as stimuli to immediate actions or decisions, but as bases for remote deductions, the most explicit and accurate knowledge of their meaning then becomes indispensable. Extemporized analysis does not yield it, and neither do any of the sciences, since they all study objects of quite a different sort. It is philosophy alone which scientifically investigates the meaning and the varieties of possible subjects of application of such predicates of criticism as true, valid, clear, right, good, beautiful, sublime, etc.; and this task involves a good deal more than would appear at first sight. For instance, with regard to the predicate True, it involves not only analysing its meaning accurately, but also analysing the import of such modifiers of it as Necessarily, Certainly, Possibly, Probably.

And it involves also a classification of the logical kinds of entities of which truth can be predicated—that is to say, of propositions, and an accurate account of the import of each kind. This means an analysis of all such fundamental categories as Causation, Teleology, Space, Time, Identity, Substance, and so on. Nothing short of all this constitutes an adequate instrument of epistemic criticism and the fashioning of that instrument, and of corresponding instruments of æsthetic, ethical, and other types of criticism is the task of philosophy.

Philosophy may thus be defined as the general theory of criticism. Man picks his course through life by a process of evaluation which is at first unaware of itself and immediately practical. Criticism—which, of course, does not mean only adverse criticism—is the later stage in man's development, at which the evaluations are conscious and formulated, and therefore no longer necessarily incorporated immediately into life. The possibility of such delay itself makes possible the criticism of criticisms, which is what goes by the name of philosophizing. The final product of the philosophizing process is a philosophy, i.e. a general theory of criticism in all fields. Criticism which is self-conscious and systematic in the sense that it possesses full and clear knowledge of the meaning and implications of its predicates may thus be described as applied philosophy. When, on the contrary, criticism is not equipped with such knowledge, it is blind and haphazard. What can be said of it then, is only that it implies a philosophy and, almost unavoidably, one replete with contradictions.

From this it becomes evident that the task of philosophy and that of criticism are distinct in that it is not the task of philosophy to apply value-predicates to concrete facts, while, on the other hand, there is a realm in which the philosopher, like the scientist, is critic. That realm is the realm of claims to truth, so far as they concern propositions about facts within the field of his own subject-matter. The difference in this regard between the philosopher and the scientist is only that the philosopher is critic of the truth of propositions about truth and other values; whereas the scientist is critic of the truth only of propositions about matters other than truth or other values.

As to the possibility of contact and mutual service between philosophy and science, it seems to me, on the one hand, that their respective subject-matters are completely distinct, and I should therefore fully endorse the assertion of the physicist, Von Laue, that "one of the marks of a correct theory of knowledge is that it is invariant with respect to changes of physical theory" (*Die Relativitätstheorie*, vol. ii, p. 42). On the other hand, one of the things which as a matter of psychological fact is bound to be of great service to the philosopher in constructing a correct theory of knowledge, is acquaintance with the epistemic aspects of the scientific theories through the changes in which his epistemology is itself to remain invariant. The scientist, in his work, uses the various epistemic categories. At times he finds that their application to a novel problem in his field demands some analysis of their essential import. He then improvises so much of an epistemological analysis as the particular case requires. Such analyses, while for the most part very limited in scope, are likely, nevertheless, to be quite sound so far as they go just because they have immediately in view some very definite case; and one test of the soundness of a general epistemology will therefore be its including as special cases the particular analyses which the scientist's immediate needs suggested and certified.

On the other hand, if an epistemology is clear and determinate enough to have discernible bearings on concrete epistemic problems, it may conceivably come to render valuable service to the theoretical scientist by freeing his improvised epistemic tools from accidental limitations, or by proffering to him some tool for which he may be groping. Doing this, however, would not at all be a case of philosophy's adding to the content or to the generality of the propositions of the science concerned. That is something which philosophy, I think, never does.

The view formulated of the general nature and task of philosophy leaves out some problems which philosophers have commonly discussed, for instance, those of the origin and development of matter, life, and mind. But it seems to me that such questions fall completely within the domain of natural science. Only, natural science is not yet far enough advanced to answer them as it already can others of the same type in geology or paleontology. Certainly the answers which philosophers have proposed to questions of the sort mentioned have never been anything but speculations. They have, it is true, often started from the facts already ascertained by science; but they have quickly left those facts so far behind as to reach a point where even an estimation of relative probabilities is wholly out of the question. Answers of this sort have no claim to the name of knowledge. They represent only the particular suppositions which, among those not clearly forbidden by known facts, happened most to appeal to the temperaments of the persons who made them. They constitute private faiths, stated often in more or less naturalistic language, but hardly more closely related to knowledge properly so-called than are, for instance, the creation myths found in various religions.

The ontological problem, on the contrary, I regard as truly falling within the proper domain of philosophy, because I hold the predicate Real to be a critical, i.e. an evaluative, predicate, and not, as has been generally assumed, a descriptive one. On this rests the ontological liberalism of the sudden advent of which on my psychological horizon I have already said something, and the logical aspects of which will be set forth in the sequel.

If philosophy, in respect of subject-matter, differs radically from the sciences, I believe, on the contrary, that in respect of method it is, or rather should be, like science; for both philosophy and science are attempts to know, and man has so far discovered only one trustworthy road to knowledge in whatever field, the road, namely, called Scientific Method. The general nature of scientific method is well understood, but the manner in which it is to be applied to philosophical inquiries is still in the minds of many a matter of doubt. Obviously philosophy, like science, should start from facts, and test the hypotheses it frames by observing whether or not they fit the facts. But for philosophy, it seems to me that the relevant facts are language-facts, since, according to the conception of it previously indicated, its hypotheses all ultimately concern the meaning of predicates of value or of status in respect of value. The language-facts which are philosophy's data consist of common phrases where the particular term which happens to be under scrutiny is, not talked about, but used, and used in a manner admittedly correct. All well-educated persons know the meaning of the words of their language, in the sense that they are able both to use them correctly and to understand sentences in which they occur; but not in the sense of being able to give the explicit analysis of their meaning which philosophy seeks. The meaning as intuited in correct usage, however, constitutes the fact which is to be analysed, and which any hypothesis must fit that purports to state what the word considered means. The test of its fitting is whether it can be substituted for the word in any phrase where it occurs, without changing the meaning which the phrase has to language intuition. This is to say that the accounts which philosophers give of the meaning of the various critical predicates must be discoveries, not inventions. For if the philosopher arbitrarily prescribes meanings for terms already in common use, he is then only manufacturing a new language out of old words, not solving any problems. Arbitrary prescription of meaning for an existing word is permissible only within the linguistic penumbra between the characters which the correct usage of the word clearly implies and those which it clearly rules out. Technical terms, of course, are another matter. They are sometimes necessary, and should then be defined accurately; but as Whewell has justly pointed out, even such definitions are seldom wholly arbitrary, for if they are not merely to create idle concepts remaining insulated from all reality, they must be so framed as to make true certain propositions of fact and false certain others in which the word defined is to figure. Towards technical terms in philosophy, however, I must confess to an attitude of great suspicion, traceable perhaps to Professor Royce's admonitions in regard to some early terminological wild oats of my own. It seems to me that too often the use of technical terms has tended only to embalm some philosophical problem. A name given to it comes to pass for the solution, and henceforth easily serves as an abracadabra wherewith to make metaphysical rabbits come out of the cosmic hat. If we asked a stage magician how rabbits can come out of a hat that contained none, and he should reply that they "emerge," we should be well enough aware that he had but given a name to the fact we wished him to explain. But when the word Emergence is imported into philosophy, it is easy to forget that it explains nothing, and is, on the contrary, the very label which designates a particular sort of ignorance.

The conception now outlined of the proper task of philosophy, and of what scientific method means as applied to that task, indicates the general theme of my philosophical creed. The implications of that theme, in respect to the typical problems of the several branches of philosophy, remain to be exhibited. The ontological problem will be considered first.

Any ontology reduced to its simplest statement is obviously a proposition of the form "To be is to be X," or "To be real is to be X"; but the two forms are not equivalent. Any proposition of the first form, such as "To be is to be perceived," or "To be is to be material," is *a priori* false if taken literally, since what it does is to subsume being-in-general under one of its own species. Such a proposal is obviously as absurd as would be that of stuffing the whole of a building into one only of its rooms, since the name of the other "rooms" of Being must then, in violation of the good usage of those names, either be made to signify some part of one's own room or else be declared so many synonyms for the word Nothing. We may, of course, if we wish, confine ourselves wholly to one room, but we cannot logically force others to do so, nor any more refute their claim that other rooms exist than they can themselves then prove that claim to us.

The absurdity just mentioned, however, is not involved in any ontology stated in the form "To be real is to be X," for such a proposition merely divides the total realm of Being into two sub-classes. One of them, asserted to constitute Reality, is Being which has the character X; and the other, consisting of Being which lacks that character, is said to be Appearance or Unreality. In the case of an ontology so stated the question is only whether in fact it is true or false that to be real is to be X.

To answer this question we must, conformably to the method described above, consider a number of ordinary cases of the manner in which the word Real is actually used. For instance, it would be said that Spain is a real country, but Utopia is not; that the table-top appears trapezoidal, but is really rectangular, although for the painter it is really trapezoidal; that the table appears solid, but is really a cloud of electrons. Again, one commonly speaks of what one really means, really feels, really imagines, really wants, really is doing; of the realization of one's dreams, and of the possibility of considering dreams as the only realities. In considering such cases of the way in which the word Real is used, it soon, I think, becomes obvious that being real, like being mayor or governor, is a status occupied by something, not a quality discernible in the thing. The same thing is called real by one person and not by another; or by ourselves at one time and not at another. But, unlike being mayor, being real is a status of relation to somebody's valuation, not of relation to other objects.

Of the various hypotheses as to the meaning of the word Real that have been proposed by philosophers, the one which seems to me to have come nearest to fitting the facts is that which asserts "reality" to mean that of which we must take account for our purposes. But it does not quite fit, inasmuch as we are not only purposive, planning, rational beings, but also to some extent the very opposite. To that opposite self of ours, the Real is not, as for our teleological self, the orderly and rational aspect of Being, but on the contrary its chaotic, irrational, unpredictable, novel aspect, since it is that aspect which brings to us the immediate and intrinsic values of adventure, excitement, strong emotion, strange feeling. Properly has it been asked:

> Ist die Vernunft allein getauft?
> Sind die Leidenschaften Heiden?

The word Real cannot, therefore, be defined in terms exclusively of instrumental value. The analysis of its meaning, which seems to me to fit accurately all the facts, is rather this: Real is the predicate applied by any person to anything, to mean that that thing has at the moment value for him, positive or negative, intrinsic or instrumental. This, I believe, is the only meaning of

Real that remains invariant through all changes of attitude or interest, and through all the varieties of objects to which at different times we apply the term. Reality is thus objective in the sense that it is of objects of reference that it is predicable, and subjective in the sense that what it predicates of such objects is their being of a nature which, at the time, has for us value, whether positive or negative, intrinsic or instrumental.

The other views of the nature of reality that have been formulated in the past appear to me to bear to this one something like the relation of species to a genus. They are deducible from it by specifying as supreme some one of the typical interests of which man is capable. That view itself is rooted in a taste for the most inclusive, universal, and objective view-point possible; and that taste is not obligatory on any one else. Obviously, in the very nature of that view, I can have no logical quarrel with the ontological position of another, but only with the logic of his claim to have "proved" that position or "disproved" some other.

In the realm of Epistemology I find myself similarly led to a view for which the only objective constants are relational schemata, with the consequent need for the intervention of a logically arbitrary choice by the individual. The general nature of that view will be indicated by an outline of the answer I would propose to the problem of truth, and then by briefer statements on such problems as that of objective reference, of the internality of relations, and of causation.

The knowledge possessed by man represents facts which were there to be known, but it represents no less interests in man which noticed the facts, or which moved him to search for such as would satisfy these interests. Indeed, so insistent are they that when neither accident nor search brings to man that which would satisfy them, he creates it if he can. A microscope is one instance and the concept of the electron another. Man's knowledge has thus two poles, one objective and the other subjective; and its instruments, as Whewell justly says, are observation and definition. The theory of truth which alone seems to me adequate is determined by such considerations. Needless to say, the word Truth is used here to denote something predicable of propositions, and not as a synonym of the word Fact, which, so far as I can see, means merely the import of a true proposition.

Every proposition asserted in good faith serves either to answer or to forestall a question. That question in each case assumes some state of affairs not itself regarded as in doubt, but giving rise to a doubt which the question indicates, and which the proposition claims to remove. Thus the question, "Does this piece of ore weigh 1 lb.?" assumes that something is before us, that it is a piece of ore, and that it has weight. The doubt raised is whether that weight is 1 lb.; and the proposition "This piece of ore weighs 1 lb." claims to remove that doubt. When propositions are viewed in this way, Subject and Predicate simply mean *Datum* and *Dubitatum*; and every proposition, whether relational or not, which is asserted in good faith, then declares a similarity or dissimilarity between something defined and something observable—between the characters connoted by one term and the characters concretely present in the thing which is denoted by the other term. In the proposition just considered, for instance, the assertion is that one of the characters observable in the thing denoted by the subject, "This piece of ore," is the same as the character connoted by the predicate, "weighing 1 lb." Had the proposition been existential instead of descriptive, the terms would merely have been inverted. The question would have been, "Is there something weighing 1 lb.?" and the proposition would have been an assertion about the character connoted by the term "weighing 1 lb.," to the effect that it is concretely observable in the piece of ore pointed to. In short, descriptive propositions predicate the "what" of the given "this"; existential propositions, on the contrary, predicate the "this" of the given "what."

Leaving existential propositions out of further account here for the sake of simplicity, it is obvious that the truth or falsity of the proposition, "This piece of ore weighs 1 lb.," depends, among other things, on the meaning of the term 1 lb. That meaning, however, is ultimately assigned to it by verbal definition—that is, it is of the nature of a resolution as to what the word shall be used to mean. Such a resolution is logically arbitrary in the sense that it is neither true nor false, but merely made. Until it has been made and stated, the proposition containing the term 1 lb. remains completely ambiguous, and therefore neither true nor false. Each person, however, is logically at entire liberty to define his terms as he pleases. Intelligibility depends on their being assigned a definite meaning, not on that meaning being the same as that which they already have in the language spoken by others. Assigning them the latter meaning is only a matter of convenience, since others are seldom willing to go to the trouble of learning a new language merely to have the privilege of understanding us.

But the truth of propositions is dependent in another and less obvious way upon a choice by the individual. Once the character meant by the predicate has been specified, there remains the task of comparing it with the character concretely present in the thing. However, this comparison of a meant character with a concrete character may always be made by a variety of methods. For instance, the comparison of the weight of the piece of ore with the weight defined as 1 lb. might be made by means of the unaided hand, or of the postmaster's scales, or of the chemist's or the jeweller's scales. One of these methods may pronounce the two weights equal, and another not; and therefore, until one particular test of the sameness of the two weights has been specified, the proposition, which asserts them to be "the same," remains ambiguous and is neither true nor false. Moreover—and this is where relativity to the individual again enters—I believe that no one sort of test is intrinsically and *a priori* better than any other, but that the particular sort of test we specify in a given case is wholly a matter of our purposes in that case.

Of course, in the example considered, we have a strong inclination to believe that the use of the most sensitive balance will yield a closer approach to "absolute" truth, but I think this is an illusion. First, it must be noted that a "more sensitive" balance does not mean a more "truthful" balance, but merely one which calls unequal all the weights which another so calls, and in addition many weights which the other, on the contrary, calls equal. But second, the only question to which the use of the most sensitive balance is essentially relevant is whether the two weights compared are substitutable for *every* purpose. If, however, our question is not this, but only whether the two weights are substitutable for one particular purpose, e.g. that of mailing the piece of ore, and the post-office balance says Yes, then the fact that a more sensitive balance says that they are not substitutable for certain other purposes is completely irrelevant. The use of the more sensitive balance yields, not a truer answer to our question, but merely an answer to an additional question which we did not ask, and at a price in additional time, care, trouble, etc. In other words, the more sensitive balance not only does not more truly answer the question of the substitutability of the two weights for mailing purposes, but it cannot even answer it at all, except in abstraction from other purposes, such as the saving of time and trouble, which in the instance considered also are ours. Lastly, it may be observed that even substitutability for every isolated purpose, does not define equality in abstraction from purpose but in terms of it. To generalize purpose is one thing, and to eliminate it from the definition another.

Our purposes in each case thus determine the sort of test of "sameness" to be used, but they do not in the least determine the outcome of the test, which may be either favourable or unfavourable to them. I should therefore emphatically disagree with any view that would define the truth of a proposition as the expediency, for our purposes, of believing it. The belief, I should insist, is not true because it works; but it works because it is belief in a true proposition, the truth of it being defined as indicated above, in terms of a test (viz., weighing the piece of ore), which is distinct from and antecedent to that constituted by the proposition's capacity to make us succeed in our purpose (of getting the piece of ore transported without cost to the recipient) if we take the proposition as guide to action in the attempt (viz., if we mail the piece of ore with postage for 1 lb.). I therefore do not regard myself as a pragmatist.

There is yet a third extra-logical factor to which the truth of any proposition is relative—namely, the constitution of the observer who is to make the comparison of the meant character and the concrete character. Even when, as in the instance considered, the sameness or difference of the two is defined in terms of the verdict of some instrument, that verdict itself has to be read by the unaided senses of an observer; and inasmuch as the sense organs of various people sometimes differ enough for them to perceive diversely even very simple matters, the specifying of some particular observer is necessary to make the proposition completely unambiguous.

It seems to me, then, that the truth of any proposition must be defined as the sameness, according to some specified test by some specified observer, of the character which one of the terms of the proposition is specified as connoting, and the concrete character of the entity denoted by the other term. Truth is thus in every case relative to three factors, the specification of each of which is logically arbitrary—that is, their specification is a matter of the individual's taste, pleasure, convenience, or purpose in the particular case. Once the three factors have been specified, however, the truth or falsity of the proposition then is a bare matter of observation and not any further of taste.

Passing now to the problem of objective reference, it would, I believe, commonly be stated in some such form as this: How can a thought entertained by some mind know or refer to an object not itself at that time literally present in that mind? But it seems to me that the mystery which this "self-transcendence" or "objective reference" of thought, as just described, is felt to involve, is gratuitously packed at the outset into the very terms used to formulate the problem. A thought is tacitly assumed to be something which is essentially in a mind, while an object is assumed to be something essentially outside a mind, or at least outside a given mind at a given time. A mind is thus taken as a sort of closed box, with thoughts walled in and objects walled out. More or less unconscious assumptions of this sort, which obviously render the problem insoluble, seem to me traceable to a firm grasping of the Berkeleyan train of thought, coupled with an equally firm clinging to one's natural and more or less naïve realism.

But obviously thoughts and objects cannot, without absurdity, be so conceived as to render impossible the admitted fact of "objective reference," and any such assumptions as the above must therefore be given up. The task which the problem of objective reference then really sets us is that of discovering what exactly and literally we mean when we speak of an "object" and of a "thought"; and it seems to me that here again the answer has to be framed in relational terms. Starting with the notion of Signification (reference, meaning), which I would allow each to define as he may please in psychological, physiological, behaviouristic, or other terms, I should only say that "object" and "thought" are names for certain logical statuses in respect of Signification. More specifically, the status of being object is that of being signified without also signifying—that is, to be object means neither more nor less than to function as terminus *ad quem* of reference or signification; it is simply to be something indicated. To be a thought, on the other hand, is to discharge at the moment the function of at once signifying and being signified, i.e. it is to be an instrument of signification or reference.

I am ready to admit that the correctness of these two hypotheses as to the meaning of the words Object and Thought is far from being intuitively evident. But this does not mean very much. The test of the correctness of a hypothesis concerning the meaning of a word is the possibility of substituting the proposed definition for the word in any phrase where it occurs, without altering the intuited meaning of the phrase. This test, however, presupposes that we have as clear an intuition of the meaning of the proposed definition as we have of the meaning of the word defined; and this is not likely to be the case when the definition, as in the present instance, is framed in highly abstract terms. The only test then remaining is to note whether the definition proposed for the term permits and precludes all the inferences which our intuition of the meaning of the term itself beyond question permits and precludes. I believe that the definitions of Object and Thought which I have proposed satisfies this test.

Even granting this, however, it may still be objected that to deal with the problem of objective reference as I have done is to give "only" a verbal solution of it. But to my mind this would be like saying that the problem how an uncle can have a nephew is only verbally solved when one has pointed out that being an uncle is a purely relational predicate which means having a nephew; and insisting that a real, as distinguished from a verbal, solution must point to some internal character in the men who are uncles, the presence of which in them explains their avuncularity. In short, the very essence of my contention is that "object" and "thought" are, like the terms "uncle" and "nephew," purely relational terms, which imply nothing whatever about the intrinsic nature of the entities at any time so labelled beyond the capacity to enter into the sort of relation considered. Of what actual traits such a capacity itself consists is a legitimate question; but it is irrelevant to that of the special inferences which can be based on the fact that at a given time a given entity does have the status of "object" or of "thought."

If we accept as premises the view of truth that has been outlined, and that of the nature of objects and thoughts just set forth, such a problem as that of the existence of an "external" world takes on an aspect different from that which it usually presents. An existential proposition remains ambiguous, and therefore neither true nor false as long as one has not specified some particular test of the presence or absence at any point of reference of the characters defining the nature of that which is asserted to exist. An existential proposition, if meaningful, thus merely asserts that if some specified test of their presence were used, those characters would be found present at some place, or at a particular place, within some specified denotational system. The denotational system, or "reference frame," may be a spatio-temporal one; but it may be an order system of some other sort, for instance, the system of the rational integers. I am very far from asserting that, except in special cases, "to exist" means "to be observed"; but I do assert that no existential proposition can be given meaning except in terms of the supposititious observation of the outcome of a theoretically performable test; and that no existential proposition is known to be true except through the actual performance of the test and observation of its outcome, unless, of course, the truth of the proposition be logically implied by other existential propositions themselves in that way known to be true.

In the light of such considerations, the problem of the "existence of an external world" is seen to be hopelessly ambiguous until one has given some non-figurative definition of what one means by "external," and specified some test of the existence of something "external" that will be theoretically performable in the sense of not requiring that even a hypothetical observer shall observe without observing. If these specifications are furnished, the assertion of the "existence of an external world" then has a meaning; and if the test specified is actually performed, the truth or falsity of the assertion is then known. But I think that if one endeavours to furnish the required specifications one soon becomes conscious that either the question as to the existence of an external world is really absurd or else that the answer to it is so obvious as to be doubted by no one.

A certain opinion on the problem of the internality of relations obviously pervades the epistemological doctrine so far outlined. Most summarily stated that opinion is as follows. An assertion, such as that the nature or the existence of things is independent of their relations, is much too sweeping to be merely accepted or rejected. If, for instance, we have in mind the relation of "likeness " obtaining between two patches of colour, it is obvious that that relation cannot be altered without altering the colour of at least one of the patches. On the other hand, it is also obvious that if what we have in mind is the relation between them of ''being ten inches apart," that relation can, under certain conditions, be changed to that of "being eleven inches apart" without altering the colour of the patches. What can be said in general, then, is that some relations are internal to certain aspects of things and others are not—that is, some relations can be altered and leave their terms nevertheless unaltered in some specified respect. Again, some relations cannot be altered without altering their terms in some stated respect. Until the respect and often the degree of alteration considered in the terms is specified, as well as the relation itself, nothing more than this can be said.

Of the various special problems in the field of epistemology, I have studied that of the nature and observability of causal connection more minutely and at greater length than any other. Almost every discussion of this problem that I have read seems to me pervaded throughout by a confusion of the two notions of Cause and Law. The conclusion to which I have found myself led is that the notion of law, or of generality, or of recurrence, is in no way involved in that of cause, but that the causal relation is on the contrary essentially a relation between individual events. To the extent that the individual events involved in a number of causal facts exhibit likenesses, generalization is possible. Generalizations so obtained are causal laws. They are laws because they are propositions about a class of resembling facts; and they are causal because each of these facts individually and in its own right is a causal fact. A given individual event is said to have been the cause of a given other if it was the only change which occurred in the immediate environment of that other immediately before it. This, which Hume calls a "Rule by which to judge of causes and effects," and Mill a "Method of experimental inquiry," is, on the contrary, the very definition of Cause. The observing of that which it specifies is the observing of the causal relation itself, and not at all an instrument for the discovery of something other than what is then observed. When Hume denies that causal connection is observable, what he is really denying is only that causal connection is a third fact between the cause and the effect, of the same sort as themselves— namely, sensuous. However, causal connection is not a sensation but a relation, and according to Hume himself relations are observable. It consists, I hold, of the relation defined above, and the observing of its presence offers no difficulty different from that involved in observing a case of any other sort of only-one-ness. The causal relation, moreover, is not a two- but a three-term relation. It always involves the environment of an object, some change in that environment, and the resulting change in the object. It is therefore impossible to take up the circumstances into the cause, as Mill at one place attempts to do in flagrant contradiction of his own characterization of the cause as the single difference in the circumstances.

In the field of the philosophy of religion, the question of the legitimate scope of faith in the lives of reflective and informed persons has long seemed to me to have been definitely and conclusively answered by the essential parts of the famous essay which William James unfortunately called "The Will to Believe." Concerning that question, I have therefore only to set forth what I take to be the essential import of this variously interpreted essay. Its peculiar contribution lies, I think, in having called attention to the existence of questions of a certain sort. They are questions which interest us, which have important bearings on our lives, and as to which suspense of judgment is precluded by the fact that we have to act at once on the issues they raise; but they are at the same time questions concerning the answers to which we have no evidence whatever either *pro* or *contra*. Since refusing to decide such a question is automatically to have decided it in a given way, and by hypothesis information on which to decide it is totally lacking, the decision not only may but must be purely a matter of hopes or fears. It is obvious that in believing concerning such a question whatever we please, whatever we already happen to, or whatever we can make ourselves believe, we violate no canon of logic, of evidence, or of intellectual integrity. Anyone who were to call upon us to modify or to give up our belief concerning a question of the type specified would have, to support his call, no more evidence than ourselves of the truth or falsity or probability of the belief, since by hypothesis none whatever is available at the time. The religious or other dogmas about which we legitimately may, if we can, believe whatever pleases us, are thus at the time always wholly outside the realm of proof or evidence, and therefore any endeavour to show even that a belief has some degree of probability automatically admits either that the arguments adduced are spurious or else that the matter is not one belonging to the legitimate sphere of faith. That is, for religion to argue its dogmas is either futile or suicidal. These considerations appear to me both to warrant and to demand, concerning such religious dogmas as may constitute instances of the kind specified, an attitude on the part of a rational man of complete liberalism.

In ethics it appears to me that every judgment of Right or Wrong essentially asserts that what is so judged does or does not conform to a standard; and the judgment remains ambiguous so long as that standard has not been specified. No standard that one specifies, however, can itself be said to be right or wrong, high or low, good or bad, since all these terms acquire a meaning only after some standard has been specified. Ethical standards are thus logically arbitrary. The will or the welfare of the majority or of the individual, or of the stronger, or of the weaker, or of the more intelligent, and so on, is a possible standard; and each of these has, in fact, been used as the measure of right and wrong by some persons at some time. But it is meaningless to speak of any one of these possible standards as "the right one," since "right" means only conforming to some adopted standard. To appeal to the testimony of the majority, for instance, or to effects upon their welfare, in order to prove that something is right, is only to pick arbitrarily as standard the judgment or the welfare of a group of people for whom one happens to have regard; and such an appeal proves nothing to anyone who happens not to have such regard. Thoroughgoing selfishness may be proved to a person to be at times inexpedient, but one cannot prove to him that it is wrong, except on the assumption that the misery of others is not to him a matter of indifference. But that it is, or is not, is a bare matter of fact in each case, which no argument can touch. All that can be said is that most of us, in fact, do care to a greater or lesser extent whether others suffer, and care the more, the more concretely present before us is that suffering. But this proves nothing to those, if any, who care not at all.

As regards the meaning of Good, it has always seemed to me that Hedonism alone carries the analysis to its final stage. Whether anything whatever could be called good which brought no sort of pleasure to anybody directly or indirectly now or ever, is a question to which I cannot conceive of any but a negative answer. On the other hand, if something, whether directly or indirectly, does some time bring pleasure to someone, it seems to me impossible to deny that it is to that extent and in so far good. Perfectionism is confronted by the necessity of specifying which direction of change is to be called progress and which retrogression; and I know of no way of doing this, except ultimately in terms of increase of happiness for somebody at some time. People, however, are not all constituted alike, and what the actual and possible sources of happiness are for each is a matter of bare fact. In this field, too, I thus find myself led to conclude that every critical judgment is ultimately relative to individual verdicts wholly alogical in nature. The problem of the freedom of the will in ethics is, for me, disposed of by the theory of causation outlined, which defines determinism essentially in terms of the individual and not in terms of some "necessity" supposedly external to him.

In æsthetics, analogous trains of thought have led me to similarly relativistic views. Before summarizing them, however, I feel that I must pause to acknowledge the very great debt which I owe to Professor Santayana's writings on the philosophy of art and of beauty. Little as my conclusions in this field may perhaps commend themselves to him, I believe that I might never have reached any at all had it not been for what I learned in the study of many pages on æsthetics from his pen, where an extraordinarily subtle insight time and again comes to expression in the most arresting words. In no other branch of philosophy am I conscious of so great an obligation to the work of a contemporary writer.

One of the central problems of æsthetics is that of the nature of Art. Art, it seems to me, cannot possibly be defined in terms of beauty. The existence of works of art which are ugly, and are yet asserted by their makers to be exactly as they meant them to be, would by itself bar the way to such a definition, even if the direct observation of the state of consciousness out of which works of art are born did not plainly do so. Art, I believe, is the expression of feeling through the creation of an object, when the creative act is critically controlled in the light of the requirement that the object shall, if æsthetically contemplated, exactly reflect back the expressed feeling to the object's maker, or to others whose constitution may be similar to his. To say that something is a good work of art is only to say that it does just that. On the other hand, to say that an object (whether natural or a product of skill) is beautiful, is to say that when it is æsthetically contemplated the feelings which it yields are pleasant. Æsthetic feelings are any feelings that are obtained through æsthetic contemplation. Æsthetic contemplation itself is most adequately described in brief as a "listening" with our capacity for feeling. Judgments of beauty are objective only in the sense that it is truly of objects, and not of our feelings, that beauty is predicable. They are subjective and relative, however, in the sense that what is predicated of the object when it is called beautiful is its status in respect to the pleasure of the æsthetically contemplative beholder. Judgments of beauty, and so-called canons of beauty, have therefore no binding character at all; and such general acceptance as they may meet signifies only that the original or acquired taste of certain more or less numerous beholders happens to coincide.

Such, then, in the principal branches of philosophy, are the grounds upon which is based the liberalistic creed which I profess. These grounds are not set forth as a proof of its articles, but rather to dispose of arguments which would commonly be supposed to forbid such a creed.

PRINCIPAL PUBLICATIONS

Causation and the Types of Necessity, pp. 132. University of Washington Press, Seattle, 1924.

"A Liberalistic View of Truth," *Philosophical Review*, November 1925.

Articles in *Journal of Philosophy*, *International Journal of Ethics*, and *Philosophical Review*.

Philosophy of Art (Lincoln MacVeagh, 1929).

IN VESTIGIIS VERITATIS

By WALTER G. EVERETT

Born 1860; Head of Department of Philosophy, Brown University,
Providence, R.I.

IN VESTIGIIS VERITATIS

Why are our beliefs what they are? Anyone with whom thinking has been the chief occupation of life must often have reflected upon the forces that determine men's beliefs. These determining factors are obviously not always conscious, nor are the reasons we give for our beliefs always the real reasons for their genesis and development within the mind. Certain dominant influences are clear. They begin in childhood with the steady impact of tradition and habit upon the plastic organism. The pressure exerted by institutions and by social groups is soon effectively in operation. Commitments to a career and to the practical necessities of a livelihood prove hostages to belief as well as to fortune. The rôle of emotion and desire, too, is important. With not a few, beliefs are largely objectified emotions and wishes. As the ancient oracles were inclined to speak according to indications given by the interested consultants, so the result of reflection is often predetermined by desire. No wonder truth wins its way slowly! One might well despair if it were the creature of a day, and had not the long career of the ages.

Even those who are stimulated to self-criticism by the very nature of their task, and who are made aware of all the factors determining our human credos, do not escape altogether the more subtle forms of rationalization. We may be committed by our own theories or our published views. It would be well if a "statute of limitation" applied to all philosophical utterances, so that in five years, or at least in ten, they would automatically "cease and determine," and could be claimed as one's own again only after a thorough re-examination.

One who attempts a review and statement of his philosophical beliefs may well invoke the spirit of candour and disinterestedness, of detachment and objectivity, for the undertaking involves issues which are unaffected by our desires or our inclinations. In practical matters these may well turn the scales. But to fix in advance the price at which we will accept a theory of the world is to erect a barrier against all clear insight. Not in the temper which makes claims or demands can one discern the structure and meaning of things, or catch the movement and colour of reality. "Jede Absicht der Einsicht droht."

The system that formed the background of my intellectual life and gave me my earliest impulse to reflection was that of the orthodox theology of the nineteenth century before it was touched by the scientific illumination which followed the publication of Darwin's works. I distinctly remember pausing in my play one morning in the 'sixties, when I was a small child, to listen to a talk between my father and another clergyman about a new theory of man's appearance on the planet. What impressed me at the time was that it connected man not merely with the animal kingdom in general, but with one interesting type in particular, that "with tail and pointed ears, arboreal in its habits." Thereafter I often heard and read of the theory, always to its utter confusion. The theological literature which came into the home, and which I seized upon with eagerness, made the theory seem untenable and even absurd.

One intellectual service at least this environment rendered. It gave me familiarity with abstract ideas and encouraged discussion of high themes. I became, in fact, something of an expert in the manipulation of theological ideas, and still recall the commendation with which my exegesis of a difficult text was received by a visiting clergyman, one of the more human of these good men, with whom any lad might feel free to talk. Although I would not willingly subject any child to the acute fears which this theological system caused me at times, I have often wished that all the students whom I teach might have had the benefit of some training which compelled them to raise their minds above the level of the immediately practical and the commonplace. My revolt in youth against the system was not primarily intellectual. It was rather a matter of taste, an instinctive recoil from certain practices that prevailed in religious circles. Especially was the effort of zealous believers to penetrate to the sanctuary of one's most intimate thoughts and aspirations repugnant to me. These I felt were not to be rudely dragged to the light for inspection, or proclaimed from the house-top. Rather were they, like an avowal of love, only to be breathed into a sympathetic ear in some quiet hour of rare confidence. But despite these infelicities, the old theology remained for many years my philosophy of the world and of human life, for I knew no other. That I accepted it so long without modification argues, I think, a not too suspicious or sceptical nature. It is now a far cry back through the gradual changes of the years to that earlier system of thought. I have not been able to find shelter even in the half-way houses of liberal orthodoxy, where the dwellers have been unwilling, as it has seemed to me, to pay the price of making them permanently habitable.

In the 'eighties a college course in most American institutions did not greatly aid the process of intellectual reconstruction. For two and a half years my time was chiefly occupied with mathematics and the classics, the latter taught as a linguistic discipline with little regard to the civilizations which the languages represented. Only later, through private studies, did I discover the meaning of Greece and Rome. The courses in mental and moral philosophy of the senior year were so limited in method and content that they contributed little to one's knowledge of the history of thought or to an understanding of contemporary movements. Worst of all, perhaps, almost no reading in the subject was required. At the end of the course I had no acquaintance with the works of the great thinkers. The first writers who stimulated me to critical reflection were John Fiske and Matthew Arnold. The latter rendered much the same service at one stage of my development that Emerson had rendered to the young men of an earlier generation. Of science I knew almost nothing. It would have fared ill with my philosophical interests, which had been compelled to work "on an empty stomach," had I not enjoyed the instruction and friendship of a great teacher, one of the greatest that America has produced in his power to capture the interest and arouse the enthusiasm of students for the things of the mind. This man was E. Benjamin Andrews. To him in large measure I owe my career. Although he taught history and economics, philosophy was his central interest. In almost every lecture it broke through the material with which he was immediately dealing, and flashed forth some insight of large or universal significance.

A position as tutor in a private family, held for some time after graduation, gave me needed opportunity for general reading. Some four years later Dr. Andrews, who had just become President of Brown University, asked me to return to the institution as an instructor. Thereafter for several years I combined the teaching of Greek or Latin with the study of philosophy. During this period I translated the *Pyrrhonic Hypotyposes* of Sextus Empiricus. The primary purpose of this was to gain mastery of all the material it contains for the preparation of my thesis on Greek Scepticism.

Germany was still the Mecca of graduate students, and as soon as I had taken the doctorate I spent a year at the Universities of Berlin and Strassburg. In Berlin I pursued courses under Paulsen, Simmel, and Diels, then just succeeding Zeller in Greek philosophy. Work under Windelband in Strassburg greatly influenced my study and teaching of the history of philosophy.

Returning from Germany in 1896 to take the professorship made vacant by the resignation of James Seth, I entered upon the work of teaching without any sense of final commitment in the matter of philosophical creeds. I should, however, doubtless have described my position as that of a critical realist. The system of thought then attracting most attention in America was Royce's idealism. This made its appeal in attempting to offer a logical theory of the necessary form of reality, and in exhibiting the universe as one spiritual life-process. At the same time this system did not too easily compromise with the emotional or practical interests either of individuals or of groups, and it left the character of experience largely for empirical determination, thus assuring freedom to science.

In idealism *c'est le premier pas qui coûte*. This first step consists in somehow reducing the object of thought or experience to the same nature as the process which knows it. All things are experiences of some mind. Nothing is independent of consciousness. If this be admitted, the rest follows of necessity. Obviously objects do not owe their existence, their ontological status, to the experience of finite minds which are occupied with them only in brief spans of time, and often withdraw their attention. In order to have secure and permanent existence they must therefore be within the compass of an all-embracing knower.

This epistemological argument, which reduces everything to mental processes, left me unconvinced. That mind is the universal and sole knower of the world, that all reality of which we can think or speak, imagine or dream, is by these processes so far brought within the realm of experience, is incontestible. This "ego-centric predicament," to use Professor Perry's phrase, is indeed the A B C of reflection, the first and most obvious fact about human knowledge. But this initial relationship does not determine the predicates applicable to the objects themselves. It only describes the instrument or net with which we, as knowers or experiencers of the world, catch all elements of reality, the most obtrusive and the most elusive alike. And I could not believe that what is thus caught in the universal net of consciousness is necessarily of the same nature as the net in which it is caught. This no more seemed to follow than it follows that, because one catches fish with steel hooks, the fish themselves are therefore made of steel. Indeed, one of the most primary and necessary tasks of knowledge in our world of intercourse is precisely that of distinguishing between objects which are in themselves possessed of consciousness and those which are without it. I also perceived that a change in nomenclature did not effect a change in our practical contacts with reality. Experiences of value remained what they were before. In an idealistic universe, mire and dirt were no less potent to soil; rotting flesh and swarming maggots lost none of their repulsiveness. I was thus driven back to a realistic position.

I have asked myself whether my early experiences partly predetermined my choice of realism. As a lad I had roamed the fields and forests with a freedom enjoyed by few. I dealt vigorously with the external world, manipulating its objects to my own ends with no doubt of their non-mental character. They were clearly marked off from the animal kingdom which I knew and loved, and in which I recognized varying types of consciousness. I observed and made acquaintance with the farmers—those unwitting realists of the soil—who wrested a simple livelihood from their cross-grained farms. They would unhesitatingly have rejected the idea, had I been able to propose it, that the infinite variety of their world could be significantly described by a predicate derived from the mere fact that they were having a conscious experience of it. Were these early habits of mind an influence in placing me among the "tough" rather than the "tender-minded" philosophers? I cannot say. Certainly they fostered no visionary attitude. I have to confess that even to-day most metaphysical idealisms seem to me to have caught some fantasy of a dream-hour, which, loath to surrender, they have attempted to imprison in the chains of an ingenious logic.

Pragmatism did not greatly influence me. On the one hand, the truth it contained seemed already current in all sound thinking, while, on the other, it was peculiarly liable to misapprehension and misuse. It was doubtless possible to state the chief principle of the doctrine in such a way as to offer little ground for criticism. The fruitful working of ideas might be found in their satisfaction of all the intellectual tests that in any given case could be applied; the factors of sentiment and immediate satisfaction of felt needs, other than the need for truth, might exercise no influence in determining the value of evidence. But those outside of philosophical circles who at once seized upon it were tempted to make it the justification for believing whatever might be immediately useful, pleasant, or comforting to believe, without regard to other evidence.

The lack of scientific training in my college education left lacunæ of which I was keenly aware. With wider reading I soon discovered a strong interest in certain sciences, especially biology and medicine. The development of medicine from early Greek times to the present day proved for me one of the most fascinating and instructive chapters in the history of science. Biology I found was busy with questions that had direct application to ethics, and also extended to wider issues in philosophy. These influences, and others to be noted in due course, turned my thought to a series of problems both scientific and philosophical in their significance.

For one thing, I grew increasingly distrustful of the commonly accepted dichotomy of mind and matter. The terms in which the second member of the dichotomy is often described—"mere matter," "dead matter," or "blind force"—make it a pauper by definition, and rob it of any possibility of fruitfulness in the process of evolution. The abstract concepts of mind and matter are then applied to reality, with the result that a sharp disjunction, an either-or with the alternatives, "either dead matter or perfect mind, either blind force or a planning, creative consciousness akin to our own," must be the principle of explanation to be applied to the world. But opposites which are valid for certain phases of our experience—light and darkness, summer and winter, and the like—cannot be applied in the same sense to reality. Nature in its unceasing movement transcends and annuls them; else we might be permanently caught in the one or the other, fixed, perchance, in a prison-house of darkness or congealed by frost. Nature contains both opposites, but is contained by neither.

The hypothesis that primitive organic forms arose from the inorganic has, I have long believed, a clear right of way as against any other view. The difficulty of conceiving a different origin of life is well-nigh insuperable. Whence and how the seeds of life could be injected into matter from without, baffles the imagination, and finds no analogue in any known process of nature. Wherever these processes are open to observation they are self-contained, subject only to the influence of environment. The idea which has been suggested by some, that life floated in upon the earth from without, if there were any grounds for its acceptance, would at most show that exceedingly low forms of life existed elsewhere. The *a priori* dictum that life can only come from life is as idle as other such dicta with regard to the possible and impossible. What is possible in this realm can only be determined by the event. Reality is its sole measure and determinant. It may be that scientists, even by the most skilful manipulation, will not succeed in producing life in the laboratory. But Nature's laboratory is far ampler and better equipped. She has time—thousands of millions of years—and can make endless trials under conditions which man can never reproduce. The same considerations apply to the appearance of consciousness. The dogma that only like can produce like would in the last analysis compel one to accept a

Platonic museum of forms and prototypes as antedating and conditioning the generation of all the species of life known to us. Aristotle's criticism of the Platonic ideas as having an existence apart from concrete reality would apply, and we should have the same doubling of the forms to be explained. All novelty would be excluded. Yet novelty is one of the most obvious facts in nature. Genuine novelties are produced even in the inorganic realm. The chemist builds up synthetic compounds that have never existed before. In living beings the novelties which attract attention do not occur *uno saltu*. They represent exceedingly long-continued minimal emergences which even the trained scientist can only imperfectly detect and describe.

My attention to the mind-body problem has been stimulated by many years of service as trustee of a mental hospital. This position has involved the duty of frequent visits to every ward. What was at first undertaken as an obligation has become a matter of absorbing interest as well as of spontaneous solicitude for the inmates. Visits to other hospitals in this country and in Europe have enabled me to see practically every form of mental disease and defect, from the commonest types of manic-depressive insanity and dementia precox, to such cases of physical malformation as are illustrated by a group of children, with almost bird-like heads, segregated in the Salpêtrière in Paris. Like all who have ever reflected upon the problem, I long ago recognized that we have no knowledge of minds of any kind save in the most intimate union with bodies, and that it is impossible to form any conception of a mind sundered from this union. No effort of the imagination can picture a disembodied spirit. Even those which mediums introduce to favoured circles are clothed in some tenuous or wraith-like material. One is tempted to suggest that the triviality of their utterances may be due to the unsubstantiality of their organic structure. But in mental hospitals the unity of mind and body leaps to the eye with striking distinctness. It is also true that the drives and impulsions of human nature are revealed in the various psychoses with a clearness nowhere else exhibited. The old dualism made possible the idea that the insane were people whose minds had somehow gone wrong, but whose bodily organs and functions remained quite unimpaired. Even when this appears superficially to be the case, we are amply justified in believing that a physical correlate of the mental malady exists. The greatly increased attention now given to the physical examination and diagnosis of mental patients often reveals some hitherto unsuspected disease or functional disturbance. Man, I firmly believe, is a thinking, feeling, and willing organism whose complex structure is one thing, not two. There would be no objection to such phrases as thinking and feeling bodies or spiritual animals on the one hand, to corporeal minds or incarnate spirits on the other, were it not for the fact that these modes of expression imply a priority of one element and its subsequent union with the other. We can indeed abstract from this unitary organism and can make either mind or body an object of thought. In this sense, and in this only, are they two things. But this abstraction for purposes of thought no more proves the duality of the self than does the fact that we similarly abstract the qualities of the rose—its colour and its perfume—prove that the rose itself is two things and not one. We may then say: No organism, no mind; different types of organism, different types of mind; to each individual organism, an individual mind. And, as far as our present knowledge goes, in order to establish the existence anywhere of a mind or minds akin to our own, we should have to prove the existence of organisms that are akin. The old anthropomorphic—or better, perhaps, anthropopsychic—beliefs which still persist so tenaciously found their support in a dualism that assumed the capacity of minds to function independently of organisms. But not one authentic example of this has ever been brought to light.

The interpretation of the self indicated above, does not, I conceive, involve any slight or peril to its higher and more characteristic powers. These are activities of the organism as truly as are the lower and more animal functions. Indeed, just these are the meaning and value of the human organism. And its environment, it must be remembered, is enormously extended in comparison with that of lower organisms. Not only does it range nature with a vastly lengthened tether and with acuter perception, but includes in its span wide areas of cultural-historical life, and emergent social structures of increasing complexity and determining influence. The capacity for rational and moral judgments cannot, I think, be explained as a mechanism which operates without regard to logical and ethical situations—that is, an environment in which the true and the good are conditioning factors in the life of the organism as real as are food and drink.

I was indebted to an early study of Schopenhauer for his clear and forceful statement of the doctrine of the grades of being. Quite apart from any consideration of the validity of his own metaphysics, it at once seemed to me an important but neglected principle. Certainly no other classical philosopher has dealt with it so fruitfully. Many years before one heard of emergent evolution or creative synthesis, it affected my attitude to the problem of development, and also to that of naturalism. I distrusted the systems that, by the magic of a single formula, sought to transcend the real and vital differences that reality presents, whether this formula was an abstraction from the highest or the lowest grade; whether, as in idealism, it magnanimously offered to exalt everything to the rank of mind, or, as in materialism, it invidiously threatened to degrade everything to the level of inorganic stuff. Further, as I believed in the genetic continuity of nature's processes and did not believe in miracles, I insisted that there was a naturalistic view which would do justice to all the higher grades of being, whereas the naturalism then current was, in the eyes of its critics and perhaps in those of its chief advocates, able to function intelligibly only when well coated with dirt and slime. I therefore avowed my belief in what, for lack of a better term, I called in the class room a larger or higher naturalism. Questions as to nature or the natural admit of no answer whatever that is meaningful until the sphere to which they apply is defined. Then the differentia which mark off the chosen sphere from others must determine the account to be given. If at one level this account must be in purely physical terms, at others it must include all that is essential and characteristic of what has been won in the process of development. Such an account of human life will find the intellectual and moral, the æsthetic and religious experiences as "natural" as the movement of physical bodies, the growth of plants, or the instinctive activities of animals. To man it is natural even to fly. It has long been a native impulse to "take the wings of the morning," and the means to the realization of this cherished dream have been invented as the result of scientific curiosity inherent in man's mind. So, too, courage and heroism, sympathy and unselfishness become in choice spirits the expression of their deepest cravings; and all the works of grace in all the saints are in as true a sense "natural" as the evil deeds of the criminal.

Philosophy is not in a position to determine the details of fact or explanation of the evolutionary process. Here it must be the humble pupil of science. It is equally clear, however, that the descriptive accounts of science yield no account of values. To be sure, the scientist is also a man of human passions and interests, and from this human point of view he cannot be debarred from indicating the losses and disasters, the gains and triumphs which he discovers. In the old theology, creation was the signal display of supernatural power. As evolution has gradually displaced the earlier picture of the sudden advent of terrestrial life, there has been an effort to make the new view an equally obedient and useful *ancilla theologiæ*. But those who best know the details of evolution might well hesitate to give unqualified approval to the new servant. A commission of experts would, I am confident, approve the earlier plan of Adam's decorous entrance upon the stage in the full possession of human traits. Even the birth of Eve, the pains attendant upon which were assuaged by the happy device of twilight sleep, commends itself to one's impartial judgment as a small price for the male to pay for an unsophisti-cated but enterprising companion who would permanently relieve him of the travail incident to the perpetuation of the race. The appearance of animals by creative fiat would have been admirable on general grounds, and would have had the advantage that a discriminating taste might have refused passports into life to certain undesirable types which the democratic procedure of evolution has freely admitted. By contrast, the processes of evolution, judged strictly as methods of intelligence and fore-sight, make a rather sorry showing. In the words of a distinguished biologist: "The whole multimillennial course of evolution, with its innumerable *impasses* and *culs de sac*, its abject and tragic failures, would seem rather to be one vast monument to their colossal and hesitating inadequacy, blindness, and stupidity."[1] Popular encomiums of evolution, on the contrary, fix attention only on certain selected features or results.

My thought was early focused on the problem of value as the central problem of philosophy. The first literature on the subject that came to my attention was that of the Austrian school. I used the term in teaching for many years before the writing of *Moral Values*, but attempted no formal statement of my ideas until the preparation of a paper for the meeting of the American Philosophical Association in 1906.[2] In ethics the concept had the obvious advantage of relating the subject in a significant and fruitful way to other fields of value which furnish the very material with which the moral life is compelled to work. The method I had hit upon and developed seemed to succeed in making students feel that the subject was vital, in fact was of the very essence of their own life-purpose. Despite frequent reports of diminishing interest in ethics in American universities, I still believe that, for teaching purposes, it is a truly great academic discipline.

I shall not attempt any recapitulation of the points of my ethical theory. It will be sufficient for the present purpose to say that the central thesis I have tried to maintain is that the content of morality is a content of various specific interests or values primarily not designated as moral. Hence my table of human values. The moral task *par excellence* is the criticism and organization of these values in the structure of individual and social life. Ethics thus becomes in its wider scope a critical study of civilization. The intimate connection of ethics with the other fields of value necessitated a fresh interpretation of the relationship existing between the various humanistic sciences. On this problem

[1] W. M. Wheeler, *Proceedings of the Sixth International Congress of Philosophy*, p. 91.

[2] An abstract of this paper appeared in the *Journal of Philosophy*, January 31, 1907. This attracted the attention of Fouillée in France. See his *Morale des Idées-Forces*, Introduction, p. xlvi.

I searched in vain for a satisfactory statement. The defects of the common departmental view which divided the sphere of experience between them, much after the method of settlers staking out land claims, were evident. But a satisfactory theory that gave to each of these sciences its complete freedom without conflict with any other, I could nowhere find. Although the topic occupies but a few pages of the Introduction to *Moral Values*, I still think it to be one of the best theoretical insights of the book. It was in the way here outlined that I was able to gain fruitful insight into such complex relations as those of ethics and economics, of ethics and æsthetics, and of morality and religion.

One challenging question concerning the foundation or the metaphysic of morals solicits attention. Reality has brought man upon the terrestrial stage, has determined his environment, has given him his equipment for life, and nursed him through the long ages of infancy. Does it also promise continuous direction of his career? Does the cosmos indicate the plan and the method of his future development? Or has it produced in man a unique creation for which there are no models elsewhere, no patterns for his guidance? And if this be the true alternative, must he count the gifts of intelligence and appreciation which work within him as his sole legacy for the accomplishment of his purposes and the realization of his ideals? It would doubtless be comforting could we be assured that the universe deals with men according to strict standards of value, that a clear principle of worth determines everywhere the incidence of birth and death together with all the down-sittings and up-risings of earthly fortune. We could then be assured that unworthy types that may come into being will be thrust down to speedy extinction, and that all who flourish do so because of intrinsic excellence.

But the statement of this hypothesis meets the refutation of hard experience. The cosmic struggle for survival has too often been what Huxley called it, "the gladiatorial theory of existence." The destructive processes of nature give no hint of discriminative selection. One individual is taken and another left without regard to their moral and spiritual worth. It would fare ill with our ideals of sympathy, of justice, and love, were we to rest their validity for human life upon the evidence of their operation in the cosmos. Only in man, and to a slight degree in the animal world, is there evidence that these sentiments come into play. The devastating hurricane is not malicious, nor is the favouring breeze an expression of good will. The micro-organisms that kill by the millions do not hate their victims, nor do the beneficent ones love those to whom they bring relief.

The evidence which we can at present command compels the belief that man's life on this planet is a unique phenomenon in the universe, and that he will in vain consult the stars or the heavens above to chart his course. If he thinks to find patterns there for what should be here, he sees only the visions which his own thought and imagination have created. Our race is thrown back upon what it can discover through its own nature and its own needs. If reality conveys to man any message, it would seem to be just this call to self-direction and even to struggle against such forces in the cosmos as oppose his ideals. He must renounce the ruthless methods of nature in order that he may be himself. This does not mean, however, that we can disregard nature. We are directly dependent upon it, and we may even detect here and there principles in its operations that we can utilize. In particular, the rigorous destruction of the unfit, which keeps the averages of animal species at so high a level, suggests that if standards of human excellence, intellectual, moral, and social, are to be maintained and advanced, some attention must be given to the selective process. Civilization unquestionably offers a degree of protection to all its members, even to the lowest and least valuable types. And if the mean shelter these find is not too poor to prevent rapid multiplication, which has rarely if ever been the case, civilization is attempting an emergence above lower forms in contradiction to the principle which governed its origin. Submergence rather than emergence would appear to be in prospect. But when methods for the accomplishment of the desired end are to be considered, then we must sharply repudiate nature's ways and find those consistent with the dictates of humanity. Wisdom must find marriage with love.

The ultimate principles applicable to morality, then, I hold to be those discoverable in the life of man, and in nature as far as it is presented to observation and study. These are the parts of reality open to our direct examination. Of the totality of things, our knowledge is too limited to yield any truths that can shed light upon the specific problems of the moral order. The universe, as far as we are able to glimpse its structure, exhibits a measure of order and regularity and at the same time an infinite variety of detail. Uniqueness of the individual parts is one of its most striking features. Could thought penetrate the entire scheme of things, it by no means follows that we should then be in possession of knowledge that would make at all clearer the path humanity should pursue in development of its own life and destiny.

Philosophy is, in the final reckoning, a way of life. Thought roams far afield, but there is always a home-coming, when account must be taken of the human significance of the journey. The applications of philosophy to life then gain their rightful hearing. My interest in the theoretical problems of ethics had been keen, but once these had found the best statement I could give, my attention was drawn increasingly to the actual moral order exhibited in social life and institutions. Here was a challenging situation. Large areas of human activity seemed almost untouched by ethical ideals. They presented a standing contradiction of generally accepted moral standards—in short, were unmoralized. Some of these unmoralized activities had been commonly considered as outside of the moral province, as matters over which man does not exercise control. And where it was recognized that they are within the sphere of possible control, and are of high importance for human welfare, the very magnitude and complexity of the issues discouraged courageous thought and action. Among such issues to which I every year devote attention in the class room are militarism, population, poverty, and, far more fundamental to these than is commonly assumed, the problems of sex.

What degree of progress in general may we reasonably hope for humanity? On this question neither an easy-going optimism nor a dark pessimism seems warranted by what we know of the past. Every genuine advance will, we may be sure, bring some new and difficult problem in its train. But before the twilight of man's long day on this planet, be it a thousand million years or less, it seems reasonable to anticipate an advance to higher levels of effort. This in itself is no insignificant gain. The plane at which mankind fights its unceasing battle determines the values realized. It makes a vast difference whether the struggles of an individual or of a people are for mere subsistence or for the durable values of life to which the means of living should minister.[1]

I turn again afresh to the problem of value, but approach it from a different angle and with other questions in mind. Shall values be regarded as objective, ready-made, as it were, and awaiting man's act of appropriation, or as existing only when the act of appropriation and appreciation is present? This much debated question may be regarded, in part at least, as one of terms and definitions. It might be agreed, for example, to use value for the objective things and conditions which are essential to the experience of value. The common use of language lends a measure of support to such usage. This is especially true in the case of economic values. In the language of the market-place, things possess value. The same holds true of æsthetic objects generally, although we are here perhaps more keenly aware how largely value depends upon what the conscious subject brings to the act of æsthetic perception. However, it is clear that without conscious subjects there would be no value at all. The presence of such a subject is always presupposed. Even the most hardened trader of the mart knows how speedily his values will diminish or disappear, once attention or desire is withdrawn. I prefer, therefore, with many others to regard value as involving its actual experience. In this way justice can be done to both the subjective and objective factors. Certainly there need be no disparagement of the objective conditions of value, nor to their authority in the determination of such values as the true and the good, which no desire or caprice of the individual subject can change.

[1] A fuller discussion of the subject is given in my address, "The Problem of Progress," as President of the Eastern Division of the American Philosophical Association, before a joint meeting of the Eastern and Western Divisions in New York City, December 1922. See the *Philosophical Review*, March 1923.

Between positive value, the good, and reality we cannot establish an equation. Reality is positive being, never non-being, whereas negative value or evil is as real as positive value. To parts of reality we necessarily apply the terms of a negative valuation. Theodicies have struggled in vain to escape this conclusion or to soften its consequences. Evil cannot be construed as the mere privation of good, or simply as good in the making. As an experience it is the polar opposite of good. The agonized sufferer who prays for extinction knows well that what he suffers is not mere loss of the accustomed joys or satisfactions of existence. The suggestion would appear to him or to an onlooker as a cruel mockery. What I have said of other opposites of experience, however, applies here also. The opposition we experience does not bind reality in fixed and changeless states. It passes from good to evil and from evil to good; out of evil may spring some good, and out of good, some evil.

The sharp differentiation of the point of view of a science of value from that of the physical sciences is obvious. Descriptive judgments of science never yield value judgments. They are concerned with the relations existing between the elements of reality, such as the connections of time and space, the cause of change, and the resemblance of forms. Despite this inherent limitation of science, a misinterpretation is not uncommon. Because science finds in the world a certain type of intelligibility or rationality—that is, structures susceptible of understanding and formulation in so-called laws—it is concluded that reality is rational in the sense of conforming to or satisfying human ideals of value. But this is an application of the idea of scientific rationality or intelligibility to quite another sphere. Discovered and established in the connections and interrelations of things and events, it is now applied uncritically to the sphere of values. The two spheres are not the same, nor is the vindication of the principle in the one a vindication of it in the other. To science a destructive storm, an epidemic of disease, or an earthquake is as intelligible or rational as is a day of exquisite beauty, a community enjoying health, or a countryside smiling with its rich harvests. Good and evil are equally intelligible. But, from the point of view of human values, evil is irrational, a negation, something to be resisted, because destructive of precisely what we seek by human effort to create and preserve.

To the problem of evil, I am therefore compelled to give a degree of importance which it does not commonly receive. I accept the tragic view of life, in the sense that its inevitable struggle and conflict involve at times disaster and irreparable loss.

"Tout est dangereux ici-bas," said Voltaire. And, long before, the father of tragedy had declared:

> No mortal thro' this life shall go
> For ever portionless of woe.
> Alas! Alas!
> It comes to all, or swift or slow.

Experience has never been able to gainsay this truth. Any philosophy that disregards it, seems to me to lack penetration or to have sought refuge in a defence mechanism. I am constantly astounded at the facile way in which optimistic systems, whether of philosophy or of theology, attempt to dispose of this fundamental dualism. If there are any true standards of value, if men really care for the things they profess to count precious—care not only for themselves but also for their fellows—then to accept the view that whatever is, is good, that "all's well with the world," seems to me no less than a repudiation of avowed standards and a stultification of intelligence. Frankly, one would like to believe otherwise. But if experience teaches anything, it teaches that we are all compelled to believe a thousand things that we would gladly have different from what they are. The old theology was here true to the facts. Granted all its presuppositions, it was strictly logical in its thinking. A personal devil was as necessary to the explanation of the actual world as was a personal deity. Without desiring to rehabilitate a discarded *persona dramatis*, one may rightly insist that, robbed of this rôle, the drama loses all verisimilitude. This repudiation of a frank recognition of evil was a change far more momentous for theology than it is commonly accounted. It marked a decline in intellectual rigour, the loss of a firm hold on reality, an ominous trifling with grave issues.

The procedure which selects from the world only the good elements, and out of this material alone constructs a scheme of things entire, celebrates an empty triumph, for its creation corresponds with no world of our experience. Perfection of the universe is sometimes affirmed on the ground that compensation will be made to each individual sufferer. This belief draws cheques in its favour on the unknown to the point of credulity. To be satisfactory, it must extend its system of rebates to all individuals of the brute creation. It must also show that such evils as moral and spiritual degradation are all ultimately good. When perfection is located, not in the experience of finite beings, but in an absolute experience which utilizes the evils of finite life for its own enrichment, our most dispassionate judgment registers a protest. One thinks of the issue so pithily stated by James, when he pictures the hypothesis of millions of beings kept permanently happy "on the one simple condition that a certain lost soul on the far-off edge of things should lead a life of lonely torture." With James one must add, "How hideous a thing would be its enjoyment when deliberately accepted as the fruit of such a bargain." A master of the show who desired to have real tragedies enacted for his delectation would not be an object of religious veneration.

The tragic view of life, in the sense stated, is not pessimism. Life may still amply justify itself, still be worth the burning of the candle. The idea that the universe must be either perfectly beneficent to man or completely hostile and fiendish, finds not the slightest support either in logic or in experience; not in logic, because it ignores the endless series of possibilities between these extremes; and not in experience, because our surest judgment concerning the actual order of things is its varied and opposing value-content. Good in parts, in parts it is evil.

Can we distinguish between evils that ought and evils that ought not to be? Dare we say that some should not be eliminated from human experience, whereas others ought, nay, must, be rooted out? Such a distinction we are compelled, I think, to make. No reflective mind would perhaps deliberately affirm that physical death on this planet ought to cease and our mortality at once put on immortality, even though such a thing were possible. The change would result in a starving population or in checking the fresh stream of life. In this case the world would soon present the unlovely spectacle of a senile or stagnant race. Similarly, all risk, hazard, and danger, which inevitably bring evil, could not be excluded without changing the whole structure of nature and of human life. On the other hand, such evils as gross ignorance and superstition, injustice and cruelty, certain types of disease and suffering, prostitution, and war, could be diminished and even destroyed with only those readjustments that humanity could profitably make. No fundamental reconstruction of the world order would be involved. Against evils of this kind we feel bound to wage uncompromising warfare.

And, finally, what of religion? How fares now this dominant force of my childhood and youth? Does it still survive under a changed form? Certainly I have never escaped its influence. For decades scarcely a day has passed without serious reflection on some aspect of the problem. I have observed with care the manifestations of religion in all kinds of people under all sorts of conditions, and I have attempted to put every possible question to the religious experience of the race. A gradual process of reconstruction such as has taken place in my life of thought and emotion allows time for readjustment. However radical the changes effected in this way, the spirit was never left homeless. The view I am to sketch will doubtless seem to not a few to rob life of its supports and its consolations. "I could not live with such beliefs," would be their first impulsive cry. They fail, however, to reckon with man's capacity for readjustment or with his tenacious hold on the living world.

For an enduring heart have the gods given to the children of men.

The undying element in religion—to deal summarily with so great a theme—is found in man's relation to the universe. And, as a totality of things, a whole of reality, is involved in the object of religious thought, so its subjective aim is a wholeness of life. What is demanded in religion, then, is both a settling of one's intellectual account with reality, as far as this is possible, and the winning of a practical and emotional attitude that is vital and pervasive, an enhancement of the values of inner experience. It early became clear to me that a religious belief or faith must satisfy the same criteria of reasonableness as our beliefs or faiths in other spheres. Certain significant features of the matter I find recorded in notes made long ago: (1) Faith must be founded upon knowledge; (2) although a projection of thought beyond knowledge, it must be consistent with what we know; (3) faith lacks the certainty of knowledge, otherwise it would cease to be faith; (4) all beliefs or faiths must be held subject to correction by the discovery of new knowledge; (5) in certain practical spheres faith is an essential condition of the realization and validity of its object, whereas the general structure of reality is independent of our desires and our wills.

With the passing of all anthropomorphic elements in my belief it was evident that every specific idea and form of speech in traditional theology was a creation of the poetic imagination, a religious symbolism. But I found significance in this as a medium for the expression of aspirations and emotions when no prose could utter the full meaning of the heart. To many it is perhaps a necessity, a healing experience, a genuine catharsis. Especially is this true in sorrow or tragedy when our impotence is made manifest, and scarcely less in the great consummations of life when we are conscious of enjoying some bounty of the universe beyond our own creating. But the full fruition of symbolism is only attained when we know that it is symbolism, and are able with complete freedom to surrender ourselves to its sway without the intrusion of the intellectual demand for truth. The critical tests of historical, scientific, and philosophical veracity no longer find place; the letter would indeed kill. Had we to submit the great hymns of the church to such examination, scarcely a line could be consistently sung. But here we move freely in the realm of poetry, where all peddling exactitude is forgotten. Lange, in his chief work, somewhere asks: "Who shall convict Raphael's Madonna of error, or who shall refute a mass of Palæstrina?" Who indeed? Their truth lies only in their fitness to express emotions and ideals, not in any conformity to external reality. Symbolism, of course, may go quite mad, and by its elaboration of complex and intricate forms be in need of so much explanation and justification that it again enters the intellectual arena, where it is unfitted to contend.

But a positive content of reality as we immediately know it has gradually shaped itself *sub specie universi*. If tragic, as I have insisted, the world is also marvellous, fascinating, rich in possibilities. Every part of nature offers its processes and its myriad forms for interested study and contemplation. Every species of plant and animal life is a field for observation and experiment. Even a single species is capable of engaging for a lifetime the mind that once enters upon the discovery of its secrets. So have men found delight in the understanding of things unseen by the eye of the ordinary observer. These are the contributions of science to religion. What science can never give, because it moves in a different sphere, is a vindication, or even aid toward vindication, of traditional theology.

But it is the unfolding of the drama of human existence that most of all fills the mind and feeds the imagination. If the development of a single character in biography or in drama and romance can prove of absorbing interest, what must be said of the inexhaustible possibilities offered by the unceasing stream of human life? The gifts of genius that enrich all subsequent ages, the heroic spirits who win a forward step for the race by high endeavour, the kindly souls who make daily life more gracious—all these glorify the humble ways of earth in which we walk. To possess as far as possible the values of this our real world, and to seek to extend them to others—this, in the language of religion, is to live to the glory of God. All these values have the character of a gift or largess which no design or effort of individuals could provide. Little by little these things have become for me alike the glory of the universe and the glory of man. Religion thus lives in every ray of sunshine, in every gleam of beauty, and in every warm pulse of human love. These things, too, are happily beyond the shadows of doubt, and safe from the devouring teeth of criticism.

The affinities with historical thought of the view I have briefly suggested will be clear to all students. In common with mysticism, both classical and Christian, it holds the inapplicability to ultimate reality of all the specific predicates drawn from finite being. In consequence, it agrees with mysticism in affirming the symbolic character of current religious thought and language. And it further emphasizes the contemplative appreciation of nature and of human life that mysticism at its best has always cultivated. It differs with mysticism, however, in its estimate of the significance of those states of emotion or ecstasy to which the mystics have looked for an illumination of reality that is denied the intellect. These states, I hold, exhibit certain capacities of the subject, and may at times enhance inner experience without extending knowledge of the object of religion. At their worst they tend to illusion, to imaginative flights that have lost relation with reality. If I were to choose a single phrase to characterize my thought, it would be the *amor dei intellectualis* of Spinoza. It is *amor* because it is a warm and joyous appreciation; it is *amor intellectualis* because it is not the love of human affection, but demands a quickened perception and understanding; and it is *amor dei* because all its objects are referred to the being and substance of reality, or to nature in Spinoza's meaning of the term.

In Christianity I have never ceased to find a principle of permanent value. It matters not that it was no new discovery in the spiritual history of the race. Indeed, its wide extension is evidence of its universal appeal. But the founder of Christianity captured the idea anew for Western civilization, and announced it with fresh insight and power. If one turns from this ideal of love and universal brotherhood to the Christian cosmology, the basis of its theological system, quite a different judgment must be rendered. This cosmology represents a view of the world that has long ceased to exist save as a tradition specially guarded from the stream of thought. As to a divine order, a kingdom of righteousness and love, of which the religious spirit has dreamed, this, if it is to exist at all, must be an emergence of future development. It can be realized only through the devotion and service of those who ardently care for its coming. To rest in the assurance of its present existence, save in embryo, I regard as an illusion that often endangers its establishment. Christianity is not a completed achievement. It is rather a challenge, a task, and also a test of the spirit of man.

It would be an intolerable presumption for anyone to assume an escape from all the presuppositions, prejudices, and errors that beset the work of the philosopher. How difficult this work is, and how incomplete, he of all men is most keenly aware. It involves not merely logical thinking, but also a clear perception of facts and a just appraisal of their relative significance. No dialectical subtlety can make amends for failure in these latter details. The best one can do is to give to his fellows with perfect frankness and clarity the total impression which the world has made upon him, in the hope that other hands will correct and enlarge the picture. The same reflection applies to the corporate thinking of any age or generation. Our own time has been a period of rapid discovery and illumination. But it is still a question how much we have won. Some errors we have surely escaped; into others we have doubtless fallen. Here, too, we must hope that, in Xenophanes's phrase, men "will gradually find out what is better."

The future, like other dimensions of the unknown, is hidden from us. But the philosopher is the friend of the unknown. He eagerly desires to make its acquaintance. Nor does he condition his introduction to it by stipulating what its character must be. If, when his lamp which lights so narrow a circle, and that but dimly, is threatened with extinction, there should be for him, beyond all expectation and prescience, some great surprise of illumination, he would gladly bid it welcome and advance to probe the secrets it revealed.

PRINCIPAL PUBLICATIONS

Moral Values (Henry Holt & Co., New York, 1918). English Edition,
Wm. Heinemann, London, 1920. Japanese Translation by Tseo
Kimura, Meguro & Co., Tokyo, 1929.

Various Articles, Addresses, Reviews, and Mental Hospital Reports,
among which are:

"The Evaluation of Life," *Philosophical Review,* July 1898,
pp. 382–393.

"The Concept of the Good," *Philosophical Review,* Sept. 1898,
pp. 505–517.

"The Relation of Ethics to Religion," *Int. Journal of Ethics,* vol. xx,
pp. 479–493.

Le Contenu et l'Organization de la Valeur dans la Vie Morale.
(Congrès des Sociétés Philosophiques, décembre, 1921,
pp. 489–502.

"The Problem of Progress," *Philosophical Review,* March 1923,
pp. 125–153.

THE IMPERSONAL POINT OF VIEW AND THE PERSONAL

By WARNER FITE

Born 1867; Stuart Professor of Ethics, Princeton University.

THE IMPERSONAL POINT OF VIEW AND
THE PERSONAL

In the first chapter of his *Experience and Nature* Professor Dewey attempts a task in which (as he himself has best shown) all others have failed; in which he also fails; and in which, as I think, he was bound to fail. Under the title of "Experience and Philosophic Method," what he undertakes to do is to lay a solid foundation for philosophy—to define a philosophical starting-point, or, in common terms, to establish a basis of fact—which shall be once for all independent of personal presuppositions, interpretations, prejudices. In this Professor Dewey is faithful to the academic tradition, which looks for truth and reality in the impersonal. Your true academicist is careful to confine himself to the third person or to the impersonal "It is so." "It is so" rather than "I think so," because the use of the "I" implies an immodest intrusion of his unworthy self into a realm divinely impersonal. His feeling is that his personal motives and prejudices should have no bearing whatever upon what he is to call real.

My own feeling is just the opposite. When I write "I think so," I feel that for what I say I am claiming no more authority than that of my sinful and erring self; and that I am warning my reader to take it only for what it is worth. If I should write "It is so," I could not but feel that I were speaking with the voice of God —since only God can properly say "It is so." And so far am I from supposing that the personal prejudices of philosophers have no bearing upon truth that I think I should better know the truth—I should know better what they see—if they were less careful to conceal their prejudices from their readers, but no less from themselves, out of deference to academic respectability; if they would tell me what they see, and not what belongs to "the logic of their position," or to the part they have chosen to play. The task is not easy, *crede experto*. But a mind without prejudice—it may be a *tabula rasa*, a mirror, a cinematograph, a phonograph, or any of those other contrivances which psychologists substitute for mind, but it will see nothing.

Hence my *Credo* will be a statement of prejudice; or, if you please, a presentation of the ideas which I find congenial, which I like to entertain, towards which I feel hospitable. I will not say that these ideas form a harmonious social circle. There may even be those among them which have not yet been introduced to one another. And that they should form a system, God forbid! But if this seems to any reader an incredulous *Credo*, or perhaps only an impudent scepticism, let me suggest that in the end he may find it all too credulous. It is always possible that scepticism is but another name for faith—and conversely. Your man of science is neither credulous nor sceptical; he simply records facts.

For in speaking here of "ideas" I am adopting a convention of the learned. In my opinion there are no such entities as "ideas." By entertaining ideas I do not mean that I am collecting pictures: I mean, rather, that I am grasping, or at least glimpsing, aspects of reality; and a "mere idea," which grasps no reality, I regard as a mere word or phrase. And if this seems to imply a universe of loosely indefinite reality, generously revealing itself in various forms to the many varieties of ideas, as the God, or the divine, of William James reveals himself to the varieties of religious experience—well, yes, this implication may as well be admitted. The only alternative that I can discover is some sort of absolute—absolute mind, absolute matter, absolute God, or absolute event—which sooner or later turns all ideas into nonsense.

After an honest attempt I have not succeeded in stating my *Credo* in the form of an "intellectual autobiography," as called for by the idea of these essays. I cannot disentangle an intellectual autobiography from an autobiography rather intimately personal and somewhat uncertain in my own mind. As for the "individualism" which is to be found in all that I have printed for many years past, I cannot remember when I was not an individualist or when I was not confronted with the inconvenience of being one. But it occurs to me that for the ideas about knowledge which appear in this essay I can find a definite starting-point in the reading, more than twenty years ago, of Royce's lecture on "Physical and Social Reality" in the second series of

The World and the Individual. And this leads me to offer a few
details which may serve as a setting.

I was born in Philadelphia in 1867, graduated from Haverford
College (A.B.) in 1889, and received the degree of Ph.D. from
the University of Pennsylvania in 1894. My interest in philosophy
was definitely initiated by reading Martineau's *Types of Ethical
Theory* in my last year at Haverford; it was restored some fifteen
years later, after I had been ready to abandon philosophy for
anything else, by reading Royce. Meanwhile, I had studied three
years with Fullerton at Pennsylvania, during the first of which
I was also a student at the Philadelphia (Episcopal) Divinity
School. I had also spent two years (1891–93) in Germany, hearing
among others Paulsen, Ebbinghaus, Dilthey, Lasson, Von
Gizycki, Simmel, and Stumpf. I say "hearing" advisedly—I
seem to have heard Beethoven and Wagner to more effect.
Fullerton was really my only teacher of philosophy, and to him
I owe a vigorous training in dialectics, perhaps the absorbing
interest in the nature of knowing which has never left me, and
I do not know how much more. I rewarded his efforts some years
later by a sharply critical review of *The World We Live In*; and
it is now a great pleasure to recall the warm-hearted, even
affectionate, letter that I received from him in reply to mine
deploring the fact that I could not review the book otherwise.

But among those to whom I owe much I should name Professor
Dewey, who has kept my imagination busy with an ever-develop-
ing "situation" for years past. To the graduate student seeking a
subject for a thesis, my standing recommendation (unfortunately
not thus far accepted) is a study of the philosophy of Professor
Dewey, not, indeed, as a method of sharpening his teeth, but as
the best way of realizing in present terms the ramifications and
implications of philosophical problems. But whether from wrong-
headedness or what not, I seem to have been nobody's disciple.
More shocking, then, will be the confession that more than
anywhere else have I found what is personally congenial and
suggestive in the disorderly philosophy scattered through the
essays, novels, and poems of Miguel de Unamuno, who calls

himself a *paradojista*, or paradoxist. His *paradojismo*, to the
effect, as I take it, that the real is the paradoxical (paradoxical,
of course, from the standpoint of logical and scientific analysis),
I am disposed to elevate into a metaphysical principle, belonging
to the conception of reality as personal. For in the world of
persons all the real beings are paradoxical; and the only strictly
rational beings are such things as typewriters and gasolene
engines.

My circle of prejudices may then be roughly summarized
by saying that for me only persons are real and only persons
are significant. All impersonal things, including the objects
presented by science, are abstractions, constructions, fancies.
These abstractions I take to be ways of talking about the world
and of dealing with it which serve as highly useful and even
indispensable instruments of communication; but they are never
quite adequate; and they never stand for more than "so to
speak," "as it were," or "as if."

But to state that persons are real, as if each of us had arrived
at finality, is to state the case too plumply—which of us can
boast of more than of trying to be a person? It will be better,
then, to state the prejudice as a preference for the personal point
of view. And here I refer to the age-long antithesis between soul
and body, between the inner life and the outer fact, between
subjective and objective. What is the meaning of "subjective"
and "objective" in terms of human experience? For me the
meaning is this: taking any human activity or situation, what
is the difference between being the agent (or patient) of the
situation and the observer of it? What is the difference between
running from a bear and seeing another run from a bear; between
being ill and visiting the sick; between being a parent, actively
responsible for the welfare of one's children, and giving to parents
neighbourly advice; between being a child reading a story, and
writing stories for children; between being a dog and owning a
dog (or between being a pig and having a taste for pork); between
being a professor and figuring as a professor; between living in
the past and noting (another's) memory behaviour; or, finally,

between being in love and watching a pair of lovers (all the difference, it seems, between tragedy and comedy)?

The difference of point of view I describe as the difference between personal experience and impersonal observation—or between experience and observation. Impersonal experience I regard as denatured experience; personal observation is something more than observation. The difference is also a difference between an inside view of a situation and an outside view—for me a difference between reality and appearance. Personal experience, inner reality, impersonal observation, outer appearance —for me in each of these expressions the adjective serves only to bring out the meaning of the noun. The connections of noun and adjective will then serve to mark my metaphysical prejudice and to show what I mean by a preference for the personal point of view. The realities of human life I find revealed in the inside view: in some such inside view I look for the realities of the universe.

Latter-day realism makes light of the distinction between subjective and objective. Realism graduating into behaviourism cancels the distinction. There is a story of a drunken man who was advised by a waggish friend to take the first of two cabs standing at the door of his club, because the second cab "wasn't there." Realists, offering similar advice, explain that the second cab is labelled "consciousness," or the inner life. For myself, then, this distinction, this conflict between inner and outer, is not only real; it is the tragic conflict which alone gives meaning to life, and which alone gives birth to philosophy. If the distinction were effectively cancelled I wonder what philosophers (including realists and behaviourists) would have to talk about? If all were impersonally objective, science would suffice; there would be no questions peculiarly "philosophical."

Accordingly, when I say that only persons are real and only persons are significant, I mean that for me the person marks the *type and direction* of what is real. The only conceivable thing-in-itself is a person. The typical experience of reality is one person's experience of another person. Truth is a personal experience—there is no impersonal truth. Beauty is the expression of a personal impression—there is no impersonal beauty. Morality (and this was the thesis of my *Moral Philosophy*) covers all of the personal life—and there is no impersonal morality.

In the philosophical directory I suppose that this point of view would be called "personalism," or "personal idealism." For myself, I prefer not to name it. Only let it not be called "subjectivism"; for me it is realism.

To make clear the implications of my metaphysical prejudice (let me call it now my point of view) I need a background of contrast in a point of view resolutely "objective." This I find presented very significantly in Professor Dewey's *Experience and Nature*. And very significantly for me, because, in the endeavour to make the vocabulary of philosophy intelligible to myself, I find that I am obliged to refer each of its seemingly abstract terms to what Mr. Dewey calls a "social situation"; and in reading Mr. Dewey I seem to have found the peculiar social situations corresponding respectively to "subjective" and "objective."

The various "subjective" prejudices to which I subscribe I find conveniently summarized by Mr. Dewey under "the genteel tradition." Now, "the genteel tradition," which is an inheritance from Plato and Aristotle, represents that form of social order, conceived by both of them to be divinely ordained, in which there is a sharp distinction and separation between a lower class of labourers and artisans, who do all the work, and an upper class of hereditary aristocrats who tell them what to do, live upon the fruits of their labour, and are thus enabled to spend their own lives in the enjoyment of contemplation. In such an order of society there is a clear separation between knowing and doing; and since the knowing is the special privilege of a favoured and ruling class it comes to be invested with an "honorific" significance. All idealistic metaphysics, of whatever kind, is a projection upon reality of this class-tradition. To this desire of creating an "honorific," and therefore invidious, distinction, Mr. Dewey attributes all of those ideas, logical, ethical, æsthetic, metaphysical, or religious, which form a part of the traditional "higher culture," but more especially those that lay emphasis upon "the inner life," or the life of thought; or upon intimately personal experience as the realization of value and the revelation of reality; or upon the peculiar sacredness and binding power of personal and intimate relations.

The genteel tradition—*versus*—— How shall we name the tradition represented by Professor Dewey? I shall call it the tradition of the man on the street. And this not as an epithet (all of us are many times men on the street), but as a description of the "social situation" and point of view that explain the meaning of "objective." It might be described as the point of view of the market place or of the agora; in Southern Europe of the café; not of the club, because a club is exclusive. In general, it is the point of view of "the public." [1]

The genteel tradition represents, correspondingly, the point of view of private life. The phrase suggests, indeed, an aristocratic class-distinction, but as we study its implications as developed by Mr. Dewey we see that any common labourer resenting gossip about his wife, any slave claiming his soul as his own, any person whatever attaching importance to his consciousness of self, would be representing the genteel tradition. To incur this reproach it is not necessary to say, "I am better than thou," but only, "I am different from thou—I am myself." "The genteel tradition" covers all differences to which personal importance is attached—that is, all individual differences which are conceived as other than socially "functional."

This means that Mr. Dewey shares the "social" point of view which has dominated all of our thinking for a generation or more past: the view which describes all of the realities of human life as "social" and attributes to "individualism" all that is false and vicious. Here, therefore, I pause to ask whether "social" is the right word to use. It is true that "society" and "social" have come to be little more than algebraic signs, *de*noting the group as against the individual, the larger group as against the smaller, and *con*noting little or nothing. Yet there remains

---

[1] When this was written I had not heard of *The Public and its Problems*, Mr. Dewey's last book, which I have not yet read.

a moral implication, namely, that there is more fellowship ("social" being derived from *socius*, a fellow or companion), more sympathy, more humanity, in the numerically larger relations than in the smaller. It seems to be forgotten that while "social" marks a distinction from "individual," it marks also a distinction from "political," and that the commonest use of the term outside of philosophy and sociology is to distinguish social relations from business relations. These considerations seem to me to reverse the moral implication, and to remind us that relations are more properly and intensively social to the extent that they are personal. There is more of human sympathy and fellowship within the family or the group of intimate personal friends than there is among the members of a club; more within the club than among the men on the street. Among the stockholders of a railway company, a "social institution" *par excellence*, there is practically none.

Hence I suggest that Mr. Dewey's "social" point of view would be better described as the point of view of "the public." What I have in mind is two familiar "situations," standing for a familiar difference of point of view: the home situation and the street situation; the point of view of "the private citizen," in the privacy of his home, of his circle of friends, or of his meditations, and the point of view of "the public." The public view is the objective view.

It is commonly assumed that the point of view of primitive man is purely and completely objective. The primitive man is untroubled by any consciousness of self; he seems happily free from the corrupting influence of private life. It seems that Mr. Dewey prefers to take his illustrations from primitive life, explaining the meaning of art, for example, by reference to the (public) ceremonial dance. Primitive life offers a conspicuous illustration of social solidarity. Yet I think it will be more instructive to describe it as the point of view of classical antiquity. Though deprecating the genteel tradition, Mr. Dewey has much to say about the Greeks; and his attention is fixed upon the fact (very significant for an analysis of the objective motive) that it was the Greeks who introduced the scientific point of view.

Now, what first strikes the eye in looking at Greek life is that it was peculiarly and exclusively public life. What we know of Athenian civilization leaves us with the impression that it was a civilization made up entirely of men on the street—or in the agora or market-place. Of course we know that Socrates sometimes went home to sleep, and therefore that private life existed as a sort of brute fact. But it is a fact of which the corresponding point of view is seemingly unrepresented in Greek literature—as it is clearly *not* unrepresented in English literature. And all of the Greek political philosophy is for the purpose of assuring us that, whatever be the status of private life as a brute fact, no one can be conceived really to live, to have the right to life, or to be treated as a living being, except as he functions as a member of recognized standing in the city-state. The Greek city-state and the objective point of view—the connection is surely not without significance.

In any case, it seems that for Mr. Dewey, as for the Greeks, all that is good in life—and all that is real life—is public life. For him the ideal human community may be conceived to be, not perhaps a life without distinctions, but at any rate one great stream of life, in which there may be for brief distances lateral canals (in which is performed some kind of "readjusting" function which I do not understand), flowing from the main stream and into it again, but no quiet pools. A stagnant pool—this is his conception of the subjective and personal; no one really lives except in the current. To change the figure, we may note the difference between the newer style of village or suburban town in the United States and the older style of forty or so years ago, or the style of an English rural community to-day. In the newer style fences, walls, hedges, which mark off one's private ground and protect it from the eyes of the public—all these have vanished. This protection was part of the genteel tradition; it is now seen to be hostile to public spirit. The good citizen is he who treats his carefully tended gardens as a part of the public domain, and leaves them unscreened for public enjoyment. The implication is that his soul, as belonging to the same domain, should be similarly unscreened.

But for me the interesting point in all of this is not the social aspect, but the metaphysical. Every "social situation" has its metaphysical implications. And in Mr. Dewey's philosophy, as in every other, it seems that the good and the real, the moral and the true, are bound in the end to come to the same thing, as against the evil and the unreal, the immoral and the false, which also come to the same thing. Thus it comes about that the subjective, or private, point of view is not only morally false, it is illusory from the point of view of reality. The real world is one continuous and homogeneous world, objective and public. Man, as Mr. Dewey tells us again and again, is continuous with nature. He is not marked off by any "inner life," or "consciousness," from the rest of the organic world. The "inner life," in short, is a fiction. Just as Society is one unbroken stream of life, so also is Nature. And as Society is a public affair, to be viewed from the street, so again is Nature; to be viewed from "out there," and not from "in here"—"in here" being nowhere. Or, in terms of "experience," there is one unbroken stream of experience. It is irrelevant to ask, Whose experience? Private experience, experience regarded as in any way peculiar to you or to me, is an illusion and an impertinence. "Personality," it almost seems, is an insult to Nature. All real experience is public experience. The only real world is what Fullerton called "everybody's world."

And this is a way of saying that the "objective" motive of Mr. Dewey's philosophy is the motive underlying modern empirical science. The modern scientist's "appeal to experience," as he terms it, is an appeal to public experience—namely, to what anyone who is in possession of his senses may be expected to see. He may refer you to "expert observers," but in his view they are "trained observers"—made and not born. No "scientific authority" claims for himself, in theory at least, the powers of a prophet or a genius. It is no inner revelation to which he appeals, but only, in the end, to what anyone will see who looks carefully. Has the use of antitoxine lowered the death-rate in diphtheria? To any sufficiently industrious investigator the facts speak for themselves. They are public and need only to be pointed to.

And this gives us in one word Dewey's own conception of experience. The philosophic method, or method of getting at experience, is, he tells us, the *denotative* method, or the method of *pointing*.

By the same token "religious experience"—and I should say that all æsthetic experience lies in this direction—must be excluded from the world of experience. Such experience partakes of the nature of a private revelation and implies a personal capacity to receive. Even of æsthetic impressions it may be said that, to whatever degree communicable, each is in the last analysis a uniquely personal impression. In any case it seems that neither religious experiences nor æsthetic impressions are to be verified by simple denotation. The communication of them, so far as they are communicable, depends upon sympathetic insight. But if the measure of experience is denotative—what you can point to—this will mean that religious and æsthetic experience, so far as it is private, is neither experience of reality nor, in the end, real experience. All real experience is public experience.

Returning, then, to my own prejudices (which being unscientific cannot be stated so neatly), I come to my moral prejudices, the first of which is that all moral questions are resolvable into the question, What is it to live? As I have just suggested, it is a conception of what constitutes life that underlies all of any man's philosophy. But I do not ask, What is life? but, What is it to live? If you, my reader, could elect to live abundantly, what would that be? For Mr. Dewey, as I understand him, it would be to share the communal, public life of something like the Greek city-state.

For myself, it is towards the private life that I look for what it is to live. To me "the only deeply satisfying things are the personal intimacies. All of the casual 'social' goods are of value only as they retain the flavour of the personal (which, curiously, they always make a pretence of doing). And all of the ostensibly impersonal interests, such as an interest in books, in scientific investigation, in social reform and commercial enterprise— which, it seems, are necessary to give breadth and substance to life—these again take on the quality of life just so far as they furnish the subject-matter of intimate intercourse. . . . And it seems to me that he who in this human sense is at home in the world, who in the circle of family and kin finds an ever-satisfying affection and understanding, and in his friends an intelligence ever responsive to his tastes, has the best that life has to offer; and that he who lacks these lacks everything."

This I repeat from my *Moral Philosophy* (pp. 285–86). But lest the picture of life seems too "otiose" (Mr. Dewey's word), let me say that not more than the next man can I conceive myself to live without something to do which is worth the doing. Yet I refuse to identify life with "work." I might not improperly say that for me life is leisure. But by "leisure" I should then mean, not the absence of action, effort, struggle, but the presence of thought. It is this that converts work into life. For myself it seems that any task, however difficult or exhausting, or however mean, becomes interesting and the living of life, when I can do it from the point of view of leisure, putting my thought into it and guiding it by my thought. This for me is the experience of "activity"; to be distinguished from work without thought, dictated by the economy of thought, which is "business efficiency."

The gospel of work, the gospel of efficiency, the gospel of success—all of these stand for views of life from the "public" point of view. The same is true of the conception of life as a "career" (or possibly as a "mission") which is so often presented as something idealistic and edifying. To speak of one's life as a career is to think of human life as a dramatic spectacle in which each of us plays his part. This histrionic conception of life is to be found in widespread currency and in forms hardly to be suspected. For Professor Hocking an important function of human life is the making of "history"; and this involves the making of war. One need not deny that history makes interesting reading, but to *be* a character in history, a figure in a pageant, a part in a play—this, if we pause to think of it, is to find ourselves in the position of poor Augusto Pérez in Unamuno's novel, *Niebla*, when Augusto discovers that he is only a character in a novel which Unamuno has written for others to read.

Yet from my point of view to live is indeed to be self-centred —I should insist upon that. To be self-centred, however, need not imply an attitude either of self-contentment or of exclusiveness. For me, I might say, there is no life without love—we live by communion with our fellows; and he who loves can never be self-contained. And the more that I can make my own the experience of life of my fellows, the richer my own life will be. There may be persons who find satisfaction in "drawing a line," who pride themselves upon the persons whom they do *not* know and the things they do *not* understand; but that seems to me very stupid. I find, however, that sooner or later something like a line, not located necessarily here or there, is drawn for me (as for other persons) by the fact of fatigue. Up to a certain point in a conversation, in an enterprise, in anything you please, I can mean what I say and mean what I do; beyond that point I begin to be oppressed by the sense of playing a part. This creates for me an issue between "public" and "private"—a moral issue, in the presence of which I do not hesitate to prefer "the genteel tradition."

Let me explain, however, what the genteel tradition means for me. In his *Realm of Mind* Professor Woodbridge describes the mind as a phonograph. Mind, he tells us, is translation; and the phonograph "translates" the surface of a disc into sound. Professor Woodbridge has doubtless observed that we are a nation of phonographs, engaged very conspicuously in translating the advertising pages of the newspapers into purchases profitable for the advertisers. I fancy that every self-observant person knows what it is to be a phonograph. For myself, when I have been teaching two hours and then, without intermission, go on talking for a third hour, I know precisely how a phonograph must feel. And so, if I must stand for a genteel tradition, let it be this: I do not wish to be a phonograph, I cannot conceive this to be the ideal of life of my fellow-men.

This is not to pass judgment upon those who are interested in public life, or upon those who are engaged in business. Leaving politics aside, I do believe, with Plato (and with many a business man), that trade is essentially demoralizing, i.e. de-moralizing;

and trade rather than industry. The fact that trade is necessary need not alter the statement. But while I consent to live, indirectly, on the profits of trade, I cannot very well say that my soul is above it. And I might find many a form of business interesting if I could treat it—not indeed as a game, but—as a scientific problem, soberly utilitarian. My quarrel is with those who find in business and politics the essence of religion and brotherly love. Chief among these are the orthodox political philosophers who, accepting the inspiration of Plato and Aristotle, and the Greek city-state as a revelation of the will of God, find in the state, or in "society"—in the life of the "public"—both the organic unity and the source of all the moral life. To my view the nearer you get to the state the farther you have left morality behind; and (with the preamble to our Constitution) I prefer to regard the state as simply a necessary and useful institution for the transaction of our common business—which may involve much or little, from the building of prisons to the building of railroads, or the building of churches, as determined by circumstances and by the personnel of the citizens. The unity typified by Greek city-state I regard as one of the characteristic fictions of scientific method. The Greek state marks the type of ordered society demanded by the needs of administration. To the Greeks (say, to the Athenians) I fancy that the city-state could more or less justify its claims to be the organization, the unity, and even the source of the moral life. This was because the Greek city-state was tiny, and because the imagination of the Greek citizen was of necessity (as compared with the range of view afforded by modern conditions) narrowly provincial. His art, his literature, his religion—every part of his life found its chief source of inspiration in local tradition and local opinion. The modern situation is wholly different. For us of to-day the city-state is hardly more pertinent as a moral ideal than the polity of Abraham, Isaac, and Jacob.

But what I would chiefly communicate here, if I can, is the contrast, a contrast amounting to different orders of being, that I find between human life as viewed from the inside and from the outside; from the two "social situations," private and public;

and the peculiarly devastating transformations wrought by publicity. Some years ago I spent several days in a divorce court waiting for a case to be heard in which I was interested. What I learned was that, granting if you like that half of the persons who appear in the divorce court are morally negligible, it is the court that makes divorce discreditable; it is the "social institution" that converts what in so many cases is tragic or simply pitiable into something disgraceful. If married life generally were subjected to a similar publicity (and why not, if marriage is a "social," i.e. a public institution?), marriage itself would be made repulsive and ridiculous. Any private life is in danger of this when it becomes subject-matter for the newspapers. But to me this impersonal situation—for us, paradoxically, the result of modern means of "communication"—is not merely demoralizing and devitalizing, it is also (if I may coin a word) curiously de-realizing. When I survey the row of faces of those sitting opposite me in the subway, it is not merely that I find them depressingly vacuous; I am thinking all the time how easy it would be to conceive these persons, in Berkeleian fashion, as so many ideas in my mind, as so many features of the subway picture which have no existence outside of the subway. And yet I know that each of those faces stands for an individual life quite as significant, for anything that I can say, as my own.

And nothing is more constantly interesting to me than the difference in what I seem to get from a person, almost any person, when he is talking to me alone, under conditions which imply a friendly confidence, and when I meet him in a group of even half a dozen persons. The private conversation is likely to be a revelation, not merely of moral estimates and desires, but of ideas and beliefs. I have had a scientific physician pledge me to secrecy and then tell me of cures that he had known to be wrought by Christian Science. I have more than once been in a group of sober, intelligent men, each of whom, after one had broken the ice, testified to remarkable "psychic phenomena" (which I find it very difficult to accept) that he himself had witnessed. And I have been at times both surprised and deeply interested to discover in philosophical colleagues an attitude towards religion, amounting to a sort of religious belief, which was not remotely suggested by their published writings. All of this suggests to me that the Freudian theory of repressions, so far from pointing to anything abnormal or exceptional, states simply the rule of what we call "social" life. Social life, so far as it becomes public life, is not so much communication as repression. If I ask a casual acquaintance what he thinks about this or that, his answer is more likely to tell me what he will stand for, or what he conceives to be logically respectable. We don't tell all we think, least of all what engages our thoughts most deeply. And this not merely because we fear ridicule, but because it is so difficult to say what we think and it raises so many questions; and if we made it a rule to say what we think, just imagine the confusion of social life! Hence we adapt our conversation to what will serve the purpose. Surely this cannot be without significance for the logic of the "objective" view.

It will doubtless be admitted, as among the unimportant observations, that every man's view of the world of fact is surrounded by a "halo," or a "fringe," of imagination and super-stition. My own conviction is that this so-called "fringe" is for each of us the very body of the garment of his life, the world in which he lives as distinct from the world in which he does busi-ness with his neighbour.[1] In the history of the human spirit I suspect that the consciousness of fact has ever been the smallest part of life. Or to borrow two phrases from Fullerton, the real world, "the world we live in," is for each of us his own private world; "everybody's world," the public world, is an artificial construction for practical purposes.

With this I have already passed from my moral prejudices to the corresponding "intellectual" prejudices. Coming, then, to the conception of "experience," I will say that for me all genuine experience is personal experience. And I believe that at bottom this is the meaning and the persuasive aspect of the modern scientist's appeal to experience. Mr. Dewey says somewhere that the modern appeal to experience was an appeal "from occult

[1] See *Moral Philosophy*, §§ 35, 41, 57.

essences and causes" to scientific method. But why not call it
the appeal to the personal presence? Did this thing really happen?
The reply of experience is, Yes, I was there. Or Jones, who told
me—and you know Jones—saw it himself. And if this reply be
rejected as coming only from uncritical common sense, then I
invite a study of the typical form, illustrated by almost any
scientific monograph, employed by the empirical scientist in
explaining the derivation of a theory from fact: in 182– A discovered that, etc.; in 185– B found by experiment; meanwhile
C had noted, etc. It seems that the whole purpose is to carry the
story back to the personal experience of responsible persons,
of persons whom in some sense we know and whose experience
we may then be expected to share. And this means, if you pause
to think of it, that in the last analysis the scientific appeal to
experience is an appeal, not merely to personal experience, but
to poetic experience.

As experience is personal, so also is truth. In my *Moral Philosophy*, a chapter on truth is entitled, "The Experience of Truth."
The purpose of the title was to suggest what I conceive to be the
question of truth. It is not, When do I *have* the truth? or even,
When *is* this the truth? It does not mean, When does this result
that I have reached accord with the criterion of truth? Such
is precisely the kind of question contemplated in the issue between
the coherence-theory of truth and the correspondence-theory.
Following the coherence-theory I may say, This statement of the
situation is internally consistent—in the sense, perhaps, that
it satisfies the law of contradiction—therefore it is true. Following the correspondence-theory I may say that the statement
accords with the facts. But I may say either or both without
seeing anything of the object. The fact of "coherence," or of
"correspondence," may be only added source of mystification.
And my own question is, When do I *see* the truth—when do I
see this to be true? Or (as I shall put it a little later) When *am* I
in the presence of something real?

The answer that I have given is, When imagination is satisfied. I will not say that this answer does more than develop the
meaning of the question, but I doubt whether philosophical

analysis ever does more than this. I am certain that it offers no
logical criterion, and it is not my purpose to offer a criterion.
A criterion (useful in its place) is a substitute for an experience.
What I am trying to do is to grasp and to communicate an
experience. What is it to see the truth? But what is it,
after confusion and doubt, perhaps—to see that a musical
composition, such as the Brahms symphony in C minor,
is real music, significant music, and not a wandering association of tones? To my mind the two questions are of the
same order.

After truth, logic. In my teaching of philosophy it has been
my chief aim to convince my students, having in mind the gibes
of the irreverent, that philosophers, however unusual their
vocabulary and point of view, were dealing with the realities of
human experience, only at a deeper level. But alas! in the effort
to convince my students my own faith has been shaken. And
to-day nothing seems to me to be more of a travesty upon experience, more of a caricature upon thought, than what is called
"logic," especially the formal, or syllogistic, logic. The syllogistic logic is not even a good game. At the end of a course in
the syllogism, what has a student learned? So far as I can discover,
only some very simple geometrical relations between circles
which a child of five could not be conceived to doubt. If this
be logic, there is surely more logic in chess. The chess-board
situation is a trifle closer to social life than the syllogism is to
thought; and chess problems are incomparably more difficult
than most of the "exercises" in logic.

Meanwhile, I should say that logic stands for an experience—
namely, the experience of necessity, or of necessary connection;
such an experience as seems to worry the soul of Kant in his
Prolegomena. Now your textbook in logic is likely to begin with
a series of definitions relating to terms, including the distinction
between the "extensive" meaning of terms and their "intensive"
meaning, between their "denotation" and their "connotation."
The system of logic is then built upon the extensive meaning—
that is, upon a scheme of classification which may be just as
convenient as the alphabetical classification of a directory, and

just as meaningless from any other point of view; and the intensive meaning is quietly discarded as impracticable, as indeed it is. But this is to disregard all that is experientially "logical," all of that sense of necessary implication and inner connection which a logically curious mind, unacquainted with the literature of logic, would expect to have unfolded to him in a book on logic. And for the secret of this connection, if we are to find it, where shall we look? My answer would be, In the personality and situation of him for whom the connection is necessary and "logical." The only logical connection is a personal connection, the only logical necessity is a personal necessity. As for events, granting if you like that events show a uniformity of succession, nothing "logically follows." What "logically follows" follows only for a mind so constituted that it does so follow. And thus the logical connection is of the same order as the æsthetic connection.

I do not forget that from the point of view of the newer realism, and of Mr. Dewey, this is talking nonsense. For Mr. Dewey, as I understand him, "logic" resolves itself into "method," or scientific method—a method of getting from a given event to any other; and logic regarded as a science of thought (in the older phrasing) and ethics of belief, is part of the illusion of "consciousness." Now I have a wholesome respect for method, as indeed I have for all things practical. We cannot live, rather we cannot get along in the world, by logic alone. But I seem to see a difference, a difference extending to every part of human life, between thinking and methodizing, between believing and accepting. And I am never more conscious of the difference than in reading a logically respectable philosophical essay. The author begins with a statement of foundations—basic facts or basic principles—which are to compel acceptance. From this as an anchorage he extends his chain of argument, making each link irrefrangible as he proceeds, giving to the chain, perhaps, a further anchorage on the way. At points he pauses to recapitulate: "we now see that, since A is B, and B is C, etc."—the very word "since" making me wonder whether he sees anything but "the logic of his position." In the end his point is: the foundations are immovable, the chain is irrefrangible, therefore by all the laws of method you are obliged— to believe or merely to accept?

For if I believe it will not be in deference to the method, but because, possibly in spite of the method, he has succeeded in conveying to me his vision of the situation—he has communicated an experience. And getting the experience I know that he is thinking and not merely talking, and that he is facing something real. The method may (or may not) aid in communicating the experience, but the "criterion" of belief will never be more than this: when I have got before me the point of view as a whole, with all of its ramifications and interconnections, do I find it convincing—am I also in the presence of reality?

From believing I come, by a change of terms, to knowing. Mr. Dewey makes it very clear that for him knowing is method —method of getting from one event to another. It is no immediate grasp of an object—no mystical experience. For him, indeed, immediate knowing is a contradiction in terms; things that are immediate are not known, but merely "given." It may then serve to put the question squarely if I say that for me knowing is an experience precisely (if you like) "mystical." And I will also say that for me the most significant use of the verb "to know" in any literature is that of Genesis iv. 1, where we are told that "Adam knew Eve his wife, and she conceived, etc." And then we may remember that the mystical union of the mystics is presented as a union of perfect knowledge, and yet for the most part in imagery suggesting that the sexual union is never far from the thought. But, leaving aside the sexual aspect, which raises very interesting questions of its own, I will put the matter more soberly, as follows: knowing is an experience of personal intimacy. Let the personal implication be as much diluted, or merely adumbrated, as you please, what we mean by knowing can never be impersonal. This means that knowing is an intimacy between persons. Formulated in grammatical terms, it would mean that the verb "to know" requires both (1) a personal subject, and (2) a personal object.

(1) A personal subject: this means that knowledge is not method, but experience—knowledge is "mystical." And if the

distinction itself seems mystical (as indeed it must seem), let us fix our attention upon the implications of "method." The analysis of "method" is likely to ignore the fact that the method in question is the method of a living, thinking person. Yet it is bound to ignore this fact; for to methodize any task is precisely to put it into shape to be performed by any person whatever, or by no person. For modern industry makes it fairly clear that anything that can be reduced to method, like the various forms of accounting, can also be reduced to machinery. If scientific investigation could be really methodized we could dispense with the scientist. Meanwhile, scientific investigation remains a personal experience, often a highly dramatic experience. What is it to be a scientist —from the inside? What is the meaning of his motives, of his hopes and fears, of his background of presuppositions, or *Weltanschauung*? What is the quality of his imagination? At the least he is hardly so disinterested as required by "method"; and at bottom it seems that the "secret" of scientific discovery remains as incommunicable in terms of method—the experience is as much of a mystical experience as the experience of artistic creation.

(2) The experience of knowing, I say, is to be looked for in the knowing of persons; and this means that impersonal "things" are dealt with rather than known. If it be objected that the knowing of persons is strangely irrelevant to any of the necessities of knowing "as such," I will suggest that the strangeness may be due to what I have elsewhere called "the scientific prepossession"; which (having always in mind an ordered society) assigns the special function of knowing to the scientist, conceives the object of knowledge in terms of the special kind of things that he deals with, and thus closes our eyes to the greater part of waking human experience, all of it an experience of knowing. How is the knowing of persons different from the knowing of things, and what has the former to say to the latter? So far as I can see, this question is hardly asked. In the philosophical literature the knowing of persons is a curious, but never a central, chapter. In the history of epistemology the question is virtually ignored. And yet—I have space for only one suggestion—when I wish to know

why my neighbour does this or that, I ask him. If delicacy forbids, and if I am still curious, I quietly observe him; I put two and two together; and perhaps I try a trick of experiment in the form of a seemingly innocent question. That is to say, I use scientific method. The natural scientist, for obvious reasons, is confined to scientific method; he can expect nothing from direct communication. Does this mean, however, that direct communication would be foreign to the motives contained in his desire to know? Or simply that, communication being impossible, he takes the only course available; and then that the "things" he knows are for him as a man the things relatively distant and incommunicable, the things that he cannot know very well, and are converted into impersonal "things" by his method of dealing with them? The latter is my own suggestion, for which I seem to find support in the following. If my neighbour be many rather than one I resort to economic statistics; and thereby I seem clearly to transform them from so many human neighbours, each exercising his personal choice, into impersonal objects of science governed by natural, even by physical law. Yet meanwhile they remain, as "things in themselves," so many human beings.

To bring the topic to a close, I will put the whole matter into terms suggested by the familiar claim of empiricism to the effect that reality is something "present" or "presented." What is it, then, that would realize my desire to know? My answer will be, To find myself *in the presence of* the object; or to get the object into *my presence*. But "my presence"—this is not a question of spatial or temporal location. Cæsar was murdered at the foot of Pompey's statue, but surely not "in the presence of" the statue! The train bearing away my departing guest leaves the station, say, in my presence; but when, lying awake in the small hours, I hear the initiatory puffs of a distant locomotive and recognize them as coming from the "owl" train leaving the junction-station three miles away, that train is also leaving in my presence; and if I could but get into my imagination the whole scene of Cæsar's murder, as clearly as though I were there, Cæsar would be murdered in my presence. "My presence," in short, is a question of the range and power of my imagination.

But what would it be, finally, to be in the presence of reality? Empirical science tells us that we are in the presence of the real when the facts correspond to and verify our hypotheses. But if they simply "correspond," do they then verify the hypothesis or merely echo it? A scientist facing a correspondence unbroken and unqualified would feel, I think, that the facts were mocking him. No, it seems that if you are to be in the presence of reality the facts must not merely "correspond," they must *respond*—with verifications which say, "True, but here is an aspect to the situation which you have not yet considered." This means that the process of "trial and error" must be something like a conversation. But then, what is it to be in the presence of reality? I will repeat here from page 274 of my *Moral Philosophy* an illustration used there in connection with the logic of resurrection and spirit-manifestation: "Suppose that a dead friend of yours appeared to you—say in your sleep. Suppose that you then had an old-time heart-to-heart talk with him—a real conversation, not a Platonic or Berkeleian 'dialogue' in which it is the chief function of one person to say 'Very true!' to the other, but a conversation in which each response stands for fresh thought." Then, I suggest, you would be in the presence of the real; and so far as you failed to get a personal object and a "conversation" you would be not quite face to face with the real. In other words, I should say that the experience of meeting another person and conversing with him is a far more conclusive experience of an other-than-yourself than any "stubbornness of fact" or "resistance of matter."

In coming to the end of my allotted space I realize that I have not succeeded in presenting the point of view in a manner rounded and conclusive. So many considerations have had to be omitted. But I doubt if I could make the story rounded and conclusive in many times the space. There remains, however, a question, the question which, I suspect, everyone who ventures to talk about philosophy dreads most to have asked him—because it is the most vital and searching of all questions: And what is your religion? For myself I can suggest only my idea of religion.

And I can best come to it by repeating the passage in which Pater explains to us "the essence of humanism": the belief, namely, that

> nothing which has ever interested living men and women can wholly lose its vitality—no language they have spoken, nor oracle beside which they have hushed their voices, no dream which has once been entertained by actual human minds, nothing about which they have ever been passionate or expended time and zeal.

Nothing about which they have ever been passionate or expended time and zeal! When I ask myself what it is to live, inevitably I am carried back over the nearly fifty years since as a boy of eleven I first began to work for my living. Except for being thrust upon the world rather early (partly because more than one school had found me impossible), I am not sure that the circumstances of my life have been on the whole either less fortunate or more fortunate than those of other men I know; and I am convinced that for what it is to live the circumstances of life make little difference. And yet as I go back and try to get the feeling of the years as they were passing, one after another, each different from the last, each with its own forward-looking tensity of doubt and expectation, it seems to me that to live is to live through—in the same breath to enjoy and to suffer—a tragic experience. And of those who have no "tragic sense of life" (in the words of Miguel de Unamuno) I have to wonder how they can ever have been passionate or expended time and zeal. But from this I am carried back over the vast expanse of human life, partly and dimly revealed in what is called history. And having in mind what it is to live, I feel that to think of this human life as "social progress"—from the "public" point of view—is inconceivably trivial. I can think only of the countless men and women who have been passionate and have expended time and zeal; for whom, as for you and me, life has been a tragic experience. And then I think that if I could conceive of a realm of being in which none of those lives would ever lose its vitality, in which no soul which has been passionate would ever cease to live—a realm of being not by any stretch of imagination to be put within the boundaries of the natural world—if I could see this, then I should know that I had found a rational universe, a real universe, a spiritual universe, and a universe religiously significant.

PRINCIPAL PUBLICATIONS

Individualism: Four Lectures on the Significance of Consciousness for Social Relations. New York, Longmans, Green, & Company, 1911.

Moral Philosophy: The Critical View of Life. New York, The Dial Press, 1925.

SOME SECOND PRINCIPLES

By W. E. HOCKING

Born 1873; Harvard University, Cambridge, Mass.

SOME SECOND PRINCIPLES

It is, I believe, both natural and usual that a vigorous religious trait in one generation should promote a philosophical trait in the next. The peculiar colouring of immediacy which belongs to religion, the pervasive sense of an unevident value in existence, cannot be precisely transmitted. But it is sure to be recognized, thought about, sought after. It is also almost as sure to be critically regarded at some time or other, to be analysed and explained away or rejected, as a preliminary to independent building. This was my own very ordinary experience.

The religion of my parents was concrete, vivid, and regulatory. It created a substantial and, on the whole, auspicious atmosphere around us. It furnished plenty of food for imagination, aspiration, and incipient rebellion. The world we were taught to live in was certainly not dull nor tediously safe, nor limited in its possibilities. Its unreachable places were not believed to be solitary or waste: they were the fields of a teeming though unexplored cosmical life. Bunyan and Milton were understood to be fanciful enough, but not wholly false to the situation.

The opportunities of life, under this view of things, were such as to elicit ambition and therewith a desire to know: I sympathized with our first parents. The ambition was not so much for scientific inquiry as for awakening: there seemed to be the possibility of an endless series of awakenings—or of convalescences. (Perhaps of the two a convalescence appeared the more desirable, as more gradual, deliberate, and serene. There were two such in my childhood, attended with dreams both alluring and terrible, such as one cannot yet forget, and with strange clarities and doublings of self-consciousness, such as one recalls without being able to recover.) In any case, the guise in which religion then appeared to me was that of something enviable, and the more so as it was something to be definitely and personally achieved. One had to take one's solitary way to gain it, and if one's search were successful, the result was not more a natural consequence than a boon from life to the seeker. It was both at once, as if growth up to this point had been a sub-voluntary occurrence, whereas the last stage of growth had been accomplished with one's own co-operation. In it, something happened to one; and after it had happened, one could never again be just the same.

This, of course, is literally true of every significant happening. But the religious happening, as we thought of it, seemed a radical one, like the passing of the soul-function through some critical value which changed its sign. By it there was acquired no emancipation from any ill of fortune, but a new immunity from overthrow in any of them. William James's phrase is precisely accurate: the type of security achieved was "compatible with every relative danger"—whatever evil could happen otherwise could happen now. But it remains surprising to me that James regarded this sort of security as meaningless, "making no difference," when its whole point was that misfortune had become relative—that is to say, relatively unimportant. If the change was subjective, it was as if one entered into his heritage of health which set the ills of experience at true pictorial distance: they found their focus, and one had become adequate to one's world.

For such a view of things, naturalism in any form was not a matter of debate; it was simply a pathetic blindness and impoverishment, the outlook of a brain which had failed to ripen.

In this parental transmission there was another strand. My father was a physician, said to be skilled in diagnosis, and in this interest, as well as others, a lifelong student and reader. His practice took him out of his office for several hours of each day; and from the age of ten or thereabout I was called upon to take my school books into the office, surrounded by his books, instruments, and drugs. I soon began to find an interest in the books of medicine: they became my first independent field of curiosity. I dipped into the forbidden *materia medica*. One experiment in this field bade fair to be costly. There was in current use at this time, as an inhalant for certain pulmonary diseases, a mixture of oxygen with other gases. During one of my solitary sessions I undertook to inhale the gas, and finding the effects pleasant, continued to do so until I lost consciousness. I was found, perhaps soon after, by an entering patient. Thus in many ways the dependence of the mind on the body, the sensitive and fragile nature of the mental flame, made its impression and strengthened the growing conception of man as an animal organism, quite without any clear sense of antagonism to the dominant supernatural outlook. My father himself, in full view of all this, was sternly pious—that was sufficient at the time.

It was partly through this medical browsing that I was prepared to appreciate my first philosopher. In the 'eighties, Herbert Spencer was still the great name in English philosophy. At the moment when reflection came on me, I fell under his spell. In our household he was, as I promptly learned, a forbidden writer; nevertheless I made my secret way through *First Principles*. As a lad of fifteen I had nothing to oppose to his plausible dialectic. Thoroughly against my will, and with a sense of unmeasured inner tragedy, Spencer convinced me. For years I plodded through his volumes. It was an unmixed discipleship, and so far an experience of great intellectual joy. Spencer had the truth—such modest truth as was to be had. He had written blank mystery over the original splendour of the uncharted world. His view demanded unqualified resignation to the outlook of animal death—to me a sweeping desolation; for I had been seized almost violently with a sense of the uniqueness of individual life and I could hardly endure the thought of annihilation. But Spencer's philosophy explained all things, the extra-beliefs of religion among them, only too well.

My interests for a number of years were dominantly scientific and mathematical. I entered training for a career in engineering. I spent four years in field- and map-work connected with surveying and the civil engineering department of a Western railroad. In the Iowa State College at Ames I studied physics, chemistry, and economics, worked in the laboratories, and became absorbed in the calculus. In the earlier routine of the schools I had taken particular pleasure in geometry, and I continued for a number of years to read independently in mathematics.

This reading has not yet gone far enough to make the unravelling of advanced physical theory a pastime. But it has sufficed for two things: to dispel fear in the presence of a mass of the esoteric symbols of mathematics, and to render me immune to a certain over-estimation of the value of mathematical method in philosophy by which the non-mathematical are widely victimized.

Almost everything fitted into Spencer's outlook. There were three exceptions which I now recall. There was a book, J. B. Stallo's *Concepts and Theories of Modern Physics*, which made some of Spencer's discussion of physical ultimates appear elementary and unimaginative: this was the beginning of disillusionment.

Then there was a simple human performance, a bit of personal unselfishness in my behalf which disturbed the wooden fabric of Spencer's theory of altruism. The matter was of no great moment, but it distinctly failed to smack of evolution. It appeared to me then as a sample of an irrational factor, which I recognized as shot through the fabric of Western civilization, and as constituting its chief claim to be a place worth living in. This judgment began to work havoc in my sense of the finality of the naturalistic scheme.

The last of these disturbing factors was a picture of the human mind so veracious as to command confidence and so living as to shame the physiological apparatus of Spencerian psychology. That was William James's *Principles*, of 1890, a book which I happened to pick up in browsing through shelves of the library at Ames. I cannot say what its argumentative value was at the time; it proved nothing, so far as I recall—it was merely a release; it left all the systematic work to do. But it irrigated certain tracts that had become desert. I began to regain confidence that the mystic's sense of the universe is in substance a true sense, quite apart from his theological symbols. I was sure that the real world is more like the world of James's imagination than like that of Spencer's, and from that time it became my first business to define the difference and to capture some rational account of it.

I did not then know that this would become my life's occupation: I thought that with James's guidance my philosophy could shortly be settled. I came to Harvard to find James. James was not there; for two years he was absent in Europe. But other great teachers were there, of whom I had not known.

George Herbert Palmer was teaching the history of philosophy and ethics as few men have ever taught them. In teaching them he conveyed his own metaphysics, largely through occasional and unforgettable sentences, which as someone well put it, "continued to glow in the dark of the mind." Santayana was there: I heard him, admired his adroit intelligence and deft phrases, felt his essence inwardly repugnant to my own, and, with the intolerance of a young bigot, avoided him, to my great loss. Dickinson Miller introduced me to the argument of idealism and gave me an opportunity to re-read Spencer under wise direction. Münsterberg was there: in due time I entered his seminary, and through him and through the reading of Windelband began to touch the massiveness of German learning. Royce was there: I listened to his lectures on metaphysics and felt power and more than power—a certain intellectual majesty and moral greatness. I was attracted to his view and held by the massive dignity of his thought without being wholly persuaded by his argument.

My prevalent state was one of unrest and impatience. I was hoping for systematic truth. Instead, I was gathering here and there an idea, listening to thinkers whose views conflicted and who seemed to be resigned to that situation. I wanted to be convinced of something, and the best reasoners left me critical and unsatisfied.

When James came, in 1901, I went to him with the enthusiasm of deferred hope. He read his marvellous manuscript on religious experience. The stuff of that work was grist to my mill: James was indeed a liberator, and in his presence life was in the saddle. Yet James's method, or lack of method, and his results left me confused and unsatisfied. My days of discipleship had passed with the passing of Spencer's domination, and with the most ardent desire to do so, I could not again become the disciple of any. Remembering these earlier years at Harvard I have ceased, as a teacher, to expect to produce assent in men between twenty and thirty.

It was in the natural order of things that one began to look toward Germany, where the texture of thought seemed at once so fine and so powerful, where, as one believed, there had been at least once an adequate profundity and technique. Harvard gave me the opportunity to study in Germany as Walker Fellow. I would like to detail, if it were possible, my obligation to Natorp, Husserl, Paulsen, Dilthey, Simmel, Windelband, Rickert; and my still deeper obligation to Kant, Fichte, and Hegel, whom I began to study minutely. I must particularly mention the value of Husserl's discipline, and his insistence on the importance of Hume and Mill. I returned to Harvard with a new power to appreciate its guidance.

James was at this period developing and driving abreast his pragmatism and pluralism in seminary courses for advanced students. He was recommending Charles Peirce's *Tychism*, according to which such order as there is in the world "results from chance coming and survival of the more coherent." This view "eliminates the 'problem of evil' from theology" and "goes with empiricism, personalism, democracy, freedom." The temptation is strong to dwell upon William James and drop the prosaic theme of this paper; perhaps I may serve both interests by quoting from a letter I wrote to him at the close of his course of 1903-4, indicating some comments his lectures had roused:

Are not all systems arrogant simplifications? What is materialism but a simplification, resolved to do justice to our natural ties at all costs? What is idealism but a simplification? What is monism? A simplification at the expense of the abundance and surprise of life. What is pluralism? It, too, is a simplification which values the richness and drama of living too deeply to fill in the connectives. All the structural red-ink and lettering in which the architectural engineer delights are for the architectural artist an abomination: they burden and spoil his picture. The philosophical synthesizer must be a strong man; whoever writes a plausible philosophical thesis must be a strong man. These are the tyrants of truth. . . .

A word about "arising." I doubt whether any empirical notion of "coming into being" can be framed. Empirically we know that we have before us a plurality of things, and that this plurality varies. The things are not labelled, however, with regard to their origin or destination. Why suppose that any of them has twinkled into existence first at a distance, and then has come together with others? Things do indeed appear to twinkle into being; but they do it before our eyes. To me, things seem to grow out of one another. A *mind* seems to be a brooding-place where being is continually hatched from previous being. The only security I feel in the universe is that nothing can come into being except under such conditions, and hence always with respect to what has been before. This hypothesis gives scope for any sort of freedom and individualism that can be of interest to anyone. . . .

Royce was concerned with bringing the sciences into comradely relations to philosophy, and especially with exploring the consequences of the *rapprochement* between logic and mathematics. I find these remarks in a lecture note: "Philosophic efforts since Kant have remained incomplete by lack of the study of the processes of thought embodied in the living sciences, and of such categories as number, quantity, space, time, cause, continuity. . . . The mathematician, in so far as he consciously distinguishes significant from trivial problems, and ideal systems, is a philosopher. The philosopher, in so far as he seeks exactness of logical method in his reflection, must meanwhile aim to be within his limits a mathematician." This was to me welcome doctrine. Under Royce's guidance I studied the concept of number, and conceived the idea of writing a "morphology of experience" in which the mathematical idea of a "group" should serve to define and explain the distinct boundaries of the several sciences.

In pursuit of this project, I began to investigate some of the primary relations between physics, psychology, and sociology. Here the problem of the knowledge of minds other than our own proved fruitful enough to occupy me during the period of my doctorate. The results took shape in a *Philosophy of Communication*, Part I, of which there was never a Part II.

It is impossible now to trace the sources of convictions that grew during this time, some of which have remained. One such, which came to me with the force of an intuition, was that the supposed isolation of minds is an illusion; that we share identical objects, and in so doing actually merge or coalesce in our being; that whatever meaning can be attached to the phrase, to be *within the mind* of another, is realized in the actual situation. For Nature is veritably a common object; there is but one Nature —not one for each person: and while for every pair of communicating minds perspectives and qualities differ, space itself is identical, and continuously identical.

This judgment puts an end to subjectivism of a solipsistic variety; but it might accord with a mutual subjectivism, in which the objectivity of a physical object lies in the circumstance that other minds agree in perceiving it. This I rejected on the ground of another conviction, that the kind of knowing which we call empirical is a sign of dependence. The obedient observation of fact, which belongs to the empirical attitude, implies that we are recipients of an activity from without. That objectivity of the physical world whereby we consider it as not-ourselves is due to its source in this active non-ego, not to the fact that it is shared by each one with other equally passive or receptive knowers.

So far, my theory of knowledge was realistic. But what we receive, we also retain and reproduce. In memory and imagination, we show an activity which answers immediately to the impressed action. There is some positive reason for thinking that this creative capacity of ours is of the same sort as that impressed activity; and this consideration became the ground, or one ground, for a third belief—namely, that the active non-ego is a self. It is through our primary relations with this self that our relations with other finite selves become, in the first place, consciously personal. Our first and persistent object of knowledge is the active self; our other objects are derivative.

In this underlying and substantial self I recognized the Absolute of Royce's teaching. But I further recognized it as the object of that mystic experience whose significance James had begun to do justice to. With this identification, a great strand of speculative and religious tradition could be interpreted and saved for human as well as philosophic uses. Royce's dominantly negative attitude towards mysticism, which he so profoundly interpreted, becomes unnecessary.[1]

But if this too lengthy narrative has had any value, it has now reached the point at which further pursuit is unprofitable. There is something about thinking which dissolves away its historical roots, even to the personal knowledge of the thinker. So, in spite of a warning from my daemon that the thing is bound to be a set of rough logs rather than a building, let me set down some of the views to which I have come, simply as materials for a philosophy. For the most part, they are not provable; nor are they in any general sense axiomatic. They are merely *my* axioms— judgments for which I no longer need proof. But they are also judgments which, by proof or otherwise, I should like to recommend to others.

1. The principle of *ambiguous simplicity*.—Neither the world nor anything in the world is unambiguously complex or unambiguously simple.

The world is not cleverly put together, in such wise that a gifted man by sufficient ingenuity can guess its structure. It lends itself freely to analysis, and in this analysis ingenuity and wit have free scope. But, on the one hand, the task of analysis is never done; and were we to depend on it for our bearings we should necessarily despair of any result. Atomism is a necessary expedient in physics: in philosophy it is a will-o'-the-wisp. There are no indivisible units of the world in space and time: there are no ultimate ions or sub-ions of which we can say, these are the last refinement of Nature's subtlety. Strange that anyone should think contemporary physics to be in touch, at last, with the most minute phenomena! Atomism means hopelessness.

On the other hand, complexity is never the whole truth, not even of the world as a whole. Like a self, the world has an aspect of complete simplicity. The possibility of metaphysical knowledge depends on the presence within the intricate mesh of things of

---

[1] I may say that in his last, as yet unpublished, lectures on Metaphysics, 1915–16, Royce's attitude has gravitated far toward that appreciation which his lifelong interest in mysticism foreshadowed.

various comprehensive simplicities, and at last as a unity which is accessible, and, indeed, a persistent datum of consciousness.

2. The principle of *initial empiricism.*—Everything that is worth knowing about the world, including metaphysical knowledge, is to be known in experience; for experience is metaphysical —it is dealing with reality. This does not exclude a .priori knowledge, for experience contains a priori elements which subsequent reflection brings to light. Thus a priori knowledge is the last in order of time to be recognized and isolated.

It must be observed that experiencing is an art, not a gift. Receptivity to the accessible gamut of being has no resemblance to an inalienable and automatic sensorium. A lethargic empiricism which "waits to be shown" will report a truncated world shorn of most of the characters which make experience tolerable—in particular, of its connections and unities. Empirical knowledge has sometimes been credited with the advantage of bringing minds to an agreement on facts, whereas a priori knowledge is discredited by a fatal disagreement as to what is "self-evident." By this test empiricism must be still more discredited; for what one finds, another finds a myth! Compare the "given" manifold of Kant with the "given" of Avenarius or of Münsterberg. There can be no agreement on what is given, when givenness is the object of a state of ideal mental vacuity; for philosophers will always vary in their capacities for becoming dramatically inane. Experiencing is not impressionism: it is the receptivity of an ideally active mind.

With this understanding we may assert that from the first experience presents wholes as well as parts. Empiricism cannot consist, then, in going from the parts to the whole. Empirical knowledge grows from a sketch, in which the whole is outlined and parts are placed by internal development of structure and detail. Induction and generalization do not proceed *in vacuo*: the shapes they assume are *elicited* by the preconceived whole.

In this process one's conception of the whole is altered. Induction finds anew the premiss which defined the data for that induction, and to this extent is circular; but each induction gives it a better definition. Thus there is a principle of alternation in knowledge, as well as in the life of the will.

The pragmatic method represents half of the truth: universals are to be discovered *in rebus*. Principles of law, for example, are to be found at work in the decisions of particular cases: the meaning of the generality is to be seen in its power to do this work. The other half of the truth is that the particulars mean the universal: the cases are of interest for the light they throw on the principles of law. Aristotle's conception of the nature of the political state is nowhere more penetrating (or more Platonic) than when he describes it as an arrangement for the progressive discovery of the nature of justice by way of the public discussion of examples. The law is no more for the sake of the case than the case for the sake of the law. Our conception of the universal grows; but it remains the same universal—we are dealing with an eternal object. It is as much our human business to enjoy the contemplation of that object as to apply or embody it in practice; in fact, embodiment cannot flourish without contemplation. Here I part company with the purely pragmatic or instrumental conception of the universal, and of the business of life.

In another direction I am parting company with both Hume and Kant, who agreed that the categories are not found in experience. I cannot adopt the view that the material of experience awaits the ordering work of mind to assume its consistent and intelligible form, partly because on Kant's own principles the material of experience, as well as the thing itself, is a meaningless conception without the categories. It is the object which is given to us and not merely the material for the construction of the object; and our possession of the category as an idea is a result of its prior presence in the world of objects. On this basis, which reverses Kant's view, the ontological argument holds good for all the categories, so far as they are logically irreducible, i.e. the presence of the idea in us implies the existence of the corresponding character in reality. Thus Kant is consistent in attacking the ontological argument: it is the central enemy of his system.

There are many thinkers who feel obliged to be Kantian with

regard to our social experience who are not Kantians anywhere else; because, as they assume, other mind than our own is not given, and in the nature of the case cannot be given. We can only *interpret* our world as social, imposing upon its plain, natural stuff, object for me, the new category of other-observers, so that nature becomes *object for us*. My conviction is that this extension of the Kantian principle is its sufficient refutation. For the imposition of a private category upon a given stuff leaves the situation private, and directly contradicts the meaning of social existence. It assumes that the social relation cannot be experienced but only *meant*; but if this is true we cannot so much as mean social experience, and the category disappears. In whatever sense we mean the social object, it is *there* for our experience; in relation to at least one such other self, our idea and our experience fuse.

3. The principle of *inclusive rationality*.—Experience is the initial form of all knowledge, and experience presents a world of data. But there is nothing in experience which is mere fact or datum.

This is to say, not that all which exists is rational, but that there is a reason for the positive and irrational character which runs through things—reason has the last and inclusive word. Hard as it is to maintain philosophical courage in view of the expanding scope of what appear to be ultimate matters of fact, from the existence of anything at all to the last details of scientific discovery, we can certainly not *prove* that these things must be taken for ever with a pure natural piety; for the proof would rob that piety of its purity. Neither dare we *assume* that anything is just blankly there. For if we begin with this assumption, we can give no reason for not admitting more of the same sort, and finally "accepting the universe" in complete intellectual abasement. The understandableness of things is a necessary assumption.

It may be taken as a corollary of this principle that the world unity is not dead. A pure datum might easily be a dead fact, such as material atoms were once conceived to be, impenetrable, unchanging self-existence; and any such dead fact must be a pure datum. To deny that there is any mere datum is to deny that there is any being which can neither account for itself nor be accounted for by other being. The inclusive being would be sponsor for itself and for other beings.

It is, indeed, impossible, as Spencer alleges, to avoid assuming self-existence somewhere. But it is an error to suppose, as this proposition suggests, that it is a matter of complete logical indifference where you assume self-existence. The self-existent must be intelligible to itself if not to us; self-existence, then, must go with self-consciousness.

It follows that there is no *telos* without a *nous*, and no world of essences without a subject.

4. *Tentative mysticism.*—Our thought is never, in point of time, adequate to its total object.

This is not, as Bradley held, because relations are irrational and we must think in relations. Nor is it, as Spinoza thought, because determination is negation. Nor is it, as Bergson teaches, because concepts are rigid while reality is fluid. It is because the concepts we have to employ for our predicates emerge to our ken in an experience which is selective: the one can only be characterized by way of that repeated effort of induction which yields the starting-point for a new revision.

We never know finally what the real is. Nevertheless there are certain predicates which we may apply to it, because they are subject to a parallel unfinishedness. As reality eludes description in terms of other categories, so does the *self*. Various systems of psychology may be worked out, internally consistent, mutually inconsistent, and all inadequate. If we characterize the real as a self, we express the unknown in terms of a commensurate unknown, an infinitude of the same order. We do not destroy its mystery, but we render intelligible its qualitative relation to human thought.

There is an obverse of this tentative mysticism which, if we liked technical designations better than we do, we might call *explorative pluralism*, namely, that just in so far as the One eludes definitive characterization, the sphere of the clearly definable remains plural and open towards future experience. The One has a character, and is thus no *ex post facto* form or omni-hospitable afterthought; but our knowledge of it must grow by that type of recurrent induction in which the instances are never all in.

Thus the world is a one, but for our handling a many. The self, likewise, is a one; but its unity splinters against the growing variety of the situations it has to meet. It is a will, and also a bundle of instincts; its programme of life is not deduced from a preformed purpose, but the purpose slowly arrives at a sense of its own substance through the pursuit of a vast variety of goods not overtly related, and always ready to send out independent branches. So, too, with the principles of our conduct: the one commandment does not displace the value of the many counsels; the manifold injunctions of Deuteronomy and Paul eke out the simplicity of Moses and Jesus; and no concentration of ethical essence in Kant or elsewhere can render useless the irresponsibly numerous sayings of Ptah Hotep or Confucius or Epictetus. Second principles remain for our philosophy more wieldable than the first principle, and on the whole more useful, provided always that they are *well known to be second*; for in that case the life of the first principle is in them to animate them, to discover their limitations and keep them in place. And they become contributory to the next, and more adequate, formulation of the one.

5. *The union of value and fact.*—The great dualities must be treated like other forms of pluralism for explorative purposes, but in most of them we have something better than a blank postulate that the two aspects of things belong together.

In the case of value and fact, we have a clue to their union in the enjoyment which is inseparable from being alive, and especially from *knowing*. Objects are *goods* simply in their character as objects of cognition, whatever their further relations to our purposes may be. As related to our health, disease is not a good; but as an object of scientific interest disease is as good as anything else in the world. Pain itself, taken simply as intense sensation, is so far good—and there is an art of so taking it. The knowledge of persons as scientific objects has a peculiarly iridescent value-quality, inasmuch as it is attended with a sense of self-defeat which can be suppressed only at the expense of *malaise* of conscience; for the adequate knowledge of persons is attended by a specific value called love, and conversely, any purely "objective" psychological observation of persons fails precisely of objectivity. Cognition and value are co-extensive; and the more adequate cognition has the higher degree of worth.

Evil is in no sense abolished by the pervasive presence of good in cognition: the world is as good and as bad as we find it to be. But the proportion between evil and good for us is a function of our voluntary adjustment; and the question of importance for theory as well as for practice is whether there is anything in the nature of the world which decrees that our findings of good must be moderate. For myself, I cannot believe that the principle of temperance has any metaphysical standing. The finding of good has its conditions, not its limits.

These conditions seem to be mainly twofold. First, a rather ruthless and uncompromising objectivity of mind. For value has to be discovered, not derived from our inner hunger; craving rises to the level of what the world offers—it would be preposterous to limit that offering to the original meanness of subjective craving. Second, a conscious recovery of the practical presuppositions which live in "subconsciousness." For the value-sense, as well as thought, has its a priori elements which come to light only through subsequent reflection. Discoveries, or recoveries, of this sort may express themselves in the form of paradox, as that seeking implies some sort of finding. Though these paradoxes constitute an apparent mockery of the seeker, they indicate a condition without which life for a rational being is not worth living. For rational life rises to the pursuit of goods which can be gained only at the end of infinite time; and if satisfaction must be thus deferred, the "pleasure of pursuit" becomes the blind pleasure of the fool. What is necessary is a present attainment which makes the continuance of pursuit, not superfluous, but eternally endurable. To discern that one is in presence of a goal, though not the final goal, is a remedy for despair; and such "anticipation of attainment," which I take to be the essence of religion, is an achievement which the practical mystic reports and undertakes to make available. No one can pass judgment on the value of existence without considering the report of the genuine mystic.

These reflections are sadly unfinished; but a finished set of reflections would misrepresent an unfinished philosophy.

PRINCIPAL PUBLICATIONS

The Meaning of God in Human Experience. 1912.
Human Nature and Its Remaking. 1918.
Morale and Its Enemies. 1918.
Man and The State. 1926.
Law and Rights. 1926.
The Self, Its Body, and Freedom. 1928.
Types of Philosophy. 1929.

THE WAY OF OPINION

By THEODORE DE LAGUNA

Born 1876; Professor of Philosophy, Bryn Mawr College, Penn.

THE WAY OF OPINION

THERE is an element of scepticism in all philosophy, and the degree of emphasis which is given to this element is largely determined by the accidents of personal and social history. In America the sceptical element has never been prominent. The moral seriousness of democratic life has kept it in abeyance. In pragmatism, as well as in neo-Hegelianism, it might easily have bulked larger; and it would not require a very perverse ingenuity to exhibit William James and Josiah Royce as descendents of Ænesidemus. That is not how they viewed themselves, however, and it is not in that direction that their influence has mainly tended. The realistic movement of recent years is even more decidedly dogmatic in temper, and had its origin in a revolt against certain idealistic theories—notably that of the essentiality of relations—which were believed to have sceptical implications.

It happens that my own thought during this last quarter-century has belonged to the fringe and not the centre of American philosophy; and its general tendency has been in the direction of a more and more radical scepticism. That, too, is, of course, largely a matter of emphasis, and it would not be hard to show that every doubt had a core of conviction; but the doubts remain, and in my own mind they have become increasingly prominent. The beginnings of the tendency are probably to be found in a long and painful endeavour to escape from the trammels of the Lutheran pietism in which I was brought up. I found it exceedingly hard to win freedom of thought, and probably should never have succeeded if I had not, in my middle twenties, been plucked away from home influences and set down for a time in the midst of a people of alien race to think my way to a clear self-consciousness. It was fortunate for me that I had come under the instruction of two teachers of great ability and strongly opposed views. Both, indeed, were idealists; but one (Howison) was a deeply religious neo-Kantian, while the other (McGilvary) was passing through a phase of left-wing Hegelianism. Either alone would doubtless have made me a disciple, and I should have passed from the faith of my boyhood to a new faith no less constraining; but between the two I was left to flounder—awkwardly enough, but at liberty.

The ambition of philosophers of the grand style has been to organize science into a system of reason, starting from definite data in the form either of self-evident principles or of particular contents of sensation, and proceeding step by step without logical circularity. For part of the system the universal premises were alone to be used, and the procedure was to be rigidly deductive and certain. This part of the design has now shrunk to the limits of pure mathematics, and there is a general conviction—which I share—that all pure mathematics is deducible from logical principles the denial of which is nonsense, and which may therefore be regarded as tautological. For the remaining part the particulars of sense were to be included, and the procedure was to be fundamentally inductive and to be confined to probabilities. So-called rationalists and empiricists have differed as to the relative extent of the two parts of the system; but the general design is common to both. To my mind the design, so far at least as it is concerned with knowledge of real existence, is chimerical. The history of science gives it no support. Human reason is never simply constructive, but always reconstructive. Science, like common sense, is at all times a going concern. There are no Cartesian doubts, no fresh beginnings. Reflection takes its rise, not from axioms and sense-data, but from habitual expectations and prejudices. We have always a multitude of general beliefs in accordance with which we interpret each new matter of fact; and though any one of these beliefs may at some time be called in question, this is always on the supposition of the acceptance of a host of others. Science, accordingly, can never be a system of judgments with one-way relations of implication. Our judgments support one another. And when, as occasionally happens, they contradict one another, there is no ultimate standard of imperishable truth by which they can be tested. The only standard is the vague and shifting standard afforded by our beliefs in general.

It is the demand for a system of reason that has shaped our

theories of induction. These theories have sprung from the assumption that men must somehow be able to draw conclusions from particulars of sensation, *plus* at most some a priori principles of logic. It has been generally admitted that induction, as thus conceived, could yield no certain results, but it has been confidently assumed that it could yield probabilities. This I believe to be a mistake. If we had to start from particular facts and logical principles alone, we could never make the least advance toward an understanding of the world. There is no reasoning except deductive reasoning. General principles having special relevance to the matter in hand must always be assumed. The belief in peculiar processes of induction, by which we might pass from singular to general propositions, and from these to propositions of higher and higher generality, is a pure delusion.

We are all familiar with the conception of the world as a grab-bag containing balls, the colours of which we have to learn by experience. We know at the outset that there are balls in the bag, but prior to actual examination we know nothing about their colours. We have no reason to suppose that all are of one colour, or that there are many colours, or, in the latter case, what the proportion and distribution of the various colours may be. That is to say, prior to examination of the balls the colour of each ball is a separate and distinct atomic fact. Under these conditions it has been supposed that if, as a matter of fact, the first n balls taken from the top of the bag were all black, there would be an appreciable probability that the next ball would be black. If black balls were not relatively numerous (it is argued) it would be improbable that n balls in succession would be found to be black; and since the first n were actually black this is evidence that black balls were indeed relatively numerous, and so there is a probability that the next ball, or any other hitherto unexamined ball, will be black. This, however, will not hold. What has been observed is that in the given region of the bag a certain number of black balls occurred; but there is nothing to delimit this region, and, furthermore, all those black balls have been removed and are no longer liable to be chosen. On the given supposition no conclusion follows.

Of course in real life the suppositions would be very different. If I pulled twenty black balls in succession out of a bag, I should be very strongly inclined to expect that the next one would be black. I should be inclined from the outset to regard the presence of the balls in the sack, not as a multitude of atomic facts, but as a unitary phenomenon calling for a more or less uniform explanation; and I should quickly begin to regard the blackness of the balls as a characterization of their source. I should, then, draw an inference; but it would not be an inference derived from particulars and logical principles alone.

It is only very slowly that I have been brought to this position, and yet it is hard to recall the steps by which it was reached. Logical speculation has a way of continually reabsorbing its premises as it goes along, so that at each stage the results present themselves as something primitive and underived. It is a straining after the self-evident, and in the measure in which it succeeds it vanishes. For the same reason it is hard to recommend a logical theory to another, whose own speculation has not definitely prepared the way for it. If it is not obvious, it is paradoxical. In the present case the leading influences have been two: first, the study of the classical English theories of induction, especially those of Bacon, Hume, Mill, and Whewell; and, secondly, certain features of the pragmatism of James and Dewey. Add to these the analysis of particular alleged inductive arguments, which never revealed any reasoning except deductive reasoning. I was interested to find that Lalande, after a much wider study of the history of inductive theories than mine, was tempted to accept a similar conclusion: that there is no way of providing a logical justification for inductive inference. Lalande, to be sure, has suggested the possibility of an ethical justification. Induction, so far as he can see, is an unsound method of procedure; nevertheless we may be morally bound, for the sake of the practical consequences, to reason inductively, as if such reasoning were sound. That hardly seems to me to be a way out. I cannot see my way to an obligation to reason badly.

That the older theories of induction will not hold—that, in particular, Mill's attempt to lay down canons of inductive proof

is a failure—is now widely recognized, although the hope is not
renounced of finding something satisfactory to take their place.
But to my mind the failures of the past are not simply negative
facts; they illustrate very clearly the position which I have taken.
Consider, for example, Mill's method of difference. According to
the canon, one single circumstance is to change. As a matter of
fact, in every instance countless circumstances are changing;
but the great mass of these we ignore as irrelevant. Only experience, however, can tell us what is relevant, and our judgments
as to possible relevancy often turn out to be ill-founded. But let
us suppose, for the sake of argument, that the conditions are
satisfied and that it is known that only one relevant circumstance
has changed. No basis for any significant generalization is yet
given. We must know also which among the *unchanged* conditions
were essential to the occurrence of the phenomenon. Otherwise
the experiment tells us nothing with regard to any other concrete
case. If the experiment warrants a logical conclusion, that is
because it is interpreted in the light of general principles derived
from previous experience. The same sort of comment is called
for by Mill's other methods. Standing alone, they are worthless.
It is only when brought into the historical continuity of human
experience that they amount to anything.

Among the most interesting of recent attempts at the validation
of induction is that of Russell in his little volume, *The Problems
of Philosophy*. I single it out for mention here because, during the
last fifteen years, Russell's logical theories have occupied a good
deal of my attention, and the study of them has had much to
do with shaping my own views. Russell proposes to found
induction on an independent and fundamental a priori principle
of reason. The principle of induction, he says, cannot be established
by experience, because we must possess and apply it in order to
prove anything by means of experience. His statement of the
principle runs as follows: "(*a*) When a thing of a certain sort *A*
has been found to be associated with a thing of a certain other
sort *B*, and has never been found dissociated from a thing of
the sort *B*, the greater the number of cases in which *A* and *B*
have been associated, the greater is the probability that they

will be associated in a fresh case in which one of them is known to be present; (*b*) under the same circumstances, a sufficient number of cases of association will make the probability of a fresh association nearly a certainty, and will make it approach certainty without limit" (p. 103). What has impressed me as significant is the fact that, if this principle be assumed as axiomatic, it does not in the least help us to draw any inductive inference; for it affords no means of determining even vaguely or approximately how many instances of the concomitance of *A* and *B* are necessary to establish the conclusion with any appreciable degree of probability. A million instances may be barely enough to excuse a faint surmise. To say that as the number of instances increases the probability increases, is to say, in effect, nothing at all. Similarly, it is idle to assert that with a "sufficient" number of instances the probability closely approaches certainty, for there is nothing to indicate, even in the vaguest way, what a sufficient number may be. Perhaps two would be enough. Perhaps the number of the sands of the seashore would be inadequate.

This is the sort of consideration that has brought many men to the confession that inductive reasoning is a mystery, and that has brought me to the conviction that it is a myth. Russell, I believe, had set himself an impossible task, which he felt constrained to accomplish; for he aimed to set up a system of reason, for which inductive proof is essential. Finding it impossible to justify induction otherwise, he sought to found it upon a special axiom. But there is no axiom of induction; and if there were it would not be of the slightest service to us.

A like reflection arises in connection with the principle of the uniformity of nature, which others have tried to use as a basis for scientific induction. This principle, in itself considered—that is, apart from the specific uniformities which men have already learned—contributes nothing at all to any inductive argument. To know merely that nature is uniform is to know nothing with respect to any particular alleged uniformity, such as the conservation of mass or the atomic weight of lead. Any of these may turn out to be imperfect, and the uniformity of nature will nevertheless remain unimpaired. Since, then, nothing can contradict it, nothing can be inferred from it. It is not this perfect, but utterly abstract, uniformity that we use in our reasonings; it is the uniformity embodied in the questionable, but particular and concrete, laws of nature with which previous experience has acquainted us. The upbuilding of human knowledge is a continuous evolution.

The relation of this view to pragmatism is too close to be overlooked, and the direct influence of William James in its formation was doubtless very great. As a young man I heard the lecture at the University of California, in which James's pragmatism was first proclaimed; and during the following years, in which my thoughts were deeply unsettled, his writings became my principal study. I always found in him much that roused my opposition; there was, perhaps, no single doctrine of his that seemed to me wholly acceptable; but the evolutionary conception of human knowledge which underlay his particular theories impressed me as being exceedingly important and fruitful. My first book, *Dogmatism and Evolution* (written in collaboration with my wife), contained an appreciation of pragmatism from this point of view.

There was another feature of James's pragmatism that impressed me—namely, the prominence given to beliefs, as opposed to knowledge. On James's part this was, perhaps, mostly a matter of convenience. It is hard, if not impossible, to find examples of knowledge which the reader can be counted upon to admit; for the tribe of sceptics, if not numerous, is at any rate well distributed. But though we may fail to recognize knowledge, there is no such difficulty with regard to belief—that is a familiar enough phenomenon. Hence it was good pedagogical, as well as controversial, policy to let epistemology take its start from belief rather than from knowledge as such. But there was involved the further reflection that the hard-and-fast distinction between knowledge and belief, as it has been maintained in the rationalistic tradition from Plato down, will not hold. The only tenable distinction is one of degree, not of kind.

The characteristic mark of knowledge has been its objective certainty. When we know, we believe very strongly; we are very certain of the truth of our belief. But more than this is regarded as being necessary for knowledge. The most intense and unswerving belief may be erroneous, while knowledge is necessarily true. That a man has no doubts may mean only that he is thoroughly mistaken. What we know must be not only certain to us, but certain in itself. This notion of objective certainty involves, I believe, a serious confusion. For the certainty that knowledge requires is not merely truth: to believe the truth is only to have a right opinion. Such certainty is not reducible to the relation of logical implication, for that relation can subsist between false propositions as well as true. We may formally define the certain in itself as that which is necessarily certain to all rational beings who understand it and who understand the grounds upon which it is based. But there is no way to bring all rational beings to such a test. Our expectation as to a general assent must be based upon our own actual assent. We may subject the matter to a critical review; we may take all possible precautions against emotional aberration; we may demonstrate to ourselves and others over and over again. But all that leaves the certainty mine or yours or theirs; it does not depersonalize it.

Shall we say that the actual condition of science is intolerable? We recognize that it is no system of reason, that it involves assumptions which have their roots, not in factual data nor in axiomatic principles, but in habits and associations. But does this mean that science must be refounded, that its present condition is sadly precarious, and that only when logical grounds have completely replaced all merely psychological grounds will its conclusions have real probability? I do not see that we are driven to adopt any such position. The condition of science appears to me to be excellent; and if it were not I do not see what reason we should have to hope for any considerable betterment. If the conclusions of science, taken generally, have not a high degree of probability as they stand, what probability can there be that any future demonstrations will increase their probability? Scientific knowledge has the best claim to the title that any beliefs can have. It is reflective, critical, subjected to continual review and to verification and correction on every hand. The personal reference remains, but it is reduced to the last degree of tenuity.

Nevertheless it remains, and this may be seen in the form which the progress of science takes—the same form which we observe in the history of human standards generally, even those which are most flagrantly emotional and subjective. There is a series of shifts from one orthodoxy to another, marked by a conflict of parties, liberal and conservative. We have recently seen the scientific world divided in this way over the theory of relativity. The same phenomenon regularly takes place on a smaller scale whenever any less profound revision of the accepted laws of nature is attempted.

It would be a mistake to suppose that in such a case the settlement is reached by rational procedures alone—unless the term "rational" is stretched to cover all processes by which we form more and more comprehensive views of things. When exceptions to a law are noted and repeatedly verified, the law is not necessarily revised, much less given up. It is always possible to refer a discrepancy between expectation and observation to the action of unknown disturbing causes. A scientific law, be it remembered, describes what happens "other things being equal," and other things may easily not be equal. So long, then, as the principle continues to do its great work of co-ordinating our experiences, occasional exceptions do not weaken its authority. We accept them, as the conservative man of affairs accepts the evils incidental to the operation of our political constitution and machinery of trade. But when do the exceptions become more than occasional? When do they impeach the validity of the principle and make revision imperative? How do the weaknesses of the old theory compare in seriousness with those of the new theories that are advanced? Division on these questions is largely determined by sentiment and character and personal associations. And the division is healed and a new orthodoxy reached, not when all the difficulties are logically disposed of, but when it is generally felt that the discrepancies that remain are no more than we are bound to expect.

One of the chief preoccupations of two generations of philosophers has been the nature of truth. It has been assumed without question that truth has a nature—that is to say, that there is a common property which all true propositions possess and which all false propositions lack. I have become convinced that this assumption is groundless: that truth has no nature, and that there is no property whatsoever that is common to, and peculiar to, true propositions. Truth, I believe, is an expression which has meaning only "in use." When a given proposition is said to be true, we know what that means; but, as I understand the matter, there is no meaning of truth in general—there is no room for a theory of truth.

I was predisposed to this opinion as a result of the spirited controversy between pragmatists and absolute idealists which enlivened the early years of the century, and which died away in futile countercharges and restatements. Both sides, it seemed to me, were guilty of radical inconsistencies. Both were strong in refutation, but neither was able to give a straightforward and consistent account of its own position. The suspicion arose that there was a very simple and familiar reason for this: that the controversy was over a shadow, and that, to speak strictly, there was no theory of truth to be established.

Truth appears as a predicate which may be affirmed or denied of any proposition, as the predicate "yellow" may be affirmed or denied of a given object of perception. But there is this remarkable difference. However the proposition, "This is yellow," may be restated or transformed, "yellow" remains a constituent and is never simply dropped. Yet that is exactly what happens to the predicate of truth. To affirm that a given proposition is true is precisely equivalent to affirming the proposition itself. If it is true that the given object is yellow, then it *is* yellow; and conversely. Similarly of the predicate of falsity. It purports to be the negative of "truth"; but as a matter of fact it is the equivalent of negation in general. To say that it is false that the object is yellow is simply to declare that it is *not* yellow. This is all that the explanation of truth or falsity in any particular case amounts to. They have no general meaning. If they had, that meaning could not be eliminated without change in the implications of what is asserted. In the above example, "this" is the subject, and the predicate asserted of it is "yellow." To take, instead of "this," a proposition as the subject, and to predicate truth of this proposition, is a mere form of speech. The real subject and predicate remain what they were before. The quality of truth is an idol of the market-place.

It is worthy of note that when formulæ are constructed, from which the predicate "true" or "false" cannot be eliminated, the formulæ are nonsensical. This is illustrated by the verbal para doxes to which the name of Epimenides is attached; but the principle is of wider extent. In the case of the formula, "This is false," where "this" is supposed to denote the formula itself, the difficulty is not confined to determining whether the formula is in fact true or false; it is primarily a matter of interpretation, and the same difficulty arises in connection with the formula, "This is true." When in either case we try to determine *what* is affirmed to be false or true and thus to eliminate the predicate of truth or falsity, we are unable to do so. In the latter case, for example, what is affirmed to be true is simply that *this is true*, and the predicate that was to be eliminated is left on our hands.

The usual course in dealing with these paradoxes has been different, and it has resulted in uniform failure. The secret has been thought to be that no real proposition can directly or indirectly refer to itself, or even that it can never be applicable, however indirectly, to itself. The proposition that every proposition contains a universal is doubtless true, but, according to this way of thinking, it would be a mistake to try to apply it to itself. In place of such an application, one must have a distinct, but analogous, proposition on a higher level, so to speak; and one must have other analogous propositions on higher and higher levels without end. Such a theory may be plausible, but it can never be made logically secure. There must always, at some point or other, be an express or tacit resort to a reducing principle, which refers to all levels and belongs to none. The difficulty is thus only postponed, and ultimately the whole scheme collapses in utter futility. But no such scheme is necessary. There is no reason why a proposition should not be asserted of propositions in general, or why it should not be applied to itself. The paradox of Epimenides lies in the *predicate*—a predicate which is intelligible only when it can be eliminated, and which here cannot be eliminated.

Just as the distinction between truth and falsity is at bottom an illusion of language, so the distinction between appearance and reality, together with the great historical opposition between realism and idealism, reduces to a similar illusion. The real is that which really exists, i.e. that which may truly be said to exist. The apparent is that which certain evidence leads us to suppose to exist. There is no mutual exclusion involved in these definitions. The real may or may not be apparent; the apparent may or may not be real. Reality, moreover, has in it the same absolute ambiguity that truth has. What reality means depends upon what is affirmed to be real. In any particular case we know what it means; but there is no universal common content involved. There is, for example, nothing in common between the reality of Shakespeare's genius and the reality of the planet Neptune. Again, the real figures as the object of possible knowledge, while the apparent is the object of belief. Just as the attempt to distinguish knowledge definitely from belief breaks down, so does the attempt to set up an absolute reality in opposition to mere appearance issue in a total failure.

The general position which has been outlined above has gradually made its determining influence felt in all the particular departments of philosophy in which I have been actively interested. It used to be assumed that all problems, with few exceptions, had solutions, just as it was supposed that diseases, with few exceptions, had cures. We might not know the solution or the cure, but it was there to be known and our task was to find it. We have learned to have very little faith in cures; and for my part I have as little faith in solutions. In particular, questions of the form, "What is the relation between A and B?" seldom admit of a definite answer. When it is asked, for example, what the relation between soul and body or between mental and physical events is, I am disposed to reply that there is no one uniform relation involved, and that the search for such a relation yields only self-deception and disappointment. If this is in itself a solution of the problem, let us make the most of it.

Science is so far from being a system of reason that it has not even the external appearance of a system. Our knowledge grows in spots, and the enlarging spots interpenetrate and fuse—like grease-spots, as James wittily remarked; however, there are large areas which are only imperfectly connected with one another, and between which we pass with a sense of an abrupt hiatus. Comte made this a cardinal principle of his philosophy, and declared that between the higher and lower sciences of his hierarchy there was a gulf fixed. Chemistry was not reducible to physics, nor biology to chemistry. Radically new concepts, as well as new methods, were in each case involved.

As a young man I used to wonder—as many others have wondered—whether Comte's divisions were really absolute: whether they might not be overcome, and whether, if this was not to happen, the reason did not lie merely in a great difference of complexity. It now seems to me that the recent history of physics and chemistry goes a long way toward answering these questions—mainly by revising them. If we ask whether the chemistry of 1850 or 1900 was reducible to the physics of 1850 or 1900, the answer is doubtless in the negative. Nevertheless the gap between chemistry and physics has been materially cut down. This has involved a profound modification of chemical conceptions and—what is more important for our present purposes—an equally profound modification of physical conceptions. If the two sciences are ever to be really continuous, it is not likely to be by the reduction of chemical phenomena to physical terms as we now know them. The physics which is also a chemistry will be a strangely altered physics—how different from the present we have no means of conceiving. If biology also is to be brought into the union, the new science, while historically continuous with that of the present day, may easily differ from it as profoundly as our science differs from that of Empedocles.

Here, I take it, lies the weakness of materialism. It is the same sort of weakness that belonged to Descartes's thesis, that all physics is reducible to geometry. One may twist one's words so as to find in the general theory of relativity a partial verification of the thesis; for has not one great force been reduced to a spatial conformation in things? It is a verification which would have shocked Descartes. When it is claimed that all mental phenomena are describable and explicable in physical terms, the claim is silly if the physical terms are understood to be closely related to those now familiar to us, and it is empty if the terms may differ from these to an undetermined extent. If "physical" is defined so as to connote merely an agreement with the principle of the uniformity of nature, the claim is equally empty of significance; for that principle, as we have seen, is purely formal and contains no information whatsoever. Materialism can only be made plausible by being allowed to mean as little as possible. When it ceases to be indefinite it becomes ridiculous.

Much the same thing has to be said of spiritualism. It sees a gulf where materialism sees nothing but continuity; and it has as little claim upon our respect. It assumes a fixity of concepts which history is far from suggesting; and at the same time it indulges in the utmost vagueness. If we only knew what the "soul" meant! The soul is a name which has moral and religious associations of the utmost importance—not all of them very wholesome or desirable, to be sure. For the understanding of ourselves and the world we live in, it is nearly worthless. Leave the term undefined, and disbelief in the soul seems monstrous. Define it, and it is a mystery how such an entity can perform any of the functions that are assigned to it. It is an organism without organs. There is mental heredity, the transmission of characteristics from soul to soul; but there is no continuity between a given soul and the souls from which it inherits.

A sceptic learns to avoid such embarrassments by not pretending to know too much. Ultimate questions are for him useless questions, because the asking of them strains our conceptions to the breaking-point. All our science of nature is limited by conditions of which we are at best only dimly aware. In all reasoning from experience we assume the irrelevance of a multitude of factors, any of which may be found by later observation to be essential. When we speak of *the* specific heat of mercury, of *the* atomic weight of lead, of *the* distance between the earth and the moon at a given instant, we give hostages to fortune. We must, of course, speak in just such ways—we must take risks, we must give hostages. But we need not, while we give them, fancy ourselves free.

Such elementary considerations as these have gone far to determine my attitude towards some of the newer movements in philosophy, notably those connected with *Gestalttheorie* and emergent evolution. *Gestalttheorie* has been generally regarded as having to do with psychological phenomena, but it is intended by its principal advocates to be equally concerned with physical and social phenomena. Can the action of wholes be explained by the behaviour of their parts? To me the question has no precise significance. The whole may or may not act in a way which we should never have expected from our previous acquaintance with the parts. The relational structure may or may not involve essential conditions that lie beyond the limits of our scientific experience. From the point of view of method, *Gestalttheorie* is amply justified—unless, indeed, it is used to choke off all further analysis. But nothing has a nature of its own, apart from the configurations into which it enters. All behaviour takes place under specific environing conditions; and the notion of the nature, or characteristic behaviour, of a thing is a construct from its reactions under all the conditions in which we observe it. The study of wholes carries with it, therefore, an enlargement of our conception of the parts. Whether, therefore, the whole is explained by the parts or not depends largely upon the accident whether the parts have been previously studied in analogous wholes.

Gestalttheorie owes its real significance—which I take to be very great—to the specific dogmatisms which it opposes, and to the new lines of experimentation which it has accordingly initiated. If a generation of comparative psychologists had not tried to evaluate the intelligence of animals by testing their ability to learn to use devices entirely unrelated to their whole previous experience and habits, there would have been much less point in the suggestion that if intelligence is to be measured it must be given an opportunity to act.

Emergent evolution is surprising evolution. Every attempt to make anything more out of it ends in tautology or in unhistorical dogmatism. The new laws that are cited arise admittedly in accordance with older laws, and are accordingly embraced by them. The new entities are either new configurations (of which I have just spoken) or new elements; and in the latter case there is nothing to show how deep the novelty goes. To characterize the appearance of life where the necessary conditions of life have not always existed as "emergence" implies that we know well what organisms are and what the inorganic is, and that no continuous transition from the one to the other is possible—that there is a hard-and-fast line between the living and the lifeless. We know nothing of the sort. The same may be said of the rise of consciousness. That lies outside the field of our knowledge, and there is nothing to gain by trying to capitalize our ignorance with a word.

It can be argued with equal plausibility that we know nothing about the universe and that all that we know is about the universe. Obviously a distinction is called for. Every affirmation of a law of nature is a characterization of the world we live in. Every affirmation that a particular event has occurred or will occur implies the denial of a law of nature—namely, the law that such an event cannot occur. Granted, then, that we have any knowledge at all, it would seem that we must have knowledge of the universe. The difficulty lies in the fact that all laws of nature, as we know them, are subject to limitations which we do not know. Our experience is circumscribed, and when we vaguely assume that what lies beyond the horizon is to all intents and purposes like what lies close at hand, we expose ourselves to contradiction, and, as a matter of fact, a widening experience not infrequently contradicts us. There is no possible means of

discounting this possibility, or of precisely and sufficiently defining the actual limits of the world as we are acquainted with it.
In this sense, then, we know nothing about the universe.

Our explanations of things run in two directions. Sometimes
we analyse things into their parts, and account for the behaviour
of the wholes in terms of the behaviour of the parts. Sometimes
we regard things in relation to larger wholes, and find the explanation of their behaviour in their environment. Thus we reach
smaller and smaller elements and larger and larger systems. It is
to be observed that the mere breaking up of things into parts
adds nothing to our understanding of them. I can go on till
doomsday describing the irregularities of a common brick, and
science be no whit advanced by the performance. The only parts
worth considering are relevant parts—that is to say, parts that are
relevant to the understanding of some specific mode of behaviour
of the whole. Similarly, it is not every larger whole that counts.
We can find such things *ad libitum* and be as ignorant as before.
The case is not altered, but is, if anything, more obvious, if the
parts or larger wholes are essentially hypothetical. The breaking
up and the compounding are alike step-by-step procedures. We
have no means of advancing either to an absolute element or to
an absolute whole.

All cosmologies are figures of speech. To take them literally
is to make nonsense of them. Plato's conception of the universe
as an animal organism—an organism without an environment—is
typical. The common theistic conception of a creator and his
work, involving an infinite intelligence for which no problems
exist and an infinite power adapting means to ends, is also
typical. Such conceptions have, I believe, no value at all for the
purposes of theoretical explanation. There is no science of the
universe, and there is no science of God.

From a logical standpoint, cosmologies are the result of an
ignoring of the historical limitations of human knowledge.
However, they commonly have motives of another order altogether: they are expressions of the religious spirit. The belief,
for example, that the universe is an animate being is held, not
because of tangible evidence that can be offered for it—though

men who hold it may seek to bolster up their faith with proofs—but because it seems to the believer to ascribe the highest possible value to the world in which we live and the life we lead in it.

What I have to say about religion and its relation to philosophy is very much what a multitude of other men, in and out of the Christian Church, are saying. For the fixing of my thoughts on the subject I owe much to a brief association with the psychologist Irving King, a member of the Society of Friends. I supposed at the time that King must be regarded as extremely heretical by the fellow-members of his Church, and only much later learned that the Society of Friends is not a Church, that it has no creed, and that King's theories are in great part virtually a generalization of views widely held by thoughtful members of the Society. This I say by way of acknowledgment and not with the intention of offering my views as anything but my own.

To regard the contents of a religious faith as consisting of so many scientific or philosophical theories is almost inevitably to condemn them, but it involves, I believe, a very serious misapprehension. What a belief amounts to depends upon the experience that has gone to the formation of it. Now the amount of experience that is represented by religious dogma is enormous. In a way, it may be said to be co-extensive with human life itself. It is, in short, experience of the values of things, and especially of those things which are felt to make existence most worth while, not only for the individual, but for the society of which he is a member. The fact is not to be overlooked that the logical relevancy of the experience to the particular dogmas that arise out of it is always questionable; but the more important fact is that, in their way, the dogmas do sum up and represent the experience. The conception of a heavenly father, for example, is not sufficiently disposed of when it is labelled "anthropomorphism."

It is correct enough, so far as it goes, to speak of religion as a means of getting good things. It is always that, but it is more than that. What is fundamental is the conception of the good things that are to be secured, the happiness that is to be enjoyed. It is this conception that pervades the rites and ceremonies and expresses itself in the particular articles of faith.

Thus in a hunting people the religion may centre in festivals that secure the reproduction of the totem animal; in an agricultural people, where the annual crops stand out as the most important thing in life, we find the feasts of the sowing and the harvest prominent; when success in battle seems to be all in all, it is a god of battles that is worshipped; and as the conviction forces itself upon men's minds that no such external goods, but wisdom, justice, and charity are of supreme value, the great ethical religions arise.

One of the most striking features of the rapidly shifting scene of the last few centuries has been the way in which one scientific theory after another, which the great majority of sincere believers have regarded as undermining the very foundations of Christianity, has found its way to general acceptance, and yet Christianty has continued to flourish. The first great example was the Copernican theory; a recent example, which even now does not belong entirely to the past, is the theory of the evolutionary origin of species. If in the year 1850 a representative group of men from any Christian denomination had been asked whether it was inconsistent with their faith to hold that man has descended from a brute ancestry, they would with practical unanimity have answered in the affirmative. Yet there is now a great body of educated Christians for whom transformism is a commonplace, and who are no more weakened in their faith by it than they are by the reflection that the earth goes round the sun.

The reason for this phenomenon is, I suppose, that what is really essential to Christianity has not been materially disturbed —namely, the moral experience of Christian people. A creed, as such, is a relatively external manifestation of an inner spirit. It is a partly rational, more largely imaginative construction, a conceiving how the world must be constituted and governed if the real values in life are what the worshippers have found them to be. Such a construction is always framed in conceptual terms which the common consciousness of the time takes for granted as unimpeachable, but which may to any extent be modified by later scientific and philosophical reflection. So long as Christian men and women retain a consciousness of supreme moral obligation, and so long as that obligation includes a recognition of love, or charity, toward all as the guiding principle of the best life, their religion will be far from extinction.

PRINCIPAL PUBLICATIONS

Dogmatism and Evolution (with Grace A. de Laguna). 1910.
Introduction to the Science of Ethics. 1914.
The Factors of Social Evolution. 1926.
Three papers on "The Nature of Space," in the *Journal of Philosophy*, vol. xix.

MY DEVELOPMENT AND PRESENT CREED

By JOSEPH ALEXANDER LEIGHTON

Born 1870; Professor of Philosophy, Ohio State University.

MY DEVELOPMENT AND PRESENT CREED

I. My Intellectual History

As an undergraduate, the studies which influenced most power-
fully my intellectual development were chemistry, biology, and
historical geology. From chemistry I gained an appreciation of
exact scientific procedure; biology and geology quickened my
imagination with a sense of the vastness and complexity of the
march of life. In philosophy I was most influenced by Aristotle's
Ethics, Leibniz, Kant, and Green. It was, I think, Green's
Prolegomena to Ethics which, more than any other influence,
turned me in the direction of philosophy as a vocation—not his
metaphysics, but his reverence for the free spirit and his noble
passion for social liberty and progress.

But I hesitated between biology and philosophy as major
interests. I think it was the accident of receiving a graduate
scholarship in philosophy at Cornell that turned me definitely
toward philosophy. It has always been difficult for me to confine
myself to any one field. I am as much interested in geology,
geography, anthropology, cultural history, and literature as I am
in technical philosophy.

The summer after graduation I read with enthralled interest
James's *Psychology*. This book permanently influenced me. I
have always since felt much sympathy with James's views—his
pluralism, temporalism, and meliorism, his vivid appreciation
of the individual.

At Cornell I devoted myself chiefly to the history of philosophy,
logic, and ethics. The thinkers who most influenced me at that
time were Plato, Aristotle, Leibniz, Fichte, Hegel, and Bradley.
I felt then that an adequate philosophy must be based on a
synthesis of the cosmology of Leibniz with the cultural or historical philosophy of Hegel. Of course the Aristotelian *motif* is
obvious in Leibniz. The monads are modernized entelechies. I
was much influenced by Bradley's brilliant *Logic*. I did not then
fully appreciate Bosanquet's contribution to epistemological and
metaphysical logic.

It was an exciting event to find Bradley's *Appearance and Reality* at the publisher's. But, in one respect, I was disappointed in it and in his later writings. While Bradley made it very clear that finite centres are not illusory, that the Absolute is nothing apart from its appearances, I could make little of his Absolute—the utterly harmonious, timeless Experience. To me, this is the great stumbling-block in Bradley, less so in Bosanquet, because he does not say very much about the Absolute. When Bradley says that the statement that the Absolute progresses is either blasphemous or unmeaning, I quite fail to follow. What is there unmeaning in supposing that the whole of being might grow or shrink in value? How can one say that the Absolute is nothing apart from finite centres and then deny that the expansion or decay of finite centres has the least bit of significance for the Absolute? James is right in insisting that, if personal lives have any real significance, then change is not sheer illusion. It does not follow, of course, that there cannot be a changeless order or structure of reality.

As for the blasphemy, one is simply puzzled. If the heart of religion be to affirm the reality of goodness through every aspect of one's being, where is the irreverence in believing that goodness may increase? I thought, when I read them, that Bosanquet's two volumes, *The Principle of Individuality and Value* and *The Value and Destiny of the Individual*, were a more constructive contribution to the interpretation of reality than Bradley's *Appearance and Reality*. I still think so. What I owe to these thinkers is a more adequate conception of the notions that have lain at the heart of my thinking since about my seventeenth year—individuality and value.

Bosanquet's further contribution lies in his rich and penetrating insight into the significance of the historical cultural life. He is a British Hegel and, in some respects, a better-balanced one. The strength of the idealistic movement lies in its knowledge and appreciation of the historic and social cultural life of humanity, and here Bosanquet is at his best.

On the other hand, in their social philosophy they exaggerate the significance of the social *ethos*—the institutions, the traditions, the objective spiritual structures—and minimize the value of the individual. It is somewhat strange that philosophers who have developed the notion of *individuality*, as the criterion both of reality and value, should assume such an attitude of lofty indifference to the uniqueness of the human individual.

Of course, this over-emphasis on the social *ethos* is a reaction against the abstract individualism of the eighteenth century—of the rationalists and utilitarians. Also, perhaps, the notion of a timeless Absolute has something to do with it.

At any rate, at no stage in my own thought could I accept this attitude of apparent indifference to the uniqueness and value of the *individual person*, any more than I could accept a timeless Absolute.

My friend and teacher, Creighton, said I misunderstood the idealists on these points; well I have continued in this misunderstanding, if it be such.

My feeling for the philosophical significance of cultural history was strengthened by my studies in the history of religion and theology at the Episcopal Theological School at Cambridge, Massachusetts. The school had two remarkable teachers, A. V. G. Allen, the author of *The Continuity of Christian Thought*, and Henry S. Nash. They were remarkable in their union of historical learning and philosophical insight with an enlightened religious mysticism. I afterwards went to Berlin and Tübingen, where I did not find their equals. Indeed, my sojourn in Germany brought no new philosophical stimulation. In this respect it was disappointing. Of course I enjoyed and profited by the acquaintance with German university life. The influence of Hegel on my thought was increased by taking a seminary in Hegel with Josiah Royce. I saw then (and I still hold) that Hegel's greatness lies in his extraordinary knowledge of, and insight into, the history of culture and the dependence of the human individual on the cultural *milieu*; his weakness lies in his frequent arbitrary and fanciful distortion of cultural history (cultural phylogenesis) and individual development (cultural ontogenesis) to fit the scheme of his dialectic method. There is a dialectic in the spiritual history of man the group and man the individual. But the history of man and of the individual are too complex, too full of contingencies (so far as one can see) to be threaded out on the Hegelian or any other dialectic.

Among the recent and living writers I have been most impressed by the work of the German philosophers of culture, especially by Rickert, Windelband, and Scheler; also by Eucken's treatment of the various life systems or cultural syntagma. I confess that Husserl's phenomenology seems to me, notwithstanding its acuteness, thin-spun and verbalistic. I admire the massive contribution of S. Alexander. I acknowledge stimulus from the writings of James Ward, Josiah Royce, John Dewey, Alexius von Meinong, Bertrand Russell, and Bergson. Among the latest English works, that of Professor Whitehead impresses me as most significant, but I do not profess fully to understand it.

I think my own views have closest affinity with Royce's philosophy. I believe he strikes a better balance between the individual and the social than do Bradley and Bosanquet. Among the poets my favourites, because of their human and philosophical interests, are the Greek dramatists, Shakespeare, Goethe, Shelley, Wordsworth, Matthew Arnold, Browning, and Whitman. For his sheer artistry I have always loved Keats.

To sum up: the great thinkers who have influenced me most are Plato, Aristotle, Leibniz, Hegel, Bradley, Bosanquet, James, and Royce.

I proceed to a brief statement of my present views.

II. The Theory of Knowledge

Knowing is just as truly a natural event as breathing or digesting. The problems of knowledge and its unique prerogatives are simply the consequence of this peculiarity; it is through knowing that we become aware of what is done to us and what we do. But this peculiarity is not a sufficient ground for making such a pother over the mystery of the transcendence of the object of knowing and of the mind's leap over the yawning chasm, as some epistemologists do. A natural and workable theory of knowledge will be found by keeping our way between the fallacies of subjectivistic mentalism and a pan-objectivism that denies anything unique in the cognitive relation. I find the matter rather simple. Clearly, if the objects of knowledge were constituted by the knowing of them, there would be no meaning in knowing. The uniqueness of the cognitive relation being abolished there would be nothing more to say. To say that cognition and the objects are compresent is not enough. Knowing, then, implies that the cognitive process does not constitute its data. These are given in cognition. They consist of sensory data and the native constitution of the mind as cognitive. In both cases what is known is not anything that we can say must exist, just as it is known, apart from its being known. Humanism is unavoidable. We cannot escape, in our knowing, from the conditioning structure of the psychophysical human organism. We cannot know the thing-in-itself. The quest for the maximum objectivity in knowing is just the enterprise of reducing the personal equation and looking at the objects as far as possible in the light of universally human conditions of perception and of the logical organization of sensory and other data (by other data one means here the data of the affective-emotional life of the human organism itself). This is to me the established result of Kantian and post-Kantian idealism. When the pragmatist claims to be the only Simon-pure humanist he makes himself ridiculous. Idealism is universal or objective humanism. Hence, in a sense, all our knowledge is of *appearances*—that is, of things as they appear to human organisms and of the relations that are found by the human thinking apparatus. Scientific knowing is the knowing of appearances, cleansed, as far as may be, from particular occasional and personal idiosyncracies. This is what reality is—namely, the most universal, fundamental, impersonally viewed systematic totality of appearances.

I am willing to say that knowledge rests on faith—namely, on the faith that the conjoint world of things and selves as it appears to us is a veridical appearance. Reality can mean nothing more than the maximally comprehensive or organized totality of the appearances. The "laws" of the relations among its elements are the ways in which these elements are interdependent. But this faith that the appearances are real is justified, in so far as the taking of the appearances and their relations as real enables us to get along, to find our way about, to live and enjoy the conjoint world of things and selves. Since we have appeared in precisely this world and do, on the whole, live out our little days in it, since every dog among us has his day, our faith is partially justified. How could it be otherwise? Man is the offspring of the cosmos, and the better he knows his cosmos the more successfully he lives in it. In the most comprehensive sense, knowing is a human instrument. Thus far I agree with the pragmatists. But, while it is man's cosmos, there is in it a partial and ever growing harmony between the structure of mind in man and the nature of the whole which is responsive to the activity of mind. I am an empiricist in the sense that I hold that all our data and our ways of acquiring the data are empirically known. The coherence theory or criterion of truth is itself the most inclusive statement of the empirical structure of mind functioning in a world—that is, the mind is, as a matter of fact, so constituted that when it is attempting to think clearly and adequately to organize its data it cannot rest in contradictions and inconsistencies. That is the way the mind is made. Thus coherence is an absolute criterion just so far as it will work. But there are many different sets of judgments that are not inconsistent with one another, while on the other hand we cannot find any positive relation between them. I, for instance, find no inconsistency between the theory of relativity and my belief that I am to some extent a self-determining being. Both are probably true, but what their positive relation may be I do not now see. Each belief organizes and interprets satisfactorily certain data; but these data belong to such different realms that I fail to see their mutual interdependencies.

For me, the tests of truth are complex: (1) Negatively two contradictory judgments cannot both be true; they may both be false; or they may be partially true and partially false. (2) Positively a judgment is true if and when, eliminating the personal equation, it expresses qualities-in-relation which are based on some unavoidable experience (that is, unavoidable under standardized or test conditions). The term "experience" is to be understood in the most liberal sense. The data of the moral, æsthetic, and religious experiences have as good a right to a hearing as the ordinary sense data. That they do not get this hearing in an age obsessed by mathematical and physical method only shows that this age of "science," like all ages of culture, has its own idols of the market-place.

Knowledge is conditioned by social culture, although not so much so as conduct. But the world we recognize, even in its "physical" forms, is an expression of forms of thinking and belief that have social validity. Our concepts of space-time, matter, causation, process, as well as our moral and æsthetic concepts, are assumed to be socially valid. It is a curious fact that even philosophers have generally assumed, without much critical inquiry, that there are other minds like their own. Even the sceptics do this, otherwise they would not express themselves. The situation is this—we assume, whether we are Trobriand Islanders, Pragmatists, Realists, or Idealists, that there is a public realm of space-time, matter, motion, life, etc., which is accessible to all of us, and that there is a *normal* mentality that enables us to communicate with one another through standardized physical instruments and conventional symbols. All communication is symbolic and rests upon the twofold faith in a community of the physical realm and a community of minds. And our concepts of the structure and behaviour of this twofold community are conditioned by our environing culture system which, in turn, undergoes slow and almost imperceptible alteration by the explorative probings and happy guesses of exceptionally endowed minds. But the community of minds is logically prior to the physical community.

I think that, as our cultural heritage increases, our knowledge and our resulting practical controls must take place more and more through the increasing organization and co-operation of individual minds. The day of the lonely genius is wellnigh, perhaps altogether, past.

I look forward to the time when science and philosophy will both be matters of planetary co-operation. But this time must wait, I suppose, upon a more effective organization of economic and administrative instruments. On the other hand, I believe that to increase the work of intellectual planetary co-operation will facilitate the coming of the day when mankind will become one community. The absolute sovereign state is an anachronism and the greatest menace to the economic and spiritual welfare of the planetary community that now exists. While I should be sorry to see all diversity extinguished and all peoples merged into a standardized mob, I am an internationalist. If the leading nations of this earth do not learn to pull together they will severally commit cultural suicide.

A world language is a great desideratum, but no linguistic artefact seems to hold out much promise. Perhaps a simplified English will fill the bill.

III. Theory of Reality

The real universe, in the sense above defined, is a hierarchical system of individual wholes. It is not "really" made up solely either of "point instants," "electrons," or "persons." I cannot help regarding all abstract qualitative monisms, materialistic, energetic, or mentalistic, as philosophical juvenilities. Empirical reality (I know naught of any other) is complex and rich in structure. There are in it physical configurations of electro-magnetic character. There are vital configurations that probably are not the mathematical products of mere electro-magnetic configuration; there are reflective wholes (persons) that are qualitatively richer than mere animal configurations; there are in persons, super-reflective powers (the æsthetic, moral, and religious) which it seems to me indicate that man at his highest reach of being has richer and more immediate relations with the whole of reality than any lower order of individual. This last is the life of spiritual values which surely, no less than lower modes of response, are effective and valid responses to a quality of the cosmos.

I would put it this way: reality consists of a hierarchy of organizing forms, dynamic structures or centres of organizing activity (like Aristotle's immanent forms).[1] The richer forms cannot be explained as arising from accidental collocations of the lower forms. That a rational value-creating and value-enjoying mind is nothing but an accidental by-product of electronic configurations is to me wholly unwarranted.

I welcome the doctrine of emergent evolution as the explicit recognition that the richer wholes or individualities cannot be reduced to the poorer. Where I quarrel with it is its failure to recognize that to say the higher emerges, but is not mechanically caused by the lower, is to admit that evolution is not an ultimate explanatory principle at all. Either all the higher forms have emerged from the lower—and there was a time when the former were not and then the higher are by-products of the lower—or the higher have not really emerged from the lower and evolution is merely a description, not an explanation. Indeed, when I contemplate the fascinating structural plans of the electron-proton in the atoms and the quantic jumps, there, too, I see that the merely physical is organized. The atom is a minute ultra-microscopic stellar cosmos. The organism is a much richer microcosmos, and so on we go, until in cultural humanity we reach the richest dynamic organizing formative principle. It is possible, though on the whole not to me probable, that the electro-magnetic is vital. I say improbable, because the modes of behaviour seem to me qualitatively and not just quantitatively different.

I have called these organizing forms *individua* or *monads* in *Man and the Cosmos*. The term *Monad* is, however, subject to misunderstanding. Leibniz was on the right track in holding that the constituents of reality are organizing centres of activity; but he went astray in making each monad a windowless self-existent substance. This mistake led to the artificial doctrine of the pre-established harmony of the various perspectives. It is correct to say that each individuum reflects the universe and is a mirror of it. But it does so because it is in dynamic and passional relation with the other individua. If the individua are in mutual

[1] If I apprehend him rightly, some such notion seems implied in Dr. Whitehead's *organic mechanism*.

commerce, then not only new individuals of one type, but new types of individuals may be generated, may emerge, and there is real creative evolution. With Leibniz's closed monads there could be no emergence of new types of individuality and value. Now, empirically these new types of individuality and value do seem to emerge. But their emergence is a finite temporal expression of the character of the whole cosmos. The cosmos, in its organic wholeness, can never have been merely spatio-temporal or even solely electro-magnetic. The hierarchy of empirical individua has its real ground in the nature of the living whole. This is what I mean when, in *Man and the Cosmos*, I say that there is a *hierarchy of orders*, all of which are levels or stages in the all-sustaining order of the whole. From the eternal or ultimate ground, for which no reason can be given (it always just is), there emerge, in finite temporal series, successive hierarchies of individuality and value.

The most significant all-inclusive quality of man is that he is the *creator of cultures*; of complex, continuing systems of social cultures—complexes of manners and customs, organizations of social-relationship, etiquettes, laws, arts fine and applied, myths, sciences (systematized methodical myths), and religions. He who knows only one culture knows none well. Our machine culture is new, all-pervasive and, spiritually and æsthetically, somewhat poverty-stricken. There have been other and richer cultures. Some of them still survive with great stubbornness. All our problems, concepts, methods, and valuations are interwoven and have emerged into being with our culture. Our concepts and valuations are mixed because our culture is a mixture, not a unified synthesis. The philosophy of comparative culture will deliver us from naïve parochialism. If it introduces an historical relativism it supports a humanism. It may be objected that this standpoint is a sheer historical relativism or scepticism. I think otherwise. Granted the mutual relativity of social cultures and selves, the central point is that cultures are at once the expressions and the media for the realization of self-hood or personality. The self-transcendence of the natural biological self-hood, through active participation in the cultural life, is the self-realization of personality. In this respect Royce has stated the true view. Speaking of the relation between the general idealistic attitude and the colouring given to one's philosophy by one's individuality, he says: "This does not mean that the truth is at the mercy of private caprice, or that any man is his own measure of all things, without reference to other men. It *does* mean that the whole of philosophy can only exist in an essentially social form as the synthesis of many—yes, ideally speaking, of an infinite number—of individual and personal points of view, whose diversity will be due to the fact that the truth must mirror various aspects of its constitution in various ways to the diverse individuals. The world, in other words, interprets itself through us—that is, through whatever rational individuals there can be. Inadequate our individual interpretations, indeed, always remain. But they need not be monotonously inadequate. They must properly supplement one another." (*Lectures on Modern Idealism*, p. 242.)

And again, after speaking of the effort of logical and ethical and empirical inquiries to define common categories, he adds, "But when the best has been done to discover the common features of our various experiences and ideals, a most significant aspect of the universe will have been inevitably omitted in every such investigation. And this will be precisely the aspect of individuality in the universe. If the world is essentially a life of will and of thought coming to an individual consciousness of itself in and through various personalities whose social unity rests upon their very variety, the work of discovering the truth can never exhaustively be reduced to the work of finding out what these various personalities find or will merely in common. They all in common mean, intend, experience, and think the universe. They are all, therefore, as Leibniz said, mirrors of the universe. But since the universe is, from this point of view, just the system of living mirrors itself, what is common to the various world pictures is never the whole truth." (*Ibid.*, p. 243.) "A philosophy is essentially concerned with a unity of truth which can only be expressed through the variety of individual points of view." (*Ibid.*, p. 244.) In short, the last word of objective idealism is that the universe is a living whole which expresses and realizes itself in and through an endless (to us) multitude of individualities or personalities.

The crown of metaphysics for me is "metahistorics," the metaphysics of culture. The universe is dynamic; even the ultimate reality traffics in time and is creative. There is cosmic change. In other words, change, life, belong to the very life of the cosmos. Any such mechanical scheme as Spencer's is ridiculously false. Life and mind are primordial constituents of the universe, not accidental by-products. But reality is not, and never was nor will be, disembodied mind.

IV. ETHICS AND SOCIAL PHILOSOPHY

The term "moral" may be used in two senses—a narrower and a wider one. In the narrower sense, "moral" denotes these active attitudes and their affective and intellectual sources which have to do with right social relationships. Right social relationships all have their roots in reverence for personality; personality meaning here a harmonious or integral self-hood. In the wider sense, "moral" may be used to include all values that minister to, and reside in, personality. In this wider sense, it includes æsthetic and intellectual fulfilment and has its culmination in the vision and devotion to the ideal of perfect value. My colleague, Professor Sabine, says that the concept of personality would better be abandoned in social philosophy, since a person is a subject of "rights" and suggests the contrast between the individual and the state. The historic rights-philosophy has done its work. To continue it is to overlook the fact that the ethical problem is one of multiple relations between individuals in many group relations. He would put "interests" in the place of "rights." I agree in principle, but I do not see why the term "personality" should be abandoned. A personality is a socialized individual, a psychic unit functioning and satisfying its interests in many group relations. A person is nothing worth while except in social relationships. Every interest of an individual involves social relationships. I would say that the fundamental concept of ethical and social philosophy, and the one which expresses both the fact and the ideal, is personality-in-community, psychic individuality realized in many social individual wholes.

V. RELIGION

There is no self-realization or happiness for a reflective being except in devotion to super-personal causes, to social and super-social (æsthetic and intellectual) ends. I think Bosanquet is right in saying that wherever a man loyally throws the centre of his action and being outside himself there is true religion. While I cannot accept the claim that classical Christianity was an isolated supernatural revelation, I think its doctrine, that he that seeketh his life shall lose it, and he that loseth his life shall find it, is the highest spiritual principle revealed, not *to*, but *in* man. I find much the same principle in Platonism, and perhaps the highest Buddhism is not far from it. The paradox of paradoxes in our human world is that while values come alive only in persons, while the richest and deepest individuality and value is realized in persons, they do seem to be cast as aimless to the void. I cannot feel that the arguments for immortality, in the sense of the continuity of the individual life, are very strong. On the other hand, inasmuch as the richest reality and the fullest value inhere in spiritual individuality, inasmuch as the whole creation seems to move to, and find its fullest meaning in, the production of persons, I hold, as a matter of reasonable faith, to the perduration of spiritual individuality. Every man is a child of his time and culture. But it is given to man "in his own solitariness" (as Dr. Whitehead puts it) to react to the whole of things. This attitude of the individual spirit toward the whole of things—cosmic emotion and its imaginative setting—is his religion. Religion is a person's ultimate escape, release, redemption from his own solitariness. This must vary with the culture and the individuality of the spirit. But whatever it be—a Christian theism, a cosmic pantheism, an æsthetic mysticism, or an ethical mysticism—that there is such an individual communion with and worship of the spirit of the whole is significant. The universe which engenders and seems to engulf these varied individualities is qualified by them. They cannot be sheer illusions. A merely humanitarian or "humanistic" religion is no religion at all.

The social factor in religion is of immense importance, but is apt to be over-emphasized these days. After all, spiritual religion is not either a political, ecclesiastical, or psychological system of police control. Spiritual religion has being in man only when he reaches mature self-consciousness. It is not a crowd-engendered emotional cataclysm. Nor is it merely escape from the world of "reality" into a realm of sheer make-believe, an illusory compensation for the stings and arrows of outrageous fortune. These notions of religion have arisen from rather crude social psychologies or too exclusive dwelling on psychiatric data. Spiritual religion is the total attitude of the mature spirit in man to the whole. It is not mere emotion nor mere pragmatic practicality. It is the imaginative and intuitive affirmation of the unity and supremacy of the highest life-values.

So long as man is man he will be religious. The highest form of religion is mysticism, in the sense that worshipful communion with the supreme unity of values has its roots in the immediate inner attitude of the person.

VI. Practical Applications

I may take space to say that I am much concerned with the headlong movement of our American capitalistic industrialism and democracy. We may be headed for a tremendous disaster, when we have burned up the major part of our natural resources, have speeded up quantity production and instalment buying until every one's future is mortgaged for several years in advance and we have all become slaves of the capitalistic state. I am convinced that what this country needs most is more general and intelligent interest in productively useless matters—in art, play (I do not mean professionalized college football), speculation. Our education seems to me scrappy, sloppy, superficial. There is neither continuity, consecutiveness, nor coherence in the work done; consequently there is no appreciation of thoroughness, nor of relationships nor meanings. The things learned are largely chaotic jumbles of raw facts (which are often not facts), retained sufficiently long in the mind to add to the sum-total of time credits. The time credit is the only principle of unification in our education. There is not developed any sense for generalizations, relationships, meanings, values. Our education is too crassly pragmatic and episodic.

I see no way out except by a concerted effort to foster cultural ideals by abandoning our chaotic elective system (which is not a system) and establishing in the college a well-organized, coherent curriculum in liberal arts, built around an extensive and intensive study of two great phases in the history of culture.

Perhaps, if this could be done, its influence might seep down into the secondary schools in which, on the whole, it seems to me the work is rather bad in its intellectual and spiritual effects now. It consists chiefly in cafeteria displays to please the supposed tastes of the children and their parents who do not know what they want. The chief criteria of choice of studies are too often what will be immediately useful in one's vocation, or ornamental for social display, or easy to get by with. The disinterested impulse to muse upon, to speculate, to contemplate, is conspicuous mostly by its absence.

I do not think that American philosophers, with the exception of Royce, Dewey, and Adams, have shown a sufficient appreciation of the points of view and problems of a *Philosophy of Culture* or *Civilization*. They seem to me, on the whole, too much obsessed with the methods either of descriptive individual and social psychology or of natural science.

I hold that the central task of Philosophy, as the analysis and synoptic science of values (or selves), is not with psychological introspection of the poor passing moments of our individual consciousness nor with overt muscular behaviour. It is rather with those massive and enduring and also changing social complexes which I have called in *Man and the Cosmos* "social culture systems," or objective spiritual structures (Mr. Adams's term). One might take the history of art and of religion and morals as his point of departure. But until one has worked his way into at least two systems of culture, so as to be able to compare them, he is not in a position to philosophize profitably concerning human values and the nature of mind. I would, if I could, make the study of two cultures—say the Greek and the Modern, the basis of the liberal arts course.

Our education is not only scrappy, it is one-sided. We emphasize but two things, bookish learning of facts and theories and mathematico-physical analyses. The æsthetic factor is still woefully neglected. Although there has been some improvement, we need to balance empirical and rationalistic analysis with the cultivation of the power of intuitive imagination; to cultivate the impulse to feel ourselves into and enjoy beauteous and significant wholes—a sunset touch, a chorus ending from Euripides, a sonnet, a lyric, a drama, a painting, a noble architectural or sculptural figure, the stars, the lives of organisms, human personalities. There is not only creative expression in the fashioning of words, musical sounds, pigments, wood, stone, and steel, there is creative enjoyment in which we fill out, creatively, our own personalities in the æsthetic experience. Living should be a rich, full-bodied art, and we are, as a people, such rank instrumentalists that we sacrifice the art of living to the machinery that should subserve living.

There is frequent clamour to-day that philosophy should be practical, that it should be put to work to give guidance for social reconstruction; it should furnish an applied theory of culture, education, the ends and values of social life. I agree heartily to this, and I have much sympathy with Mr. Dewey and his disciples on this score. My chief quarrel is not with the programme, but with the way in which it is carried out, especially by the "educators," who are, or at least claim to be, his disciples. I think that in their social philosophy the actual tendencies of American industrialism and democracy are accepted somewhat uncritically, and play too large a rôle.

I hold that philosophy fails of its mission if it be not applied in social philosophy to our actual problems. Probably the most influential single book in the history of thought is Plato's *Republic*,

Plato certainly wrote as a social reformer. A philosopher who has not, or is not seeking, a working social ideal is not of much use; but we must beware of cheap and easy social philosophies.

SUMMARY

In brief, then, the universe for me is an organic whole, a living system. Its real constituents are active individual wholes, principles of organizing activity. It is a creative whole; at the highest known level it flowers in the creative cultural life of personality-in-community. New values emerge by the transmutation of older values. It may be a growing universe, but, if so, its growth is the empirical realization of individualities and values that are grounded in its eternally real possibilities. The spirit of the whole, the cosmic individuality, does not emerge, in a chaos hitherto devoid of it, at some juncture in time. Deity is not just a (possibly) emerging level higher than humanity. We have a good right to believe that the realization of interpersonal and spiritual values is the highest empirical expression of the secret of the whole, which must be a community of selves.

PRINCIPAL PUBLICATIONS

Typical Modern Conceptions of God: The Absolute of German Romantic Idealism and of English Evolutionary Agnosticism. (Longmans, Green & Company. 1902. Pp. 190.)

Man and the Cosmos: An Introduction to Metaphysics. (D. Appleton & Company. 1922. Pp. xi + 578).

The Field of Philosophy: An Introduction to the Study of Philosophy. Fourth edition. (D. Appleton & Company. 1924. Pp. x + 584.)

Religion and the Mind of To-day. (D. Appleton & Company. 1924. Pp. x + 372.)

The Individual and the Social Order: An Introduction to Ethics and Social Philosophy. (D. Appleton & Company. 1926. Pp. xxx + 578.)

Individuality and Education: A Democratic Philosophy of Education. (D. Appleton & Company. 1928. Pp. ix + 204.)

INDEX

GEORGE ALLEN & UNWIN LTD
LONDON: 40 MUSEUM STREET, W.C.1
CAPE TOWN: 73 ST. GEORGE'S STREET
SYDNEY, N.S.W.: WYNYARD SQUARE
AUCKLAND, N.Z.: 41 ALBERT STREET
TORONTO: 77 WELLINGTON STREET, WEST

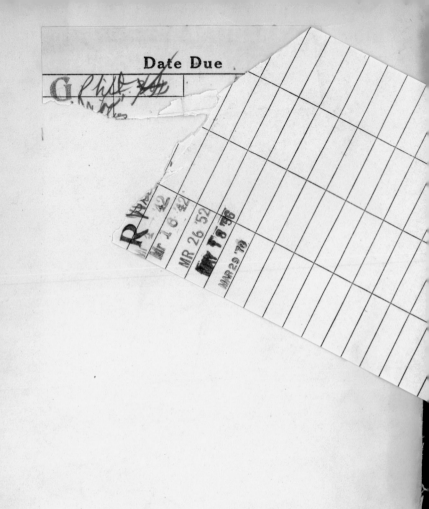